BRITISH WORKPLACE INDUSTRIAL RELATIONS 1980–1984

The DE/ESRC/PSI/ACAS Surveys

Neil Millward and Mark Stevens

Gower

Published by
Gower Publishing Company Limited
Gower House
Croft Road
Aldershot
Hants GU11 3HR
England

Gower Publishing Company
Old Post Road
Brookfield
Vermont 05036
USA

British Library Cataloguing Publication Data

Millward, Neil
    British workplace industrial relations
    1980–1984 : the DE/ESRC/PSI/ACAS surveys.
    1. Industrial relations—Great Britain
    I. Title   II. Stevens, Mark
    331′.0941   HD8391

Library of Congress Cataloging-in-Publication Data

Millward, Neil
    British workplace industrial relations, 1980–1984.

    Includes index.
    1. Industrial relations—Great Britain.
    I. Stevens, Mark, 1947–   .   II. Title.
    HD8391.M55   1986   331′.0941   86–25625

ISBN 0 566 05391 8
     0 566 05396 9 Pbk

Contents

TECHNICAL APPENDIX 319

Foreword

Whilst many factors influence the nature of relationships between employees and their employers, it is increasingly recognised that systematic information is an important component for their development, both at the level of the individual workplace and at the national level. In the past much of the discussion and debate about industrial relations was based upon fragmented information and partial analysis. The first systematic survey of employment relations issues was undertaken for the Donovan Commission. Two other national surveys followed shortly afterwards. But these surveys never became part of a systematic series.

The idea of establishing a series of Workplace Industrial Relations Surveys was developed in the late 1970s in the Department of Employment to remedy this lack of systematic data and to make possible the analysis of change and continuity over time. The Economic and Social Research Council and the Policy Studies Institute, with the support of the Leverhulme Trust, felt that such a national series would provide unique and invaluable information for the analysis of both research and policy issues. As a consequence these organisations not only made a substantial financial contribution to the first survey but also made important inputs to the design, content and analyses.

The publication of the report on the first survey had a very favourable reception from commentators in the serious press and in journals concerned with the study and practice of industrial relations. One reviewer called it the most important book in the area since the publication of the Donovan report. In addition, however, to the initial analysis, the survey has formed the basis for studies of a wide range of topics including part-time working, trade union mark-ups, joint consultation, outworking, share-ownership, personnel management, and pay structures. It has also generated a variety of linked studies on employee relations at the enterprise level and on the methodology of workplace surveys. Many of these studies were funded by the ESRC.

The reception given to the first survey and the many uses and publications which have resulted from it encouraged the continuation and development of the series. The second survey was carried out in

1984 with funding from the original three sponsors and also from the Advisory, Conciliation and Arbitration Service. The design for the second survey was in all essential respects similar to the first survey in order to provide a sound basis for the measurement of change. In terms of content, a substantial core of common questions was retained but a new topic area, concerned with technical change, was introduced into the survey and two other topics, employment practices and pay determination, were dealt with in more detail than in the first survey. In addition, an experimental panel element was built into the design.

The Second Workplace Industrial Relations Survey has been carried out under the guidance of a Steering Committee, which I have had the privilege of chairing, composed of representatives of the sponsoring bodies. The members of this committee were Professor George Bain, Francis Butler, Chris Caswill, John Cullinane, Bill Daniel, and Bill Hawes. I am grateful to them, not only for making an important contribution to the survey, but also for the tolerance they have shown for each others' differing interests in the enterprise and for their determination to co-operate for the greater good. The major responsibility for the design, execution and analysis of the research has, however, rested with the research team: Neil Millward and Mark Stevens from the Department of Employment, Bill Daniel from the Policy Studies Institute and Colin Airey of SCPR. They have shown a determination in undertaking the work and a commitment to the series which has gone well beyond the bounds of duty or contract. It has been for me a pleasure to work with those who also share a belief that information is an essential component for rational discussion and analysis of employment matters.

There are two initial publications setting out the results of the second survey: one by W W Daniel, addressing itelf to the material on new technology; and this volume by Neil Millward and Mark Stevens, to which Bill Daniel has also made an important contribution. The book provides a comprehensive overview and descriptive analysis of the survey data and sets out in a lucid and objective manner a wealth of material on employment and industrial relations in British workplaces in 1984. More importantly, however, the authors have been able to identify, in a rigorous manner, changes and developments over previous years. This is the first time that such systematic monitoring has been possible and it is perhaps appropriate that the results should appear 21 years after the Donovan Commission was established.

Besides the publication of the two general volumes and further articles that their authors are producing, a number of other analyses of the data are being undertaken with funding from the ESRC; these include work on management organisation, employment practices, wage levels, and labour relations and economic performance. In addition, there will be a special analysis of the panel data. As with the first survey, the data are deposited at the ESRC Data Archive and will, I am sure, provide an important source of information for both researchers and practitioners over future years.

The hope is that the series will continue so that comprehensive data will be available to policy makers, policy analysts and researchers on the changing and developing patterns of employment relations and associated issues across the British economy. Whilst such an enterprise is costly, its value seems to me to have been amply demonstrated. I have no doubt that readers of this volume and users of the data on which it is based will agree.

Peter Brannen
Chairman, Steering Committee for the Workplace
Industrial Relations Surveys .

Authors' Note

Many people have contributed to the enterprise of which this book is an outcome. Most importantly, since the surveys upon which it is based were voluntary, we owe a great debt of thanks to the respondents who participated in the survey. Both managers and trade union representatives – nearly 5000 of them in each of the surveys – gave generously of their time to complete the lengthy schedule of questions that we had devised, and made considerable efforts to ensure that their answers were factually accurate. In thanking them for their pains, we do so on behalf of all those that benefit from the availability of the survey data: the four sponsoring bodies; analysts of the data like ourselves and many other researchers who access it through the ESRC Data Archive; and you, the readers of this report and of the many other publications that will undoubtedly arise from continuing use of the data.

In the body of the book we refer to *our* surveys and *our* respondents. This is partly a linguistic convenience. It should not be taken as an indicator of proprietorial claims to the data; we welcome informed use of the data by other researchers and constructive dialogue about interpretations of it. But it does indicate an attachment to the value of the data that we are describing. Numerous people have cooperated with us to make it such a valuable resource. We should particularly like to thank Colin Airey and Jude England of Social and Community Planning Research for their sterling work throughout the project, but particularly the design and fieldwork phases of the 1984 survey, Denise Lievesley of the Survey Methods Centre for her advice on sample design and weighting, Steve Elder for his data-processing work and the interviewers, coders and office staff at SCPR who all provided essential contributions. At the data analysis stage we were helped by staff of the Policy Studies Institute, particularly Karen McKinnon, in processing the results. During the production of this book we received the valued support of family, friends and colleagues. Finally, our thanks go to Bill Daniel for carrying out the analysis for and drafting Chapters 2 and 9 of this book. Without this assistance we could never have adhered to the gruelling publication timetable set for us by the Survey's Steering Committee.

In bringing a report of this nature to publication within two years of the end of fieldwork, a year less than we managed on the 1980 survey, we are conscious of its limitations. There are a few questions on which we have not reported; and there are many topics and issues which deserve a much deeper analysis than has been possible within our timetable. We hope, however, that what we have presented will provide a useful input into public discussion of industrial relations in Britain and a starting point for further exploration, by us and others, of the invaluable source of information which the survey datasets comprise. Naturally, we take full responsibility for any errors and omissions in the material presented here. We must also make it clear that the interpretations of the survey results, and any views expressed, are ours and should not be taken as representing those of any of the four sponsoring bodies.

Neil Millward
Mark Stevens

Social Science Branch
Department of Employment
July 1986

List of Tables

Notes on Tables Used in the Text

All tables contain results from the 1980 and 1984 cross-sectional samples unless otherwise specified in the table heading.

General conventions adopted in tables
§   Unweighted base too low for percentages (see Note A).
( )   Percentages should be treated with caution (see Note B).
..   Data not available (see Note J).
*   Fewer than 0. 5 per cent
—   Zero

Notes on tables

(A) Unweighted base is fewer than 20 and therefore too low for percentages.

(B) Unweighted base is 20 or more but fewer than 50; percentages should be treated with caution.

(C) Column and row percentages do not always add to 100 owing to the rounding of decimal points.

(D) The proportions in subsidiary categories do not always add to the proportion in a composite category owing to the rounding of decimal points. For example, in 71 per cent of cases in 1984 shop stewards of the same employer, but from various workplaces organised primary picketing and in 69 per cent of cases stewards at the picketed workplace organised it and in three per cent of cases it was organised by stewards based elsewhere.

(E) Column and row percentages sometimes add to more than 100 because more than one answer was possible.

(F) The proportions in subsidiary categories do not always add to the proportion in a composite category because more than one answer was possible. For example, although strike action among white-collar workers was reported in 14 per cent of workplaces in 1983/84 and non-strike action in 12 per cent, *either* form of action was reported in 18 per cent of workplaces.

(G) The base numbers for the individual categories in a variable do not add to the total base number because the necessary information was not provided in a number of cases.

(H) The weighted base numbers for the individual categories in a variable may not add to the total weighted base number owing to the rounding of decimal points.

(J) The data is not available because either the question was not asked, or it was asked of a different respondent, or the question was asked in a sufficiently different form to make strict comparisons difficult, or the category is not applicable.

(K) Column percentages sometimes add to more than 100 as data from more than one respondent are used for each category of response. For example, either blue-collar or white-collar worker representatives in 76 per cent of cases said they were 'very satisfied' or 'quite satisfied' with the working of their pay disputes procedure in 1984, while in 29 per cent of cases some form of dissatisfaction was expressed.

(L) The base numbers for the individual categories in a variable do not add to the total base number because only an illustrative range of categories was included. For example, in our analysis of trade union organisation we use a variable which shows the union to which our worker representative respondents belonged. It includes a column for all representatives but provides more detailed information for only the four or five unions with sufficient numbers of observations among our sample.

The different sources of information

As is the case with the text, where data are presented in tables without the source of the information being identified it will have been provided by the management respondent. Where 1980 data are used and the source is identified as the manual or the non-manual worker representative without any further qualification, it will be the primary worker representative.

Unless otherwise specified the information used for breakdown variables, such as number employed at establishment, size of total organisation, industrial sector, ownership and trade union membership density, will be that provided by managers.

1 Introduction

Change and stability in the structures and practices of British workplace industrial relations are the twin themes of this book. Whilst they are not new themes, the nature of our evidence is new. For the first time in Britain, we are able to call upon systematic, large-scale survey evidence about industrial relations practices for two points in time – and the surveys which generated that evidence were specifically designed for the purpose of measuring change.[1]

In our report on the first survey,[2] we drew attention to the lack of authoritative, national data on industrial relations practices for the illumination and evaluation of industrial relations issues. We expressed the hope that the 1980 survey would be the first in a series of similar surveys. It is a hope that received support in many quarters. Reviews of our report on the first survey, in the national press, in learned journals and in a wide variety of other publications, generally welcomed the notion of a series of surveys on the lines of the 1980 survey. This encouraged the three original sponsors, the Department of Employment, the Economic and Social Research Council and the Policy Studies Institute (with funds from the Leverhulme Trust), to commission a second survey, this time with an additional sponsor – the Advisory, Conciliation and Arbitration Service. Within weeks of the publication of the first survey report arrangements were made for the joint funding of the second survey and serious design work began.

The survey design
With the measurement of change as a primary objective, many of the decisions that had had to be made for the first survey quite naturally made themselves for the second. Obviously we had to concentrate on the same types of question – predominantly factual questions about formal structures and practices. In terms of design, we clearly had to maintain the establishment as our unit of data collection and analysis. For the widest possible comparisons we also had to maintain, if possible, the same comprehensive coverage of sizes and types of establishment as was contained in the achieved sample for the first survey. And we had to interview at least one of the same type of respondent as we had in 1980. With these fundamental characteristics

kept constant there were still many possibilities for variation and choice in the design of the second survey, choices which would impact on the comparability of the results. Below we outline the most important of these choices and variations to give the reader the relevant technical background with which to evaluate the material presented in the chapters that follow this one. For the interested reader further detail on these topics is contained in the Technical Appendix.

The sample

With the *establishment* or *workplace* firmly fixed as our unit of interest, our obvious requirement in terms of a sampling frame was for one as similar as possible to that used for the 1980 survey. In 1979, when preparations for the 1980 survey were well under way, the most comprehensive and up-to-date sampling frame of workplaces had been the 1977 *Census of Employment*; similarly in late 1983, when we needed to approach employers for interviews for the second survey, the results of the 1981 *Census of Employment* had just become available. There was, however, a difference between the two censuses, the 1977 one being dated April of that year, the 1981 version being moved to September. With fieldwork for the 1984 survey occurring at roughly the same time of year as previously, the result was that we were using a slightly more up-to-date sampling frame: two and a half years old instead of three. This had two effects. It slightly reduced the number of establishments that had closed down or dropped below our threshold of 25 employees by the time we required an interview, thus reducing slightly the required size of our initial drawn sample. There was thus a minor effect upon the size of the 'unproductive' part of the sample, but it was small in comparison with other effects, to be detailed later. The other effect of the more up-to-date frame was not merely an operational one: the 1984 sample could contain establishments which were either set up or had grown to 25 or more employees between three and two and a half years previously, thus increasing the proportion of 'young' workplaces. In fact, the proportion of establishments in the sample which had been carrying out their current main activity for three years or less changed little, being 1.5 per cent in 1980 and 1.7 per cent in 1984, and many of these cases would have been either establishments that had moved address or had changed their main activity. We therefore judge that having a slightly more up-to-date sampling frame for the 1984 survey had no material effect on the 1984 results or upon comparisons between the two surveys.

No major changes were made in the scope or design of the sample. As before it was limited to workplaces with 25 or more employees, the decision to include establishments down to this relatively small size having been well justified by the 1980 results.[3] Again the survey covered England, Wales and Scotland and its industrial coverage was all manufacturing and services, both public and private sector. However, whereas in 1980 the coal mining industry was excluded from the achieved sample, although included in the sample scope, in 1984 it was excluded at the sample issue stage because of the widespread stoppage of work in that industry (and hence lack of potentially available interviewees) throughout the fieldwork period. The industrial coverage of the two surveys is thus identical.

However, we did make one minor modification to the sample design. The sample was again an unclustered, stratified one with size (number of employees) being the basis of stratification. To enable comparisons between large and small establishments to be made, and to increase the accuracy of estimates of employees covered by particular practices or arrangements, we oversampled large establishments, as before. But methodological work on the results of the 1980 survey had suggested that a slight improvement in the accuracy of *employee* estimates could be obtained without noticeably sacrificing the accuracy of *establishment-based* estimates by marginally reducing the sampling fraction for smaller units. This modification was made. The sampling fractions thus used varied from one in 92 for the smallest establishments (25 to 49 employees) to one in 3.3 for the largest (1000 or more employees), a slightly wider range than in 1980. The general principle of weighting the data to compensate for the oversampling of larger establishments is maintained. Details are given later in this chapter and in the Technical Appendix.

Fortuitously, the achieved sample in 1984 was very similar in size to the 1980 sample: 2019 compared with 2040 previously.[4] The intention had been to achieve about 1850 cases from the sample taken from the 1981 census compared to a target of 2000 for the first survey. In 1984 the target of 1850 was overshot considerably, largely because of a higher than anticipated response rate of 77 per cent.

A new feature of the second survey was the inclusion of a separate sample drawn from those establishments where interviews were successfully carried out in 1980. The target for this 'deliberate panel' sample was 150 cases, bringing the overall total to 2000, as for the first survey. It was also anticipated that a number of cases in the main, independently-drawn sample would also have been interviewed in 1980, especially amongst larger establishments which were deliberately sampled with much greater probability. Extensive comparisons were made between the address lists of the two surveys and 96 cases were identified as such 'chance repeats'. By combining these 96 'chance repeats' with the 139 achieved 'deliberate panel' cases the survey dataset contains 235 establishments that were interviewed in both 1980 and 1984. We refer to this panel sample of 235 cases at various points in the text because it can shed light on some features of the pattern of change which the main cross-sectional sample cannot. The size of the panel was, quite deliberately, kept small because it represented something of an experiment in survey practice as applied to organisational units. In consequence, and also because the range of weighting factors is very large,[5] results from it are subject to much greater sampling errors than results from the main sample. Despite the small size of the panel sample, there might at first sight appear to be some advantage in combining the deliberate panel cases with the main sample; this we have not done because the panel sample is not representative of the 1984 population of workplaces, but rather of those that existed in 1977, when our first sampling frame was constructed, *and had survived until 1984*, having 25 or more employees in 1977, 1980 and 1984. With this minimum size threshold being operated at three different points in time – and given the volatility of employment size, particularly in the private sector – it should be no surprise that our panel sample has many fewer small workplaces, after correctly weighting for selection probabilities, than the main samples in both 1980 and 1984. Until further methodological work has been done on the panel sample it seems sensible to restrict its use to illustrating possible patterns of change amongst larger workplaces, rather than to arrive at any definite judgements about those patterns.

In all respects other than the method of selection of the address, panel cases were treated in exactly the same way as cases that formed part of the main independent sample: in particular, the same survey instructions and questionnaires were used and there was no attempt to provide interviewers in 1984 with information from the same establishment obtained[6] in 1980. Because the two parts of the sample were treated identically we continue with our account of the survey design without the need to distinguish between them.

The respondents

The 1980 survey design specified between one and five respondents to be interviewed in each selected workplace: up to two representatives of management and up to three employee representatives. In 1984 a further management representative was added and one of the worker representatives was dropped.

The key role of the *senior person at the establishment dealing with industrial relations, employee relations or personnel matters* remained our *primary management respondent*. As in 1980, we expected there to be cases where such a person would be unable to answer all sections of the questionnaire and would call on the help of, or refer the interviewer to, a colleague. In 1980 there were 165 such cases where a *secondary management respondent* was interviewed; in 1984 there were 220. In four of these cases there was an additional secondary management respondent, an eventuality that had been allowed for, but did not occur, in 1980. As before, a complete management interview (plus a completed *Basic Workforce Data Sheet*) was compulsory for an address to be counted as productive; the bulk of data provided by secondary management respondents, where present, was consolidated into the primary respondent's questionnaire.

At some workplaces belonging to larger organisations, especially in the public sector, interviewers were unable to obtain information at the sampled address and were referred to people at other levels of the organisation, usually an area or headquarters office. There were 207 such cases, an increase of a fifth from 1980.

The additional management respondent interviewed in 1984 was referred to as a *Works (or Production) Manager*. This role was added to the design to complement information obtained from the primary respondent where the primary respondent was clearly in the industrial relations or personnel function, rather than being a general manager. The main use of this additional questionnaire was in a specific topic area, the introduction of advanced technological change, which was new in the 1984 survey. As the title implies, works manager interviews were only sought if the establishment was engaged in manufacturing. Of the 2019 cases in the main sample, 561 were engaged in manufacturing.[7] In 196 of these the primary management respondent was not an industrial relations or personnel specialist and therefore no works management interview was required. Of the remainder, 15 had no works manager at the site and interviews were obtained in 259, a response rate of 74 per cent.

Interviews with worker representatives were an important part of the design of the first survey, providing information that added to or complemented the data obtained from management. For the second survey we confined the number of possible worker representative interviews to two and slightly restricted the circumstances in which they were required. As before, the circumstances were based upon data collected during the course of management interviews and worker representative interviews were sought with the knowledge, and often help, of management. In establishments with recognised trade unions for manual workers an interview was sought with the *senior shop steward (or similar lay representative)* of the negotiating group which represented the largest number of manual workers. Similarly, where non-manual unions or staff associations were recognised, the senior lay representative of the largest non-manual negotiating group was sought for interview.[8]

Manual worker representatives were interviewed in 79 per cent of cases where an interview was required, compared with 84 per cent in 1980. Corresponding response rates for non-manual representatives were 82 per cent in 1984 and 85 per cent earlier. As before, refusal by management to allow the interview was the single most common reason for non-response. Refusal by worker representatives themselves accounted for four per cent of cases in 1984, compared with only one per cent in 1980. In a very small number of cases, as in 1980, the appropriate representative of the largest negotiating group was not available and an interview was obtained with a representative of the second largest negotiating group.

In total the main sample generated 2519 completed questionnaires for management respondents (including 17 works manager questionnaires not counted above in cases where they were not strictly required) and 1859 worker representatives (910 manual, 949 non-manual). Interviews took place over the period mid-March to early October 1984, with about three quarters in the four months April to July. The median interview date in mid-May was very close to the median interview date for the 1980 survey, although for various practical reasons the second half of the sample took longer to complete. Interviews typically lasted about the same as they had on the first survey, that is about an hour and a half for the main management interview, three quarters of an hour for worker representatives and the same for works managers.

Interview content and structure
The content and structure of the 1984 questionnaires followed quite closely the lines of the first survey. None of the major topics covered in 1980 was dropped, although on a few topics there was more limited questioning.[9] Others were expanded on matters of detail and a completely new topic area was added. This concerned the methods of, and reactions to, the introduction of advanced technological change and was dealt with in somewhat different ways for manual and non-manual workers. It involved substantial questioning in the main management questionnaire and, for manual workers only, in the works manager questionnaire, besides more limited questioning in the two worker representative questionnaires. This important topic, with the added advantage of the rest of the survey data as analytical background, is the subject of a separate publication.[10]

Besides the above-mentioned new topic, two of the original topics received substantially expanded questioning. One of these was the subject of employment practices, where recent research had indicated a lack of extensive data which could be allied to the characteristics of employing establishments. The other was that of pay levels and pay determination, an area of recurrent interest where again the combination of some more detailed questioning plus the existing background characteristics of workplaces would provide a rich source of research material.

A general impression of the degree of change in the questionnaire content between the two surveys is given by the fact that about two thirds of the questions in the 1984 survey were repeated, usually verbatim, from the 1980 questionnaires. These 'core' questions form the basis for most of the analysis of change in this report.[11]

Although the *establishment* or *workplace* provided the focus of data collection, our initial design catered for, and the 1980 survey confirmed, variation in many industrial relations practices *within* establishments. The key analytical distinction between *manual* and *non-manual* workers was maintained, along with the occasional subdivisions of the workforce into male and female and full-time and part-time employees. We also kept strictly to the original notion of *negotiating groups or bargaining units*, that is, groups of employees with common representational arrangements involving a trade union or group of unions *recognised* by management for collective bargaining.

Weighting
As mentioned earlier, the design of our sample involved the selection of workplaces with different sampling fractions, with larger workplaces having higher probabilities of selection than smaller workplaces. In broad terms, the weights applied in this report to the raw survey data were those necessary to restore the numbers of cases in each size band to their proper proportions according to the census. For convenience the results have again been weighted back to a base of 2000 establishments. We have, however, incorporated a modification to this basic principle which compensates for the under-representation of small establishments near the minimum size threshold and improves the accuracy of employee estimates. This modification was not made to the results contained in our report on the 1980 survey.[12] In consequence, figures for the 1980 survey given in this report may differ from those given in that report and in other publications based upon the original weighting scheme. Nevertheless, the important point when using the results from the two surveys to monitor change is to use weighting schemes that are strictly comparable.[13] This we have done.

Accuracy of the results
The results of the 1984 survey, as with all surveys, are subject to sampling errors, reflecting the possibility that the various measures such as proportions and averages computed from the sample may not correspond to those of the population from which the sample was

drawn. Because of the disproportionate sampling of large establishments the sampling errors in both the surveys were greater than would have been the case if simple random sampling had been used. We estimate that the design increased sampling errors by about 25 per cent for both surveys. Given the virtually identical sample sizes, the sampling errors for the two surveys are for practical purposes the same. In Table 1.1 we give the approximate sampling error attached to a selection of proportions for each survey, assuming a 95 per cent confidence level. These are the sampling errors attached to a single estimate for either the 1980 survey or the 1984 survey. The sampling errors attached to measures of *change* have to encompass the sampling error attached to both surveys and therefore are computed differently. These are shown in the second half of the table.

Table 1.1   Sample errors for estimates derived from each of the two surveys and for differences between the two surveys

| | Percentage found by survey | | | |
	10 or 90	20 or 80	30 or 70	50
Sampling error for single estimate (per cent)	1.6	2.3	2.5	2.8

| | Difference in percentages between the two surveys (for whichever percentage is the more extreme) | | | |
	10 or 90	20 or 80	30 or 70	50
Sampling error for the difference (per cent)	2.3	3.0	3.5	3.8

Let us illustrate both of these calculations in turn. If a particular characteristic was found among 30 per cent of the sample in the 1984 survey sample (or, indeed, the 1980 sample) its sampling error would be (from the table) 2.5 per cent. We could therefore be 95 per cent certain that the true proportion in the whole population was within the range 27.5 per cent to 32.5 per cent. Suppose this characteristic showed a change from 24 per cent in 1980 to 29 per cent in 1984. Using the more extreme of the two figures, the 24 per cent, and taking the nearest column in the table we would have a sampling error for the difference of 3.0 per cent. Thus we could be 95 per cent confident that our change between the two surveys of some five per cent was not due to sampling error but represented a real change in the population over the period between the two surveys. Naturally, measures of character-istics of subsamples – and of change from a subsample in 1980 to the same subsample in 1984 – are subject to greater sampling errors. We have taken this into account when reporting changes in the body of this report.

But sampling error is only one of the possible sources of error in survey research. Measurement error can arise from imprecision of the questions asked, misinterpretation of instructions by interviewers and of the questions by respondents, coding errors by interviewers or coders and many other sources. Fortunately, these largely unquantifi-able sources of error can be discounted when the interest is in aggregate change between two surveys of nearly identical design and with standardised execution in the field. The use of the same research organisation to carry out the two surveys undoubtedly helped to minimise the introduction of new and unquantifiable sources of error at the fieldwork and data-processing stages of the work.

The choice of respondents for the analysis

Multiple-respondent surveys, such as both of the surveys in our series, widen the possibilities for analysis, because they allow a wider range of questioning and because many of the questions may be asked of more than one respondent. In the 1984 survey something less than two fifths of the questions were put to both our main management respondents and to worker representatives. In such cases the answers of the two sets of respondents can be compared as a check on the reliability of the information obtained, provided the question is a factual one, as most of them are in our case. Our practice in this book, as in the earlier one, has been to confine ourselves to a single account of the topic in question, usually that of the management respondent. This is largely because we have a primary management respondent for every case in the survey, whereas we only have worker representatives for a subsample. Generally we have satisfied ourselves that the two sets of responses have a similar distribution (among establishments where worker representatives were interviewed) before doing this. Where the distributions were different we have generally pointed out the differences, especially if the patterns in relation to other variables were different. Exceptionally, we have combined information from the two sets of respondents to give what we consider to be a more reliable measure of the phenomenon in question. This was done in the case of industrial action, as indeed we did on the first survey. A fuller account of our reasons for doing that is available in the earlier book[14] and we have found nothing in the 1984 results that suggests changing the practice.

The same issues arise anew from our inclusion of an additional respondent in the 1984 survey – the works or production manager in manufacturing plants with specialist personnel management. This additional interview was added, in these highly selected and atypical circumstances, to enrich our data on the introduction of advanced technical change. The analysis of those data is reported separately[15] and contains extensive comparisons between personnel managers' and works managers' responses to many of the questions on that particular topic. We have not repeated that analysis in this volume.

The context of change

In interpreting changes in industrial relations practices between 1980 and 1984, as measured by our survey data, we have had to bear in mind the changing context of British industial relations over the period. Against the background of an unchanged government for the period from 1979 to the present, there were substantial changes in both the legislative and economic contexts of industrial relations. Our first survey was carried out prior to the present government's first piece of industrial relations legislation, the Employment Act 1980; our second survey was conducted after its second legislative initiative, the Employment Act 1982, had been in operation for some time. The government's third initiative of direct relevance to our subject, the Trade Union Act 1984, was enacted towards the end of our interview programme, but most of its provisions came into force well after completion of the survey. In essence, then, the 1980 and 1982 Acts are the ones of relevance to our study of industrial relations change over the period mid-1980 to mid-1984. They covered a wide range of matters including: trade union ballots on the election of worker representatives; industrial action; picketing; unfair dismissal; trade union membership; trade union recognition; and the closed shop.[16] On some of these matters our survey data have a fairly direct connection with the legal changes that were made; on others the connection between what was measured by the survey questions and the legal changes is a tenuous one. In any event the legal changes were amongst many other influences that bore upon the matters in question and the attribution of a direct causal connection between the legislation and any specific change in industrial relations behaviour, practices or structures is difficult. We mention the possiblility of such connections, where appropriate, in the substantive chapters that follow.

Another important part of the context for our analysis of industrial relations change is the changing economic and, particularly, employment situation in Britain over the period. Employment in Great Britain fell from 22.5 million employees to 20.9 million between June 1980 and June 1984 in the economy as a whole, a drop of some seven per cent. The Workplace Industrial Relations Surveys (WIRS) do not, of course, cover the whole economy, the major exclusions being agriculture and coal mining and all small establishments. The drop in employment in the WIRS 'population' is unlikely to be greatly different from the seven per cent figure[17] and, in fact, the 1984 WIRS sample experienced a drop in employment from 1980 to 1984 of nine per cent.[18] Some of the loss of employment in the economy as a whole is accounted for by closures of whole workplaces, particularly in manufacturing. These, of course, will not have been interviewed in 1984. But the major part of the change in employment structure between 1980 and 1984 is represented by changes in the employment size of establishments existing in both 1980 and 1984 and this is reflected in our survey data. Another and perhaps more illuminating way of looking at the change is to take percentage change figures comparing each establishment's size in 1980 with its size in 1984. These figures form the basis of Table 1.2.

Looking at the first row of Table 1.2 the preponderance of establishments with declining employment numbers is clear. While there were roughly as many establishments that shrank by 20 per cent or more (13 per cent) as grew by 20 per cent or more (15 per cent), there were many more that showed moderate declines of between five per cent and 20 per cent in the four years (22 per cent of the sample) than showed growth of the same degree (13 per cent). Workplaces with stable workforces (showing changes of less than five per cent over four years) accounted for 17 per cent of the sample. Unfortunately, but not surprisingly, quite a substantial number of respondents (17 per cent) were unable to provide precise numbers for their 1980 workforce, but this does not appear to invalidate the **patterns** of employment change shown in the rest of the table, although it does mean that the individual percentages should be used cautiously.

Looked at by size of establishment in 1984, the pattern of change in employment size since 1980 is such that the largest establishments are the most likely to have shrunk or remained stable. Very few large workplaces showed sizeable growth. This is entirely consonant with what is known from other sources[19] about the changing size distribution of workplaces. It also fits with the shift in the size distribution of our two samples, the 1984 sample having fewer large workplaces than the 1980 sample.

More illuminating is the next part of the table indicating in which parts of economy the changes occurred. In private sector manufacturing the picture is of very substantial changes in both directions, but with a clear predominance of cases with declining numbers of employees. Private sector services were somewhat more stable, with a slight preponderance of growing establishments. This again is what

Table 1.2   Percentage change in number of employees, 1980 to 1984, for various types of establishment

Row percentages

	Decrease of 20% or more	Decrease of 5% to 20%	Stable	Increase of 5% to 20%	Increase of 20% or more	Under 25 employees in 1980	New establishment since 1980	No information on 1980 size	Unweighted base	Weighted base
						6[1]			2019	2000
All establishments	13	22	17	13	15	6[1]	2	17	2019	2000
Number of employees at establishment										
25–49	12	23	17	15	13	11	3	18	353	1039
50–99	14	23	17	12	23	2	*	11	362	494
100–199	16	19	15	15	12	2	2	21	362	260
200–499	18	19	17	10	15	1	1	22	362	145
500–999	21	20	16	10	15	1	1	19	295	40
1000–1999	17	36	17	7	3	*	*	19	202	17
2000 or more	22	25	24	12	4	–	–	14	83	6
Broad sector										
Private manufacturing	29	19	9	10	22	6	2	9	592	424
Private services	12	19	14	17	18	8	2	19	597	843
Nationalised industries	9	26	35	4	7	1	*	19	196	106
Public services	5	29	22	14	9	6	1	20	634	627
Proportion of workforce who are manual										
More than 70%	13	24	17	11	15	7	1	19	645	667[2]
From 31% to 70%	19	22	15	12	14	6	3	16	627	649
Up to 30%	8	22	18	17	17	5	2	16	747	683
Proportion of workforce who are part-time										
More than 40%	6	20	23	14	11	10	3	23	262	383
From 6% to 40%	11	26	16	14	15	5	1	15	659	721
Up to 5%	19	21	14	12	17	6	3	15	1015	820
Proportion of workforce who are female										
More than 70%	7	22	22	14	15	9	1	18	352	478
From 31% to 70%	11	26	15	17	15	4	1	15	670	632
Up to 30%	20	22	15	11	17	8	3	12	803	755
Primary market for products or services[3]										
Local or regional	15	20	14	16	15	8	2	17	287	478
National	19	21	17	10	18	5	2	14	395	307
International	20	19	14	15	19	8	6	8	221	161
Not answered	16	17	12	13	22	9	2	19	212	209
Number of competitors[3]										
None	12	31	23	9	10	1	–	15	158	116
Between 1 and 5	16	18	15	17	20	10	2	12	387	363
More than 5	20	18	13	12	17	7	3	15	478	549
Not answered	9	19	11	14	22	8	*	25	92	126

[1] See Note C.   [2] See Note G.   [3] Base is all industrial and commercial establishments.

one would expect from national statistical sources on employment. In the public sector employment stability or slight decline is the rule, with the nationalised industries having particularly stable employment numbers.

The next three portions of Table 1.2 cover individual worker characteristics and again clearly reflect shifts in the pattern of employment that are well documented in national statistics. Establishments with predominantly non-manual (white-collar) workforces were slightly more likely to have expanded, and were less likely to have declined substantially, than other workplaces. Headquarters establishments, with a large preponderance of non-manual employees, were also more likely to have grown than other establishments that were part of multi-establishment organisations. Workplaces with high proportions of part-time workers were very much less likely to have contracted than those with moderate or low proportions of part-timers. And, closely related because most part-time workers are female, workplaces with predominantly female workforces were much less likely than other workplaces to have contracted. These shifts are in fact somewhat understated in this analysis because our measurement of the workforce characteristic (such as the proportion of females) uses the 1984 data which already incorporate the changes in composition since 1980. If we just compare the composition of our 1980 and 1984 samples with respect to these same characteristics – and using the same arbitrary cut-off points for the categories – some of these trends are again apparent; in particular the decline in workplaces with predominantly manual workforces which fell from 41 per cent of our sample in 1980 to 33 per cent in 1984 (using the 70 per cent manual cut-off shown in Table 1.2). Alternatively, we see the same trend using our data in a more direct way, simply adding up the weighted totals of manual and non-manual workers in our sample and expressing the aggregate number of manual workers as a percentage of the grand total. On this basis, 53 per cent of all workers covered by the survey were classified as manual in 1980, whereas in 1984 the proportion was 46 per cent. Using the same method of calculation the proportion of part-time employees rose from 14 per cent in 1980 to 16 per cent in 1984; the relative decline in male employment matched this.

Another compositional change which might be inferred from other national sample survey sources[20] (for example the Labour Force Surveys) is also manifested in our results, namely that the proportion of workplaces with a substantial proportion of ethnic minority workers (10 per cent was the cut-off used in both surveys) dropped slightly from 8 per cent in 1980 to 5 per cent in 1984. Such workplaces were also more likely to have shrunk substantially when we used similar measures to those given in Table 1.2.

So far the changes discussed might have been inferred from other sources, although we should stress that analysing the characteristics of the employed population and analysing the characteristics of workplaces are quite different forms of analysis and could well exhibit different trends.[21] However, further light on the changing context of industrial relations over the period covered by our research can be shed by looking at responses to a number of background questions asked in both surveys as well as some new questions that can be related to the changing employment picture.

First of all, the relative decline of private sector employment compared with the public sector, already mentioned in our discussion of Table 1.2, is further illustrated by the fact that private sector establishments declined from 68 per cent of our sample in 1980 to 63 per cent in 1984. Employment in private sector establishments shrank from 64 per cent to 57 per cent of all employees covered by the sample, again confirming the trend identified earlier. Within the private sector, foreign-owned establishments represented seven per cent of cases in both surveys, although in employment terms there were differences in the amount of change between foreign-owned and British-owned plants. Foreign-owned establishments were more likely to have made severe workforce reductions over the period 1980 to 1984 and less likely to have kept their employment constant (within five per cent of the 1980 figure). But they were equally as likely as British-owned establishments to have grown in employment terms. While some of the explanation of these differences could lie in the industries in which foreign-owned firms are concentrated, some of it may also lie in differences in industrial relations and employment practices between these two portions of the private sector. We make occasional reference to foreign ownership in our analysis in subsequent chapters and its importance is highlighted in Daniel's companion volume on the introduction of advanced technology.[22]

A further aspect of the changing pattern of ownership in the private sector is shown by responses to a question asked in both surveys concerning changes in the ownership of sampled establishments. In 1980 we asked about changes of ownership in the past three years whereas in 1984 we asked about the previous four years so that we would catch all changes in the period between the two surveys. The actual proportions are therefore not strictly comparable, although allowing for the different periods suggests that the rate of change in the ownership of private sector workplaces did not alter substantially between the three years up to 1980 and the four years up to 1984. (The recent wave of takeovers and mergers was, of course, subsequent to our 1984 survey, as was much of the government's privatisation programme.) But changes in ownership were certainly widespread in the period 1980 to 1984: 18 per cent of our private sector sample had experienced them. Of these the great majority were takeovers or mergers, but there were also significant numbers of buyouts by management or by employees as a whole, as well as transfers between firms. Both of these latter forms of change were insignificant in our results[23] covering the period 1977 to 1980.

Many aspects of the changing economic environment for industry and commerce between 1980 and 1984 have been well documented elsewhere and the period leading up to when our first survey was conducted can be summarised as being the start of a rapid decline in gross domestic product and, especially, in manufacturing output. Both of these measures of economic activity had ceased to fall by early 1981 and had recovered substantially by the time of our 1984 survey. This change of circumstances is reflected in our management respondents' subjective assessments of the trend in the output of their establishment over the previous year.[24] Whereas in 1980 a third of respondents reported that demand was falling, in 1984 only one in ten respondents reported that sales were falling. Interestingly, and reassuringly, this dramatic change in economic conditions did not affect managers' assessments of the **relative** economic performance of their establishment compared with their competitors in the same industry – the proportions saying their establishment was above, about average or below average were virtually identical for the two surveys.

Of the remaining contextual data from the survey that are worth mentioning before the start of our analysis proper, two items were shown earlier in Table 1.2. The first of these concerns the type of market for the establishment's main products or services, the main distinction being between local (or regional) markets, national (UK) and international markets. Table 1.2 shows no very marked differences between the employment experience, 1980 to 1984, of establishments supplying these different types of market. But if there is a relationship it is a slightly greater tendency for establishments selling to international markets to have been more likely to have expanded their workforces over the previous four years than establishments selling to the UK market. The second market characteristic we measured was the number of competitors for the establishment's main products or services and the relationship between this variable and the four-year change in employment is again shown in Table 1.2. Here the pattern is clearer. Establishments in a monopoly situation (many of them part of nationalised industries) were much more likely to have stable or slightly declining workforces than establishments supplying competitive markets. The latter were much more likely to have reduced their workforces by 20 per cent or more over the previous four years; indeed, about a quarter of them had done so if we ignore cases where the 1980 employment size was not available. Using another measure of employment change, the change over the previous twelve months (roughly mid-1983 to mid-1984) showed this same pattern of greater stability for establishments in monopoly markets.

Two general points emerge from the above discussion. The first is that the economic circumstances of British workplaces had changed substantially between our two surveys and that such data as our survey contains on these circumstances appears to fit very well with the picture shown by other statistical sources. The second point is that our survey questions on the economic and employment background of establishments in our sample appear to have worked well. They therefore provide scope for explanation, albeit partial, of many of the changes in industrial relations practices and institutions that are our focus of interest in this book.

The contents of the book and some conventions used
As with most reports on multi-purpose surveys, the sequence of the substantive chapters is to some extent arbitrary and many of the chapters can be read independently of each other. In broad terms we have followed the sequence of topics used in the earlier book, which also generally followed the sequence of questioning in our interviews. In Chapter 2 we examine data from the two surveys on how management at establishment and higher organisational levels organised themselves for industrial relations purposes and on the qualifications and experience of those most closely involved. Chapter 3 covers various features of trade union membership and representation, particularly where trade unions are recognised by management, while Chapter 4 covers a particular form of trade union representation – the closed shop. In Chapter 5 we use information from trade union representatives to look at changes in the nature of the trade union branches to which their members belong, as well as inter-union structures at workplace and higher levels. Chapter 6 deals with formal methods of communication and consultation irrespective of the presence of trade unions. Industrial relations procedures and their use form the focus of Chapter 7. In Chapter 8 we analyse data from a number of questions, many of them asked for the first time, on employment practices, including various types of 'non-core' or 'marginal' worker. Chapter 9 deals with pay determination and payment systems as well as the scope of collective bargaining with trade unions. Finally, Chapter 10 deals with industrial action. The book ends with a general summary, highlighting the twin themes of

change and stability and some of the implications of the results.

As in the previous book, tables and text use information reported by our primary management respondents unless otherwise specified. We have introduced presentation of the results from questions used in the interview schedules by either direct quotation of the question or by incorporation of the gist of the question in the text. We have not, however, reproduced the interview schedules either in their entirety or in part. This is due to lack of space: the interview schedules from the 1984 survey alone amounted to some 188 pages and for some purposes it would be necessary to compare the wording used in the two surveys. Copies of the two sets of questionnaires, as well as the data from the two surveys, are available from the ESRC Data Archive at the University of Essex.[25]

Notes and references

1. A recent book by Batstone might appear to contradict this claim to novelty, since it contains survey evidence from 1983 and compares that with earlier data from the 'Warwick survey'. See Batstone E (1984) *Working Order: Workplace Industrial Relations over Two Decades*, Blackwell, Oxford; Brown W (ed.) (1981) *The Changing Contours of British Industrial Relations*, Blackwell, Oxford. However, Batstone's 1983 survey was a postal survey of only larger manufacturing plants, using an unsatisfactory sampling frame and having a response rate of about 50 per cent, yielding 133 usable questionnaires. We do not consider that this provides a firm empirical base and we have therefore not made extensive comparisons between his results and ours.

2. Daniel W W and Millward N (1983) *Workplace Industrial Relations in Britain: The DE/PSI/SSRC Survey*, Heinemann Educational Books, London, p.1. The book has recently been reprinted as *Workplace Industrial Relations in Britain: the DE/PSI/ESRC Survey*, Gower, Aldershot.

3. See, for example, Daniel W W and Millward N (1983) *op. cit.* p.6.

4. The 2019 establishments at which interviews were carried out in 1984 employed 954,669 employees, approximately one in 16 of those employed in the population of census units from which the sample was drawn.

5. The range is much greater than for the main sample because for the 'chance repeats' the probability of occurrence in the sample is the multiple of the two selection probabilities, one for selection in 1980, and the other for selection in 1984.

6. Strictly speaking, interviewers were given five items of information about each panel address from the 1980 data: its size, region and industry coding and whether primary manual or non-manual worker representatives had been interviewed. This was to help confirm that the correct establishment had been identified.

7. This is less than the 624 manufacturing cases shown in some tables in the body of the book because the 624 is based upon the *Standard Industrial Classification, 1980*, which classifies establishments to manufacturing even if they are only the headquarters or administrative offices of a manufacturing concern.

8. In 1980, worker representatives were also interviewed in circumstances where trade unions were not recognised but there was some other type of formal representation. See Daniel W W and Millward N (1983) *op. cit.* p.8.

9. There was more limited questioning on a number of aspects of trade union branch organisation and on the characteristics of shop steward combine committees.

Furthermore, a small section of questions about employers' use of homeworkers and outworkers was omitted because extensive work on this topic was being pursued through other sources. See Hakim C (1985) *Employers' use of outwork: a study using the 1980 Workplace Industrial Relations Survey and the 1981 National Survey of Homeworking*, Research Paper No. 44, Department of Employment, London; Hakim C (1987 forthcoming) *Homeworking in Britain*, Department of Employment, London.

10. Daniel W W (1986 forthcoming) *Workplace Industrial Relations and Technical Change*.

11. Millward N and Stevens M (1984) *The Workplace Industrial Relations Survey (WIRS) Series: a guide to questions in the 1980 and 1984 questionnaires*, Department of Employment, London. This guide is available from the ESRC Data Archive as part of the 1984 survey documentation.

12. Daniel W W and Millward N (1983) *op. cit.*

13. For all descriptive and most analytic purposes this second weighting scheme is preferable to that originally attached to the 1980 dataset and all users of the dataset via the ESRC Data Archive are recommended to use it and its equivalent on the 1984 dataset. Details are given in the Data Archive's documentation of the two surveys. Further adjustments to the weighting scheme used for the 1984 data have been contemplated, but await the availability of the 1984 Census of Employment size analysis.

14. Daniel W W and Millward N (1983) *op. cit.* pp.13 and pp.214-217.8.

15. Daniel W W (1986 forthcoming) *op. cit.*

16. The legal changes are summarised in: Department of Employment (1980) 'Employment Act 1980' *Employment Gazette*, August, pp. 876-7; Department of Employment (1982) 'The Employment Act 1982' *Employment Gazette*, November, pp. 473-6.

17. Because of delays in processing the 1984 Census of Employment, we cannot give a precise figure for the WIRS population, that is excluding workplaces or census units employing less than 25 employees.

18. This figure is based upon only the 83 per cent of the 1984 sample who provided 1980 employment data, but the data are more complete in private manufacturing, the sector where employment losses were greatest, and so it seems unlikely that there is significant bias in this result.

19. See, for example, Business Statistics Office (1979 and 1984) 'Analysis of United Kingdom manufacturing (local) units by employment size', *Business Monitor PA 1003*, HMSO, London.

20. Barber A (1985) 'Ethnic origin and economic status' *Employment Gazette*, December, pp. 467-77; Brown C (1984) *Black and White Britain*, Heinemann Educational Books, London.

21. For example, part-time employment could have increased relative to full-time employment without the much lower rate of contraction of workplaces with high concentrations of part-timers apparent in Table 1.2.

22. Daniel W W (1986 forthcoming) *op. cit.*

23. Strict comparisons between the 1980 and 1984 responses to the question on changes of ownership cannot be made because of the shift from an open question in 1980 to a question with pre-coded responses in 1984.

24. There was a minor change in wording from 'demand for main product or service' to 'value of sales of main product or service'. This is unlikely to have affected results, although the change of wording helped to reduce the non-response rate for the question, confirming the desirability of the change.

25. Enquiries should be made to The Director, ESRC Data Archive, University of Essex, Wivenhoe Park, Colchester, Essex CO4 3SQ quoting Study Nos. 1575 for the 1980 survey and 2060 for the 1984 survey.

2 Management Organisation for Industrial Relations★

We were struck in our 1980 survey by the persisting rarity of professional personnel management in Britain.[1] In most workplaces personnel work was done by managers who in no sense of the word could be called specialists. Only about a half of the managers who spent a major part of their time on personnel matters had job titles that identified them as personnel managers in even the broad meaning of the term. Moreover, only a half of the personnel specialists had any formal qualifications for the work and by far the most common type of qualification was membership of an occupational association on its own. The most common type of preparation for personnel management was on-the-job experience or training in the establishment or organisation where managers were working. That was the case even when the job was done by a specialist. More frequently, personnel work was done by general managers or specialists in other management functions for whom personnel management was a minor part of their work. The sense of pervasive amateurism with which we were left by our 1980 findings was heightened by the expectations with which we came to our analysis. We had expected to find that professional personnel management was spreading as a result of the codification and formalisation of British industrial relations during the 1970s, encouraged by the growth of employment legislation.

Much changed between 1980 and 1984 that could have influenced the position of personnel management. But we would have been surprised if we had found a major change over the four-year period in the general distribution of personnel managers as measured by the proportion of workplaces that had personnel specialists or in the extent to which those specialists were professionally qualified. And so it proved to be the case (see Table 2.1). We found that 15 per cent of our workplaces in 1980 employed personnel specialists on site.[2] In 1984 that proportion remained 15 per cent. In 1980, a third of our principal management respondents, selected on the basis that they were the most senior person with responsibility for personnel or industrial relations matters[3] at the workplace, said that they spent a

★W W Daniel is principal author of this chapter.

Table 2.1   The distribution of specialist personnel managers

Percentages

	All establishments	Number of employees at establishment						
		25–49	50–99	100–199	200–499	500–999	1000–1999	2000 or more
Whether personnel in job title								
1980	15	5	12	25	52	74	86	92
Unweighted base	*1868*	*340*	*339*	*353*	*343*	*233*	*138*	*122*
Weighted base	*1831[1]*	*936*	*456*	*239*	*138*	*38*	*17*	*9*
1984	15	4	12	29	54	68	85	96
Unweighted base	*1794*	*311*	*315*	*313*	*321*	*267*	*192*	*75*
Weighted base	*1779*	*933*	*432*	*229*	*130*	*36*	*16*	*5*
Time spent on personnel matters								
1980								
Major part of time	33	21	32	46	72	85	93	95
1984								
More than a quarter	42	31	42	55	79	81	95	99
More than a half	22	11	18	37	59	72	90	94

Base: workplaces where respondents worked at the establishment

[1] See Note H.

Table 2.2 Personnel specialism and the job titles of respondents in relation to number of non-manual workers, 1984

Percentages

| | All establishments | Number of non-manual workers employed at establishment | | | | | | | Total employees |
		1–24	25–49	50–99	100–199	200–499	500–999	1000 or more	
Personnel specialist	15	3	14	28	48	60	75	91	47
Personnel in job title	13	3	13	26	43	51	64	79	41
Industrial/labour/employee/ staff relations in job title	2	*	1	2	5	9	11	12	6
Time spent on personnel/IR matters									
More than a quarter	42	32	34	60	74	82	85	97	68
More than a half	22	11	16	38	57	68	80	94	53
Base: workplaces with non-manual workers where respondents worked at the establishment									
Unweighted	*1791*	*391*	*288*	*287*	*278*	*277*	*158*	*112*	*1791*
Weighted	*1772[1]*	*854*	*468*	*244*	*119*	*62*	*16*	*10*	*1772*

[1] See Note H.

major part of their time on personnel matters. In 1984 we could not resist the temptation to improve upon the question by making it more precise and asking people what proportion of their time they spent upon personnel matters, even though that meant that we could not make strict comparisons with 1980. We found that 42 per cent of our respondents said that they spent more than a quarter of their time on personnel work, while 22 per cent said that they spent more than a half of their time upon such matters.

Variations in the distribution of personnel specialists in 1984
As in 1980, by far the strongest influence upon the extent to which workplaces had personnel specialists was their size, as measured by the number of people employed at the establishment. As the presence of a personnel specialist was so strongly associated with size, the number of employees at workplaces where there was a personnel specialist was very substantially higher than the number of workplaces having a specialist. Forty-seven per cent of non-manual workers had a personnel specialist at their workplace and that was true for 41 per cent of manual workers. It appeared that the number of non-manual workers employed was slightly more important than the number of manual workers. Table 2.2 shows the pattern for non-manual grades. We included among personnel specialists both respondents who had the word *personnel* in their job titles and respondents who had the phrases *industrial relations* or *staff relations* or *labour relations* or *employee relations* in their job titles. Only the large workplaces had a substantial proportion who fell into the second category and, unless otherwise specified, we use the term *personnel* generically in this chapter to include both categories.

Of course, the fact that only 15 per cent of workplaces had personnel specialists and just under a half of all employees were covered by personnel specialists at their workplaces does not mean that all other workers and workplaces were deprived of the benefit of professional personnel management. Some will have been employed at workplaces belonging to organisations that had personnel managers at a higher administrative level with responsibility for their workplace. On the other hand, our analysis in relation to whether workplaces were independent enterprises or parts of larger groups showed that, when workplaces of similar size were compared, those that belonged to groups were generally more likely to have personnel specialists on site. In consequence, it did not appear that the coverage of personnel management that we found could be explained away by any tendency for large organisations to centralise their personnel services away from workplaces.[4]

Generally, the critical size associated with a big increase in the employment of a personnel specialist on site was over 100 non-manual workers on the payroll, or over 100 manual workers, or, very neatly, over 200 workers in total. In relation to broad sector, private services stood out as being least likely to employ personnel specialists (see Table 2.3). Workplaces in that sector were least likely to have anyone with a personnel title, least likely to have someone who spent a substantial part of their time on personnel work, and when they had personnel specialists, they were least likely to be qualified, as we show later in the chapter. The contrast was most marked when larger workplaces were compared. Larger establishments engaged in manufacturing and public services were twice as likely as private service counterparts to have someone who spent three quarters of his/her time on personnel management. The public service sector was less likely than average to employ someone with a personnel title but more likely than average to have someone who spent a substantial amount of time on personnel work. It is likely that the distinctive position of that sector arose largely from the distinctive nomenclature used for people doing personnel work in parts of the sector.[5]

Table 2.3   Employment of personnel specialists in relation to sector among establishments employing 200 or more manual workers, 1984

Percentages

	Private manufacturing	Private services	Public services
Time spent on personnel			
More than three-quarters	72	(37)[1]	67
Job title			
Personnel/Industrial relations	85	(51)	55
Base: workplaces employing 200 or more manual workers and where respondents worked at the establishment			
Unweighted	*265*	*48*	*120*
Weighted	*36*	*8*	*18*

[1] See Note B.

Apart from size and sector, the strongest and most striking sources of variation in the employment of personnel specialists were, first, the nationality of workplaces in the private sector and, secondly, the extent to which establishments used advanced technology. Workplaces that belonged to overseas companies were very much more likely to employ personnel specialists than their domestically-owned counterparts. The contrast remained marked when we compared workplaces of similar size and when we compared British workplaces that belonged to multi-establishment enterprises with foreign-owned counterparts. Moreover, it appeared that the contrast was substantially more marked in relation to the number of manual workers employed as compared with variations in relation to the number of non–manual workers. That is to say, foreign-owned workplaces were particularly more likely to employ personnel specialists to manage a given number of manual workers. For example, medium-sized workplaces belonging to overseas companies were twice as likely to have personnel specialists, as domestic counterparts. Among the smallest workplaces the contrast was even greater. In Daniel's companion volume[6] on the introduction of technical change, it is shown that foreign-owned workplaces consistently out-performed British establishments in their use of technological resources both in the office and on the shop floor. It appeared that foreign-owned workplaces were also well ahead of British counterparts in their arrangements to manage human resources, especially manual workers. As we summarise later in this chapter, it was also found that the role of personnel management in the introduction of advanced technology tended to be modest. Nevertheless, when we analysed the extent to which specialist personnel managers were employed in relation to the use of computers and word processors in the office and of microelectronic technology on the shop floor, we found that the greater the use of advanced technology the more widely were personnel managers employed – and the trend was very marked.

The qualifications, experience and staff of people doing personnel work

Our two surveys give some indication of an increase during the early 1980s in the extent to which workplace personnel specialists had formal qualifications relevant to the function (see Table 2.4). In 1980, 49 per cent of specialists reported that they had formal qualifications for the job.[7] By 1984 that proportion had risen to 58 per cent. Moreover, there also appeared to be a substantial upgrading in the level of qualifications held by personnel specialists. More had degrees of some kind and more had relevant degrees (see Table 2.5). Nevertheless, it remained the case that only about a third of all those who spent a substantial amount of time on personnel duties had any formal qualification in personnel, and that was true for only just over a half of the personnel specialists. It was more difficult for us to make strict comparisons between non-specialists who spent a major part of their time in personnel work because of the change in the nature of our questioning to identify how much time respondents devoted to personnel.

As personnel specialists were so very much more common in larger

Table 2.4   The formal qualifications of personnel managers

Percentages

	All respondents		Personnel/IR specialist		Non-specialist	
	1980	1984	1980	1984	1980	1984
Professional/educational qualifications	29	30	49	58	16[1]	19
Support staff	53	51	48	54	57	50
Two or more years' experience in the work	84	95	89	95	82	95
Base: respondents who worked at the establishment and spent a major part of their time on personnel in 1980, a quarter or more of their time in 1984						
Unweighted	1055	1279	711	786	344	493
Weighted	608	894	244	259	364	635

[1] The base for 1980 non-specialists is people saying they spent a major part of their time on personnel matters while the corresponding base for 1984 is those spending a quarter or more of their time on personnel matters.

Table 2.5   Qualifications and staff of people doing personnel work

Percentages

	Personnel specialists working at establishments	
	1980	1984
Any formal qualification	49	58
Nature of qualification		
Member of professional association – no other formal qualification	26	27
Degree/diploma in business/ management/social science	9	14
Degree/diploma in personnel/ industrial relations	7	8
Other degree/diploma/certificate	2	9
Not stated	2	2
Base: personnel specialists who worked at the establishment		
Unweighted	711	801
Weighted	244	274

workplaces, it was also the case that people with personnel qualifications very much more frequently fulfilled the function in larger workplaces. In consequence, the proportion of employees at workplaces where personnel work was done by someone with formal qualifications for the job was substantially higher than the proportion of workplaces having a qualified personnel manager. When analysis was confined to establishments where our management respondents spent a major part of their time on personnel matters, nearly a half of non-manual workers enjoyed the benefit of having a qualified personnel manager at the place where they worked (see Table 2.6) and that was true for only a slightly smaller proportion of manual workers. It was surprising, though, that although personnel specialists were more common in larger workplaces, there was no tendency for personnel managers to be more likely to be qualified in larger establishments, when analysis was confined to workplaces with personnel specialists.

Still confining the analysis to workplaces that had personnel specialists, private services again stood out as the sector where personnel managers were least likely to be qualified. Even when larger workplaces were compared, only about a half of the personnel specialists in private service establishments were qualified compared with about three quarters of counterparts in private manufacturing and public services. Personnel specialists in private services were also very much less likely to have support staff. When the low level of qualification of personnel specialists in the private sector and the lack of support staff were added to the relative rarity of specialists in that sector, then its distinctiveness became even more marked.

In the private sector as a whole, the personnel specialists more frequently employed by workplaces belonging to overseas companies were also more likely to have formal qualifications than their counterparts in British workplaces, thereby magnifying the competitive advantage of foreign-owned workplaces in terms of personnel expertise. While workplaces with recognised trade unions were no more likely to have personnel specialists than those where there were no recognised unions, we found more marked differences in the extent to which personnel specialists in the two types of workplace had qualifications and support staff. Personnel specialists at workplaces where unions were recognised were substantially more likely to have staff to help them and formal qualifications. That was the case in relation to the recognition of both manual and non-manual unions and it remained true, although less marked, when we confined the analysis to workplaces of similar size (see Table 2.7). It did appear that the recognition of trade unions required workplaces to make a greater investment in personnel expertise.

The activities and responsibilities of personnel managers
When in 1980 we looked at the reports of our respondents of the extent to which a checklist of seven responsibilities or activities formed part of their job, we did not find their answers particularly instructive. The limitation of the questioning appeared to be that

Table 2.6 Qualifications and staff of people doing personnel work in relation to numbers of non-manual workers, 1984

Percentages

	All establishments	Number of non-manual workers employed at establishment							All non-manual employees
		1–24	25–49	50–99	100–199	200–499	500–999	1000 or more	
Professional/educational qualifications	30	24	25	29	42	57	57	73	47
Support staff	51	51	38	51	66	70	75	84	66
Two or more years' experience in the work	95	97	92	94	96	98	98	97	96
Base: respondents working at establishment who spent a quarter or more of their time on personnel matters									
Unweighted	1279	177	149	214	236	247	148	108	1279
Weighted	894	354	207	165	93	51	14	10	894

Table 2.7 **Qualifications and staff of people doing personnel work in relation to trade union recognition at medium-sized workplaces**

Percentages

	Manual union recognised	Manual union not recognised
Professional/educational qualification	25	20
Support staff	48	40
Two or more years' experience in the work	97	97
Base: workplaces employing between 50 and 199 manual workers and where respondent worked at establishment		
Unweighted	*353*	*85*
Weighted	*220*	*83*

people were able to report, for instance, that settling terms and conditions of employment formed part of their responsibilities on the basis of very different forms and levels of involvement. It seemed likely that what varied was the nature of involvement rather than whether there was any involvement at all. Our analysis, however, of people's reports in 1984 compared with 1980 suggests that there was some change in the priorities of personnel managers over that period. It appeared, first, that slightly more were involved in systems of pay and job evaluation. Secondly, a very high proportion of managers in 1984 (84 per cent) reported responsibility for industrial relations procedures. This compared with 56 per cent in 1980 who reported being responsible for *setting up* industrial relations procedures.[8] The difference is strikingly large and, given the actual increase in the existence of procedures documented in Chapter 7, it seems very likely that formal procedures have become a more widespread responsibility of managers involved in personnel and industrial relations work. It appears that the process of formalisation or codification of industrial relations that occurred during the 1970s, encouraged by the employment legislation of the decade, continued during the early part of the 1980s. Whether the industrial relations legislation of that period gave a further boost to the process, we cannot be certain. But the accounts, that we report at the end of the chapter, of the impact of industrial relations legislation upon personnel work during the early 1980s and the growth of formality in procedures described in Chapter 7 certainly suggest that it played a role in the changing pattern of personnel priorities.

Focusing upon the variations in the 1984 reports, there was, as in

Table 2.8   Respondents' activities and responsibilities

Percentages

	All respondents		Personnel specialists		Other job title	
	1980	1984	1980	1984	1980	1984
Disciplinary cases	92	90	96	93	91	90
Recruitment	90	89	93	91	89	88
Training	80	83	78	78	80	84
Settling/negotiating terms of employment	62	68	79	91	59	64
Job evaluation/grading	58	67	70	75	56	66
Industrial relations procedures[2]	56	84	78	95	52	82
Responsibility for systems of pay	49	53	41	67	51	50
Base: workplaces where respondents worked at the establishment						
Unweighted	*1868*	*1794*	*763*	*801*	*1105*	*993*
Weighted	*1831[1]*	*1779*	*278*	*274*	*1552*	*1505*

[1] See Note H.
[2] *Setting up* procedures in 1980. See Note 8 at end of Chapter.

1980, no very marked pattern. More specialists than non-specialists reported being involved in settling pay and conditions, in establishing industrial relations procedures and in systems of pay and job evaluation or grading. Fewer reported being involved in training. When analysis was confined to specialists, public services stood out as the sector where workplace personnel managers were least involved in systems of pay, doubtless reflecting the extent of centralisation of matters concerned with pay in that sector (see Chapter 9). The private services sector was notable for the small extent to which personnel managers were concerned with training. In the private sector generally, personnel managers working at establishments belonging to overseas companies were more involved than counterparts elsewhere in training and in systems of pay. There was surprisingly little difference in the responsibilities reported by personnel managers depending upon whether or not trade unions were recognised at their workplaces. We look further at the activities and responsibilities of personnel managers in the next section when we consider matters about which workplace personnel specialists consulted senior personnel managers at higher levels in their organisations.

Line relationships between personnel specialists at workplace level and personnel managers at other establishments in their organisations

The personnel specialists in our sample worked at the establishment level. The large majority of workplaces in our sample belonged to larger organisations. In some of those the personnel expertise was provided at a higher level in the organisation where specialist personnel managers will have serviced a number of establishments in the group. Indeed, seven per cent of our management interviews were with managers who did not work at the establishment to which the interview referred.[9] Even in cases where establishments had their own specialists they frequently reported to a superordinate personnel manager at a higher level in the organisation, generally at head office level. We asked our personnel specialists whether they had contact with a manager or director at a higher level and at a separate establishment in their organisation who spent a major part of his time on personnel or industrial relations matters. In cases where they did have such contact we asked how frequently it occurred, what topics they consulted senior managers about and the level at which the senior manager operated.

The answers enabled us to establish some measure of the centralisation of personnel management within organisations that operated a number of workplaces. There are, of course, generally two main options open to organisations so far as the lines of responsibility relating to local personnel managers are concerned. First, they may make local personnel managers responsible exclusively to general managers at workplace level. According to that option, the only line of responsibility running between establishments at different levels in the organisation goes through general managers. Alternatively, local personnel managers may be responsible for implementing personnel policies decided at a higher level and for that purpose they may have a line relationship with a senior personnel manager at regional office or divisional office or head office, as well as a staff relationship to local general managers. Our findings suggested that the second type of arrangement was more common and personnel management tended to be centralised in multi-establishment organisations. The majority of our local personnel specialists had contact with a senior personnel manager at another establishment. Contact with that manager was generally very frequent. The senior manager was most commonly located at head office. Table 2.9 summarises the details. Nationalised industries stood out as the sector where personnel management was most heavily centralised. That pattern was consistent with our analysis throughout the study. We found, for instance, that not only was pay determination most highly centralised in nationalised industries,[10] but so were decisions on the introduction and implementation of new machines in the office and on the shop floor.[11] Over three quarters of our personnel specialists at workplaces belonging to nationalised industries reported contact with a senior personnel manager at a higher level in the organisation and over a half of those managers had contact with the senior manager at least once a week.

Table 2.9 Extent to which personnel specialists had a line relationship with a personnel manager at another establishment, 1984

	All establishments	Private manufacturing	Private services	Nationalised industries	Public services
Existence of superordinate					
Reports to personnel manager outside establishment	58	59	62	(78)[1]	41
Frequency of contact					
Once a week	55	48	57	(57)	67
Level of superordinate					
Head office	59	59	46	(52)	92
Intermediate level	41	41	54	(48)	8
Base: personnel specialists who worked at establishments (other than head offices) belonging to larger organisations					
Unweighted	*547*	*293*	*102*	*48*	*104*
Weighted	*171*[2]	*65*	*65*	*10*	*32*

[1] See Note B.
[2] See Note H.

Even then they were often dealing with a senior manager at divisional or regional level rather than at head office.

Independently of sector, there was also a strong tendency for personnel management to be more highly centralised the larger the size of the total enterprise to which the workplace belonged. In contrast, the size of the workplace itself did not appear to have any independent association with the extent of centralisation. The extent to which personnel management was centralised was one feature of its organisation that did not vary systematically in relation to the nationality of the ownership of the workplace. Similarly, there did not appear to be any independent association between centralisation and the level of trade union organisation at workplaces.

It was on matters to do with industrial relations procedures, disciplinary cases and pay and conditions that local personnel managers most frequently consulted senior personnel managers elsewhere, relative to the general range of their responsibilities (see Table 2.10). The prominence of industrial relations procedures among the items in which head or higher offices showed most interest reflected both the increased extent and coverage of formal procedures reported in Chapter 7 and the increased involvement in procedures among local managers, reported earlier in this chapter. The extent of

Table 2.10 Matters about which personnel specialists consulted with superordinate personnel managers at a higher level in the organisation, 1984

	Part of respondent's responsibilities	Subjects of consultation at a higher level	Most frequent subject of consultation
Disciplinary cases	92	77	25[1]
Recruitment	90	48	6
Training	78	44	3
Settling/negotiating terms of employment	91	73	22
Job evaluation/ grading	75	49	4
Industrial relations procedures	95	79	30
Responsibility for systems of pay	67	51	6
Staff or manpower planning	86	60	9
Base: personnel specialists who worked at establishments belonging to larger organisations			
Unweighted	*558*	*558*	*558*
Weighted	*208*	*208*	*208*

[1] See Note E.

interest in disciplinary cases almost certainly reflected just how far large employers have become concerned to avoid the implications of tribunal cases arising out of such issues since the introduction of unfair dismissal legislation. The only surprise about the frequency with which matters concerning pay and conditions was mentioned was that it was the third most common rather than the first. Indeed, the chief significance in its position was in highlighting the importance assumed by industrial relations procedures and disciplinary cases over the recent period.

Representation of the personnel function on the board

Of at least symbolic importance as a measure of the importance an enterprise attaches to personnel management is whether or not that function is represented on its top governing body, or board of directors in the case of companies in the private sector and nationalised industries. If we found that there was a fall in the extent of board representation during the early 1980s that would certainly be a symbol of decline in the influence of personnel management in the affairs of enterprises. If, on the other hand, we found a rise, that would constitute a counter-argument. In the event we found little evidence of any change (see Table 2.11).

In the private sector and the trading parts of the public sector, we asked a number of questions about the representation of personnel and industrial relations on boards of directors. But the key characteristics of enterprises that we wanted to identify were incorporated in two questions. First, we asked whether there was anyone on the board

Table 2.11   Representation of the personnel function on the board

Percentages

	Total	Number employed by organisation			
		25–499[1]	500–1999	2000–9999	10 000 or more
Any representation on the board					
1980	71	59	71	76	79
1984	73	66	68	68	85
Specialist representation					
1980	42	11	39	46	64
1984	43	8	40	49	70
Base: part of private sector, nationalised industry or state-owned company					
Unweighted	*1190[2]*	*172*	*207*	*239*	*459*
Weighted	*1019*	*295*	*154*	*191*	*289*

[1] Bands for this variable in 1980 were one employee greater, e.g. 25–500, 501–2000.
[2] Bases shown are for 1984 only.

who had responsibility for personnel or industrial relations or both. Secondly, we asked whether there was anyone who had specialist responsibility for either or both of those functions: that is to say, one or both of the functions was their main job. In 1980, we found that 71 per cent of relevant establishments reported some representation. In 1984 the corresponding figure was 73 per cent. In 1980, 42 per cent reported specialist representation compared with 43 per cent in 1984. The apparent slight increase in representation fell well short of being statistically significant.

As we argued in our earlier analysis, exploring sources of variation in levels of board representation through our data was not very satisfactory because whether or not there was personnel representation on the board tended to depend upon the characteristics of **enterprises** while we chiefly collected the characteristics of **establishments** which were often at best only proxies for the traits of the total organisation of which they were part.[12] The chief feature of the pattern that emerged from our analysis in relation to our information that we collected about workplaces was that there was surprisingly little association between the extent to which professional personnel management was well established at the workplace and the extent to which it was represented on the board. First, and at the simplest level, we found no tendency for workplaces that had professional personnel managers to be more likely to be parts of enterprises that had personnel representation on their boards. Secondly, there were a number of ways in which the pattern of representation on the board differed from the pattern of representation at the workplace. Board representation increased strongly and consistently the larger the number of people employed by the **total enterprise** (see Table 2.12) while the employment of a personnel specialist at the **workplace** was most strongly associated with the number of people employed at the workplace. Private services stood out as the sector **least** likely to employ personnel managers at the workplace level, but that sector was very much more likely than private manufacturing to have personnel representation on the board. There was little difference between workplaces that recognised trade unions and those that did not in the extent to which they employed personnel specialists at the workplace; but workplaces that recognised unions were substantially more likely to be parts of enterprises that had specialist personnel representation on the board.

Thirdly, one particular feature of workplace organisation that we found to be very strongly associated with board representation in 1980 was the most important level of collective bargaining over pay increases affecting manual workers at the establishment. Organisations that practised company bargaining were most likely to have

Table 2.12   Pattern of representation of the personnel function on the board, 1984

Percentages

	Total	Number employed by organisation			
		25–499	500–1999	2000–9999	10 000 or more
Representation					
Any representation	73	66	68	68	85
Nature of representation					
Specialist representation of personnel/IR	43	8	40	49	70
Responsibility for personnel specifically with or without other responsibilities	72	62	67	68	85
Responsibility for industrial relations specifically, with or without other responsibilities	69	60	60	63	83
Responsibilities for industrial relations and personnel carried separately by two different members	13	8	9	14	17
Base: part of private sector, nationalised industry or state owned company					
Unweighted	*1190*	*172*	*207*	*239*	*459*
Weighted	*1019*	*295*	*154*	*191*	*289*

board representation while those characterised by plant bargaining were much less likely to do so. Our 1984 results confirmed the strength of that association and revealed it to be most pronounced among larger organisations. In contrast, personnel representation at the workplace among the same organisations was more pronounced where plant bargaining was practised.

Change in the influence of personnel managers

In designing the questionnaire content for the 1984 survey it was decided to insert a small number of new questions concerning the role and influence of the personnel function. This was done to provide further evidence relevant to the issue of whether employment and industrial relations legislation had led to increased influence on the part of personnel managers, an issue upon which we commented in our first report.[13] Unfortunately, we have no corresponding data from the 1980 survey and so we cannot establish whether the answers were different from those that we would have received at that time. Our first new question in 1984 was to those of our principal management respondents who had identified themselves as personnel specialists.

We asked them whether they thought that their influence had changed and, if so, how that had come about. Secondly, we asked works managers in those manufacturing plants that had personnel departments what they thought about the changing influence of personnel managers and about the respective roles of personnel managers and departmental managers in relation to specific issues. In addition, we were able to explore through our interviews with works managers the role of personnel managers in such matters as the introduction of major technical or organisational change at the workplace.

Clearly, such limited information is unlikely to provide us with an unequivocal answer about any changes in the role and influence of personnel management. Such an answer might not be forthcoming even from a substantial study specifically designed for the purpose and using, for example, a much wider range of respondents than we already had. What information we did collect is summarised below. We shall return to the issue more generally in the final chapter of this report.

Personnel managers' accounts of changes in their influence
Nearly two thirds of the personnel managers that we interviewed (principal management respondents who had *personnel* or *industrial* or *employee relations* in their job title) felt that their influence had increased over the previous period and nearly a third thought that it had increased a lot (see Table 2.13). Only five per cent reported that the influence of personnel had decreased on balance, and the large majority of those thought that the decrease was modest. It may be that the need to maintain professional *amour propre* encouraged managers to report favourable views about the standing of their function. But the balance of view among personnel managers was so very much inclined towards an increase in influence that it would be difficult to explain all of it away in that manner. Moreover, the pattern of variation in views was very plausible.

There appeared to be few differences among the four main sectors in the extent to which personnel managers reported any increase in influence for their departments, but there were substantial differences in relation to the size of both workplaces and the enterprises of which they were part. The larger the establishment and the larger the total organisation of which it was part the more likely were personnel managers to report an increase in influence. So far as the size of the workplace was concerned it was the number of non-manual workers employed more than the number of manual workers that was associated with a reported increase in influence for personnel. In workplaces employing 1000 or more non-manual workers, 79 per cent

Table 2.13 Personnel managers' assessments of recent changes in their influence, 1984

		Number of non-manual workers at establishment							
	Total	1–9	10–24	25–49	50–99	100–199	200–499	500–999	1000 or more
									Column percentages
Increased a lot	31[1]	(29)[2]	(33)	22	33	32	34	38	59
Increased a little	31	(37)	(26)	38	32	23	31	28	20
Much the same	25	(12)	(33)	35	22	24	23	19	14
Decreased a little	4	(17)	(1)	—	2	6	1	*	3
Decreased a lot	1	—	(3)	1	1	3	2	*	*
Not stated	7	(5)	(4)	4	9	12	9	11	3
									Means
Mean score[3]	+90	(+80)	(+90)	+80	+100	+90	+100	+110	+140
Base: all personnel and industrial relations managers									
Unweighted	947	28	37	78	140	198	220	140	105
Weighted	395	45	28	94	91	68	43	14	10

[1] See Note C.
[2] See Note B.
[3] The maximum score was 200, which would have been achieved if all respondents said that their influence *increased a lot*. A score of 100 represented the equivalent of all respondents saying that their influence *increased a little*. The scores were calculated by giving an arbitrary value of +200 to *increased a lot*, +100 to *increased a little*, −100 to *decreased a little*, and −200 to *decreased a lot* and dividing the sum by the proportion who expressed views. The result was then rounded to the nearest ten.

Table 2.14   Personnel managers' accounts of changes in their influence in relation to establishment and organisation size, 1984

Mean scores[1]

	Number employed in organisation		
	25–499	500–9999	10 000 or more
Number employed at establishment			
25–99	(+50)[2]	+90	+100
100–499	(+110)	+90	+110
500–999	. .[3]	+100	+110
1000 or more	. .	+120	+130
Base: all personnel and industrial relations managers			

[1] See Note 3 to Table 2.13.
[2] See Note B.
[3] See Note J.

of personnel managers reported an increase in influence and 59 per cent reported a major increase. Table 2.14 shows how the total size of the enterprise of which the workplace was part and the size of the workplace itself were independently associated with personnel managers' reports of increased influence.

There was a marked tendency for reports of increased influence to be more common where there was recent technical change. Although the involvement of the personnel department in the introduction of technical change appeared to be modest,[14] personnel managers were nevertheless substantially more likely to report an increase in influence in workplaces that were making most use of advanced technology and where there had been recent technical change. It was also true that increased influence was reported in 67 per cent of the cases where there were redundancies in the previous year compared with 58 per cent of cases where there was no reduction in the size of the workforce. Moreover, reports of enhanced influence were also very much more common in workplaces where there had been a particularly large **increase** in the size of the workforce over the recent period.

These patterns indicate that personnel managers' accounts of changes in the influence of personnel departments over the recent period varied in systematic and plausible ways. That added weight to our judgement that the accounts did not simply represent professional self-justification on the part of personnel managers. Personnel managers' accounts of why they thought that the influence of the personnel department had increased reinforced our belief in the validity of the results (see Table 2.15). Hardly any of the managers

Table 2.15 Personnel managers' accounts of the reasons why their influence increased in the recent past, 1984

Column percentages

	Total	Private manufacturing	Private services	Nationalised industries	Public services
Enterprise or headquarters policy	38[1]	36	29	(50)[2]	58
Industrial relations/ employment legislation	25	18	39	(4)	13
Personal characteristics of key management appointment	19	26	20	(20)	10
Financial position of establishment/enterprise	15	17	12	(20)	10
Reorganisation of functions in organisation – outside establishment	11	2	15	(27)	14
Changes in personnel	7	5	7	(1)	7
Other answer	8	7	11	(2)	7
Not stated	*	1	–	–	*
Base: personnel and industrial relations managers who said that the influence of the personnel function had increased					
Unweighted	589	227	149	44	149
Weighted	245[3]	69	103	14	51

[1] See Note E.
[2] See Note B.
[3] See Note H.

who reported that the influence of the personnel department had grown did not provide a rationale for that judgement. It is true that a number of the answers pointed to decisions about change having been taken at a level outside the workplace and for reasons that were not necessarily known within the establishment. That number included reports that enterprise or headquarters policies had changed in a way that laid more emphasis upon personnel matters; that somebody appointed to a key management position attached more importance to personnel; and that there had been a reorganisation in the enterprise as a whole that resulted in personnel having more influence. Such reports tended to be more common in the public sector where personnel management was much more highly centralised. But it would have been necessary to conduct additional interviews at higher levels in the organisation to tease out the various influences from other parts of the organisation upon the changes reported by our respondents at workplace level.

The two influences upon the role of the personnel function (other than corporate management decision-making) that dominated the reports we received from our local managers were, first, the impact of industrial relations and employment legislation and, secondly, the implications of the financial position faced by the establishment in the recent period, especially the implications for the number of people employed. Of course, a decline in the role and influence of personnel management is perhaps rather unlikely in a period when there was considerable legislative change of direct consequence to the personnel function and when there were widespread changes in manpower requirements.[15] It is particularly striking that industrial relations and employment legislation should emerge as the single most common contextual factor cited as enhancing the role of personnel management. It was not possible for us to distinguish between references to the employment protection legislation of the 1970s and the industrial relations legislation of the 1980s in managers' answers shown in Table 2.15. But whatever the balance between them, our present results suggest that it might well require the repeal of earlier legislation, rather than the introduction of new, in order to remove the advantage that personnel management derived from the employment legislation of the 1970s.

The role of works managers in personnel management
One reason that is sometimes advanced to explain the relatively poor performance of British manufacturing industry is that British managers have been distracted by industrial relations issues and problems so much more than their overseas competitors. Comparative research has shown that British managers spend more time on

industrial relations matters than managers in other parts of Europe.[16] In consequence, it has been argued, they have been able to devote insufficient time to technical and production issues. It has also been argued, alternatively, that British managers have devoted insufficient time and attention to the human side of enterprise in general and to human resources in particular. Our interviews with works managers in those parts of manufacturing industry that had personnel managers enabled us to look at some features of the relationship between line management and personnel management in that sector. First, we asked works managers how much of their time they spent upon personnel issues and to what matters they particularly devoted their attention. Secondly, we were able to explore works managers' perspectives on changing patterns of influence and the involvement of personnel management in different forms of change.

So far as the amount of attention devoted to personnel issues by line managers in manufacturing was concerned, we found that works managers did spend a substantial minority of their time on personnel questions. But they tended to be more involved in such questions at workplaces where professional personnel management was less well developed. It appeared that when works managers were occupied with personnel matters, it was more because there was no-one else to do the job than because the workplace or the enterprise of which it was part generally devoted more of its time and attention to the management of people and of human resources. On average, works managers reported that they spent a quarter of their working time on personnel matters. Twenty-nine per cent said that they spent more than a quarter of their time upon such questions and 15 per cent devoted at least a half. That amount of time was only slightly less than that reported by those of our principal management respondents who were not personnel specialists.

There was a very slight tendency for works managers to spend more of their time on personnel matters the larger the size of their plant in terms of the total number of people employed, but the most interesting sources of variation were nationality of ownership, use of advanced technology and industrial sector. Works managers in British-owned factories spent substantially more time on personnel matters than counterparts in plants belonging to overseas companies. The contrast was especially marked when we compared factories of similar size. Similarly, works managers spent more time on personnel matters in workplaces which made little use of advanced technology and in declining sectors like textiles. It will be recalled that workplaces belonging to overseas companies and those that made most use of advanced technology were both particularly likely to employ professional personnel managers. The implication of this pattern is that if works managers in UK-owned plants spend more time on personnel problems than their counterparts in foreign-owned plants it was more because inadequate professional provision was made for that function in the former, rather than because personnel problems in them are more demanding. The larger manufacturing plants where we carried out interviews with works managers tended generally to have a relatively high level of trade union organisation. That reduced the scope we have to make comparisons between workplaces with differing levels of unionisation. But the comparisons that were possible provided little indication that the amount of time works managers devoted to personnel issues was directly associated with the extent of trade union organisation. The personnel matters which occupied works managers were not very dissimilar from those that formed the responsibilities of personnel managers in the plants where they worked (see Table 2.16). The only general topic to which they were less inclined to give attention was remuneration. Works managers were substantially less likely than personnel managers in the same plants to report that negotiating or settling pay and conditions and that responsibility for systems of pay and that job evaluation

Table 2.16 Comparison of works managers' and personnel managers' accounts of personnel matters with which they deal, 1984

Percentages

	Personnel managers in establishments where works managers were interviewed	Works managers
Disciplinary cases	96	97
Recruitment	94	90
Training	85	78
Settling/negotiating terms of employment	97	78
Job evaluation/ grading	78	71
Industrial relations procedures	97	90
Responsibility for systems of pay	85	55
Manpower planning	83	96
Base: manufacturing plants where works managers were interviewed		
Unweighted	276	276
Weighted	76	76

Table 2.17 Works managers' assessments of the influence of personnel and departmental managers over specified personnel issues, 1984

	Personnel managers					Departmental managers				
	Appoint-ments	Disciplinary cases	Negotiat-ions – physical conditions	Disputes, particular departments	Disputes, all manual workers	Appoint-ments	Disciplinary cases	Negotiat-ions – physical conditions	Disputes, own departments	Disputes, all manual workers
										Column percentages
A great deal	18	24[1]	18	16	25	52	43	21	13	5
Quite a lot	26	33	28	25	21	29	30	38	20	11
A fair amount	23	19	26	12	12	16	17	20	16	14
Very little	20	11	15	11	7	1	10	13	18	27
None	6	5	5	12	12	—	*	3	15	24
Not stated	7	9	8	24[2]	23	1	*	4	18	19
										Means
Mean score[3]	250	290	260	250	280	390	350	290	210	140
Base: all works managers										
Unweighted	276	276	276	276	276	276	276	276	276	276
Weighed	76	76	76	76	76	76	76	76	76	76

[1] See Note C.

[2] The high proportion of cases where respondents were not able to express a view about influence in relation to collective disputes arose because they said they had not recently or had never had collective disputes.

[3] The maximum score was 500, which would have been achieved if all works managers had responded *a great deal*. The scores were calculated by giving an arbitrary score of 500 to *a great deal*, 300 to *quite a lot*, 200 to a *fair amount*, 100 to *very little* and zero to *none* and dividing by the number who stated a view. The result was then rounded to the nearest ten.

schemes or job grading formed parts of their jobs. But the majority of works managers still included each of these items among their responsibilities and more works managers than personnel managers reported that manpower planning formed part of their job.

Works managers' accounts of relative influence of departmental managers and personnel managers upon specified issues
In our interviews with works managers in those parts of manufacturing industry with personnel departments, we asked works managers how much influence *departmental managers* (normally their direct subordinates) had over each of the following types of decision affecting people:

> *the appointment of people to their departments;*
> *disciplinary cases concerned with people in their departments;*
> *negotiations over physical working conditions in their departments;*
> *collective disputes with manual workers in their departments;*
> *and collective disputes concerning all manual workers.*

We then asked works managers how much influence the personnel department had over the same types of decision. Subsequently, we enquired separately whether they thought the influence of both departmental managers and personnel managers over such issues had increased, decreased or remained very similar during the recent period. The questions were designed to enable us to explore the relative influence of line management and specialist staff management over decisions affecting people in large manufacturing plants. The answers suggested that the influence of departmental managers varied very much from item to item while personnel managers were attributed a similar level of influence over all items. Works managers felt they had most influence over decisions affecting individuals both in relation to appointments and in relation to disciplinary cases. They thought department managers had least influence in relation to collective disputes, especially those that involved the whole of the manual workforce, but also collective disputes confined to manual workers in their departments (see Table 2.17). Indeed, works managers suggested that the personnel department had greater influence than departmental managers when it came to collective disputes. In so far as the debate about the changing influence of personnel management has focused upon the balance of power within management teams relating to issues concerned with institutional labour relations, that finding is of particular relevance.

Having asked works managers about the amount of influence exercised by departmental managers and personnel managers over different items, we went on to ask what change they felt there had

Table 2.18   Works managers' assessments of recent changes in the influence of personnel managers and departmental managers over specified personnel issues, 1984

	Personnel managers	Departmental managers
Increased a lot	11	19[1]
Increased a little	11	24
Much the same	54	42
Decreased a little	11	8
Decreased a lot	3	3
Not stated	10	3
Mean score[2]	+20	+50
Base: all works managers		
Unweighted	*276*	*276*
Weighted	*76*	*76*

[1] See Note C.
[2] See Note 3 to Table 2.13.

been in such influence. The results are shown in Table 2.18. It is clear that works managers attributed to personnel managers a lower level of increase in influence over the five specified items than the general increase in influence that personnel managers claimed for themselves. In evaluating that contrast, however, it should be borne in mind that the evaluations of works managers were focused upon the types of issue listed in Table 2.17. In contrast, the reports of personnel managers had been asked in a more general way and were supported by reference to the financial circumstances of workplaces and their implications for workforce reductions and to employment and industrial relations legislation.

In relation to the items to which we attracted their attention, the reports of works managers suggested a very modest shift in the balance of influence towards line managers. We did not, however, have the directly comparable picture from our interviews with personnel managers, because we did not have room in those interviews for the same degree of detail about this matter as was possible in the interviews with works managers.

The involvement of professional personnel managers in the introduction of major change
Through our interviews with works managers we were also able to look at the extent to which, and the ways in which, personnel departments were involved in the introduction of major change in workplaces. That analysis is reported in the companion volume to this report.[17] Here, we summarise the main findings on the role of

personnel managers in the management of change. First, it was evident that personnel management tended to be very much more frequently involved in the introduction of *organisational change* than of technical change, even *advanced technical change*. We used the term *organisational change* to describe what we called in the interview schedule *changes in the organisation of work or working practices not involving the introduction of new plant, equipment or machinery*. The term *advanced technical change* was used to describe *the introduction of new plant, machines or equipment that incorporated microelectronic technology*. It was clear from the descriptions given by respondents, certainly in manufacturing industry, that many of the *organisational changes* were productivity agreements along classical lines. It was not surprising, therefore, that personnel managers were so frequently and heavily involved in them. It remained surprising, however, that personnel managers were so little engaged in the introduction of advanced technology. According to works managers, their personnel departments were involved in only a half of cases and even when they played a role they were frequently brought in only at a later stage in the process. One of the chief reasons why personnel managers were so little involved appeared to be that they were seen as trouble-shooters to be brought in when there were difficulties with shop stewards or work groups or when the subject matter was manifestly concerned with collective agreements. As technical change, even new, unfamiliar, advanced technical change was generally popular, very rarely provoked any resistance from manual workers or their representatives and was very rarely subject to collective bargaining, then little reason was seen, apparently, to call upon the personnel department. Clearly, it was rare for the personnel department to have established a positive role for itself as expert on all the human implications of the management of major change and therefore indispensable when new advanced technology was in prospect. There was no sign from previous research on the matter, however, that that represented any change in the role or standing of personnel management in relation to the management of technical change. Indeed, our analysis earlier in this chapter showed that professional personnel management was better represented and attributed more influence the more workplaces were inclined to use advanced technology.

Moreover, our findings suggest that the two chief influences upon the changing role and importance of personnel management during the early 1980s have been the rate of redundancies and the rate of change in industrial relations legislation. It may be that the demands made upon personnel management by such developments have inhibited the growth of its role in the management of other aspects of change.

Notes and references

1. Daniel W W and Millward N (1983) *Workplace Industrial Relations in Britain: The DE/PSI/SSRC Survey*, Heinemann Educational Books, London, pp.105-28; 285-7.

2. In some instances, when we sought interviews with the senior person who had responsibility for personnel matters at the workplace, interviewers were directed to someone who carried that responsibility at a separate establishment. Seven per cent of our principal management interviews were carried out with managers who did not themselves work at the establishment to which the interview referred. That happened most frequently in the public sector. Our analysis of the characteristics of the people who carried personnel responsibilities at workplaces in the first half of this chapter is confined to those management respondents who worked at the establishments about which they were interviewed. In fact, managers who worked at places other than the sampled establishment were, as might be expected, more likely to be personnel specialists than the generality of workplace respondents. But their inclusion did not change the overall picture of stability regarding the employment of personnel specialists. Of all our principal management respondents in 1984, including those who did not work at the sampled establishment, 20 per cent were personnel specialists. The comparable figure in 1980 was 19 per cent.

3. We selected principal management respondents on the basis that they were the most senior person with responsibility for personnel or industrial relations matters at the workplace. Unless otherwise specified, we use the terms personnel and personnel specialist generically in this chapter to cover both personnel and industrial relations. In practice, as Table 2.12 shows, where respondents were specialists they were very substantially more likely to have the word *personnel* in their job title than the phrases *industrial relations; labour relations; employee relations*; or *staff relations*.

4. It was of course true, as we explained in note 2, that the proportion of our workplaces represented by personnel specialists increased from 15 to 20 per cent when we included respondents who worked at establishments separate from the ones about which they were interviewed.

5. For example, in parts of central government the term *establishment officer* was commonly used in 1984 to denote a person with personnel responsibilities.

6. Daniel W W (1986 forthcoming) *Workplace Industrial Relations and Technical Change*.

7. The figures quoted here on the proportion of personnel specialists having formal qualifications in 1980 differ radically from those given on the basis of the same data (the 1980 Workplace Industrial Relations Survey) in a recent journal article: Beaumont P B and Deaton D R (1986) 'Correlates of Specialisation and Training among Personnel Managers in Britain', *Personnel Review* Vol.15, No.2, pp.29-31. This is because the authors, incorrectly, use the data unweighted, thus exaggerating the results for the largest establishments compared with the smallest by a factor of about twenty-six. They are, in effect, using the sample survey data to generalise to a population with twenty-six times as many establishments of 2000 or more employees as were present. There is no indication in the article that the descriptive statistics presented are unweighted, although an earlier version of the paper, on which we commented to the authors at their request, did contain a statement to this effect.

8. The 1984 question was made more general than the 1980 one because such a high proportion of establishments already had procedures in 1980 that focusing on the *setting up* of procedures was no longer appropriate. Because of the change in question wording the two results are not comparable.

9. See Note 2 above.

10. See Chapter 9.

11. See Daniel W W (1986 forthcoming) *op. cit.*

12. Equally, of course, the characteristics of workplaces cannot be inferred from responses to general questions asked at enterprise, company or headquarters level.

13. Daniel W W and Millward N (1983) *op. cit.* pp.296-7.

14. Daniel W W (1986 forthcoming) *op. cit.*

15. See Chapter 8. It is of relevance to note at this point that 41 per cent of establishments had made workforce reductions in the previous 12 months and, of course, that part of the period between our two surveys did not represent the time of most widespread reductions, at least judging from the published figures of employees in employment.

16. Fogarty M (1986) *Trade Unions and British Industrial Development*, Policy Studies Institute No.653, London.

17. Daniel W W (1986 forthcoming) *op. cit.*

3   Trade Union Representation

Trade union membership

The representation of employees by trade unions and staff associations is a key feature of institutional industrial relations in Britain. Trade union membership, which in all our ensuing discussions should be taken as including membership of staff associations, forms the initial building block for many industrial relations institutions. The second is trade union recognition. We start this chapter by looking at trade union membership, showing the basic changes in the presence of union membership at our sample of workplaces and then plotting the pattern in 1984 in some detail. Because our data are more complete for 1984 than for 1980, owing to improved questionnaire design and fieldwork techniques, our analysis of the patterns of union membership concentrates on the picture in 1984. Indeed, because the WIRS series now provides the best source of information on the distribution of trade union membership among workplaces of different types, we spend some time in describing it, knowing that the material will be of general interest and a source for other research.

We began, as in 1980, by asking our management respondents whether any employees at their establishment were members of a trade union. In fact the question was asked separately for manual and for non-manual employees and in the case of the latter the question included staff associations. Table 3.1 gives the basic responses for the four main sectors of the economy, with the 1980 results alongside for comparison.

Concentrating on the overall totals for the moment, no aggregate change is apparent in the proportion of establishments that have any trade union members, the overall figure being 73 per cent for both years. If we look at manual and non-manual workers separately there does at first sight appear to be a modest increase, but this ignores the changing proportions of cases where responses were not clear-cut. The proportion of managers giving an indeterminate answer dropped very substantially in the second survey, particularly in the private services sector where trade union membership is least common. On this basis we might assume that most cases where managers said they did not know whether there were any trade union members at their

Table 3.1 Presence of trade union and staff association members

	All establishments 1980	1984	Private manufacturing 1980	1984	Private Services 1980	1984	Nationalised industries 1980	1984	Public services 1980	1984
Manual workers										
Some union members	64[1]	68	76	66	42	47	100	100	80	94
No union members	27	29	18	29	48	49	—	—	9	4
Other answer	2	1	2	2	2	2	—	—	3	1
Not known	6	2	3	3	8	2	—	—	8	1
Base: establishments with manual workers										
Unweighted	*1899*	*1853*	*734*	*580*	*521*	*515*	*130*	*191*	*514*	*567*
Weighted	*1823*	*1749*	*498*	*412*	*755*	*689*	*66*	*103*	*504*	*545*
Non-manual workers										
Some union or association members	55	58	36	34	34	35	100	100	98	100
No members	41	40	59	62	59	62	—	—	1	*
Other answer	1	1	2	2	2	1	—	—	*	—
Not known	3	1	4	1	6	2	—	—	*	*
Base: establishments with non-manual workers										
Unweighted	*2034*	*2010*	*743*	*592*	*585*	*593*	*133*	*194*	*573*	*631*
Weighted	*1987*	*1985[2]*	*503*	*424*	*854*	*836*	*68*	*105*	*562*	*621*
Any trade union or staff association members	73	73	77	67	50	53	100	100	99	100
Base: all establishments										
Unweighted	*2040*	*2019*	*743*	*592*	*587*	*597*	*134*	*196*	*576*	*634*
Weighted	*2000*	*2000*	*503*	*424*	*859*	*843*	*69*	*106*	*569*	*627*

[1] See Note C.
[2] See Note H.

workplace were cases where there were no members. This is the assumption we make in the bottom part of the table where we combine the answers about manual and non-manual employees to give an overall measure of the presence of unions at British workplaces with 25 or more employees.

Within the four main sectors shown separately in Table 3.1 there is a clear mixture of change and stability. The public sector showed little definite change, virtually all establishments having some trade union members. The only noticeable movement was a decline in the already small number of cases where public services establishments with manual workers had no manual trade union members. In 1980 there appeared to be some genuine cases of public services establishments with no manual trade union members; most of these were ones with very few manual workers and were mainly in the local authority sector. The relatively high proportion of 'not known' cases in 1980 was partly a reflection of the number of interviews in this sector that were carried out at a higher level than the sampled establishment and, even though this also happened in 1984, interviewers were better able to get definite information about trade union membership in the second survey. Any change in the public sector, then, represented a filling in of the pattern of universal trade union presence in that sector.

If stability characterised the public sector, change was more characteristic of the private sector. In private manufacturing there was a quite striking decline in the proportion of workplaces with trade union members, particularly manual trade union members for whom the proportion declined from 76 per cent to 66 per cent. Until we have analysed in depth the results of our panel sample, including the very limited data concerning panel establishments that closed down between 1980 and 1984, we can only speculate as to the causes of this decline in manual trade union membership. A main hypothesis, however, would be that it is largely due to the disproportionate closure of large, and generally therefore unionised, workplaces in manufacturing over the period. This would fit with several other pieces of data from the survey itself: the lower proportion of large manufacturing workplaces in our 1984 sample and the very small number of new manufacturing establishments above our size threshold of 25 employees, although the out-of-datedness of our sampling frame is largely responsible for the latter. Only 22 cases in our 1984 sample were private sector establishments that had been doing their main activity for less than three years; 43 per cent had manual union members compared with 54 per cent of the whole of the private sector. For non-manual workers the corresponding figures were 19 per cent and 34 per cent overall. So these very limited data do point towards new establishments being less likely to be unionised, but with such small numbers of cases the effect is hardly clear-cut. A third possible explanation of the fall in the number of unionised manufacturing establishments is that more have changed from being unionised to being non-unionised than have changed in the opposite direction. This also seems unlikely to be a sizeable effect. Indeed, an initial view of the panel data suggests that there is very little gross change at all in whether or not establishments have union members present. We feel fairly confident that it is the closure of large plants that is responsible for the bulk of the change.

In the private services sector, the overall change from 50 per cent of workplaces with any union members in 1980 to 53 per cent in 1984 is on the margins of statistical significance and in any case confused by the high levels of 'not known' cases in 1980. Of course, service sector establishments formed a larger part of the 1984 sample and so any growth in unionisation by them would have a somewhat larger impact upon the total figure. But it is interesting that the combination of the opposite trends in the two parts of the private sector – manufacturing and services – is that the difference between them is now considerably smaller. Establishments in private manufacturing were only just more than a quarter more likely to be unionised than service establishments were, whereas in 1980 they were more than a half more likely to be unionised.

Union membership density

The presence of one or more trade union members at a particular workplace, which has been our concern in the previous paragraphs, is the minimal indication of trade union presence. Where it is the case that there is only one or a handful of isolated members in an establishment the impact on management-employee relations may be nil. It is common to summarise the increasing potential impact of trade membership at a workplace by calculating its *trade union density* – the proportion of employees who are members. Other sources of information on trade union membership in Britain, such as the Department of Employment's annual figures published in the *Employment Gazette*, use a roughly similar definition, but there are some substantial difficulties in disaggregating the data received from trade union sources that limit the usefulness of that series. With the data reported here from the WIRS series the major limitations are the small numbers of observations in some industry categories and the exclusion of the smallest workplaces (those with less than 25 employees) throughout the sample. The exclusion of the smallest workplaces means that the density figures given are greater than they would be if workplaces of all sizes had been included; information from the 1984 *Social Attitudes Survey* (with which our results for larger workplaces are remarkably consistent) suggests that about 27 per cent of employees in workplaces of less than 25 employees are union members.[1] In principle it would be possible to amalgamate, on a disaggregated basis, results for small establishments from that survey with the more extensive WIRS data for larger establishments, but it is likely that there would be insufficient observations in many of the categories to make this viable. In Tables 3.2 and 3.3, then, we present trade union density estimates for larger workplaces in 23 industrial sectors, being Classes or combinations of adjacent Classes of the *Standard Industrial Classification* (Revised, 1980). These figures are calculated by summing the number of trade union members reported by management respondents in all establishments in the sector and then dividing by the sum of the number of employees in those same establishments.[2] In aggregate the results show that 58 per cent of employees in the WIRS sample were reported by management respondents to be members of trade unions or staff associations. The figure for manual workers was 67 per cent and for non-manuals 51 per cent.

Wide variations in union density between industrial sectors are evident from these two tables. The lowest average densities of 21 per cent in the Hotels, Catering and Repairs sector and the Business Services sector contrast strongly with the two highest figures of 95 and 88 per cent in the Posts and Telecommunications and the Energy and Water sectors. At the time of our 1984 survey the latter were almost exclusively publicly owned while the former were virtually all private sector. But the dominance of public or private ownership by no means accounts for all the variation between sectors shown in these two tables. Establishment size is also important, as can be inferred from the average size of plant in each sector, shown near the bottom of each table. For example, the Vehicles and Transport Equipment sector, with an average plant size of 674 employees, is largely privately owned and has the highest union membership density in manufacturing of 81 per cent. At the other end of the scale in manufacturing, Leather, Footwear and Clothing and Rubber, Plastics and Other Manufacturing have density figures below 50 per cent and average plant sizes of around 100. Generally speaking, sectors with high proportions of establishments with any trade union members also have high average densities.

Although size and ownership must explain a good deal of the variation in union density between industrial sectors, analysis by industrial sector is not in itself a very fruitful use of establishment-level data and Tables 3.2 and 3.3 are given primarily for general information and as inputs into other research agendas, largely in

Table 3.2 Trade union membership and density in manufacturing industry, 1984

	All manufacturing establishments	Metals, mineral products	Chemicals, manufactured fibres	Metal goods, mechanical engineering	Electrical & instrument engineering	Vehicles, transport equipment	Food, drink & tobacco	Textiles	Leather, footwear, clothing	Timber & furniture, paper and printing	Rubber & plastics, Other manufacturing
											Percentages
Any trade union or staff association members	67	69	56	65	71	85	54	69	64	84	39
Manual members but not non-manual	32[1]	39	19	36	14	23	21	29	33	48	21
Non-manual members but not manual	3	3	6	3	4	–	2	2	10	2	–
Manual and non-manual members	32	27	32	26	53	61	31	38	21	34	19
											Means
Average density – all workers	58	68	58	55	51	81	50	53	48	59	40
Average density – manual workers	72	79	78	66	69	93	63	60	63	76	48
Average density – non-manual workers	35	43	37	33	31	58	26	28	20	35	29
Average number of employees	147	140	211	101	239	674	183	108	116	97	106
Proportion of establishments in public sector	1	3	*	*	1	19	–	–	–	*	–
Base: establishments with specified workers present											
Unweighted	624	66	51	125	89	53	84	33	30	72	21
Weighted	428[2]	55	26	108	34	10	48	32	27	71	17

[1] See Note D.
[2] See Note H.

Table 3.3 Trade union membership and density in service industry, 1984

	All service establishments	Energy and water	Construction	Wholesale distribution	Retail distribution	Hotels, catering, repairs	Transport	Posts and telecommunications	Banking, finance & insurance	Business services	Public administration	Education	Medical services	Other services
														Percentages
Any trade union or staff association members	75	96	71	49	53	39	93	100	83	27	99	97	91	74
Manual members but non-manual	11	3[1]	48	29	9	20	47	1	1	4	3	*	—	6
Non-manual members but not-manual	17	3	3	2	3	3	5	3	59	13	56	10	20	13
Manual and non-manual members	47	89	20	19	40	16	42	96	23	9	40	87	72	55
														Means
Average density – all workers	58	88	36	32	34	21	85	95	43	21	78	69	67	49
Average density – manual workers	63	93	42	47	50	25	96	98	34	63	73	57	68	49
Average density – non-manual workers	55	82	25	19	21	13	58	91	45	14	80	75	65	50
Average number of employees per establishment	98	180	84	55	97	56	105	132	73	79	134	87	295	78
Proportion of establishments in the public sector	46	78	16	1	—	6	23	100	2	7	100	90	75	60
Base: establishments with specified workers present														
Unweighted	1394	67	68	70	127	50	91	74	83	85	188	191	152	147
Weighted	1572[2]	44	84	120	145	100	77	50	114	122	168	298	62	188

[1] See Note D.
[2] See Note H.

economics, where union density is one of many potential explanatory variables. Our data are more fruitfully employed exploring the **inter-establishment** variation in union density, along the lines previously used by Elsheikh and Bain[3] for manufacturing. Given the lack of variation within the public sector, we confine our attention to the private sector, both manufacturing and services. Table 3.4 gives various measures of unionisation, including average density, for a number of workplace characteristics, many of them similar to ones selected from the Warwick survey by Elsheikh and Bain. Given the striking similarities between our analysis using two- or three-way tables and the multi-variate regression and probit analysis using the same 1980 WIRS data reported by others,[4] we would not expect many of the relationships apparent in Table 3.4 to be rejected by subsequent, more sophisticated analysis. Until that is carried out, by us or others, the results summarised in Table 3.4 should be of interest.

The first section of the Table 3.4 deals with the results for different sizes of establishment and clearly documents one of the more familiar relationships: larger workplaces have very considerably higher union densities and the relationship is continuous, although not linear. The contrast between the smallest establishments in our survey, those with 25 to 49 employees and an average union density of 26 per cent, and the largest, having 1000 or more employees and an average density of 72 per cent, could not be more marked. But averages do not by any means tell the whole story. The distribution of union membership in the private sector is highly skewed, with over two fifths of workplaces having none at all and over a tenth (excluding the cases with missing information) having densities of 90 per cent or more. Both the zero and very high density categories have their interest. The former declines rapidly with size of establishment, with less than 5 per cent of the largest workplaces having no union members. At the other end of the spectrum there are two quite different cases: workplaces with 100 per cent density are, surprisingly, just as likely in the smaller size bands as in the larger, while densities of between 90 per cent and 99 per cent are very strongly related to size of establishment. These patterns will become more understandable when we look at the various forms of the closed shop in the next chapter. Meanwhile there are other patterns of variation in union density in the private sector that merit attention.

Our measure of **changes** in establishment size produced some particularly striking and revealing patterns in relation to trade union density. The second section of Table 3.4 distinguishes workplaces that shrank quite substantially in the period 1980 to 1984 with those that had relatively stable employment numbers over the period and

Table 3.4 Trade union density in the private sector in relation to the characteristics of workplaces, 1984

Row percentages

	Proportion of establishments with union density of:							Average density	Unweighted base	Weighted base
	0	1–24%	25–49%	50–89%	90–99%	100%	Not known			
All establishments	42	12	9	17	6	4	8	42	1189	1267
Size of establishment										
25–49 employees	52	9	7	14	5	5	7	26	223	663[1]
50–99 employees	37	16	12	18	7	2	7	30	239	338
100–199 employees	27	16	11	22	7	5	9	39	206	156
200–499 employees	23	11	10	25	8	7	13	47	210	80
500–999 employees	13	3	9	25	18	2	22	60	165	20
1000 or more employees	5	4	5	39	24	4	16	72	146	10
Change in establishment size since 1980										
Decrease of 20% or more	29	9	15	22	10	5	7	60	329	226
Decrease of less than 20%	35	13	7	20	8	10	6	48	251	241
Stable	41	16	9	14	7	3	10	45	141	152
Increase of less than 20%	50	11	8	18	2	1	9	36	136	180
Increase of 20% or more	59	10	7	13	2	1	8	21	155	244
New establishment since 1980	§[2]	§	§	§	§	§	§	§	14	27
Not known	39	15	8	18	7	4	8	37	163	196

Size of enterprise

25–99 employees	56	15	6	17	2	1	3	20	178	438
100–199 employees	57	7	13	11	5	—	7	22	77	114
200–999 employees	42	11	11	17	7	3	7	35	181	170
1000–4999 employees	33	18	9	18	7	8	4	48	262	174
5000–49999 employees	25	6	10	22	15	7	13	55	260	192
50000 or more employees	24	8	7	19	6	4	29	58	131	94
Not known	29	7	16	16	4	13	10	57	100	84

Proportion of employees who were manual

More than 70%	34	14	7	25	9	6	4	53	456	485[3]
Between 31% and 70%	41	14	14	18	4	2	4	45	387	391
Between 0 and 30%	53	7	7	7	4	4	16	25	346	390

Proportion of employees who were part-time

More than 40%	56	13	10	8	1	3	7	24	136	178
Between 6% and 40%	47	10	9	14	4	5	11	35	354	468
Between 0 and 5%	34	13	9	23	10	4	5	51	663	578

Labour costs as a proportion of sales revenue or total costs

From 0 to 24%	49	11	8	15	5	5	5	37	395	445
Between 25% and 49%	35	13	9	24	8	3	7	48	460	454
Between 50% and 74%	39	11	12	14	5	5	13	43	194	234
75% or more	50	15	5	10	1	2	11	34	37	44
No information	48	9	9	9	10	4	11	42	103	90

Base: all private sector establishments

[1] See Note H.
[2] See Note A.
[3] See Note G.

with those that grew. Those whose employment had shrunk by 20 per cent or more had an average union density of 60 per cent while those whose employment had grown by 20 per cent or more had average density of only 21 per cent. This strong negative relationship between union density and employment growth must, of course, go a long way towards explaining the very substantial fall in overall trade union density, as measured by the Department of Employment's official series, over the period 1980 to 1984. It is not just that plant closures have been concentrated in the older and highly unionised sectors of the economy; this we could not detect with our two cross-sectional samples. Nor can it be the case that large numbers of new establishments with no or few union members have replaced those that have closed. The disproportionate loss of employment among highly unionised establishments that have remained in existence throughout the period must surely be largely responsible for the aggregate decline in union membership numbers.

Workforce size is not the only measure of size that has been suggested as a possible influence upon trade union membership levels and we showed in our analysis of the 1980 survey that size of organisation, again measured by number of employees, had a strong and independent effect upon density levels.[5] When combined with the variation with respect to types of ownership the results suggested that the effect operated through both the policies of large employers towards trade unions and through the greater visibility and ease of recruitment of large numbers of workers in large organisations. Indeed, some of the greater levels of union density in the public sector than in the private sector could well be attributed to such effects. Here we are confining our analysis to the private sector and show in Table 3.4 the various measures of trade union membership density in establishments belonging to six different categories of size of organisation. There can be little doubt that there is a strong positive relationship between union density and size of organisation in the private sector: in organisations of less than 100 employees density averaged 20 per cent; in the largest organisations – those with 50,000 or more employees – density averaged about 60 per cent. The relationship is quite smooth and is mirrored by the proportion of establishments that have **no** union members, shown in the left-hand column. More detailed tabulations using both establishment and enterprise size indicate quite clearly that both of these aspects of size have effects upon union density levels, despite the fact that there is a natural degree of correlation between the two measures.[6] Moreover, when we isolated small firms of 25 to 49 employees in our sample they reported union density on average of 19 per cent, with most of this accounted for by manual trade unions. Given the positive and continuous relationship between density and organisation size, firms below our sample threshold of 25 employees could be expected to have very much lower union density on average than this.

Workforce composition also contributes substantially to the pattern of union membership in the private sector. We noted earlier that the decline in manual employment contributed to the aggregate decline in union membership; in the lower half of Table 3.4 we can see just how important the mix of manual and non-manual employment in a workplace is to its overall union membership density. Establishments with more than 70 per cent of their workforce in manual occupations had an average union density of 53 per cent whereas those with less than 30 per cent manual (more than 70 per cent non-manual) had an average density of 25 per cent. In the survey sample as a whole, 58 per cent of manual workers in the private sector were trade union members as against 26 per cent of non-manual workers. And again in Table 3.4 we can see that where workforces are predominantly non-manual the likelihood of **any** employees being trade union members is much reduced. This applies in private services as well as private manufacturing, but of course not in the public sector, excluded from our current discussion, where so much of white-collar union membership is concentrated.

Two other aspects of workforce composition have traditionally been regarded as important in explaining union membership levels, namely gender and part-time, as against full-time, working. Females and part-time workers have generally been viewed as less likely to join trade unions than males and full-time workers.[7] But because the great majority of part-time workers are female – nearly 90 per cent of them were in our 1980 survey – it is often difficult to distinguish the two effects. Indeed, the number of part-time male workers in our 1980 sample was so small, and they were so thinly dispersed among the sample of establishments, that we did not ask our 1984 respondents to distinguish between male and female part-time workers, preferring to use the space available to collect other details of the composition of the workforce. This means that at the individual level we cannot separate the effects of these two characteristics upon trade union membership.[8] We can, however, see from our results how they relate to union density at the **compositional** level, taking the proportion of the workforce who are female or part-time as our measure. From this analysis the proportion of part-timers in an establishment clearly has a negative effect on average density levels – private sector establishments with more than 40 per cent of their workforce working part-time averaged less than half the density of establishments with five per cent of their workforce working part-time (see Table 3.4). Evidence from the 1984 *Social Attitudes Survey* indicates very strongly that full-time women employees are as likely to be trade union members as full-time men employees,[9] but that part-time women employees are half as likely to be members as full-timers. The analysis of these data has so far not distinguished these differences in union membership patterns in the public and private sectors, and it is clear that proportionately more women, both full-time and part-time, are employed in the public sector. But this evidence at the individual level, combined with our evidence at the workplace level, does suggest that union density patterns are more affected by the extent and concentration of part-time working than by gender.[10]

Trade union recognition

While the presence of some trade union members at a workplace can be seen as a prerequisite for the representation of sections of the workforce, or indeed the whole workforce, to management through trade union channels, it by no means guarantees representation. The recognition by management of trade unions for negotiating pay and conditions of employment was the key expression of management's willingness to allow trade unions to represent employees that we built into our survey design. It formed the basis of our selection of worker representatives for interview and many of our interview questions were asked only where trade union recognition was reported. Because it seemed for all practical purposes to be a nonsense to ask about trade union recognition where there were no union members present, we only asked about recognition where we had a positive answer to our question about the presence of trade union members. In the analysis that follows we have assumed that, in cases where managers either did not know whether there were any union members at their workplace or gave some other answer besides a positive 'yes', unions were not recognised by management. As we have already shown in Table 3.1, such cases were much less common in our second survey than in the first. It was generally in relation to manual workers that the information was not available and mostly in the services sector in establishments with very few manual workers. In the private services sector our assumption that **don't knows** and **other answers** could be regarded as **noes** seems fully justified. In the public sector – and most of the cases arose in local authorities or services administered by them – the assumption may be more questionable. For this reason we should warn that not all of the increase in recognition in the public sector shown in Table 3.5 should be regarded as real. Some of it could well be accounted for by measurement error, although by no means all of it should be assumed to be that. It may be quite realistic to think of small groups of manual workers in 1980 in dispersed public sector establishments as not being effectively represented by trade unions

Table 3.5 Trade union recognition – 1980 and 1984

Percentages

	All establishments 1980	All establishments 1984	Private manufacturing 1980	Private manufacturing 1984	Private services 1980	Private services 1984	Public sector 1980	Public sector 1984
Establishments with recognised trade unions for manual workers:								
as a proportion of all establishments	55	62	65	55	33	38	76	91
as a proportion of establishments with manual union members	86	91	85	85	80	81	92	99
Base: establishments with manual workers								
Unweighted	1899	1853	734	580	521	515	644	758
Weighted	1823	1749	498	412	755	689	570	648
Establishments with recognised trade unions for non-manual workers:								
as a proportion of all establishments	47	54	27	26	28	30	91	98
as a proportion of establishments with non-manual union members	87	92	74	75	82	85	93	99
Base: establishments with non-manual workers								
Unweighted	2034	2010	743	592	585	593	706	825
Weighted	1987	1985[1]	503	424	854	836	631	726
Establishments with recognised trade unions for any workers:								
as a proportion of all establishments	64	66	65	56	41	44	94	99
as a proportion of establishments with any union members	88	91	84	83	81	82	95	99
Base: all establishments								
Unweighted	2040	2019	743	592	587	597	710	830
Weighted	2000	2000	503	424	859	843	638	733

[1] See Note H.

and having their pay and conditions of employment determined unilaterally by management.

Naturally these doubts about the changes in the extent of recognition, particularly for manual workers in the public sector, carry over into the overall figures for all establishments in the economy as a whole. In the private sector we have no such doubts about the reasonableness of our assumption and we therefore concentrate in the analysis that follows on that sector, first of all in relation to all workers and then separately for manual and non-manual workers.

In private manufacturing the results indicate a substantial fall in the proportion of establishments with one or more recognised unions for either manual or non-manual employees. The proportion dropped from 65 per cent in 1980 to 56 per cent in 1984. Within the engineering and vehicles sector, accounting for just over a third of all manufacturing workplaces in our sample, the drop was from 65 per cent to 52 per cent in respect of manual recognition, a striking result in view of the stereotype of engineering as one of the strongholds of manual trade unionism. In private manufacturing as a whole, virtually all of the decline was in respect of manual workers, recognition for non-manual workers in that sector remaining at its low level, compared with manuals, of about a quarter of establishments. Recognition for white-collar workers but not for manual workers remained a very rare exception in manufacturing, accounting for only one per cent of cases. But the decline in manual recognition cannot be attributed to there being fewer workplaces with union members belonging only to unrecognised unions. In 1980, 85 per cent of workplaces with manual union members had recognised manual unions; in 1984 that proportion was again 85 per cent. For non-manuals the figure also remained unchanged. The overall decline in the extent of manual recognition in manufacturing must be attributable to the falling proportion of workplaces with any manual trade union members present. And this, as we argued earlier in this chapter, appears to be predominantly a structural change arising from the disproportionate rate of closure of large manufacturing plants.

In the private services sector a different picture emerges. There was clearly no decline in union recognition and possibly a marginal increase in the proportion of establishments recognising trade unions or staff associations, the figures for 1980 and 1984 being 41 per cent and 44 per cent respectively (Table 3.5). These marginal increases were apparent for both manual and non-manual workers separately. The size of the change is insufficient to be able to attribute it to predominantly one or the other of the effects mentioned earlier.

Taking the private sector as a whole, and bearing in mind the declining portion of that engaged in manufacturing, it is possible to discern in the results some important changes in the pattern of recognition with respect to other workplace characteristics. In relation to ownership, we were able to detect no differences between independent establishments and those that were part of a group, but two other aspects of ownership did reveal differences. For both manual and non-manual workers, foreign-owned establishments showed a marginal increase in the proportion recognising appropriate trade unions. For example, 45 per cent of foreign-owned establishments in 1980 recognised one or more manual trade unions; in 1984 the corresponding figure was 54 per cent. And this increase arose entirely because a greater proportion had manual trade union members present. By contrast, none of the increased recognition in respect of non-manual workers was because more foreign-owned establishments had union members present; it was just that those that did were more likely to recognise the union or unions. This change in respect of non-manual recognition was paralleled by another aspect of ownership. Establishments that were themselves the headquarters of their organisation (but not its only establishment) were also more likely to recognise white-collar trade unions in 1984 than in 1980. This change again arose because more establishments with white-collar union members had recognised those unions, not because more establishments had union members present.

Our analysis also showed two aspects of workforce composition to be related to changes in the extent of trade union recognition, one with respect to manual workers, the other to non-manuals. In 1984 workplaces with more than 10 per cent of their employees belonging to ethnic minority groups were less likely to recognise manual trade unions than workplaces with a lower proportion of ethnic minority workers. This difference appeared to be due to the lower proportion that had any manual trade union members present. No such difference was apparent in our 1980 survey results and in this respect the position of ethnic minority workers can be regarded as having deteriorated during the period between our two surveys. Secondly, there were differences in 1984 with respect to the use of 'marginal' or 'non-core' workers. Workplaces that used either freelance workers, homeworkers, agency temps or short-term contract workers[11] were much less likely to recognise non-manual trade unions, although they were just as likely as other private sector establishments to have non-manual union members present.

Union recognition – analysing change using the panel sample
As we explained in Chapter 1, our design for the 1984 survey included an experimental panel sample – a sample of establishments inter-

viewed in both surveys. Such a sample can be put to a number of different uses: some methodological, such as diagnosing difficulties with particular survey questions; others substantive, such as investigating the causal ordering of variables or measuring variation through time. Our purpose here is to use the panel to illuminate the picture of trade union recognition already described using the cross-sectional sample. In particular we wish to see whether the pattern of **gross** changes exemplified in the panel sample can add to our analysis of the **net** changes shown by the cross-sectional sample. As this is our first use of the panel data in the book so far some introductory remarks are in order.

To begin with we need to bear in mind that the panel sample is not strictly comparable with either the 1980 or the 1984 cross-sectional sample. This is because it excludes establishments that closed down after the 1980 survey (or dropped below 25 employees by 1984) and because it excludes new establishments with 25 or more employees in 1984. These differences mean that the panel contains proportionately more large establishments than either of the cross-sectional samples. In consequence any variable that is positively related to establishment size will have a higher reading in the panel sample than in both cross-sectional samples. This is indeed the case with trade union recognition. Moreover, as the panel is relatively small and contains a much wider range of weights, any measurements using it must necessarily have much larger sampling errors than the same variables measured in the cross-sectional samples. There seems little point, then, in using the panel sample to look at net changes in trade union recognition when the cross-sectional samples can give a more accurate picture.

But in using the panel to analyse gross changes we have to be especially sure that our two measurements were made on the same unit; otherwise we could get an exaggerated picture of change because any variation in the definition of the unit (establishment) could generate a difference between the two survey measurements. This is the main reason why we regarded the inclusion of the panel sample as an experiment. The definition of an establishment – and the operationalisation of that definition by an interviewer in the field – is much more problematic than the definition and identification of individual persons, for whom there has been considerable use of panel samples in survey research. As we explain in the Technical Appendix, we did carry out a number of checks at the coding and editing stages of the 1984 survey to ensure as best we could that all panel cases had been interviewed about the same establishment in both surveys. As a result of that work a few cases were eliminated from the panel dataset. Another 24 were given codes indicating that we had doubts about whether the establishment or its main subunits had been treated consistently between the two occasions. Of these 24 cases, 19 were ones where we felt, after examination of the questionnaires, that the establishment may have been defined more widely in 1980 than in 1984, or vice versa. We have eliminated these from our analysis of trade union recognition. A further five cases had such dramatic shifts in their numbers of manual and non-manual employees that we suspected that these terms had been interpreted differently by respondents on the two occasions. As our questions on trade union recognition were asked separately for manual and non-manual employees it seemed safer to omit these too. This left us with 211 (unweighted) cases on which to perform our panel analysis, amounting to a weighted total of 181. Table 3.6 shows how these 181 cases were distributed in terms of trade union recognition on the two occasions.

Table 3.6 The presence of recognised trade unions for either manual or non-manual employees in 1980 and in 1984 using the panel sample

Numbers of cases (weighted)

	1984 Any recognised union	
	Yes	No
Any recognised union		
1980 Yes	124	4
No	9	44

Base: establishments in the panel sample with no query about the definition of the establishment

Unweighted: 211
Weighted: 181

Even taking the figures in Table 3.6 at face value, the picture is of little gross change in whether or not establishments have recognised trade unions. Taking manual and non-manual unions together, 93 per cent of establishments did not change their recognition of trade unions between 1980 and 1984. Of the small minority that did change, more recognised unions in 1984 and not in 1980 than changed in the opposite direction.

Let us look at the two types of change in turn and see what sorts of establishment were involved. We deal first with the four (weighted) workplaces where union recognition was reported in 1980 but not in 1984 – in other words, cases where recognition may have been withdrawn. In fact there were three (unweighted) cases involved. Two of them were private sector workplaces, one in manufacturing, the other in service industry. The former had union members among its predominantly manual workforce in both 1980 and 1984, but no non-manual union members in either year. The latter had an entirely white-collar workforce, virtually all of whom were trade union or staff association members in 1984. Both of these cases could properly be cases where trade union recognition was withdrawn by management. The third case was an establishment in local or central government where trade union membership density was high in 1980 (over 80 per cent overall), but neither manual nor non-manual trade union members were said to be present in 1984. With no union members present the question of recognition was not put to our management respondent and the establishment is classified as having no recognised unions in 1984. Without more information it would be difficult to determine whether trade union recognition had genuinely been withdrawn in this case or whether collective bargaining at a higher level did determine the pay and conditions of employees there but none of them happened to be members. So only two of our three cases seem to be *prima facie* cases of a withdrawal of recognition.

On the opposite side of the coin we have nine establishments (weighted) where recognition was reported in 1984 but not in 1980 – in other words, recognition appears to have been granted between the two surveys. These amounted to seven (unweighted) cases. Only one of these was in the private sector – a small manufacturing firm with a predominantly manual workforce. No manual workers were reported in 1980, but some were in 1984. Manual recognition was reported in 1984 and we have no evidence for not believing this to be a genuine case where recognition had been granted between 1980 and 1984. All the remaining six cases were public sector establishments in 1980 with some union members present at that time. In 1984, when all of them reported recognised unions for at least some employees, all reported that bargaining for the largest group of employees took place at national level, either for their organisation as a whole or on an industry-wide basis. We warned in an earlier section of this chapter that our 1980 data on recognition in the public sector might involve some measurement error because so much industrial relations activity in that sector was concentrated in centralised institutions. These public sector cases in the panel sample are, of course, included in the 1980 cross-sectional sample and it is clear that we would be unwise to regard them, perhaps any of them, as genuine cases of the granting of recognition of trade unions by management between 1980 and 1984.

In summary, the panel data suggest that the gross change in union recognition between 1980 and 1984 is virtually zero in both directions.

In the public sector we have the single case of withdrawal of recognition and a handful of cases where an apparent granting of recognition could well involve measurement error in 1980. In the private sector we have one or two believable changes in either direction, suggesting that perhaps one or two per cent of larger private sector workplaces might have withdrawn or granted recognition in the four-year period. There can be little doubt that the substantial **net** decline in trade union recognition in private manufacturing industry that we identified earlier in this chapter occurred through a change in the composition of that sector, rather than any tendency to withdraw recognition from trade unions that already had it.

Union attempts to recruit and gain recognition

So far our analysis of trade union membership and recognition has focused on whether or not these features of institutional industrial relations are present. The other side of the coin is also of interest. In our report on the 1980 survey we paid some attention to cases where there were trade union members present but none of the unions was recognised by management for negotiating purposes. Some of them had quite high membership densities and we showed that they were almost exclusively small independent establishments or small establishments belonging to medium-sized or small enterprises in the private sector.[12] This remained the case in 1984.

A rather different type of non-union establishment is that where there are no union members present and the question of recognition would presumably not have arisen. These cases, of course, are simply the residual ones in our analysis in the chapter so far, amounting to 27 per cent of all establishments (see Table 3.1) in our cross-sectional sample and 16 per cent of employees. In our second survey we inserted a few simple questions to ascertain from our management respondents whether there had been any recent attempts to unionise their establishment if they had not reported union members present at the time of interview in 1984. We asked them three questions. The first was whether, to their knowledge, any union had attempted to recruit members from the manual workforce in the last five years. Secondly, and independently of their reply to the first question, we asked them whether there had been any request for recognition in the last five years from any union or group of manual workers at their establishment. Thirdly, where there **were** recognised unions but they did not cover the whole of the manual workforce, we asked them if there had ever been a request from unions or groups of manual workers to cover any of these workers. Similar questions were asked separately in relation to non-manual workers.

In respect of manual workers with no union members present in

1984, 15 per cent of managers reported that there had been an attempt to recruit union members at their workplace in the last five years. This amounted to some four per cent of all establishments employing manual workers. As one might expect from the pattern of union density, these reported attempts at union recruitment were concentrated in establishments with sizeable numbers of manual workers. Virtually all cases were within the private sector, but there seemed to be little difference between manufacturing and services in the likelihood of recruitment attempts being made, although most of the reported cases were in private services where the bulk of non-union establishments is concentrated. The picture was similar, but not in all respects, for non-manual workers. Here there were fewer reported attempts to recruit – 10 per cent of establishments with no white-collar union members present, amounting to four per cent of all establishments employing white-collar workers. The relationship with the number of non-manual workers on site was weaker than in the case of manual workers, probably reflecting different methods of communication used for the two groups. But as with manual workers, the attempts were concentrated in the private services sector where non-union establishments are concentrated.

Given the dramatic reduction in overall trade union membership numbers in the early 1980s, it might be thought that trade unions would have tried to compensate by concentrating their recruitment campaigns in areas of expanding employment. Our 1984 survey data indicate that this was not the case in relation to wholly non-union establishments. Recruitment attempts were reported by managers in expanding and contracting workplaces with equal frequency, but those with stable workforces compared with a year previously were more likely to report attempts. This tendency was more marked for manual than for non-manual workers. But there was very definitely no tendency for recruitment attempts to be concentrated in expanding workplaces.

Generally speaking, these results do not indicate extensive attempts by unions to recruit in non-union establishments, given that our questions were about attempts within the previous five years. Moreover, they reinforce the view that attempts to gain trade union recognition are unlikely to be successful without a substantial membership base. Indeed, when we related responses on the two questions there were virtually no cases (less than ½ per cent in the private sector) where recognition had been requested by a union but there had been no attempt to recruit members.

Our third question on this subject looked at situations where management already recognised unions for some workers but not for others. We shall be looking at the detailed questions on the coverage of collective bargaining later in this chapter, but for the moment it is worth noting that the typical situation is for **all** manual workers in a workplace with recognised manual unions to be covered by those unions and only very rarely are less than half of the manual workforce covered. For non-manuals the same is true, although there are more cases, especially in the private sector, where coverage is just under 100 per cent, no doubt reflecting the exclusion of senior managerial and possibly professional employees. Thus in looking at situations with only partial coverage by recognised trade unions we are examining rather unusual types of workplace, concentrated in the private sector. They represent only eight per cent of establishments when we focus on manual workers and 12 per cent if we focus on non-manuals. In the case of manual workers most of them have trade union density below 25 per cent. They are establishments with a high proportion of their workforce in manual grades, but with a low proportion of part-time workers. They are as likely in manufacturing as in service industries. None of them are in independent or foreign-owned establishments. The non-manual cases are rather different. They occur at higher levels of union density and are somewhat more likely in manufacturing than in service industry. None of these correlations with establishment characteristics give us any strong clues as to the reasons for a section of the workforce being excluded from the collective bargaining provisions in existence for their colleagues. Only more detailed questioning about the type of employee involved could have resolved that issue, but we do have information on the way that their pay was determined. That analysis is contained in Chapter 9, where pay determination is discussed in detail. We now therefore return to our description of the survey results on the structure of collective bargaining within establishments with recognised trade unions.

Multi-unionism
In our report on the 1980 survey we pointed out how common it was in British workplaces for more than one trade union to be recognised by management in relation to manual and to non-manual workers. The complexity of representation was very strongly associated with the size of the workforce and joint negotiating arrangements were less common than separate arrangements. We examined managers' and shop stewards' reasons for preferring separate or joint negotiations and found that where there was separate bargaining it was uncommon for both managers and stewards to agree that this was the better arrangement. When we looked at the relationship between multi-unionism amongst manual workers and the incidence of recent industrial conflict we found a weak positive relationship. This was subsequently confirmed by more sophisticated analysis controlling for

Table 3.7 Number of recognised manual unions and number of manual bargaining units

	All establishments		Private manufacturing		Private services		Public sector	
	1980	1984	1980	1984	1980	1984	1980	1984
Number of recognised unions							Column percentages	
1	65	65	63	58	86	80	55[1]	62
2	18	21	18	22	8	18	23	22
3	9	8	10	14	3	2	12	8
4 or more	8	6	9	6	3	*	10	8
Not known	*	*	—	—	—	—	2	*
Number of bargaining units							Column percentages	
1	77	82	76	72	90	88	70	83
2	13	12	15	16	7	11	16	12
3	5	4	6	10	1	*	6	2
4 or more	2	2	3	3	*	*	3	2
Not known	2	1	*	—	*	*	4	1
Base: establishments with recognised unions for manual workers								
Unweighted	1375	1405	596	462	231	231	548	712
Weighted	1021	1077	324	228	256	260	441	589

[1] See Note C.

a large number of other variables simultaneously.[13] In view of this, and the widely reported preferences of foreign companies for less complex representational arrangements than are normal in British-owned workplaces, any changes in the extent of multi-unionism are of interest. We show these changes separately for the main sectors of the economy in Tables 3.7. and 3.8.

Taking the number of recognised trade unions first, there are only marginal changes in the pattern of multi-unionism for either manual or non-manual workers. Such changes as are detectable are in opposite directions for the two groups of employees. For manual workers there is a slight tendency away from establishments having three or more recognised unions, largely due to the declining importance of private manufacturing in the sample and reduced numbers of recognised unions in the public sector. For non-manuals there is an overall increase in multi-unionism, as measured by the proportion of establishments having three or more recognised unions, but here the explanation is rather different. A decline in multi-unionism in the private manufacturing sector is more than offset by a contrary trend in the public sector, where non-manual trade unionism is much more significant. None of these movements is especially marked and the pattern of variation in the number of recognised unions remained very much what it was in 1980. Multi-unionism remains a notable feature of the British industrial relations scene and is especially common for manual employees in large manufacturing plants and for non-manual workers in the public sector.

Multiple bargaining units also remain common. As Tables 3.7 and 3.8 indicate, there may have been a slight movement away from multiple bargaining units, especially in relation to manual workers in private manufacturing and in relation to both manual and non-manual workers in the public sector. Even so, in 1984 nearly a half of public sector establishments had non-manual employees in two or more separate negotiating groups.

As in 1980, the practice of negotiating with separate unions or groups of unions for different groups of employees remained more common among indigenously-owned workplaces in the private sector. In Table 3.9 we show how foreign-owned and UK-owned workplaces compare in relation to the number of bargaining units that they deal with for manual employees. The results control for size of establishment, the variable most strongly related to the existence of multiple bargaining units. An equivalent table for non-manual workers is not given because there are too few foreign-owned establishments in the sample that recognise non-manual unions to permit separate analysis by size. However, in aggregate, foreign-owned establishments were less likely to have multiple bargaining units for non-manuals than

Table 3.8 Number of recognised non-manual unions and number of non-manual bargaining units

	All establishments 1980	1984	Private manufacturing 1980	1984	Private services 1980	1984	Public sector 1980	1984
							Column percentages	
Number of recognised unions								
1	43	39	65[1]	69	68	63	28	25
2	29	28	20	21	29	32	32	27
3	12	15	13	7	2	3	16	21
4 or more	16	18	3	3	2	2	25	26
Not known	*	*	—	—	—	—	*	*
							Column percentages	
Number of bargaining units								
1	57	61	66	77	74	70	48	55
2	31	26	21	15	23	27	36	27
3	6	8	11	5	1	2	7	10
4 or more	5	3	3	3	1	1	7	5
Not known	1	2	—	—	—	*	2	3
Base: establishments with recognised unions for non-manual workers								
Unweighted	1277	1397	407	351	208	229	662	817
Weighed	943[2]	1069	134	109	236	247	572	713

[1] See Note C.
[2] See Note H.

Table 3.9 **Proportion of workplaces in the private sector with a single bargaining unit for manual workers by ownership and size of workplace, 1984**

Percentages

	All private sector	Number of employees at establishment			
		25–99	100–499	500–999	1000 or more
UK-owned establishments	79	85	69	54	46
Foreign-owned establishments	87	§[1]	(84)[2]	(65)[3]	71
Base: private sector establishments with recognised unions for manual workers					
Unweighted	*693*	*168*	*255*	*135*	*135*
Weighted	*488*	*330*	*133*	*16*	*9*

[1] See Note A.
[2] See Note B.
[3] Unweighted base is 19; percentage should be treated with additional caution.

UK-owned workplaces. There seems little doubt that in general foreign-owned firms that recognise trade unions negotiate through less complex structures than their UK counterparts.

The coverage of collective bargaining within establishments

It is not necessarily the case that when manual trade unions have achieved recognition by management in a particular workplace then all the manual workers at that establishment are covered by the settlements and agreements that follow recognition. Recognition agreements, where they formally exist, often specify groups that are, or are not, covered by the agreement. In the case of non-manual workers it is usually assumed that there are more likely to be groups of employees, such as senior managers, who are excluded from trade union representation and the settlements made with recognised unions or staff associations. Reporting the results of the Warwick survey of large manufacturing plants in 1977/78, Brown remarked upon the 'small minority of plants' for which the 'major group' of manual or non-manual workers did not comprise the whole of the manual or non-manual workforce.[14] In our first survey we did not collect any information which would enable us to measure the extent of coverage and non-coverage of recognised unions. We remedied this omission in 1984 by asking three new questions. We asked what proportion of the manual workforce at the establishment was covered by the negotiating group (or union), and where there were two groups we asked about the coverage of the largest group. Where there were more than two groups we asked about the coverage of the second largest group. Similar questions were asked in respect of non-manual negotiating groups. We focus our attention in this report on the overall coverage figures in particular and show these by broad sector in Table 3.10.

Looking initially at the figures for all establishments, it is evident that the great majority of managements that recognise trade unions do so in respect of **all** their manual workers. The same is true for non-manual workers, although the proportion is substantially less – three quarters compared with over four fifths. In only five per cent of cases was less than half of the manual workforce covered and in only six per cent of cases was less than half of the non-manual workforce covered. The pattern of coverage was very different for the four main sectors of the economy shown separately in Table 3.10. In private manufacturing 100 per cent coverage was reported in 77 per cent of cases for manual workers and a mere 33 per cent for non-manuals, presumably reflecting a very widespread exclusion of managerial employees from collective bargaining arrangements.[15] In private services 100 per cent coverage was more common, although we should remember that union recognition was much less common. Moreover, the fact that coverage for non-manuals in private services was higher than in manufacturing must in part reflect the fact that a much higher proportion of employment in the private services sector is in non-manual occupations.

In the public sector the picture is quite different. Less than 100 per cent coverage is virtually non-existent in the nationalised industries, even for non-manual employees. In the rest of the public sector, coverage is generally high, with less than half the manual workforce covered in seven per cent of cases and less than half the non-manual workforce covered in only two per cent of cases.

Coverage varied with a number of establishment characteristics, the most notable being trade union density and the complexity of negotiating arrangements. In general terms coverage exceeded union density by a substantial margin, showing that many employees have their pay and conditions of employment negotiated by trade unions while not being members of those unions. In all establishments with recognised trade unions for manual workers 95 per cent of manual workers were covered by collective agreements, compared with a membership density of 83 per cent. For non-manuals the figures were 92 per cent and 73 per cent respectively. Coverage and density were strongly correlated. For example, coverage for manual workers averaged 63 per cent in establishments where union density was under a quarter. The corresponding figure for non-manuals was 59 per cent. At the other end of the continuum, where coverage was 100 per cent, density averaged 87 per cent for manuals (86 per cent in the private sector) and 77 per cent for non-manuals (67 per cent in the private sector).

Table 3.10 Proportion of a) manual and b) non-manual workforce covered by recognised unions or groups of unions, 1984

Column percentages

	All establishments	Private manufacturing	Private services	Nationalised industries	Public services
Manual workers					
1–19 per cent	3[1]	*	3	—	4
20–49 per cent	2	3	2	—	3
50–79 per cent	3	4	4	—	2
80–99 per cent	6	15	5	1	4
100 per cent	83	77	85	99	81
Not known	3	*	1	1	5
Overall percentage covered	95	97	91	100	94
Base: establishments with recognised manual unions					
Unweighted	1405	462	231	191	521
Weighted	1077	228	260	103	486
Non-manual workers					
1–19 per cent	2[1]	10	1	—	1
20–49 per cent	4	14	8	—	1
50–79 per cent	7	27	8	1	4
80–99 per cent	11	15	11	3	12
100 per cent	74	33	72	95	79
Not known	2	1	1	—	3
Overall percentage covered	92	72	91	99	96
Base: establishments with recognised non-manual unions					
Unweighted	1397	351	229	194	623
Weighted	1069	109	247	105	608

[1] See Note C.

For manual workers coverage was 100 per cent in virtually every establishment with three or more negotiating groups, both in the public and the private sectors. For non-manuals this was not the case, the overall coverage figure for establishments with three or more groups being 97 per cent, dropping to 92 per cent in the private sector.[16] Thus it is clear that the greater the number of negotiating groups the greater the likelihood that there will not be any groups of employees left uncovered by collective bargaining.

A final statistic of interest on the coverage of collective bargaining is that which takes all employees as its base – in other words, we take employees, both manual and non-manual, covered directly by settlements made between managements and trade unions, either at workplace or higher levels, as a proportion of all employees. On this basis the overall figure for our sample was 71 per cent, indicating that some 10.7 million employees are directly covered by collective bargaining in that part of the economy covered by our 1984 survey. We have no way of estimating what coverage would be in the small establishments not covered by our sample, but clearly the proportion would be much less (because of the strong correlation between recognition and size of establishment) and the aggregate total would not be greatly increased by their inclusion.[17]

The incidence of trade union representatives at workplaces

We now turn our attention to another important aspect of trade union recognition – the presence of different types of trade union representative at the place of work. In describing our results for manual workers we shall use the most common term for such representatives, *shop steward*. For non-manuals there is no such commonly used term and we shall refer to *trade union representatives* or just *representatives*. In all cases it should be understood that we are talking about **representatives of recognised trade unions or recognised staff associations**. In the 1980 survey we did ask a few questions about the presence of trade union or staff association representatives where those bodies were **not** recognised by management for negotiating pay and conditions but were recognised in some lesser sense. We found such representatives to be rare, being reported by management in only three per cent of establishments.[18] The questions on such representatives were dropped from the 1984 interview schedules to make way for other material. What we report here, then, is the results of comparable questions asked in both 1980 and 1984 on the presence of stewards, senior stewards and convenors (and their non-manual equivalents) in workplaces with recognised trade unions or staff associations. Tables 3.11 and 3.12 show how the presence of such representatives has changed between 1980 and 1984,

Table 3.11 Presence of trade union representatives by size of workforce

Percentages

| | All establishments | | Number of manual workers employed at establishment | | | | | | | |
| | | | 1–24 | | 25–99 | | 100–499 | | 500 or more | |
	1980	1984	1980	1984	1980	1984	1980	1984	1980	1984
Manual workers represented by:										
One or more stewards at own workplace	70	65	42	37	77	78	94	90	94	97
Stewards elsewhere in organisation	..[1]	19	..	37	..	11	..	3	..	1
Full-time union official	..	7	..	12	..	4	..	3	..	1
Senior steward of 2 or more present	25	19	5	4	24	18	52	51	76	86
Full-time steward or convenor present	3	3	—	1	*	1	8	7	49	56
Base: establishments with recognised unions for manual workers										
Unweighted	*1375*	*1405*	*171*	*229*	*403*	*421*	*530*	*503*	*271*	*252*
Weighed	*1021*	*1077*	*303*	*407*	*492*	*494*	*198*	*157*	*30*	*19*

| | All establishments | | Number of non-manual workers employed at establishment | | | | | | | |
| | | | 1–24 | | 25–99 | | 100–499 | | 500 or more | |
	1980	1984	1980	1984	1980	1984	1980	1984	1980	1984
Non-manual workers represented by:										
One or more stewards at own workplace	63	67	41	48	71	76	90	94	90	84[2]
Representatives elsewhere in organisation	..	22	..	35	..	16	..	5	..	1
Full-time union official	..	5	..	8	..	4	..	2	..	*
Senior representative of 2 or more present	21	22	8	8	21	24	50	48	63	62
Full-time representative present	1	1	1	*	1	1	2	3	15	17
Base: establishments with recognised unions for non-manual workers										
Unweighted	*1277*	*1397*	*204*	*218*	*421*	*411*	*433*	*501*	*219*	*267*
Weighed	*943*	*1069*	*360*	*430*	*425*	*461*	*132*	*152*	*27*	*26*

[1] See Note J.
[2] Understates likely figure because a high percentage of respondents did not answer. See text.

Table 3.12 Presence of trade union representatives by broad sector

Percentages

	Private manufacturing 1980	Private manufacturing 1984	Private services 1980	Private services 1984	Nationalised industries 1980	Nationalised industries 1984	Public services 1980	Public services 1984
Manual workers represented by:								
One or more stewards at own workplace	84	98	73	67	86	81	54	45
Stewards elsewhere in organisation	..[1]	1	..	7	..	14	..	36
Full-time union official	..	*	..	7	..	3	..	10
Senior steward of 2 or more present	44	46	20	12	20	29	14	7
Full-time steward or convenor present	6	5	1	1	4	8	2	2
Base: establishments with recognised unions for manual workers								
Unweighted	596	462	231	231	129	191	419	521
Weighted	324	228	256	260	66	103	376	486
Non-manual workers represented by:								
One or more representatives at own workplace	69	76	49	50	59	61	68	74[2]
Representatives elsewhere in organisation	..	7	..	28	..	36	..	19
Full-time union official	..	*	..	10	..	2	..	5
Senior representative of 2 or more present	40	33	12	13	14	18	21	22
Full-time representative present	2	*	1	1	2	2	1	1
Base: establishments with recognised unions for non-manual workers								
Unweighted	407	351	208	229	130	194	532	623
Weighted	134	109	236	247	63	105	509	608

[1] See Note J.
[2] See Note 2 on Table 3.11.

with the results broken down by workforce size and by broad sector.

Overall, the results indicate that fewer establishments with recognised manual trade unions had shop stewards present in 1984 than in 1980, the proportion dropping from 70 to 65 per cent. This appears to have come about because of the changing size distribution of workplaces with recognised unions for manual employees: only workplaces with small manual workforces showed a marginal decline in the presence of stewards, but such workplaces were a much higher proportion of the distribution and have a lower chance of having stewards. On the other hand, slightly more establishments with recognised non-manual unions had workplace representatives in 1984 than in 1980, the figures being 63 per cent and 67 per cent respectively. But here the explanation is different. All size bands, but especially the smaller ones,[19] showed slight increases in the presence of representatives and all sectors except private services did too. It is therefore likely that the increased presence of non-manual union representatives is a consequence of the general strengthening of white-collar unionism of which the growth in membership, referred to earlier in this chapter, is another indication.

In terms of the **pattern** of their distribution, it is evident from Tables 3.11 and 3.12 that there has been little change. Stewards and non-manual representatives clearly remained very much more common in larger establishments than smaller ones, the proportion rising from 37 per cent of workplaces with less than 25 manual employees to 97 per cent of workplaces with 500 or more manual employees in 1984, a pattern very similar to that of 1980. For non-manuals the pattern remained similar, although with less marked contrasts. In terms of broad sectors, manual stewards were present in the great majority of private manufacturing and nationalised industry establishments with recognised unions, but in only around a half of workplaces in public services. Non-manual union representatives were present in a clear majority of workplaces recognising non-manual unions, although only a half of those in the private services sector. There have, however, been some notable shifts within particular sectors over the fours years. Manual stewards were reported in 98 per cent of private sector manufacturing plants with recognised unions in 1984 as against 84 per cent in 1980, despite the reduced proportion of large plants where they were much more common. Some of this change could reflect a decline in particular manufacturing industries where members have traditionally been serviced by full-time union officials; but a more general shift towards increased lay representation in manufacturing seems likely. Public services showed a contrary trend. There was a fall in the proportion of establishments with manual stewards from 54 per cent to 45 per cent overall – and this decline was still apparent when the size of the manual workforce was held constant in our analysis. A union policy of centralisation might be the explanation here. This interpretation receives some support from our analysis of trade union branch composition in Chapter 5. Public service unions had fewer workplace-based branches in 1984 than they did in 1980.

As an initial measure of the existence of a hierarchy among the stewards or representatives in our sample of workplaces we asked managers whether any of the stewards acted as **senior** stewards and if they were acknowledged by management as such. The presence of such senior stewards or representatives is shown in the two tables, in cases where there were at least two stewards present. Again the pattern is similar to the pattern for ordinary stewards: senior stewards are more common in workplaces with large numbers of the type of employee they represent, and particularly in manufacturing industry. In 1984 about a fifth of workplaces with recognised manual trade unions had a senior steward; a similar proportion of establishments with recognised non-manual unions had a senior trade union representative, acknowledged by management as such. Little change is evident between 1980 and 1984 other than what might be expected on the basis of structural changes in the population of establishments and particularly those with recognised unions. Indeed, it is perhaps surprising that when we analysed the presence of senior stewards in the private sector, controlling for the size of the manual workforce, there was an indication that senior stewards were becoming more common, rather than less.

Where senior shop stewards or representatives were present in an establishment we asked if any of them spent all or nearly all of their time on trade union matters. Such *full-time stewards* or *convenors* were a feature of large-scale manual employment, occurring in 70 per cent of workplaces with 1000 or more manual workers, but only three per cent of all establishments recognising manual unions in 1984 (the same proportion as in 1980). Their non-manual equivalent, often the chairmen or secretaries of large, workplace branches in the public sector, remained much less common – they were reported in a mere one per cent of workplaces overall.

Two characteristics that we identified in the 1980 survey as being strongly related to the presence of stewards, senior stewards and full-time stewards remained so in 1984. In our earlier report we remarked upon the tendency for workplaces employing a high proportion of women to have less well-developed union organisation at the workplace.[20] This remained so in 1984, taking the presence of stewards, senior stewards and full-time stewards as separate measures of union organisation. However, there was an equally strong inverse relationship with the proportion of part-time employees at the establishment. As we have mentioned before, these two characteristics ire so strongly related to each other that it would be difficult to disentangle any separate effects. But part-time employment would seem to present particular difficulties to potential shop stewards or union representatives, so that this characteristic, rather than gender, might well lie at the root of the difference.[21] Some, but not all, of the association is explicable in terms of the greater preponderence of part-time and female employees in public sector services, where establishment-level bargaining is uncommon. Indeed, the locus of pay bargaining was the second major characteristic that remained strongly related to the presence of senior and full-time stewards or representatives in 1984. For example, manual senior stewards were present in over a half of workplaces where pay was negotiated locally, compared with about an eighth of cases where it was the subject of multi-employer bargaining. Controlling for workforce size, and limiting the analysis to the private sector, left the correlation little changed.

The locus of pay bargaining, to which we give particular attention in Chapter 9, is thus one of the most important characteristics associated with the presence of a hierarchy amongst local trade union representatives and, indeed, of the presence of any representatives at workplaces with recognised trade unions. This naturally gives rise to the question of how trade union members are represented in workplaces where collective bargaining occurs at a higher level and, more broadly, where there is no representative at all at their own place of work. This was the subject of two new questions in our 1984 survey. We asked managers, where trade unions were recognised but they reported no worker representative at their workplace, whether employees were represented by stewards or representatives from outside the establishment and, if so, what sort of representatives: *lay representatives from elsewhere in their organisation* or *full-time officials of the union.* The questions were asked separately for manual and non-manual workers and the results are shown in the relevant sections of Table 3.11 and 3.12.

Representation by stewards or their equivalent elsewhere in the organisation appeared to be a largely public sector arrangement and occurred most commonly, as one would expect, in smaller establishments with, in many cases, too few members to justify having their own representative. But the arrangement was also common for non-manual union members in small establishments in the private services sector. It was reported in less than one per cent of cases where pay bargaining took place at the establishment.

Representation by full-time union officers, in the absence of workplace representatives, was reported by managers in seven per

Table 3.13 Estimates of numbers of trade union representatives and full-time representatives at establishments

Numbers

	All establishments		Private manufacturing		Private services		Public sector	
	1980	1984	1980	1984	1980	1984	1980	1984
Number of stewards/representatives								
Manual	182000	172000	95000	72000	26000	23000	62000	77000
Non-manual	135000	163000	35000	23000	14000	24000	86000	116000
Manual and non-manual	317000	335000	130000	95000	40000	47000	148000	193000
Number of full-time stewards/representatives								
Manual	3300	2900	1900	1200	400	200	1000	1600
Non-manual	900	1300	300	100	100	200	500	1000
Manual and non-manual	4200	4200	2200	1300	500	400	1500	2600
Base: all establishments								
Unweighted	2040	2019	743	592	587	597	710	830
Weighted	2000[1]	2000	503	424	859	843	637	733

[1] See Note H.

cent of establishments with recognised manual unions and five per cent of those with recognised non-manual unions. It showed a pattern somewhat similar to that for representatives from other establishments, being commonest in small workplaces. It was more common in the private services sector, although even here very much a minority practice, being reported in about a tenth of relevant workplaces. It was only in the private services sector that a significant number of managers reported that, even though they recognised trade unions, union members were not represented by anyone, either a lay representative or union official.

Numbers of lay trade union representatives

The numbers of shop stewards in industry has often been taken as an indicator of trade union strength at workplace level and there has been much speculation about the decline of the shop steward population in recent years, given the substantial fall in trade union membership. The postal survey of personnel managers in large manufacturing plants carried out by Batstone in 1983 indicated[22] that the number of manual shop stewards in that particular sector declined between early 1978 and mid 1983. Our evidence indicates a substantial decline in the number of manual stewards in private manufacturing as a whole between mid 1980 and mid 1984, but also shows the pattern of change to be quite different elsewhere in the economy. Table 3.13 gives the results.

Taking all representatives, both manual and non-manual, in the economy as a whole, our estimates indicate a slight increase in the total number from about 317,000 to around 335,000, a rise of some six per cent. This is composed of a very substantial decline in manufacturing of some 27 per cent, a substantial increase in private services of 18 per cent and a very substantial rise in the public sector of 31 per cent. In line with the changing mix of manual and non-manual employment and trade union membership in the different sectors, so the population of trade union representatives has also changed. Manufacturing industry experienced the biggest declines for both manual and non-manual stewards, while private services experienced a very big increase in non-manual representatives, reflecting both the shift towards non-manual employment in that sector and a modest increase in union recognition. In the public sector there seems little doubt that overall there has been an increase in the numbers of workplace representatives, even though our estimates may understate[23] somewhat the numbers in 1980. The result of these various changes is that non-manual union representatives were nearly as common as manual shop stewards in 1984 and a clear majority of trade union representatives in the economy as a whole were employed in public sector establishments. The stereotype of the trade union representative as a manual shop steward in manufacturing industry evidently needs revision.

It would be of interest to know how much the changes in the population of lay trade union representatives, described above, were attributable to changes in the number of union members in the different sectors or were changes in the size of representatives' 'constituencies'. To make such calculations we would need to have precisely comparable data for the numbers of union members in our two surveys and, as we explained earlier in this chapter, our information on union membership was incomplete in the first survey. It would be possible to make limited comparisons for the numbers of **full-time** union members per representative, but this would be rather partial, given the growing importance of part-time working and the substantial numbers of union members who work part-time. As an alternative we can use our 1984 information on the changes in employment size of our sampled establishments to see how changes in the numbers of union representatives might have come about. Since we are using data from the 1984 survey alone, there is no problem about incomplete union membership figures.[24] Our calculations are for the number of trade union (or staff association) members, both full-time and part-time, per union (or staff association) representative. The average figure was 23 members per steward for manuals and 21 members per representative for non-manuals. Table 3.14 shows how these ratios varied across different types of establishment.

The first part of the table confirms the well-established correlation between the number of members per steward and workforce size. Manual trade union members, for example, share their shop steward with fewer other members if they work at an establishment with few manual workers than if they work somewhere where there are many other manual workers. But as we showed earlier, they are more likely to have no steward at their workplace at all. However, even if we restrict analysis to establishments with at least one steward, the more manual workers there are present the more members there are per steward. The contrast between large and small workplaces is even greater for non-manual members, despite the fact that they are no more likely to be represented by stewards elsewhere or by full-time officials. The bottom portion of the table also indicates that it is employees, manual or non-manual, who are in a minority at their workplace who share their representative with fewer other members.

The second and third portions of Table 3.14 show how member:steward ratios varied with our two measures of changes in numbers employed. Taking change between 1980 and 1984, there was no discernible difference between workplaces that were growing, roughly

Table 3.14   Number of trade union members per representative in relation to characteristics of workplaces, 1984

Means

	Number of manual union members per steward	Number of non-manual members per representative
All establishments	23	21
Size of manual/non-manual workforce		
1–24 employees	11	9
25–99 employees	20	14
100–499 employees	25	29
500 or more employees	29	37
Change in establishment size since 1980		
Decrease of 20% or more	22	17
Decrease of less than 20%	25	18
Stable	22	22
Increase of less than 20%	23	25
Increase of 20% or more	24	27
Not known	22	24
Change in establishment size since 1983		
Decrease of 20% or more	20	16
Decrease of less than 20%	21	18
Stable	23	21
Increase of less than 20%	26	26
Increase of 20% or more	26	(18)
Not known	24	—
Proportion of employees who were manual		
More than 70%	28	13
Between 31% and 70%	20	19
Between 0 and 30%	15	25

Base: establishments with recognised unions for categories of employee mentioned in column headings and where numbers of union members and numbers of representatives were known

Unweighted	*1017*	*982*
Weighted	*658*	*631*

stable or contracting. From this we might conclude that changes in the number of shop stewards roughly followed changes in the number of union members – on the assumption that membership density **within establishments** would be relatively constant over time. But that would be to neglect the fact that union membership numbers have declined substantially, partly – if not largely – as a result of the closure of highly unionised, generally large, establishments. Taking this into account we would infer that the number of representatives has declined more slowly than the number of members. And indeed our estimates suggest a slight rise in the numbers of representatives. The strong presumption must be that, on average, union representatives in 1984 represented fewer members than they did in 1980. We have evidence for manual workers from the two cross-section samples to confirm this. The 1980 average number of **full-time** manual union members per steward was 26; adding in part-time members would obviously have increased the ratio. In 1984 the number of members (full-time and part-time) was 23 per manual steward. Unfortunately our 1980 data on non-manual union membership do not allow us to make the equivalent calculations to see if the same trend is apparent.[25]

Turning to the third section of Table 3.14, there is a fairly clear correlation between manual member:steward ratios and the one-year change in employment size. Establishments with workforce contractions of 20 per cent or more had an average ratio of 20 members per steward whereas workplaces expanding by 20 per cent or more had an average of 26. In combination with the lack of any correlation with the four-year change in size, this indicates that the absolute numbers of manual stewards react to changes in workforce size with a lag of at least a year.

The equivalent portion of the table for non-manual representatives shows a different pattern. Member:representative ratios correlate positively with both measures of employment change, suggesting that non-manual unions (most of whose members are in the public sector) take longer to react to employment changes before adjusting their numbers of workplace representatives.

The numbers and distribution of **full-time** shop stewards or convenors – to use the conventional manual terminology – have also undergone significant change in the period between our two surveys. There have been a few celebrated cases in manufacturing industry where managements have withdrawn accreditation of full-time convenors, but there is no systematic evidence to indicate whether such a phenomenon has been widespread or is offset by changes in the opposite direction. As full-time convenors are so rare and our panel sample is quite small it would not be sensible to analyse the panel data to detect changes in the numbers of convenors in particular establishments. Even using our very substantial cross-sectional samples for 1980 and 1984 involves making estimates of their numbers with sizeable sampling errors. The grossed-up figures given in the lower half of Table 3.13, which are in any case rounded to the nearest hundred, should not be interpreted too literally. But the changes in their rough orders of magnitude are probably a reasonable reflection of what happened. They point towards several findings of interest. In the first place, it is still the case that most of the lay trade union representatives working full-time or nearly full-time on union business at their place of work represent manual trade union members. Roughly two thirds of them were manual convenors in 1984 compared with nearly four fifths in 1980. Their total numbers remained roughly constant – a substantial decline in the numbers of manual convenors being offset by a growth in their non-manual counterparts. In manufacturing there appears to have been a very substantial decline in their numbers. How much of this represents a withdrawal of facilities and how much of it a consequence of the closure or contraction of large-scale, highly unionised plants, we cannot tell. But given the changes in union membership, union recognition and shop steward numbers in manufacturing that we have already described it is likely that the change in industrial structure is important.

In contrast to the substantial fall in numbers of full-time convenors in manufacturing, there appears to have been an increase in both manual and non-manual full-time workplace representatives in the public sector. The actual scale of the increase may be exaggerated in Table 3.13 for reasons mentioned earlier, but it is most unlikely that the direction of change is not as shown. In the private services sector full-time representatives remain a rarity and the only change that can be stated with some confidence is that a greater proportion of them than before represented non-manual employees.

The training of trade union representatives
In 1980 we asked a number of questions about the training of shop stewards and other trade union representatives for their work as representatives. Most of the questions were asked of both management and worker representative respondents and we found high levels of correspondence on the factual details of shop steward training. There was, naturally, less agreement about the value of such training. Most of the questions were repeated in our 1984 survey, although a few that had been asked of all respondents were confined to worker representatives. The picture of such training that we described in our first report remained largely unchanged. Our analysis of the 1984 material concentrates on the areas where change was apparent, with the briefest summary of the remainder of results.

Substantially fewer shop stewards and non-manual union representatives were trained in 1984 than in 1980. Table 3.15 gives the details. In the year up to mid-1984 21 per cent of manual stewards were reported by managers to have had some training or instruction for their jobs as stewards compared with 30 per cent in the year up to mid-1980. There was an equally large drop for non-manual representatives from 27 per cent to 18 per cent. Worker representatives' estimates corresponded very closely with those of management and

Table 3.15 Extent of training of trade union and staff associations representatives

	All establishments 1980	1984	Private manufacturing 1980	1984	Private services 1980	1984	Nationalised industries 1980	1984	Public services 1980	1984
									Column percentages	
Manual representatives										
Any trained in last year	33	29	37	28	32	26	30	35	28	31
No information	5	5	5	3	3	2	6	15	6	5
Percentage trained – mean	30	21	31	20	19	22	47	22	28	22
Base: establishments with manual worker representatives present										
Unweighted	*1137*	*1129*	*556*	*450*	*182*	*174*	*114*	*162*	*285*	*343*
Weighted	*718*	*698[1]*	*273*	*223*	*186*	*174*	*56*	*84*	*203*	*216*
									Column percentages	
Non-manual representatives										
Any trained in last year	25	28	27	21	26	31	28	19	22	30
No information	5	6	3	8	8	3	3	11	7	5
Percentage trained – mean	27	18	18	13	18	17	28	16	32	19
Base: establishments with non-manual worker representatives present										
Unweighted	*1006*	*1161*	*354*	*327*	*137*	*157*	*101*	*161*	*414*	*516*
Weighted	*592*	*720*	*93*	*83*	*117*	*124*	*37*	*64*	*345*	*449*

[1] See Note H.

showed the same downward trend. As Table 3.15 shows, the fall was experienced in the public sector generally and in private manufacturing, but not in the private services sector. The pattern of variation apparent in 1980 was maintained: larger establishments were likely to have had a higher proportion of their trade union representatives trained.

Relying on worker representatives' accounts, which in 1980 had been very much in accord with those of managers, it appeared that the great majority of training was conducted by the Trades Union Congress or by trade union colleges. Again, a substantial minority were at educational establishments with the agreement of unions and management. A clear majority of training was initiated by the trade unions. Most of it occurred during normal working hours and thus presumably with management's consent. However, according to worker representatives, management rarely decided the majority of the course content. Only eight per cent of manual worker representatives reported that this was the case for any of the courses that they or their colleagues had attended in the last year. The equivalent proportion of non-manual representatives was three per cent. It was largely in the nationalised industries where management influence was reported, a continuation of the situation in 1980.

Both managers and worker representatives evaluated the training of trade union representatives as generally helpful. Naturally, worker representatives were on the whole much more favourable in their evaluations than managers. But there was a noticeable decline in the proportion of management respondents who rated the training as *helping a great deal*. When we analysed this change by sector it was clear that most of the difference was in the public sector where managers were also inclined to rate relations between management and the relevant trade unions as unfavourable. Indeed, the correlation between managers' evaluations of non-manual representatives' training and their assessments of their relations with the non-manual unions was quite strong. In Chapter 10 we show how much more widespread industrial action was among non-manual workers in the public sector than elsewhere and clearly this experience was reflected in managers' assessments of their relations with the trade unions. Whether this clouded their assessments of the training of representatives or whether they genuinely felt that the training had been unsuccessful because there had also been conflict we cannot say. Worker representatives' evaluations of training were not dependent on the recent experience or absence of industrial action, which perhaps suggests that managers did expect benefits in this respect.

Check-off

One of the more important facilities that managements may provide to trade unions is *check-off*, the deduction of union subscriptions from members' pay. In our 1980 survey we asked about check-off as part of the section of questioning about the closed shop, since it had been assumed by researchers up to that time that there was a very strong correlation between the two practices. Our analysis of the 1980 results showed that any link between check-off and the closed shop was largely tenuous[26] and, indeed, that check-off was much more widespread than the closed shop. As a consequence, we removed our question about the existence of check-off arrangements from the section about closed shops and asked it of managers where there were any trade union members present. In 1980 managers were only asked about check-off if they reported recognised trade unions.

Extending the scope of our questions to include workplaces with union members but without unions recognised for collective bargaining purposes provided our first finding of substantive interest about check-off arrangements. In 1984 30 per cent of those with manual members (but without recognised unions) had check-off arrangements. For non-manuals the equivalent figure was 22 per cent. We might be justified, then, in extending our conclusion from the 1980 survey to inferring that there is no necessary connection between the existence of the check-off and trade union **recognition**. But, of course, establishments with recognised unions are much more likely to have check-off. In 1984, 80 per cent of workplaces with recognised manual unions did so and 82 per cent of workplaces with non-manual unions did. Both these figures were slight increases on the equivalent proportions in 1980 (75 per cent and 79 per cent respectively). When we analysed the two sets of results by size, ownership and industrial sector it became clear that the growth in the extent of check-off (in workplaces with recognised unions) was among types of establishment where it had been relatively uncommon in 1980. For example, check-off was almost universal in the public sector in 1980 and remained so in 1984. But in the private sector there was an increase for manual union members from 66 per cent of establishments with recognised unions to 75 per cent. Small independent establishments with recognised manual unions, although in the minority, showed an increase from 47 per cent to 58 per cent. The engineering industries appeared to be a particularly active sector in extending check-off for manual union members.

In both surveys our question was simply whether there was a system for deducting trade union dues from pay; we did not ask whether it applied to all unions if there were several represented, nor did we ask if the practice was applied to all members at the establishment rather than those who opted for the arrangement. However, if we assume that both of these questions would have been answered positively in all cases, then we can estimate how many employees in the whole population of workplaces covered by our 1984 survey would have had trade union subscriptions deducted from their pay at source by their employer. The aggregate figure is 40 per cent or approximately six million employees. This represents an upper bound of the estimated coverage of check-off arrangements.

Notes and references

1. Witherspoon S (1986) *The 1984 Social Attitudes Survey: A Report for the Department of Employment*, unpublished. The estimate from the Social Attitudes Survey for trade union density in workplaces with 25 or more employees is 57 per cent. This compares very closely with our overall estimate of 58 per cent.

2. Cases with no trade union members are included in both the numerator and the denominator.

3. Elsheikh F and Bain G S (1980) 'Unionisation in Britain: an inter-establishment analysis based on survey data', *British Journal of Industrial Relations*, July, pp.169-178.

4. Blanchflower D and Cubbin J (1986) 'Strike propensities at the British Workplace', *Oxford Bulletin of Economics and Statistics*, February, pp.19-39.

5. Daniel W W and Millward N (1983) *Workplace Industrial Relations in Britain: The DE/PSI/SSRC Survey*, Heinemann Educational Books, London, pp.57-58.

6. The larger establishments in our sample clearly could not belong to the smaller organisations, even if they were single, independent establishments.

7. The rationale for this is set out clearly in a recent review of American literature on the subject in Moore T S (1986) 'Are women workers hard to organize?', *Work and Occupations*, February, pp.97-111. Moore goes on to contradict, on the basis of Amercican survey evidence, the conventional wisdom that women have a lower propensity to join trade unions than men.

8. Union membership estimates for male and female full-time workers were collected separately from worker representatives, but have so far not been analysed. For the purposes of calculating membership densities they would have to be related to the numbers of such workers at the establishment as reported by management respondents, and may therefore contain inconsistencies.

9. Witherspoon S (1986) *op. cit.* The actual proportions are 52 per cent for full-time men and 50 per cent for full-time women; the difference is within the limits of sampling error.

10. In our analysis of the 1980 survey we focused upon union density among manual workers and non-manual workers separately and we reported that density in the private sector was strongly related to the proportion of women employed. See Daniel W W and Millward N (1983) *op. cit.* p.58. No analysis with respect to part-time working was reported. However, our measure of union density in the 1980 survey was unsatisfactory to the extent that we only collected union membership numbers for full-time employees. A similar defect in respect of manual workers pervades work based on the Warwick manufacturing survey of 1977/8. See Elsheikh F and Bain G S (1980) *op. cit.* They reported that the proportion of females is a significant determinant of the inter-establishment pattern of unionisation for all workers, but that the proportion of part-time employees was not.

11. These terms are explained in Chapter 8 where the extent of these different types of 'marginal' worker is examined. Nearly half of our private sector sample in 1984 used one or more of the four categories.

12. Daniel W W and Millward N (1983) *op. cit.* p.28.

13. Blanchflower D and Cubbin J (1986) *op. cit.*, p.33.

14. Brown W (ed.) (1981) *The Changing Contours of British Industrial Relations*, Blackwell, Oxford, p.5.

15. This is in sharp contrast to the results of the Warwick survey. See Brown W (ed.) (1981) *op. cit.* p.5. He implied that in 95 per cent of cases with recognised trade unions for non-manual employees at least half of the non-manual workforce was covered by pay bargaining. This compares with our figure of 75 per cent in Table 3.10. It seems unlikely that the difference is explicable in terms of change between 1978 and 1984 or in terms of the exclusion of smaller manufacturing units from the Warwick sample. We are inclined to believe that the figure reported by Brown is exaggerated and may have arisen from ambiguities in the questionnaire about the inclusion of managerial employees in questions about non-manuals.

16. This adds weight to our inference that it is largely senior managerial employees that are excluded – and this is reinforced by the fact that head offices in the private sector (where senior management are very largely concentrated) had much lower coverage.

17. Comparisons between the coverage data presented here and those derived from the *New Earnings Survey* should only be made with caution. In 1985 the *New Earnings Survey* asked for the type of negotiated collective agreement, if any, which affects the pay (and) conditions of employment of this employee, *either directly or indirectly* (our italics). Presumably the inclusion of employees whose pay was *indirectly* affected by collective bargaining increased substantially the resulting estimates of coverage. The 1985 *New Earnings Survey* report indicates that 64 per cent of full-time employees in all industries and services were covered, directly or indirectly, by collective bargaining. See Department of Employment (1985) *New Earnings Survey, Part F*, HMSO, London. There are no available figures for part-time employees, where the NES sample is less complete, and the survey contains no information on size of workplace that would allow us to make comparisons with the WIRS sample. The fact that the NES figure is lower than our figure from WIRS is an indication of the effect of including small establishments in the NES and excluding them from WIRS.

18. Daniel W W and Millward N (1983) *op. cit.* p.147.

19. Table 3.11 shows a decline from 90 per cent to 84 per cent in the largest size band, but this is entirely due to a much larger non-response to this question in 1984 than in 1980. In fact, it is largely an artifact of simplifying our coding in 1984. The 1980 question had separate non-response categories for *don't know whether any representatives present* and for *don't know how many representatives present*. There was a similar distinction for either of the two aspects of the question being *not answered*. We collapsed these four codes into two in 1984. The 1984 survey had substantial numbers of *don't know* and *not answered* responses in the 500 or more non-manual workers size band which are almost certainly cases where representatives were present but the number was not known to our respondent. In retrospect the alteration to the 1980 coding scheme was a mistake.

20. Daniel W W and Millward N (1983) *op. cit.* p.35.

21. This interpretation is supported by evidence from the 1984 *Social Attitudes Survey*. Respondents in that survey who were employed at the time of interview were asked if they had ever served as a trade union lay representative. Of those who were, or had ever been, union members a much lower proportion of part-time workers reported ever having been a union representative than full-time employees. The difference between

men and women was smaller. See Witherspoon S (1986) *op. cit.* The difference between full-time and part-time women employees is also substantiated by survey evidence from 1980. See Martin J and Roberts C (1984) *Women and Employment: A Lifetime Perspective*, HMSO, London, pp.54-58.

22. Batstone E (1984) *Working Order: Workplace Industrial Relations over Two Decades*, Blackwell, Oxford, p. 214.

23. See our earlier remarks in this chapter about the reliability of answers on trade union recognition in the public sector in 1980. Our estimates assume, of course, that establishments where managers did not report recognition did not have stewards or other union representatives because the questions were confined to stewards in workplaces with recognition.

24. There are, of course, small numbers of cases where we do not have figures for the number of union members or the numbers of representatives. Such cases have been excluded from our analysis and from Table 3.14.

25. This is because trade union and staff association membership was collected separately in 1980 and there was some evidence of double membership.

26. Daniel W W and Millward N (1983) *op. cit.* p.75-6.

4   The Closed Shop

The closed shop was one of the areas of institutional industrial relations in which our report of the results of the 1980 survey added substantially to existing information. The factual vacuum about the extent and nature of the closed shop had already been partly filled by the publication of data on the industrial distribution of the closed shop in 1978 and on the content of closed-shop agreements.[1] Our results confirmed that there had been substantial growth in the closed shop during the period since McCarthy's study[2] in the early 1960s and that the closed shop had spread to areas of non-manual employment from its traditional stronghold in industries dominated by manual employment.[3] But we were also able to show, in a way in which the methods adopted by Gennard and his colleagues could not, that the size of establishments, the size of the organisations to which establishments belonged and ownership were important sources of variation in the distribution of the practice. And we showed that the sources of variation in the distribution of the closed shop were very similar to those for trade union density and recognition – suggesting that the closed shop was the extreme end of a continuum of union membership coverage, rather than a distinct institutional form with different factors encouraging or diminishing its development.

Since our first report, the comprehensive account of Gennard's study has been published.[4] It not only maps the extent and nature of the closed shop throughout its period of growth up to the late 1970s, but includes projections of its coverage in 1982, based upon a number of assumptions about the changing structure of employment and about likely changes in the character of the closed shop itself. The picture it paints of an institution in numerical decline since the late 1970s is very much in accord with our own results, which update the record to mid-1984. But the numerical coverage of the closed shop is not the only point of interest. The legislative changes made in 1980 and 1982 concerning closed-shop arrangements could also be expected to have affected the nature of the institution. We present the evidence from our two surveys on that question after we have summarised the numerical changes.

The extent of the closed shop

A small complication arises before we can answer the apparently simple question of whether or not the coverage of the closed shop changed between mid-1980 and mid-1984. In our 1980 interviews we asked respondents, where they had already stated that trade unions were recognised at their workplace, 'Do the manual workers at this establishment normally have to be members of a union in order to have or to keep their jobs?' A similar question was asked of non-manual workers. It would have been straightforward to have repeated those questions verbatim. However, a number of respondents in our pilot interviews for the 1984 survey, conducted in late 1983, bridled at the clear-cut *yes* or *no* reply expected by such a question format and insisted that their situation of something less than compulsory trade union membership should be allowed for in our question. This we did. Instead of the earlier question, read out to respondents, interviewers showed management respondents an appropriate card containing the following five alternative arrangements for trade union membership among the manual (and non-manual) workforce:

> *All* manual workers have to be members of unions in order to get or keep their jobs.
>
> *Some* groups of manual workers have to be members of unions in order to get or keep their jobs.
>
> Management strongly recommends that *all* manual workers are members of unions.
>
> Management strongly recommends, for *some* groups of manual workers, that they are members of unions.
>
> No manual workers have to be members of unions nor is it strongly recommended that they are members.

The first two of these categories correspond precisely to the *comprehensive* and *partial* closed shop as identified by the relevant question in our 1980 schedules. The third and fourth categories we refer to here as *employer-endorsed unionism*. Table 4.1 shows how managers in the four broad sectors of the economy reported their union membership arrangements under these five categories.

As can be seen from Table 4.1, what we have called employer-endorsed unionism was reported almost as frequently as the closed shop for manual workers and in the public services sector considerably more commonly. For white-collar workers it was slightly more common than the closed shop overall, but much more common in the public services sector. Management encouragement of trade union membership has been a long-standing and well-known policy in many parts of public administration and these results testify to that.

Table 4.1 Union membership arrangements for manual and non-manual workers, 1984

	All establishments	Private manufacturing	Private services	Nationalised industries	Public services
Manual workers					
All have to be members	17	16[1]	10	68	15
Some groups have to be members	3	2	3	13	2
Management strongly recommends all are members	15	11	6	14	30
Management strongly recommends some groups are members	1	2	*	1	1
None of the above arrangements[2]	64	69	80	4	51
Not answered	*	—	*	—	1
Base: establishments with manual workers					
Unweighted	1853	580	515	191	567
Weighted	1749	412	689	103	545

Non-manual workers

All have to be members	6	1	5	28	6
Some groups have to be members	3	2	1	37	2
Management strongly recommends all are members	16	5	7	22	35
Management strongly recommends some groups are members	1	1	*	1	2
None of the above arrangements	74	91	87	19	54
Not answered	*	*	*	1	1
Base: establishments with non-manual workers					
Unweighted	*2010*	*592*	*593*	*194*	*631*
Weighted	*1985³*	*424*	*836*	*105*	*621*

[1] See Note C.
[2] Includes establishments where there were no recognised trade unions and the question was therefore not asked.
[3] See Note H.

Table 4.2 Manual union membership arrangements in 1980 and in 1984 from the panel data

Absolute numbers (weighted)

			1984		
	Comprehensive closed shop	Partial closed shop	Comprehensive employer-endorsed unionism	Partial employer-endorsed unionism	No arrangement
1980					
Comprehensive closed shop	33	—	3	*	2
Partial closed shop	*	*	1	—	—
No closed shop	*	2	18	—	18

Base: establishments with recognised unions in both 1980 and 1984 and no query about the definition of the establishment
Unweighted base: 147
Weighted base: 77

The question now arises as to whether the change in our question format, particularly the introduction of the two new categories of union membership arrangement, prevents us from measuring changes in the extent of the closed shop between our two survey periods. It could be that some managers whose situation was one of employer-endorsed unionism in 1980 might have reported a closed shop when union membership was strongly encouraged but not compulsory in a minimal sense. In this case, our measurement of the extent of the closed shop in 1980 would be an exaggeration. This appears unlikely. When we compare our estimates of the numbers of employees in the closed shop in 1980 they fall between the 1978 and 1982 estimates of Gennard and his colleagues, as we shall show later. Alternatively, the change in question wording between the two surveys could lead to an understatement of the extent of the closed shop in 1984 by drawing responses from the closed-shop category into the category *management strongly recommends all workers are members of unions*. It seems unlikely that this has happened to any major extent. To begin with, we feel the difference in wording between the two main categories of union membership arrangement is such as to clearly connote a degree of compulsion in one case and exhortation in the other. Secondly, if we counted the cases of employer-endorsed unionism as really closed shop cases – even the minority of them where all manual employees **were** union members – we would be producing estimates of the numbers of employees in the closed shop which simply did not line up with estimates of its coverage from other sources. Thirdly, our panel data indicate very little change in the existence of the manual closed shop amongst establishments existing in both 1980 and 1984. Table 4.2 shows how workplaces in our panel sample where managers reported recognised manual trade unions in both surveys responded to our two closed-shop questions.

Of the 77 weighted cases (147 unweighted), 33 reported a comprehensive manual closed shop in both surveys, 18 reported no arrangement of any type in both surveys and a further 18 reported no closed shop in 1980 and employer-endorsed unionism in 1984. Only four cases reported a change from closed shop to 'open shop' or vice versa, two in each direction. The remaining four reported a closed shop in 1980 and employer-endorsed unionism in 1984. The smallness of this last category – roughly five per cent of the cases with recognised manual unions or about two per cent of the panel sample with manual workers – suggests that any effect of the change in question wording is limited. But of course these changes in response could be quite properly reflecting a reduction in the degree of compulsion to join trade unions at these workplaces. Since the great majority of closed shops are of the post-entry type, and their

Percentages

Table 4.3 The extent of the closed shop

	All establishments 1980	All establishments 1984	Private manufacturing 1980	Private manufacturing 1984	Private services 1980	Private services 1984	Nationalised industries 1980	Nationalised industries 1984	Public services 1980	Public services 1984
Manual workers										
Any manual workers in closed shop	23	20	30	19	15	13	86	81	21	17
All manual workers in closed shop	21	17	25	16	14	10	78	68	19	15
Any in pre-entry closed shop	5	5	10	10	1	3	11	6	3	4
Proportion of manual workers in closed shop (per cent)	40	30	48	33	26	20	73	76	27	16
Base: establishments with manual workers										
Unweighted	*1899*	*1853*	*734*	*580*	*521*	*515*	*130*	*191*	*514*	*567*
Weighted	*1823*	*1749*	*498*	*412*	*755*	*689*	*66*	*103*	*504*	*545*
Non-manual workers										
Any non-manual workers in closed shop	9	9	5	3	7	6	61	66	10	8
All non-manual workers in closed shop	7	6	2	1	6	5	45	28	7	6
Any in pre-entry closed shop	1	1	1	1	1	1	9	5	*	2
Proportion of non-manual workers in closed shop (per cent)	9	8	9	5	7	6	49	51	5	5
Base: establishments with non-manual workers										
Unweighted	*2034*	*2010*	*743*	*592*	*585*	*593*	*133*	*194*	*573*	*631*
Weighted	*1987*	*1985¹*	*503*	*424*	*854*	*836*	*68*	*105*	*562*	*621*
All employees										
Any employees in closed shop	23	18	30	18	16	12	88	81	20	16
Base: all establishments										
Unweighted	*2040*	*2019*	*743*	*592*	*587*	*597*	*134*	*196*	*576*	*634*
Weighted	*2000*	*2000*	*503*	*424*	*859*	*843*	*69*	*106*	*569*	*627*

¹ See Note C.

enforcement may be rarely raised as a formal issue,[5] it seems realistic to take these cases at face value – as ones where the degree of compulsion over trade union membership had indeed weakened. For all these reasons our estimates of the coverage in the closed shop are made on the assumption that the cases reported as employer-endorsed unionism do not include cases that would have been reported as closed shops if we had used the same question wording in 1984 as in 1980. That assumption is carried through the rest of our analysis in this chapter, starting with Table 4.3 showing the changes in the extent of the closed shop between our two surveys in the four main sectors of the economy.

Taking manual and non-manual employees together, the overall proportion of workplaces where any workers were covered by a closed-shop arrangement, as reported by our managment respondents, dropped from 23 per cent to 18 per cent between 1980 and 1984. Non-manual 'closed-shop establishments' remained as uncommon as they were before, being nine per cent of the total. It was **manual** closed-shop establishments that became rarer, dropping from 23 per cent of establishments with manual workers in 1980 to 20 per cent in 1984. This change in itself is insufficient to account for the decline of five percentage points for all establishments: a further part must be because establishments with manual workers formed a smaller portion of our sample in 1984 than in 1980. This is consistent with our analysis in Chapter 1 of the changes in employment structure over the period and is illustrated in Table 4.3 by the drop in the weighted base for establishments with manual workers from 1823 to 1749 cases (91 per cent to 87 per cent of the sample).

By far the most marked change in the extent of the closed shop was its very substantial drop in private manufacturing industry. Thirty per cent of private manufacturing establishments with manual workers had a manual closed shop in 1980; 19 per cent had one in 1984. All of the main sectors of manufacturing appeared to be affected, with the notable exception of engineering and vehicle manufacture which, as we showed in Chapter 3, had particularly high union density. The decline was largely confined to comprehensive closed shops. But there was no fall in the proportion with a pre-entry closed shop, the figure remaining constant at ten per cent of establishments. It was post-entry closed shops, the 'less robust' form of the institution,[6] that became less numerous.

The most likely factor associated with the decline in the manual closed shop in private manufacturing is the changing structure of manufacturing employment. Large manufacturing plants suffered a disproportionate rate of closure and these were the sort of plants where the closed shop was most prevalent in 1980. Our panel data, limited in extent though they are, also suggest that if there was any weakening of the closed shop (as manifested in a shift from a closed shop in 1980 to employer-endorsed unionism in 1984) it was in the private manufacturing sector that it occurred.

The other main sectors of the economy – private services and the public sector – exhibited much less change in the extent of the closed shop. Although most of the figures in Table 4.3 show falls from 1980 to 1984, only the figure for manual closed shops in the public sector approaches statistical significance. Nationalised industries, the sector with the highest concentration of closed-shop establishments, showed little change, although the big drop in **comprehensive** non-manual closed shops, coupled with the slight rise in **any** non-manual closed shop, suggests a switch from comprehensive to partial coverage in that sector.

In our report on the 1980 survey we spent some considerable time charting the patterns of variation in the extent of the closed shop, using various characteristics of establishments and the organisations to which they belonged as explanatory variables. By and large these patterns persisted in the 1984 results. It was still the case in 1984 that establishments were more likely to have a manual closed shop if they were large and in the private sector, if they were in nationalised industries (irrespective of their size), if they were part of a larger enterprise (rather than single independent establishments) and if the establishment's workforce was predominantly manual and predominantly male. There did, however, appear to be changes in the strength of some of these correlations as well as some new patterns. First, the contrast between single, independent establishments and those that were part of a group appeared to have widened. Secondly, whereas in 1980 foreign-owned workplaces were marginally less likely than their British-owned, private sector counterparts to have a manual closed shop, in 1984 they were more likely to have manual closed shops, the proportions being 23 per cent for foreign-owned and 15 per cent for British-owned establishments in 1984. This, of course, could be a size-related phenomenon, but we have not investigated this further. Thirdly, the very largest establishments (those with 1000 or more **manual** employees) did appear to have experienced a greater decline in the presence of closed shops than any other size category: this is of relevance to our later discussion of the number of **employees** in closed-shop situations. Fourthly, whereas in 1980 establishments with a substantial concentration of ethnic minority workers were as likely as other establishments to have a manual closed shop, in 1984 they were considerably less likely to do so. Only seven per cent of workplaces with a tenth or more of their workforce in ethnic minority groups had a manual closed shop, compared to 20 per cent of other workplaces. The equivalent figures for non-manual closed shops in 1984 were three per cent and nine per cent. This emergence of a relationship between ethnic minority concentration and a lower incidence of closed shops, particularly manual ones, mirrors a similar emerging pattern in relation to trade union recognition, as we discussed in Chapter 3.

Numbers of employees in closed shops

So far our analysis has focused upon *establishments*, with the proportion of establishments having closed-shop arrangements of various sorts being our principal measure of interest. We now turn to a different measure of the extent of the closed shop – the proportion of *employees* covered by the arrangement. As we have already seen, most manual closed shops, the predominant type, are comprehensive ones, that is they cover all the manual workers at the workplace in question. In consequence, the *employee-coverage* of the closed shop follows the pattern of *establishment-coverage*, although this is modified to the extent that in the private sector larger establishments are much more likely to have closed shops. The results for employee coverage are also shown in Table 4.3. The overall figure for employees covered by closed-shop arrangements in 1984 is 30 per cent for manuals and eight per cent for non-manuals. Taking them together, this represents 20 per cent of all employees. The manual figure represents a substantial decline from 40 per cent to 30 per cent between 1980 and 1984; the non-manual figure is virtually unchanged.

In terms of sectors, there were no changes in the employee-coverage figures in private services or in the nationalised industries, but a fall from 27 per cent to 16 per cent of manual workers in the public services sector and a substantial fall in private manufacturing from 48 to 33 per cent of manual employees. It was in manufacturing, too, that the only sizeable fall was recorded for non-manual employees, although this barely approached statistical significance. Within the public services sector the industries most clearly affected by the fall in closed-shop coverage were transport and communications. In the private sector, surprisingly, foreign-owned establishments did not experience the decline in closed-shop membership experienced elsewhere.

So far our explanation of the decline in closed-shop membership has depended largely upon structural factors. There is, however, an important potential source of explanation **internal** to the closed-shop arrangements themselves. Not all closed shops, even comprehensive ones, entail **every** person being a member of a union: there could be new recruits to a post-entry shop who have yet to join; and there may also be certain employees who are exempt from the arrangement, as we discuss later in this chapter. We should not expect establishments with, say, a comprehensive manual closed shop to have a manual union membership density of 100 per cent in all cases. So a possible source of decline in the coverage of the closed shop is a decline in membership density in closed shops, a change which would be most easily detectable in comprehensive closed shops. Unfortunately, as we explained in Chapter 3, our measures of union membership in the first survey were incomplete; we remedied this in the second survey, but it means that we cannot answer precisely the question about possibly declining density within closed shops. But we can show how extensive that possibility is by illustrating the most important case – comprehensive manual closed shops – in 1984. Average membership density in these cases was 99 per cent.[7] Only a few establishments had less than 100 per cent membership and most of these had between 90 and 99 per cent. Furthermore, it should be borne in mind that managers were asked about union membership numbers **before** they were asked about closed-shop arrangements, so 100 per cent membership could not have been suggested by their answer on the latter. And when we analysed the reports of worker representatives on these two same questions the pattern was virtually identical. We therefore feel quite confident that declining density within comprehensive closed shops can only be a numerically trivial explanation of the decline in closed-shop coverage. The average density of 99 per cent in 1984 could hardly have been much greater in 1980.

Our estimates of the employee coverage of the closed shop have so far been stated in proportionate terms, but they can be reformulated as absolute, grossed-up numbers of employees. We have done this by combining our estimates for manual and non-manual employees and by making allowances for establishments not covered by the Workplace Industrial Relations Survey series. These results provide estimates for the whole of Great Britain and are thus directly comparable with those of Gennard and his colleagues for mid-1978 and mid-1982. The first of the two allowances that we made was to add ten per cent of the population of employees in the smallest establishments (24 employees or less) not covered by our surveys; in 1980 coverage in our establishments of 25 to 49 employees was 14 per cent and the correlation with workforce size was very strong, so the ten per cent allowance probably errs on the high side. Secondly, we added in all employees in the coal-mining industry as given by the published figures for employees in employment.[8] Naturally, this implies an assumption that the coverage of the closed shop in the coal-mining industry is complete, but that is unlikely to be far from the truth.[9] Because of sampling error and the possibly high allowance for coverage in small establishments we prefer to give the estimates as a range. We estimate the coverage of the closed shop as lying between 3.5 and 3.7 million employees in mid-1984, compared to a similarly derived estimate from our first survey of 4.7 to 4.9 million. These figures compare with Dunn and Gennard's estimates of *at least* 5.2 million in mid-1978 and 4.5 million in mid-1982.[10] The steady decline in closed-shop membership since the late 1970s seems in little doubt.

One final piece of analysis adds further weight to this conclusion before we move on to discuss the changing character of the closed shop. This uses our retrospective measures of employment size in the 1984 survey, as we did in Chapter 1 in discussing the general pattern of employment change and in Chapter 3 in analysing the changing pattern of union membership. As previously we used the employment data for the same establishment for 1980 and for 1984 to classify them into those that increased in size during the four years, those that were stable and those that shrunk. Workplaces whose labour force had shrunk by at least 20 per cent were more than **three times** as likely to have a manual closed shop as workplaces that had grown by a similar margin.

The characteristics of manual closed shops
We have so far talked of the closed shop in fairly general terms, only distinguishing being *comprehensive* and *partial*, *pre-entry* and *post-entry* closed shops and between manual and non-manual employees. A number of other characteristics of closed shops were covered in our questioning in the two surveys, some only in one survey or the other. In 1980 we asked how long new recruits to the establishment were given to join an appropriate trade union where a post-entry closed shop was in operation. In broad terms about two thirds of managers reported that new recruits were allowed about a month.[11] (Manual worker representatives tended to give a somewhat shorter period than managers.) We did not expect this picture to have changed a great deal in the period between the two surveys and the question was dropped to make way for other material. We also dropped questions on issues arising from closed-shop arrangements, these having been reported very infrequently by both managers and worker representatives in 1980, and on procedures for considering disputes about individual union membership in closed shops. Instead we asked new questions about the date of any revisions to closed-shop agreements and the date of introduction of unrevised agreements. These questions were inserted to provide information to help assess any changes that had occurred since our first survey and to provide a benchmark for the measurement of future change. The questions which we maintained in the 1984 survey from the 1980 questionnaire concerned the existence of written closed-shop agreements and of exemptions within those

agreements for particular categories of workers. It is these latter characteristics of closed shops we now turn to.[12]

Written agreements and exemptions

In 1980 we began our questioning on the details of closed-shop arrangements by asking how many arrangements were in operation for manual (or non-manual) workers at the workplace. The proportion with a single arrangement was nearly 90 per cent and so in 1984 we simplified our questionnaire by omitting this question and asking directly for details of the arrangement covering the largest group of manual (or non-manual) employees, as we had also done in 1980. First we asked whether the arrangement was supported by an agreement between the unions and management and whether this was a written or merely oral agreement. Agreements, either written or oral, were reported in 95 per cent of cases in 1984 – no change since 1980. There was, however, a change in the number reporting **written** agreements, the proportion increasing from 82 per cent to 89 per cent of manual closed-shop cases. It was largely in the private sector, where unwritten agreements had been most common in 1980, that this increase in formality occurred. As before, sectors with higher concentrations of the closed shop were more likely to have written agreements covering those arrangements.

Respondents reporting either a written or an oral agreement covering their closed shop were asked if the arrangement contained any exemptions and, if so, what those exemptions were. The responses on certain exemptions – essentially those that were contained in past or current legislation – were checked in the 1984 survey by asking for the exact wording used in the agreement so that we could be quite sure of the correct coding of the exemption. We checked the transcripts of these answers at the coding stage and found most of them to be verbatim quotations from the relevant legislation. Naturally, orally-agreed closed-shop arrangements were much less likely to have clear exemptions, but as they were in any event a very small proportion of closed shops,[13] we have not extracted them for separate analysis. Table 4.4 shows the overall comparisons between 1980 and 1984.

The pattern of specified exemptions in manual closed-shop agreements appears to have changed somewhat, but not greatly, between our two surveys. The four exemptions at the top of Table 4.4 which enshrine moral or ethical grounds for exemption remained, as a group, the most common type. The drop in the number of agreements mentioning *religious belief* and the increase in the number mentioning *conscience, deeply-held personal conviction* or *not member of a trade union before the agreement was made* is clearly a reflection of the change in

Table 4.4   Exemptions to manual closed-shop agreements

Percentages

	1980	1984
Any exemptions	57	50
Type of exemption:		
Religious belief	36[1]	20
Reasonable grounds	3	2
Conscience	11	18
Deeply-held personal conviction	..	6
Not union member before agreement made	13	17
Already member of another union	2	1
Part-time/temporary	7	7
Key or specialist post	1	3
Long service	1	2
Apprentice	4	—
Base: establishments with an agreed manual closed shop		
Unweighted	*560*	*485*
Weighted	*366*	*326*

[1] See Note F.

legislation. The *religious belief* category was contained in the unfair dismissal provisions of the Trade Union and Labour Relations Act 1974 and its amendment in 1976, subsequently repealed in 1980. The other three categories mentioned above were encompassed by the Employment Act 1980, which became law after our first survey was completed and protects employees in those categories against unfair dismissal from a closed shop. The remaining categories in Table 4.4 are ones that are not derived from the legislation in force when the agreements were made and reflect local preferences for excluding various types of employee from the arrangement. These appear to have changed little between 1980 and 1984, although the fact that no agreements in 1984 exempted *apprentices* might be a significant change from before. Taking all exemptions **except** those that only had legal status prior to the 1980 Employment Act (religious belief and reasonable grounds), the proportion of manual closed shops that contained written, agreed exemptions was 42 per cent.

Revisions to closed-shop agreements

We asked three new questions in the 1984 survey where closed shops were reported as being the subject of a written agreement between management and trade unions. First we asked if the agreement had been revised at all. If it had, we asked the year in which the most

Table 4.5 Year in which most recent version of manual closed-shop agreement was made, 1984

Column percentages

	All establishments	Private manufacturing	Private services	Public sector
Year of agreement or most recent revision				
Before 1970	10	6[1]	11	10
1970 to 1974	8	12	11	4
1975 to 1977	28	26	14	37
1978 to 1980	23	24	21	24
1981 to 1983	19	21	29	14
1984 (early)	7	2	16	3
Under revision in 1984	5	10	3	5
Base: establishments with an agreed manual closed shop and where the date of the most recent version was known				
Unweighted	391	148	65	178
Weighted	239[2]	50	73	115

[1] See Note C.
[2] See Note H.

recent revision was made. If it had not been revised we asked when the agreement had come into effect. Only a minority (37 per cent) of written, manual closed-shop agreements reported in mid-1984 had ever been revised. Of the 63 per cent which had **not** been revised, roughly one in every six pre-dated 1970 and the majority dated from the period 1975 to 1979. Table 4.5 shows the year in which the most recent version of written, manual closed-shop agreements was made by combining the dates of revised and unrevised agreements. The figures exclude a substantial number of cases (22 per cent) where the respondent was unable to put a date on the most recent form of the agreement. Most of these were unrevised agreements, largely in the public sector, so it is likely that they were older than average. The figures in Table 4.5 may, therefore, rather overstate the degree to which formal closed-shop arrangements in operation in 1984 originated from, or had been revised in, the early 1980s.

In rough terms, about a tenth of these agreements had been made before 1970, another tenth were made in the early 1970s, a quarter dated from the mid-1970s, another quarter from the late 1970s and the remaining third from 1981 to 1984, the period after the first change in closed-shop legislation by the Conservative government. Around two fifths dated from the period after the first code of practice came into effect in December 1980, recommending that closed-shop agreements should be periodically reviewed;[14] virtually all of these were revised agreements. The number of *new* manual closed shops dating from 1983 and 1984 was less than one per cent of all cases, adding a further explanatory element to our earlier results on the decline in the extent of the closed shop.

Table 4.5 gives some clear indications of which sectors of the economy were most likely to have revised their manual closed-shop agreements. Private services, where manual closed shops were least common, was the sector with more recent revisions, followed by manufacturing. The public sector, and particularly the nationalised industries, appeared to have the most extensive manual closed shops which at the time of our survey in mid-1984 still dated from the 1970s.

The comparative pattern for non-manual workers

As we showed earlier, the closed shop was a much less common feature of non-manual employment than it was for manuals. In 1984 nine per cent of establishments employing non-manual workers had a closed shop for any non-manual workers, the same proportion as in 1980. And in contrast to the pattern for manual workers, the proportion of non-manual workers in closed shops remained stable. There was also little change in the characteristics of these non-manual closed shops. The proportion of them that were the subject of written agreements remained about the same and so did the proportion of written agreements that specified exemptions. The latter was slightly higher than for manual closed-shop agreements at about 60 per cent. The changes in the pattern of exemptions was very similar to that for manual closed shops.

Some effects of the closed shop

The detailed analysis required to examine whether the closed shop as an institution, as opposed to just high trade union membership density, has widespread industrial relations and economic effects is beyond the scope of a report such as this. The Workplace Industrial Relations Survey datasets do, however, provide the best possible opportunity currently available for carrying out such an analysis in a rigorous statistical manner. With the panel sample in our current survey there is even the possibility of testing the direction of causality between, for example, the existence of the closed shop and the nature of workforce reductions.[15] But even with cross-sectional samples it is possible to examine whether there are significant associations between the existence of the closed shop and matters like the nature of recruitment and use of various methods of shedding labour. These are touched upon in Chapter 8, but a fuller analysis has yet to be attempted.

On one particular association, however, some substantial statistical work has already been carried out on the data from our 1980 survey. It used the rather minimal amount of data on pay levels for typical semi-skilled and skilled workers – data which were subjected to some fairly extensive analysis in our report on the 1980 survey. We noted that where there was a closed shop for some group of manual workers, then earnings for manual workers tended to be higher, independently of the general level of trade union membership.[16] In further multivariate analysis of these data on pay levels and various collective bargaining arrangements, including the closed shop, Stewart[17] has shown that establishments with a manual closed shop, and especially a pre-entry one, tend to pay their semi-skilled and skilled manual workers significantly above the level for non-unionised establishments. He points out, however, that there is considerable variation in the differential and that it is only a minority of establishments that pay significantly more than they would in the non-union sector. With the more detailed information on pay levels in our 1984 survey, further statistical analysis of these associations would seem worthwhile.

Notes and references
1. Gennard J, Dunn S and Wright M (1980) 'The extent of closed shop arrangements in British industry', *Employment Gazette*, January, pp.16-22; Gennard J, Dunn S and

Wright M (1979), 'The content of British closed shop agreements', *Employment Gazette*, November, pp.1088-92.

2. McCarthy W E J (1964) *The Closed Shop in Britain*, Blackwell, Oxford.

3. Daniel W W and Millward N (1983) *Workplace Industrial Relations in Britain: The DE/PSI/SSRC Survey*, Heinemann Educational Books, London, pp.60-4, 280-4.

4. Dunn S and Gennard J (1984) *The Closed Shop in British Industry*, Macmillan, London.

5. Ibid., p.112.

6. Ibid., pp.149-56.

7. For comparison, manual union density averaged 88 per cent in establishments with comprehensive *employer-endorsed unionism*.

8. Department of Employment (various dates) *Employment Gazette*.

9. Dunn and Gennard (1984) *op.cit.*, p.155. Coal mining is cited as an example of an industry most likely to secure a positive vote of more than 85 per cent in favour of continuance of an existing, traditional closed shop.

10. Ibid., p.147.

11. Daniel and Millward (1983) *op.cit.*, pp.73-4.

12. Managers who responded to our initial question about union membership arrangements by answering that they had what we have termed *employer-endorsed unionism* were also asked these follow-up questions. Such arrangements were very much less likely to be the subject of a written agreement and to have specified exemptions. No further analysis has yet been carried out on these cases.

13. In 1984, 11 per cent of orally-agreed manual closed shops were reported as having exemptions, but as this figure is on an unweighted base of 37 cases there is little or no scope for analysis in either the type of exemption or in the distribution of those exemptions.

14. Department of Employment (1980) *Code of Practice: Closed Shop Agreements and Arrangements*, pp.11-12. The recommendation for periodic review was also contained in the revised code issued in 1983.

15. In so far as the testing of causal models requires some degree of gross change, there is clearly very limited scope for such analysis with the small panel sample available; Table 4.2 shows how little gross change there was between 1980 and 1984.

16. Daniel and Millward (1983) *op.cit.*, p.274.

17. Stewart M 1987 forthcoming 'Collective bargaining arrangements, closed shops and relative pay', *Economic Journal*.

5 Trade Union Organisation

In Chapters 3 and 4 we examined several features of trade union organisation, concentrating largely upon features within the workplace. In this chapter we develop this further and move beyond the boundaries of the workplace to the wider system of trade union organisation. More specifically we explore changes in the nature of trade union branches, the methods of appointment of workplace representatives and their relationship with the outside union. We also describe the various committees and meetings by which representatives from the same and different unions relate to each other and the ways in which they changed between the two surveys. In general terms this section of questioning was much smaller in 1984 than in 1980 and although we make reference at various points to material covered in 1980 but not repeated in 1984, a fuller account is contained in our previous report.[1] Given the nature of the subject matter, we had decided in designing our 1980 survey that representatives of management would not be the most appropriate respondents for this material, a point alluded to by previous researchers in this area.[2] In 1984 we had no reason to change that decision. Consequently, the analysis which follows is based entirely on the responses of manual and non-manual representatives of recognised trade unions.

The size and composition of trade union branches
It should be emphasised that some of the results reported in this chapter relate to practices and institutions that extend **beyond** the level of our sampling unit, the workplace. For example, certain types of trade union branch, such as those that are designed to reflect the organisation of a single, large employer are clearly based upon an organisational level above the workplace. In presenting the results on such 'higher-level' phenomena we emphasise the problem of their being multiply reported in a survey of **workplaces** such as ours. Our results relate to the extent of **workplaces** where these higher-level phenomena were **reported** by representatives and **not** to the extent of the higher-level phenomena themselves. Clearly, representatives in several workplaces may be reporting the same union branch covering all or many workplaces of a single employer. In order to make

statements about the **extent** of such branches one would need a different sampling unit: union branches rather than workplaces.[3]

In the two surveys we used the term *branch* to refer to the local units **to which our worker representative respondents belonged**, although the unions themselves may have used a different term. It is likely that the larger unions were over-represented in the two survey samples, since our respondents were the senior lay representatives of the largest negotiating group at the sampled establishment. In the 1980 survey we also questioned senior representatives of the second largest negotiating group, but as this was not repeated in the 1984 survey these results are excluded from the analysis which follows.

In both 1980 and 1984 we asked about the size of trade union branches and the composition of their membership. In the 1980 survey we also asked a series of questions about branch meetings, such as their frequency, the general level of attendance and where they were held. We only make brief reference to these 1980 results[4] as comparable data were not collected in 1984.

We examined the composition of trade union branches in terms of three main types: *workplace-based branches*, where all branch members are employed at the same workplace; *single-employer branches*, where membership is drawn from more than one workplace of the same employer and *multi-employer branches*. Table 5.1 shows the overall results for **manual** unions and the results for the four unions most frequently mentioned by manual worker representatives. It is clear from the table that, despite a decline, multi-employer branches were still the most frequently reported type of manual branch in 1984, with two fifths of respondents reporting them (compared with over half in 1980). Single-employer branches were reported by a third of manual stewards, as against a quarter in 1980. Workplace-based branches occurred in one quarter of cases in 1984, compared with a fifth in 1980. Clearly, we can only be precise about the extent of **workplace-based** branches among our sample of workplaces, for the reasons discussed earlier.

These changes in the pattern of reporting were reflected in the responses of the representatives from each of the three unions based mainly in the private sector, for whom separate results are shown in the table. As in 1980, multi-employer branches were reported most frequently by representatives of the Amalgamated Union of Engineering Workers (AUEW[5]), but the proportion reporting them dropped by a third (from 96 to 68 per cent) between 1980 and 1984. By contrast, single-employer branches were reported very much more frequently in 1984 (22 per cent) than in 1980 (one per cent) and those based at the workplace were mentioned by ten per cent of stewards, more than twice as frequently as in 1980 (Table 5.1). Similarly,

Table 5.1 Size and composition of union branches (manual workers)

	All representatives 1980	All representatives 1984	TGWU 1980	TGWU 1984	GMBATU 1980	GMBATU 1984	AUEW 1980	AUEW 1984	NUPE 1980	NUPE 1984
										Numbers
Number of branch members										
Median[1]	426[2]	319	276	193	470	235	742	425	406	488
										Column percentages
1–49	11	18	11	28	3	13	*	17	10	3
50–99	5	9	10	10	3	18	3	2	4	6
100–199	9	8	9	6	11	11	1	10	12	7
200–299	7	7	7	4	10	10	8	1	4	11
300–399	4	5	4	3	5	6	1	11	6	7
400–499	3	4	2	3	7	2	2	3	7	10
500–999	12	12	16	8	9	9	22	21	7	20
1000–1999	10	9	8	12	18	6	9	3	11	9
2000–9997	8	15	5	12	8	16	6	16	11	14
Don't know/not answered	32	13	28	15	26	10	48	15	28	12
Branch composition										
Workplace-based	21	24	30	33	14	22	4	10	18	5
Single-employer	24	32	19	25	30	37	1	22	54	62
Multi-employer	54	42	51	40	57	42	96	68	29	33
Don't know/not answered	1	2	—	2	—	—	—	—	—	—
Base: manual worker representatives belonging to recognised trade unions										
Unweighted	970	910	235	189	121	126	132	121	124	140
Weighted	643[3]	554	160	129	74	69	68	47	91	93

[1] Median linearly interpolated from weighted absolute numbers, excluding don't knows.   [2] See Note C.   [3] See Note L.

representatives of both the Transport and General Workers Union (TGWU) and the General, Municipal, Boilermakers and Allied Trades Union (GMBATU) reported multi-employer branches in about two fifths of cases in 1984 compared with over a half in 1980. In 1984 single-employer branches were reported by a quarter of TGWU stewards (19 per cent in 1980) and by 37 per cent of GMBATU stewards (30 per cent in 1980). Workplace-based branches were still most common in the TGWU, reported in a third of cases in both 1980 and 1984, while the proportion of GMBATU stewards reporting them increased from 14 per cent to 22 per cent over the period. Clearly, as in 1980, representatives of the TGWU and the GMBATU were most likely to report a mixture of the three types of branches in 1984.

More generally, there was an increase of a third in the extent of workplace-based branches in both the private services sector (from 25 per cent to 33 per cent of cases) and in private manufacturing (from 21 per cent to 28 per cent). Within the nationalised industries the proportion almost doubled over the period (from 12 per cent to 21 per cent), while there was a decline within public services, from 18 per cent to 13 per cent of workplaces. In Chapter 3 we suggested that the decline in the number of manual stewards within public services may have arisen from a union policy of centralisation. Clearly, the decline in workplace-based branches within that sector adds further weight to this hypothesis. Indeed, the decline was particularly marked within the National Union of Public Employees (NUPE) where workplace-based branches were reported in just five per cent of cases in 1984 compared with 18 per cent in 1980. As in 1980, however, we found that single-employer branches were most frequently reported by representatives of NUPE, obviously reflecting the public sector concentration of the union. In fact there was an increase in reporting of single-employer branches from 54 per cent of cases in 1980 to 62 per cent in 1984. Multi-employer branches of NUPE were reported in about a third of cases in both surveys.

As in 1980, representatives of non-manual unions were much more likely to report single-employer branches than were manual representatives, obviously reflecting the public sector concentration of white-collar employees. In fact, as Table 5.2 shows, in overall terms the proportion of non-manual representatives reporting these branches increased substantially over the four-year period, from a half in 1980 to almost two thirds in 1984. The increase was particularly marked within the National and Local Government Officers Association (NALGO). Although the unweighted base is too small to draw firm conclusions, in 1984 single-employer branches were reported by the great majority of representatives of both the Civil and Public Services Association (CPSA) (two thirds in 1980) and the National

Table 5.2 Size and composition of union branches (non-manual workers)

Figures for NALGO, ASTMS, AUEW-TASS, NUT and CPSA fall under the heading "Union to which representatives belonged". The Median row values are Numbers; all other size/composition rows are Column percentages.

	All representatives		NALGO		ASTMS		AUEW-TASS		NUT		CPSA	
	1980	1984	1980	1984	1980	1984	1980	1984	1980	1984	1980	1984
Number of branch members												
Median[1]	288	328	522	634	676	332	716	399	486	519	242	228
1–49	15[2]	9	12	3	*	8	7	6	(4)[3]	(3)	(10)	(17)
50–99	5	9	2	6	2	3	*	5	(—)	(—)	(7)	(11)
100–199	9	12	7	7	2	4	9	6	(6)	(6)	(7)	(10)
200–299	6	12	8	11	7	22	*	6	(1)	(13)	(24)	(41)
300–399	5	7	6	8	1	10	2	5	(10)	(5)	(7)	(6)
400–499	5	6	8	10	3	8	1	—	(11)	(12)	(5)	(7)
500–599	9	15	11	14	27	20	31	21	(12)	(30)	(3)	(4)
1000–1999	7	6	10	5	4	9	14	4	(15)	(4)	(3)	(*)
2000–9997	7	13	22	32	2	1	—	3	(3)	(9)	(3)	(*)
Don't know/not answered	33	12	14	6	52	15	35	45	(39)	(17)	(33)	(4)
Branch composition												
Workplace-based	18	15	12	8	5	9	11	29	(4)	(3)	(12)	(5)
Single-employer	49	64	67	78	23	27	9	3	(88)	(87)	(69)	(94)
Multi-employer	26	19	16	11	68	65	81	68	(7)	(11)	(1)	(1)
Don't know/not answered	8	2	5	4	5	—	—	—	(—)	(—)	(18)	(—)
Base: non-manual worker representatives belonging to recognised trade unions												
Unweighted	921	949	164	167	128	114	53	62	42	41	32	34
Weighted	585[4]	560	104	93	40	26	21	17	83	83	28	32

[1] Median linearly interpolated from weighted absolute numbers, excluding don't knows.
[2] See Note C.
[3] See Note B.
[4] See Note L.

Union of Teachers (NUT). However, representatives within both the Association of Scientific, Technical and Managerial Staffs (ASTMS) and the Technical, Administrative and Supervisory Section (TASS) of the AUEW were still most likely to report multi-employer branches in 1984. In both of these unions two thirds of representatives gave this answer. This indicates a decline since 1980 among TASS representatives when they were reported in 81 per cent of cases, as the proportion reporting workplace-based branches increased substantially over the period, from 11 per cent to 29 per cent. Indeed, of these five white-collar unions in 1984, TASS representatives were the most likely to report workplace-based branches. More generally, and in line with the foregoing analysis, there was a decline in the extent of workplace-based branches within the public services sector from 18 per cent to 12 per cent of cases. Non-manual workplace-based branches within private manufacturing also declined over the period, from a quarter to 18 per cent of cases, but there was no detectable change within the nationalised industries (13 per cent 1980, 14 per cent 1984). By contrast, within private services the extent of workplace-based branches doubled, from 13 per cent to 27 per cent of cases, perhaps signalling a strengthening of local union organisation within this relatively unorganised sector.

The association that we demonstrated between branch size and composition on the basis of the 1980 results[6] was again apparent in 1984. Table 5.3 shows that the typical (median) branch size reported by both manual and non-manual representatives was smallest among those that said they were members of a workplace-based branch and largest among those that said they were members of a multi-employer branch. However, it is important to note that our results are likely to exaggerate the magnitude of the difference in size between workplace-based branches and those that draw members from several workplaces. This is because respondents in the latter type will be reporting the same branch (and therefore its size) more than once, thus inflating the median and the mean. Although we can be less precise about the size of these branches, or about the magnitude of the difference in size between them and workplace-based branches, the results still indicate that, in general terms, workplace-based branches are smaller than those based above the workplace. It is unlikely that the extent of multiple reporting is so substantial as to militate against this overall conclusion.

The multiple reporting of geographically-based branches is common to both our surveys. It is doubtful whether the extent of it has changed sufficiently to invalidate comparisons of branch sizes, but we cannot be sure. With this caution in mind, the results show that the reported size of single-employer branches of either manual or

Table 5.3   Size of union branches in relation to branch composition

	Manual						Non-manual						
	Workplace-based		Single-employer		Multi-employer		Workplace-based		Single-employer		Multi-employer		
	1980	1984	1980	1984	1980	1984	1980	1984	1980	1984	1980	1984	Numbers
Median[1]	39[2]	38	369	354	925	908	41	64	403	396	634	466	
													Column percentages
1–49	57	65	6	6	2	3	57	39	7	5	4	3	
50–99	17	14	5	16	1	2	17	24	3	7	3	3	
100–199	9	9	12	12	3	5	9	15	12	12	5	11	
200–299	4	4	7	9	5	9	4	4	8	14	3	12	
300–399	2	2	5	6	3	6	2	6	8	8	3	6	
400–499	3	1	5	4	3	6	3	2	8	6	2	8	
500–999	1	3	15	15	13	14	1	4	10	17	16	17	
1000–1999	3	1	7	8	15	14	3	*	10	6	6	9	
2000+	1	1	9	14	11	24	—	*	10	16	7	12	
Don't know/not answered	5	*	26	10	45	18	4	6	23	9	51	19	
Base: worker representatives belonging to recognised trade unions													
Unweighted	261	240	229	283	470	375	192	205	375	482	278	248	
Weighted	132	131	154	180	348	235	104	85	286	358	150	108	

[1] Median linearly interpolated from weighted absolute numbers, excluding don't knows.
[2] See Note C.

non-manual unions remained at about the same level in both surveys. The reported size of multi-employer branches of manual unions was also unchanged, but that for non-manual union branches of this type declined considerably between 1980 and 1984. It is also interesting to note that the size of the typical, workplace-based, manual union branch **declined** by half over the period, while the size of the typical, workplace-based non-manual union branch **increased** by half. By way of summary, then, within manual unions there was a decline in the size of workplace-based branches over the period, but a slight increase in the extent to which such branches were reported. The reported size of both single-employer and multi-employer branches was virtually unchanged, but single-employer branches were reported more frequently than previously, and, therefore, multi-employer branches were reported much less frequently. Within non-manual unions, by contrast, there was an increase in the size of workplace-based branches over the period, but a slight decline in the extent to which they were reported. The reported size of single-employer branches was unchanged but the extent to which they were reported increased substantially, and both the reported size of multi-employer branches and the extent to which they were reported declined over the period.

Given the move towards less geographically-dispersed branches in the three main **manual** unions in our sample, we would expect the overall size of branches within these particular unions to have shrunk between 1980 and 1984. Bearing in mind the caution discussed above, Table 5.1 indicates that for each union (TGWU, GMBATU and AUEW) the typical (median) reported branch size was lower in 1984 than in 1980. The shrinkage of GMBATU branches was particularly marked: in 1980 representatives typically belonged to a branch of 470 members while in 1984 it was 235. There was a substantial increase in the reporting of very small branches (1–49 members) in all three unions but, interestingly, TGWU branches with 1000 or more members were mentioned twice as frequently in 1984 than in 1980. It is notable that the reporting of smaller and less geographically-based branches among these three unions between 1980 and 1984 was associated with a substantial decline in their membership over the four-year period.[7]

By contrast, for the union with more geographically-dispersed branches in 1984 than in 1980 (NUPE) the typical branch size **increased** over the period from just over 400 to almost 500 members. As there was only a slight decline in NUPE membership between the two surveys,[8] it appears that the branch structure became more centralised over the period, towards fewer but larger branches. As the table shows, there was a decline in the reporting of very small NUPE branches (1–49 members) and the bulk of the increase was in branches with between 200 and 999 members. Taking all manual unions together, however, the typical branch size declined from 426 in 1980 to 319 in 1984.

The pattern of change for the main non-manual unions in our sample is rather different. Between 1980 and 1984, the typical size of non-manual union branches in general actually increased slightly, from 288 to 328. The increase was most marked within NALGO (from 522 to 634) and, as with NUPE, the very slight decline in membership of NALGO[9] over the four-year period, together with the move towards more geographically-based branches, points towards a centralisation of the branch structure between 1980 and 1984. By contrast, the typical ASTMS branch declined by half, from 676 in 1980 to 332 in 1984. Clearly, as the overall composition of ASTMS branches changed only slightly over the period (see Table 5.2), the fact that membership of ASTMS dropped[10] by a fifth between 1980 and 1984 suggests that the decline in branch size is due entirely to the drop in membership. The typical TASS branch also declined considerably in size, from 716 in 1980 to 399 in 1984 but, as Table 5.2 shows, workplace-based branches of TASS were reported around three times more frequently in 1984 than in 1980, and those at a higher level were reported less frequently. The 15 per cent **increase** in TASS membership[11] over the period suggests there was a change in the branch structure: a larger membership organised in more, smaller, less geographically-based branches.

It is also notable that the proportion of respondents who could give no estimate of branch size declined substantially between the two surveys. Non-response among manual representatives declined from a third to 13 per cent, and the decline among non-manual representatives was very similar (see Table 5.2). It is likely that part of the explanation for this, particularly for manuals, is precisely the changes in both the composition and size of branches over the period: the size of smaller and less geographically-dispersed branches is easier to estimate than those that are larger and more geographically-dispersed, as indicated by the data on non-response in relation to branch composition given in Table 5.3. However, we also feel that an improvement to the question itself in the second survey contributed significantly to the reduction in non-response for each type of branch in 1984. Whereas in 1980 we asked respondents to provide an estimate without prompting, in 1984 we asked them to locate their branch size within one of the nine ranges shown in Tables 5.1 to 5.3.

Although the sequence of questioning was not repeated in 1984, in our earlier book we concluded that, although geographically-based branches met more frequently than those based at the workplace in 1980, they were attended by a much smaller proportion of the membership.[12] We noted that the pattern of attendance at branch meetings appeared to be related to the ease of communication between officers and members and the ease of travel. Since geographically-dispersed branches of non-manual unions were reported more frequently in 1984 than in 1980 and their overall size changed only slightly, we can infer that attendance at branch meetings declined between 1980 and 1984, assuming that their frequency remained constant over the period. However, the results also suggest that manual union members, although fewer in numbers than earlier, may be more likely to attend branch meetings than previously, given the large decline in the reporting of multi-employer branches and the slight increase in the extent of workplace-based branches over the period.

The methods of appointment of workplace representatives

We asked our worker representative respondents how they and other lay representatives in their union were appointed at their particular place of work. As in 1980, we sought to distinguish the methods of appointment of senior stewards and 'ordinary' (i.e. non-senior) stewards. However, where there was just a single steward at the establishment this distinction obviously did not hold. In these cases, although the stewards in question were routed through the section of the questionnaire dealing with the methods of appointment of **senior** stewards, we report these results separately as they relate specifically to what we term *sole stewards*. It is important to note that the scope for comparisons across the two surveys is limited in respect of the method of appointment of workplace representatives, owing to some substantial changes to the relevant questions. In the first survey our interviewers were instructed to **read out** a list of alternative methods of appointment from which respondents were asked to choose the method which best described current practice within their workplace. The following methods of appointment were read out:

> *Show of hands*
> *Postal ballot*
> *Non-postal ballot*
> *Other method*.

However, experience gained in the first survey led us to change the structure of the question in 1984. First, we increased the range of options from which respondents could choose. Secondly, we made some slight changes to the wording of some of the options. Thirdly, we allowed respondents more time to consider their answers by instructing our interviewers to present them with a show-card on which were printed the following methods of appointment:

General feeling of meeting without a vote
Show of hands at a meeting
Voting slips
Postal ballot
Other method.

In 1984, therefore, we effectively gave respondents more options from which to choose their method of appointment than in 1980, which makes direct comparisons with similar **elements** of the questions from both surveys unreliable. With this consideration in mind, we focus mainly on the results from the 1984 survey, and make only general reference to the 1980 results. Table 5.4 shows how senior stewards, ordinary stewards and sole stewards were appointed in the case of the union to which manual and non-manual representatives belonged.

In 1980, using the slightly different question format, we found that a show of hands was by far the most common method of election for all types of representative. Table 5.4 shows that this was also the case in 1984, being reported in over half of cases of manual steward elections and between a third and a half of non-manual cases. In the great majority of cases this method was used for the election of **senior** stewards within NUPE (82 per cent), the AUEW (69 per cent) and ASTMS (76 per cent).

For either manual or non-manual appointments, *voting slips* were used in around a quarter of cases for each type of representative, being slightly more commonly used in the appointment of senior stewards. Postal ballots were mentioned much less frequently and, as in 1980, were more commonly used by non-manual unions than by manual unions. Although not directly evident from the table, there is some evidence to suggest that non-manual unions were more likely to use both postal and non-postal ballots than manual unions in 1984. This relates to our suspicion that the 1984 question format resulted in some under-reporting of methods of election which would be conventionally defined as ballots among both manual and non-manual representatives, but particularly among the latter. It is clear from Table 5.4 that over a quarter of 'ordinary' non-manual representatives and one tenth of 'ordinary' manual stewards specified a method of appointment not listed on our show-card. It is apparent from interviewers' records of 'other answers' that about a quarter of the 77 (unweighted) non-manual cases and two fifths of the 42 (unweighted) manual cases referred to some form of balloting procedure.[13] Further work on coding of these answers is in hand, but, in advance of this, it seems likely that the revision would increase the (weighted) proportion of non-manual representatives appointed by ballot more than that for manual stewards. In other words, we can be reasonably confident that our data suggest that, in 1984, non-manual representatives were more

Table 5.4 Methods of appointment of union representatives, 1984

Column percentages

	Manual unions			Non-manual unions		
	Senior representative	Ordinary representative	Sole representative	Senior representative	Ordinary representative	Sole representative
Method of appointment						
General feeling of a meeting without a vote	13[1]	14	23	22	16	25
Show of hands	58	54	51	46	36	37
Voting slips	28	24	20	27	23	26
Postal ballot	4	3	1	4	4	7
Other method	5	10	6	8	26	9
Not answered	2	4	4	3	4	4
Base: worker representatives belonging to recognised unions						
Unweighted	*721*	*721*	*190*	*788*	*788*	*161*
Weighted	*299*	*299*	*256*	*373*	*373*	*188*

[1] See Note E.

likely to have been appointed by some form of balloting procedure than manual stewards. In our earlier book, using the different question format, we reported that just such a pattern was evident in 1980.[14] Interestingly perhaps, given the preference for balloting among non-manual unions, the *general feeling of a meeting without a vote* was more commonly used as a method of appointment for non-manual representatives than for manuals and was much more commonly used in the appointment of 'sole' representatives (either manual or non-manual). This, as well as our preliminary analysis of the verbatim *other answers*, points towards sole stewards often being appointed unopposed.

Our data can be used to see whether the methods of appointment that predominate in **workplaces** also predominate for the population of **representatives**.[15] A clear majority of representatives in 1984, both manual and non-manual, were employed in establishments of less than 500 employees, where the more informal methods of appointment (*general feeling . . .* and *show of hands . . .*) were the majority practice. It seems likely, therefore, that the majority of **representatives** were appointed by such methods. However, as non-manual representatives outnumbered manual stewards (see Chapter 3) and are likely to form an increasing majority of all representatives, their greater use of formal methods of appointment (such as balloting) may at some stage lead to this becoming the majority practice.

Contact with paid officials of the union

In the 1980 survey we asked about the amount of contact between senior stewards at the workplace and full-time officers of the union at local and national level. This questioning was repeated in 1984 but we substituted the term *paid official* for *full-time official*. Broadly speaking, there was little change in the amount of contact between stewards and paid officials over the period. In 1984 three quarters of senior manual stewards reported meeting a paid official of their union in the last year, the same proportion as did so in 1980. As before, fewer non-manual representatives reported these meetings, though the proportion doing so declined slightly over the period from 63 per cent to 57 per cent. However, of those manual and non-manual representatives that had met their paid officials in 1984, they did so as often as in 1980, typically two or three times in the year prior to interview for manual stewards and twice for non-manual representatives.

There was a decline in the proportion of stewards who reported joint meetings with both their paid officials and management during the year prior to interview. Such meetings were still most frequently reported by manual representatives, being reported in about half of cases in both surveys (56 per cent 1980, 50 per cent 1984). The decline was most marked among non-manual representatives, with the proportion reporting them down by a third (from 40 to 25 per cent of cases). However, there was no change in the frequency of these meetings, both manual and non-manual representatives typically reporting that such meetings were held roughly twice in the year prior to interview.

There was more contact between workplace-based representatives (manual and non-manual) and either national union officers or the head office of their union in 1984 than in 1980. This was so in nearly all sectors and only manual stewards within private manufacturing reported less contact than previously. Overall, these meetings were still more commonly reported by non-manual representatives (50 per cent 1984, 43 per cent 1980) than by manual stewards (46 per cent 1984, 38 per cent 1980).

Intra-union shop stewards' meetings at the workplace

Our survey series provides one of the few sources of systematic and generalisable data on the ways in which shop stewards from both the same and different unions relate to each other, both within and outside the workplace. In both surveys the sequence of questions covered a variety of meetings and more formalised committees: joint shop stewards' committees and meetings at the workplace; 'combine' committees at both single-employer and multi-employer levels; and purely local arrangements such as meetings between stewards of the same union at the same workplace. We begin by outlining the findings on these 'intra-union' arrangements at the workplace and we deal with the various joint committees in subsequent sections.

In 1984 29 per cent of **all** manual representatives said there were meetings between stewards of the same union at their workplace and the same proportion of non-manual representatives did so. This reflects a decline overall since 1980 when they were reported by two fifths of all respondents in both cases. Excluding establishments where there was only a single representative of the union in question, such meetings were reported by a half of manual stewards in 1984, the same proportion that did so in 1980. With the same exclusion, the proportion of non-manual representatives reporting such meetings declined from around a half to 39 per cent over the period. In other words, taking those cases where intra-union steward meetings could have been reported, in 1984 such meetings were more frequently reported by manual stewards than by non-manual representatives, whereas in 1980 they were as frequently reported by either representative.

As in 1980, intra-union stewards' meetings were more often

reported by manual stewards the larger the manual workforce at the establishment, presumably a consequence of the greater need for co-ordination when more stewards are present. The same was also true for non-manuals. In both 1980 and 1984 manual stewards reported such meetings much more frequently in establishments with either workplace-level or single-employer-level bargaining arrangements. Meetings of non-manual representatives from the same union in 1984 were more common in cases where workplace-level bargaining was predominant. At once a month or more often, the frequency of either manual or non-manual union meetings remained unchanged between our two study periods and, although we do not have comparable data for 1984, we reported in our earlier book that in a majority of cases in 1980 such meetings were always held during working hours and that minutes were regularly taken.[16] There is little reason to suppose that these practices have changed in the intervening period.

Joint shop stewards' committees and meetings at the workplace
In addition to the sequence of questions about meetings of stewards from the **same** union at the workplace we also asked about committees and meetings of stewards from **different** unions in workplaces where workers were represented by more than one trade union. (Here, as elsewhere, we use the term *stewards* as a shorthand for stewards or representatives, although our questionnaires used different terms for manual and non-manual interviews.) However, we made some changes to the structure of the questioning about these *joint shop stewards' committees and meetings* in the 1984 survey. Effectively we condensed the two sequences of questions on *committees **and** meetings* used in the 1980 survey into a single sequence on *committees **or** meetings* in the 1984 survey. In the analysis which follows, the 1980 results have been combined to reflect the 1984 structure of questioning. Strictly speaking the results from the two surveys are not directly comparable, since respondents were given two opportunities to report either committees or meetings in 1980, while in 1984 they were given only one. This may have slightly reduced the proportions in 1984 from what they would have been using the 1980 question structure presented below. We use the single term *committee* in the following section as shorthand for *committees or meetings*.

We saw in Chapter 3 that in overall terms there was little change in the extent of multi-unionism between 1980 and 1984. Among manual workers it occurred in a minority (around one third) of workplaces with recognition, while for non-manuals it occurred in a majority (around three fifths). As in 1980, it was in a minority of multi-union establishments that *joint shop stewards' committees* were to be found.

The figures indicate an overall decline between 1980 and 1984 from 41 to 32 per cent for manuals and from 24 to 20 per cent for non-manuals. With sampling error and the change in question format there can be little confidence that there was a decline. However, we can be more confident about both the decline in the proportion of respondents from NALGO who reported joint committees, from 40 per cent to just 16 per cent, and the slight increase in such committees within ASTMS (from 26 to 32 per cent).

Some of the changes shown in Table 5.5 are such that they are unlikely to be a mere artifact of the change in question format. Of note is the decline in committees in manufacturing and the reported increase of manual committees and the decline in non-manual committees in the nationalised industries. Non-manual committees in public services also appear to be no less common in 1984 than they were in 1980.

As in 1980, both manual and non-manual representatives were more likely to report joint committees in larger establishments. This was so whether we used the total workforce as our measure of size or the size of the manual or non-manual workforce, as appropriate. In both surveys we found that the greater the number of recognised unions present, the more likely was a committee to be reported at the workplace. However, an interesting difference between the two surveys concerned the incidence of committees in relation to the number of negotiating groups at the workplace. In 1980 we found that committees were much more common in workplaces where all the manual (or non-manual) unions negotiated with management as a single group than in those where they negotiated separately or in several groups. By contrast, in 1984 the reverse was the case for manual committees, and non-manual committees were as common in workplaces with either type of negotiating arrangement.

Both manual and non-manual committees were more common in *Division 3* of the *Standard Industrial Classification* (Metal Goods, Engineering and Vehicles Industries). Interestingly, joint committees of non-manual representatives were more common in head offices of multi-establishment organisations, in foreign-owned establishments and in cases where workplace-level pay bargaining was predominant. These patterns were apparent in both surveys. However, whereas workplace-level bargaining was strongly associated with the occurrence of joint committees of manual stewards in 1980, there was no perceptible variation with respect to bargaining level in 1984.[17]

In both surveys we asked two follow-up questions about how frequently these joint committees met and when meetings were held. Unfortunately, the change in question format vitiates comparisons between the two periods, but the 1984 results can be summarised as

Table 5.5 Extent of joint shop-stewards' committees or meetings by broad sector

Percentages

	All establishments		Private manufacturing		Private services		Nationalised industries		Public services	
	1980	1984	1980	1984	1980	1984	1980	1984	1980	1984
Manual unions										
Committee or meeting reported	41	32	48	33	(32)[1]	(21)	33	46	35	28
Base: manual worker representatives belonging to recognised trade unions at establishments where workforce was represented by two or more unions										
Unweighted	605	587	324	255	44	41	63	87	174	204
Weighted	273	230	130	97	21	16	25	29	97	87
Non-manual unions										
Committee or meeting reported	24	20	42	26	(11)	(8)	36	17	21	21
Base: non-manual worker representatives belonging to recognised trade unions at establishments where workforce was represented by two or more unions										
Unweighted	615	661	190	143	45	41	81	113	299	364
Weighted	363[2]	375	44	25	38	23	30	44	252	284

[1] See Note B.
[2] See Note H.

follows. Over half of manual committees met at least once a month, while a further third met at least once every three months. Non-manual committees met much less often, about a quarter meeting at least once a month. Both manual and non-manual committees were held in working hours in over three quarters of cases, indicating a high degree of acceptance by management.

Single-employer combine committees

We now move on to present the results on shop stewards' committees and meetings which draw their members from several workplaces and thus exist at a level above the sampling unit of our surveys. In workplaces that were part of multi-establishment organisations we asked about the existence of committees of shop stewards from **different** workplaces within the **same** organisation, or what have come to be known as single-employer *combine committees*. Several examples in recent years, notably at Vickers[18] and at Lucas Aerospace,[19] have been well documented. More generally, it has been suggested that the development of single-employer union structures such as these forms part of a strategy by which trade unions can mitigate the presumed bargaining advantage accruing to employers through mergers and rationalisation.[20] Indeed, in the 1980 survey we found that the main reason for starting inter-workplace combines was to give stewards the opportunity to exchange ideas and information with representatives from other workplaces, presumably a prerequisite for such an effect.[21] However, explanations for the development or otherwise of combine committees have been hampered either by the lack of comparable data across the major sectors of the economy, or by misinterpretation of the survey data available. A recent example[22] of the latter confines the analysis to manufacturing but in using both the 1978 Warwick survey[23] and the 1980 Workplace Industrial Relations Survey has to rely on information provided by different types of respondent across the two surveys. Although the questions used were broadly similar, the former survey asked them of management respondents while the latter used worker representatives.[24] The article also confuses the unit of analysis when reporting the survey data on combine activity. Clearly, in surveys of **establishments**, it is not possible to calculate the extent of **higher-level** phenomena such as single-employer combines,[25] unless reports of the same committee from different establishments can be linked. The data can only tell us about the proportion of **workplaces** where worker representatives were reported as being **members** of them. This issue of 'multiple reporting' of combines is particularly important to recognise when presenting data over time, such as in our survey series, because the overall composition of the combines

Table 5.6 Proportion of workplaces where worker representative reported a single-employer combine committee

Percentages

	All establishments 1980	1984	Private manufacturing 1980	1984	Private services 1980	1984	Nationalised industries 1980	1984	Public services 1980	1984
Manual										
Single-employer combine committee reported	44	42	33	21	44	34	59	65	49	52
Base: manual worker representatives belonging to recognised trade unions at establishments that were part of multi-establishment organisations										
Unweighted	877	853	405	320	137	115	91	138	244	280
Weighted	557[1]	482	183	122	144	112	49	78	180	171
Non-manual										
Single-employer combine committee reported	43	41	35	30	44	40	42	37	44	43
Base: non-manual worker representatives belonging to recognised trade unions at establishments that were part of multi-establishment organisations										
Unweighted	865	912	286	241	112	102	91	130	376	439
Weighted	546	534	79	54	104	75	36	53	327	352

[1] See Note H.

themselves may have changed over the period. For example, whereas stewards at four different establishments may have reported being members of what could turn out to be the **same** single-employer combine in 1980, stewards at eight establishments might have reported this in 1984. Clearly, in this example it is not the case that the numbers of **combines** have doubled over the period. It is only by presenting other information, such as changes in the average number of workplaces belonging to multi-establishment organisations over the period, that we could begin to approach an estimate of changes in the extent of single-employer combines themselves. This issue of the unit of analysis should be borne in mind in this section on single-employer combines and in the subsequent section on multi-employer combines. Although we are comparing the responses of identical types of respondents from all the major sectors of the economy in the results presented below, it is important to remember that the results relate to the proportion of **workplaces** with **members** of single-employer combines and not to the proportion of **organisations** (or enterprises or companies) where combine committees were reported.

In general terms, the results show no perceptible change in the proportion of respondents at establishments that were part of a multi-establishment group who said they were members of a single-employer combine committee (manual or non-manual). Just over two fifths of respondents gave this answer in both surveys. However, as Table 5.6 shows, there were changes in certain sectors. In particular, there was an overall decline in the proportion of manual representatives who said they were members of combines within both the private manufacturing and private services sectors. None of the other changes approached statistical significance. Membership was still more commonly reported (by either manual or non-manual representatives) in the private services sector than in private manufacturing. The nationalised industries remained the sector in which manual combines were most frequently reported.

In 1980 we found that private sector combine meetings were more frequently reported by stewards in workplaces belonging to larger organisations while in the public sector the reverse was the case. This was also true in 1984. Regardless of sector, however, in 1984 combine meetings were more frequently reported in workplaces belonging to organisations employing 1000 or more people than in smaller organisations.

Membership of manual combines declined significantly among representatives of some of the largest trade unions, in particular the TGWU (from 53 to 33 per cent) and, to a lesser extent, the AUEW (from 32 to 25 per cent). Within the main non-manual unions, combine membership declined among NALGO representatives (from

60 to 53 per cent), but increased among representatives of ASTMS (from 34 to 46 per cent). There was a marked difference in the reporting of membership of combines between establishments with different pay bargaining arrangements. As we might expect, in both 1980 and 1984 manual representatives were more likely to report membership of single-employer combines in workplaces where single-employer pay bargaining was predominant. Although the same was true of non-manual representatives, the difference between the single-employer and multi-employer bargaining levels was less marked. Non-manual representatives were more likely to report membership of single-employer combines in both foreign-owned workplaces and in the head offices of multi-establishment organisations.

In 1980 the reported frequency of combine committee meetings was related to the predominant level of pay bargaining. Meetings were held most frequently where there was single-employer bargaining and least frequently where the locus of bargaining was at the workplace. But in 1984 meetings of manual combines were **less** frequent in workplaces with single-employer bargaining than those with other levels of bargaining. Non-manual representatives reported more frequent meetings the **higher** the level of bargaining. In other words, in 1984 non-manual combine meetings were most frequent where multi-employer bargaining was predominant and least frequent where pay negotiations took place at workplace-level. As in 1980, however, the typical reported frequency of both manual and non-manual combine meetings was at least once every three months. Meetings were held at least once a month in approaching a third of cases in 1984. Within the public services sector meetings were particularly frequent.

Multi-employer combine committees

The highest 'level' of shop steward meetings that we asked about were those involving shop stewards from workplaces belonging to several different employing organisations. Clearly, the caution we gave about the unit of analysis in relation to the reporting of our data on single-employer combine activity applies equally to these *multi-employer combines*. The data presented do not, and cannot, relate directly to the extent of multi-employer combines, but to the proportion of **workplaces** where stewards said they participated in such committees and meetings.

Manual or non-manual representatives reported membership of multi-employer combines in about one eighth of workplaces in 1980 – roughly a third of the number who reported membership of single-employer combines. The figures were broadly the same in

Table 5.7 Proportion of workplaces where worker representative reported a multi-employer combine committee

Percentages

	All establishments		Private manufacturing		Private services		Nationalised industries		Public services	
	1980	1984	1980	1984	1980	1984	1980	1984	1980	1984
Manual										
Multi-employer combine committee reported	13	11	16	10	16	10	5	9	8	13
Base: manual worker representatives belonging to recognised trade unions										
Unweighted	970	910	477	349	148	137	91	138	254	286
Weighted	643[1]	554	256	169	150	133	49	78	187	174
Non-manual										
Multi-employer combine committee reported	11	11	9	7	13	7	5	9	11	12
Base: non-manual worker representatives belonging to recognised trade unions										
Unweighted	921	949	312	250	128	122	91	130	390	447
Weighted	585	560	95	61	117	88	36	53	337	359

[1] See Note H.

1984, although there were changes in particular sectors. Table 5.7 gives the results. Substantially less manual representatives reported membership of these combines in both the private manufacturing and private services sectors as had done so in 1980, but significantly more reported membership in the nationalised industries and the public services. Membership of non-manual multi-employer combines was reported half as often in private services establishments in 1984 than in 1980, and almost twice as often in the nationalised industries. There was no change in either the private manufacturing or the public services sectors and, as Table 5.7 shows, there was a more even reporting of membership across sectors in 1984 than in 1980. As in 1980, multi-employer combines met about as frequently as single-employer combines, typically once every three months or more often.

Notes and references

1. Daniel, W W and Millward N (1983) *Workplace Industrial Relations in Britain: The DE/PSI/SSRC Survey*, Heinemann Educational Books, London, pp.82-104.

2. For example, see Brown W (Ed.) (1981) *The Changing Contours of British Industrial Relations*, Blackwell, Oxford, p.69; Terry M (1985) 'Combine Committees: Developments of the 1970s', *British Journal of Industrial Relations*, November, p.363.

3. In theory one could move from one level of analysis to the other, provided one had available the information required to calculate the probabilities of selection. This is rarely available in practice.

4. More detail is available in Daniel W W and Millward N (1983) *op. cit.*, p.85-6. However, it should be emphasised that the analysis in the earlier book is based on the unrevised weighting matrix, so the results given here may be slightly different.

5. In 1986 became the Amalgamated Engineering Union (AEU).

6. Daniel W W and Millward N (1983) *op. cit.*, pp.84-5.

7. Certification Office for Trade Unions and Employers Associations (1982 and 1986) *Annual Report of the Certification Officer*, London, Appendix 4.

8. *Ibid.*

9. *Ibid.*

10. *Ibid.*

11. *Ibid.*

12. Daniel W W and Millward N (1983) *op. cit.*, pp.85-6.

13. There seems to have been some confusion, both among respondents and at the coding stage, about the meaning of *voting slips* and *postal ballots*. We envisaged the former as referring to some form of written voting procedure where voting forms are distributed and returned via ballot boxes or their equivalent, either at a meeting especially convened or at the workplace, and with an element of secrecy attached. It was intended that the latter category should cover those forms of written voting procedure where forms are distributed and returned centrally, through a mailing system either internal or external to the workplace.

14. Daniel W W and Millward N (1983) *op. cit.*, p.88. The difference is also apparent in methods of consultation on pay offers. See Chapter 9.

15. A more precise answer to this question could be obtained by multiplying the number of representatives in each establishment by the reported method of election. This would involve assuming that the practice was uniform for workplaces with two or more 'ordinary' representatives. Further work along these lines is in progress.

16. Daniel W W and Millward N (1983) *op. cit.*, p.97.

17. They were reported in 33 per cent of cases with plant-level bargaining, 33 per cent with company-level bargaining, and 30 per cent with multi-employer-level bargaining in 1984.

18. Beynon H and Wainwright H (1979) *The Workers' Report on Vickers*, Pluto Press, London.

19. Wainwright H and Elliot D (1982) *The Lucas Plan: A New Trade Unionism in the Making?*, Allison and Busby, London.

20. Millward N and McQueeney J (1981) *Company Take-Overs, Management Organisation and Industrial Relations*, Manpower Paper No.16, Department of Employment, London; Geroski P and Knight K G (1984) 'Corporate Merger and Collective Bargaining in the UK', *Industrial Relations Journal*, Summer.

21. Daniel W W and Millward N (1983) *op. cit.*, p.102.

22. Terry M (1985) *op. cit.*

23. Brown W (Ed.) (1981) *op. cit.*

24. The author recognises that managers may only have been aware of combine committees where they impinged on management activity through collective bargaining. Terry (1985) *op. cit.*, p.363.

25. Yet this is precisely the mistake the author makes in reporting the survey material, as the following extracts show, first, in relation to the Warwick survey and, secondly, in relation to our 1980 survey: '. . . the results show that these managers were aware of such meetings, involving manual unions in slightly over a third of (multi-plant) **companies** . . .' *ibid.*, p.362. (Our emphasis) '. . . Combine committees (for non-manual workers) were identified in 38 per cent of multi-plant **firms** where a non-manual union had recognition' *ibid.*, p.364. (Our emphasis)

6 Consultation and Communication

Joint consultative committees at workplace level

One of the findings of the 1980 survey that aroused considerable interest and comment was that joint consultative committees had become more common in the period up to 1980 and specifically between 1975 and 1980. Lacking any comparable survey data for previous years, we had based that finding on a comparison between the rate of births and deaths of consultative committees as reported by managers in 1980. We had, however, warned that such comparisons might overstate the extent of growth, although not to the extent that growth was illusory. The reasons for this possible overstatement were twofold: establishments that had closed down or dropped below our sampling threshold would not be represented (and large establishments closing down might well have had consultative committees); perhaps more significantly, there might be a bias in the recall of respondents, making them exaggerate the recency of new committees and understating the extent to which committees had been abandoned. As with other topics where we have repeated questions in the survey series, no such difficulties arise in our estimates of the changes between 1980 and 1984.

As can be seen from the first row in Table 6.1, there were changes in the extent of joint consultative committees between 1980 and 1984 within particular sectors of the economy, but the net result of these changes was that overall the proportion of workplaces with a joint consultative committee remained constant at 34 per cent.

In the private sector the decline in the proportion of establishments with a joint consultative committee was most marked in manufacturing, where the fall was from 36 per cent to 30 per cent. Much of this change arises from the changing structure of the manufacturing sector. In terms of size, establishments with 500 or more employees accounted for seven per cent of the manufacturing sample in 1980 but five per cent in 1984; plants with 25 to 99 employees grew from 64 per cent to 68 per cent and of course were much less likely to have joint consultative committees than larger plants. Changes in the sectoral composition, however, do not appear to have contributed to the change within manufacturing industry; engineering (Division 3) had

Table 6.1 Proportion of establishments where managers reported a joint consultative committee

	All establishments 1980	1984	Private manufacturing 1980	1984	Private services 1980	1984	Public sector 1980	1984
Consultative committee currently exists	34	34	36	30	26	24	42	48
No longer has a consultative committee, but did within last five years	2	3	4	4	2	3	1	2
Workplace consultative committee or higher-level committee with local reps	..[1]	41	..	33	..	28	..	62
Base: all establishments								
Unweighted	2040	2019	743	592	587	597	710	830
Weighted	2000[2]	2000	503	424	859	843	637	733

[1] See Note J.
[2] See Note H.

the highest proportion of joint consultative committees in 1980 and was only average in 1984, but it had declined as a proportion of the sample meanwhile.

The pattern of change within manufacturing can to a certain extent be elaborated by the results of a question to managers without an establishment-level joint consultative committee, asking them if they had ever had one and, if so, when it was abandoned. This question was also asked in 1980. As Table 6.1 shows, manufacturing plants as a whole were no more likely to have abandoned joint consultative committees in the five years up to 1984 than in the five years up to 1980. It is possible that the birth rate for joint consultative committees dropped between the two surveys, but we have no evidence from the main sample on this – the question on the recency of creation of committees having been dropped in the 1984 survey to make room for other questions. We do, however, have very limited evidence from the panel sample about both the births and deaths of committees.[1] This indicates very little change in either direction. Of the (weighted) panel sample of 38 within private manufacturing, 32 neither introduced nor abandoned consultative committess between 1980 and 1984. Two establishments had one in 1980 but no longer had one in 1984. Four establishments did not report one in 1980 but did in 1984. On such a small base no firm conclusion can be made, but the data suggest that the **net** decline in the proportion of manufacturing workplaces with a joint consultative committee is the result of structural changes, rather than a tendency for establishments with committees to abandon them.

For manufacturing our finding of a net decline in the extent of consultative committees in large manufacturing plants contrasts with the recent evidence of Edwards,[2] who reported an increase in extent between 1978 and early 1984. But the two findings are resolved if there was an increase in the late 1970s and a decline thereafter. This would seem to be the most likely occurrence, given the data from our survey series and the changes in the structure of employment over the period.

In private services, Table 6.1 shows a more or less constant figure for the proportion of establishments with a consultative committee. It also shows a low and unchanging rate of abandonment. However, the panel data indicate a very substantial number of gross changes. Of the 66 (weighted) cases in this sector, no less than 15 reported a committee in 1984 but none in 1980. Only two cases had changed in the opposite direction. The conjunction of this gross increase with no net change suggests that private sector establishments **without** committees were more likely to have closed down or dropped below our threshold of 25 employees. This is the opposite of the situation we inferred for manufacturing. However, we should stress again that the panel dataset is small and its results only suggestive.

In the private sector as a whole, there appeared to be a connection between the existence of joint consultative committees in 1984 and their financial performance, establishments that were doing better than their competitors (according to managers' assessments) were more likely to have joint consultative committees and also more likely to have abandoned them recently if they did not have one. This was not the case in 1980; indeed, the 1980 data indicate the opposite relationship. Such a change could perhaps indicate a growing propensity on the part of management to experiment with the appropriate forms of employee involvement for their circumstances, a suggestion that we shall return to later in the chapter when other mechanisms for employee involvement are discussed.

In the public sector the increase in the presence of joint consultative committees at establishment level from 42 per cent to 48 per cent is on the margins of statistical significance at the 95 per cent confidence level and appears to be largely confined to small establishments, where joint consultative committees are less common and there is therefore a greater potential for new committees. Here the panel results show a fairly high level of gross change (22 out of 78 weighted cases), but equally split between the two directions of change. But unlike the private sector cases, the answers here do not generally fit with the 1984 question on the abandonment of committees. There must therefore be doubts about the reliability of the question in public sector workplaces, possibly arising from a confusion between consultative and other types of committee or between establishment and higher-level committees. It is to our direct questioning about the existence of higher-level committees that we now turn.

Higher-level joint committees
In workplaces that belong to multi-establishment organisations joint committees of various sorts may exist at organisational levels above the establishment and provide opportunities for workforce representatives to be consulted about issues that concern them. Such committees were the subject of some new questions in the 1984 survey and the results from them extend our knowledge of consultative machinery as a whole. Overall, in 45 per cent of workplaces belonging to larger organisations our management respondent reported the existence of a joint committee at a level above the establishment about which we were interviewing. A mere three per cent of them were reported as being only concerned with negotiation, the remainder either being concerned only with consultation (39 per cent) or with both functions. The incidence of these higher-level committees was much greater in the public sector than in the private sector and generally was greater

the larger the organisation of which the sampled workplace was a part. In nearly half the workplaces where the manager reported a higher-level committee there was also a joint consultative committee at the workplace itself. The survey questions were not designed to unravel the different functions and scope of consultative committees at different organisational levels, but we can use the questions on both types of committee to estimate the coverage of formal consultative committees, at whatever level, that have a bearing on workplace matters. To do this we have included all higher-level committees that were concerned with consultation and use the data from an additional follow-up question which asked whether any employees from the respondent's workplace sat on the higher-level committee as an employee representative. In aggregate, 45 per cent of respondents reporting a higher-level committee replied that there were representatives from their own establishment on it; naturally it was predominantly the larger establishments which had them.

The result of combining these three questions is shown in the lower half of Table 6.1, where establishments are classified as having a workplace or, where appropriate, higher-level joint consultative committee with workplace representatives. On this definition, 41 per cent of workplaces (employing 62 per cent of employees in our sample) had formal consultative machinery in 1984. Using this wider criterion for the existence of consultative machinery increases the difference between the private and public sectors, the latter having a clear majority of workplaces with consultative machinery, whereas in the former it is a minority practice, covering a third or less of workplaces. We shall give a little more detail of the workings of higher-level committees later in the chapter, but for the moment we return to the subject of workplace-level joint consultative committees and to comparisons between the two surveys.

The structure and operation of workplace-level joint consultative committees

In comparing the structure and operation of joint consultative committees in 1980 and 1984 we have data from several questions to draw upon: we asked respondents with one or more joint consultative committees how many such committees there were at their establishment; and for the two major committees the type of worker represented (manual, non-manual or both) and whether representatives were nominated by trade unions or staff associations. For the principal committee only we asked the frequency of meetings and an open-ended question about the most important matter discussed by the committee in the last year.

As far as the structure of workplace consultative committees went, it remained the case that about three quarters of establishments with any joint consultative committees had a single committee. The existence of multiple committees remained strongly related to the existence of recognised trade unions; indeed, establishments with no recognised trade unions almost invariably had a single joint consultative committee, if they had one at all. However, there is a suggestion that the distribution of multiple committees changed a little between the two surveys: the proportion of cases where there were four or more committees at the same establishment increased from four per cent to six per cent. This is attributable to an increase in the proportion of public sector establishments having four or more committees, an increase only partly offset by a decline in the proportion of private manufacturing establishments that did so. Complex consultative structures co-exist with complex collective bargaining arrangements – in the public sector in particular.

More widespread change was apparent in the types of employees represented on joint consultative committees. For practical reasons these questions were limited to the two major committees ('most important' in the view of our primary management respondent), but it is unlikely that the exclusion of the small number of third or additional committees would alter the findings. Table 6.2 shows how principal and secondary committees (in the quarter of cases where the latter existed) were divided between ones that represented only manual workers, only non-manual workers or both.

Table 6.2 Composition of principal and secondary consultative committees

Column percentages

	Principal committee		Secondary committee	
	1980	1984	1980	1984
Committee has representatives of:				
manual workers only	18	16[1]	26	16
non-manual workers only	22	33	46	54
both categories	49	52	19	27
not answered	11	0	9	3

Base: establishments where relevant committee was reported by management respondent and there were manual and non-manual employees present.

Unweighted	*1030*	*1067*	*353*	*358*
Weighted	*671*	*683*	*149*	*152*

[1] See Note C.

On principal consultative committees both manual and non-manual employees were represented in 52 per cent of cases where both categories were present. In two thirds of the remainder only non-manual employees were represented. These proportions were similar to those for 1980, although there was some increase in committees only covering non-manual workers, reflecting the general trend towards non-manual employment. What had changed was the relationship between who was represented on the principal joint consultative committee and who was represented by recognised trade unions at the same establishment. Non-manual only joint consultative committees were particularly more common in situations where both manual and non-manual unions were recognised. Correspondingly there had been a sharp decrease in the number of cases with recognised unions for both categories where there was a joint consultative committee for both categories (59 per cent in 1980 to 43 per cent in 1984). Secondary committees were still in 1984 much more likely to be for one category of employee only and usually for non-manual workers. A striking change was in the proportion of committees that had only representatives of groups that were not covered by recognised trade unions. For secondary joint consultative committees this dropped from ten per cent in 1980 to three per cent in 1984, although for principal committees the drop was less marked.

Although this might suggest some further alignment between collective bargaining and consultative channels of representation, more direct evidence on this comes from a further question about whether joint consultative committee members were nominated by trade unions or staff associations, if there were members present at the establishment. These results suggest, in fact, that trade unions have become a less important source of representatives on joint consultative committees, particularly in establishments where there are two or more committees (see Table 6.3).

On principal joint consultative committees, and of course most of these were the only committee at an establishment, the proportion of cases where **all** representatives were nominated by trade unions with members at the establishment dropped slightly, while there was a corresponding increase in cases where there was a mixture of trade union and non-union representation. On secondary committees the drop in exclusive trade union nomination was more marked (although on a smaller and therefore less reliable statistical base). Put together these changes do suggest some weakening of the position of trade unions on consultative committees at workplace level.

The results of the 1980 survey shed some initial light on the issue of whether consultative committees co-existed or overlapped with collective bargaining arrangements, an issue raised in the 1960s by

McCarthy and again by other writers since.[3] We showed that it was very common for groups of workers represented on joint consultative committees to be represented also by trade unions for collective bargaining purposes and there was[4] 'some evidence that where consultative machinery and collective bargaining machinery exist together there is some overlap in the issues with which they deal.' We took the opportunity presented by the 1984 survey to explore this overlap a little further by adding a question about whether consultative committees were used only for consultation or whether they also encompassed negotiation between management and employee representatives. Clearly there is scope for substantial disagreement about what constitutes *negotiation*, but there was a striking similarity in the pattern of responses between managers and worker representatives, enough to satisfy us that the responses could be used to examine the issue of overlap.

Principal consultative committees engaged in negotiation as well as consultation in just under a third of all cases, but the proportion was somewhat lower where there were no recognised trade unions at the establishment. The most striking relationship was with the composition of the committee. Committees representing only manual workers were the most likely to involve negotiation (43 per cent did so according to primary management respondents). Committees representing only non-manual workers involved negotiation in 30 per cent of cases while those representing both manual and non-manual employees did so in only a 24 per cent of cases. These differences

Table 6.3 Trade union representation on principal and secondary consultative committees

Column percentages

	Principal committee		Secondary committee	
	1980	1984	1980	1984
Trade unions nominate:				
all representatives	38[1]	35	46	33
some representatives	10	16	8	12
none of them	44	44	45	50
not answered	6	5	1	5

Base: establishments where relevant committee was reported by management and there were union members present.

Unweighted	949	982	340	348
Weighted	577	586	139	146

[1] See Note C.

largely reflected the presence of trade union nominees on the committees and were manifest within both the private and public sectors separately. The same general picture was apparent in relation to secondary committees where they were present.

The possibility that higher-level joint committees might also be involved in negotiating activities was also addressed by a short extra question in the 1984 survey. The majority did so, according to both managers' and worker representatives' reports. In the public sector, where presumably Whitley committees at national level would have been the committees referred to in many instances, the proportion of cases where the higher-level committee was said to involve negotiation was just over 60 per cent, while foreign-owned private sector establishments recorded substantially higher figures. In view of these results and those given earlier for establishment-level consultative committees, the picture of joint consultative committees painted by some writers of a largely passive, management-dominated talking-shop is hardly apt.

Another of the strands of evidence cited in our first report to support the impression that the practice of joint consultation had achieved something of a resurgence in the 1970s was the issues which they discussed.[5] Drawing on the evidence of managers and worker representatives we showed that **production issues, employment issues** and **pay issues** were most commonly mentioned as being the most important matters discussed by establishment-level joint consultative committees. Using an identical question and a virtually identical coding frame, the results in 1984 show a similar set of preoccupations, but also some interesting shifts between the two surveys.

To begin with, the proportion of respondents saying that nothing important had been discussed in their workplace consultative committee during the previous twelve months stayed at the low levels reported for the 1980 survey. Two per cent of managers gave this response in 1984 (three per cent in 1980); four per cent of manual worker representatives gave it (five per cent in 1980) and three per cent of non-manual representatives (eight per cent in 1980). In addition we also have data from works managers in large manufacturing plants in 1984; of these five per cent reported that their consultative committee had discussed nothing of importance in the previous year. Responses from all respondents in 1984 included a substantial number of issues not separately coded in 1980, but they were too numerous and varied to justify elaborating our coding frame; for example, 17 per cent of managers gave such 'other' responses. Ignoring these and concentrating on the separately coded answers most frequently mentioned by managers, the following changes can be observed between the two surveys. **Pay issues** declined from second to fourth place; **future trends** declined from fourth to sixth place and **working conditions** from fifth to eleventh. Two issues became more frequently cited: **employment issues** which moved up from third to second; and **industrial democracy, participation and consultation arrangements,** which was ranked sixteenth in 1980 but fourth in 1984. However, **production issues** (for example, production levels, work scheduling, increasing productivity) remained the issue most frequently mentioned by managers. Unsurprisingly, this was the issue most frequently mentioned by works managers in the 1984 survey. Worker representatives, however, were much more inclined than managers to mention **employment issues** as the most important and this was particularly marked for non-manual worker representatives.

Besides the question of the issues discussed at joint consultative committee meetings, the only other question on the operation of committees that we repeated in the 1984 survey was one concerning the frequency with which the principal (or only) committee met. Here again we rely on managers' accounts, but restrict the analysis to cases where appropriate worker representatives also reported the existence of a committee. There clearly had been changes between the two surveys. Overall, 44 per cent of managers in 1980 reported that their principal joint consultative committee (if it included manual representatives) met once a month at least. By 1984 this had dropped to 27 per cent. Private industry was the sector most affected by this change, although it occurred less noticeably in the public sector. However, committees covering non-manual workers (and whose existence was confirmed by non-manual representatives) showed no change in the frequency with which they met.

Health and safety representation
All the questions reported on in the previous sections explicitly excluded health and safety committees and reserved such committees for the scope of more specific questioning. These latter questions covered the existence of health and safety committees, as well as other methods of workforce representation on health and safety matters, the presence of health and safety committees at higher levels in multi-establishment organisations and the presence of trade union representatives on committees at either level. Only the question on health and safety representation at establishment level had been asked in 1980 and some ambiguity in the response codes had led us to make a minor revision to it in the 1984 survey. To be specific, it was unclear on the 1980 questionnaires whether the responses, *joint health and safety committee* and *workforce representatives* were mutually exclusive and it may well be that some workplaces with individual health and

Table 6.4 Most important matter discussed by principal consultative committee at establishment in the previous year. (Rank order of frequency of mention)

Rank order of frequency of mention

	Primary manager 1980	1984	Works manager 1984	Manual worker rep 1980	1984	Non-manual worker rep 1980	1984
Production issues	1	1	1	1	4	2	4
Employment issues	3	2	2	3	1	1	1
Industrial democracy/participation	16	3	18	16	16	13	20
Pay issues	2	4	3	2	3	5	10
Administrative changes	6	5	9	11	5	3	2
Future trends	4	6	5	10	11	7	5
Working conditions	5	11	7	5	6	4	9
Health and safety	9	12	14	4	2	9	8
Base: all respondents							
Unweighted	*2019*	*2040*	*185*	*505*	*487*	*450*	*552*
Weighted	*2000*	*2000*	*38*	*244*	*202*	*225*	*242*

safety representatives but no health and safety committee at the establishment were wrongly coded in 1980. This ambiguity was removed in 1984 by changing the latter response code to *no committee but workforce representatives*. Naturally, such changes make comparisons between the two surveys very hazardous and we have omitted them, except for the response signifying that there was **no** workforce representation on health and safety matters at the establishment. Taking the obverse of this response, in other words looking at the presence of some form of worker representation for health and safety matters but ignoring its type, we find that there was an increase between 1980 and 1984 from 70 per cent of establishments to 80 per cent.

The pattern of change was widespread but more heavily concentrated in types of establishment where the level of health and safety representation in 1980 was relatively low: small establishments, those without recognised trade unions and workplaces in the private services sector. In consequence there was some lessening of the disparities between types of workplace in terms of whether they had workforce representation on health and safety matters. For example, workplaces in 1984 with recognised unions were one and a half times as likely to have some form of health and safety representation as workplaces with no recognised unions, whereas in 1980 the ratio had been nearer two times. The gap had also narrowed between workplaces with large numbers of part-time employees and those with a predominantly full-time workforce. But whereas in 1980 workplaces with largely manual workforces were more likely to have health and safety representation than predominantly non-manual workplaces, in 1984 the reverse was the case. Whether this is a structural change or reflects an increased awareness of health and safety issues in non-manual employment is hard to say.

The variety of health and safety representation in 1984 is shown in Table 6.5, which incorporates the results of the additional question concerning committees at higher organisational levels. As the table shows, some form of health and safety representation was reported almost universally in the public sector, with half of establishments having individual health and safety representatives and four fifths having a health and safety committee, usually not at the establishment itself but at a higher organisational level. In the private sector as a whole, a quarter of workplaces had no form of health and safety representation at any level, while in establishments with no recognised trade unions the figure was nearly two fifths. In private sector service industries, where workplaces are generally smaller and trade unions less common, the proportion without representation was higher than in manufacturing and where there was local representation it was

Table 6.5 Method of consultation on health and safety matters at establishment and higher organisational levels, 1984

	Public sector	Private sector					25–99 employees	100–499 employees	500+ employees
	All	Manufacturing	services	Unions recognised	Unions not recognised				
									Column percentages
At the establishment:									
Joint health and safety committee	23[1]	21	33	15	31	12	14	42	78
General committee covering H&S	9	10	15	7	13	7	9	11	10
Workforce representatives but no committee	52	34	25	39	36	33	36	30	6
No representation, management decides	10	30	22	34	16	43	34	14	6
Other answer or not answered	7	5	5	5	4	6	6	3	1
									Percentages
Joint health and safety committee at establishment or higher level	80	41	43	40	57	27	37	56	87
No health and safety representation at establishment or higher level	3	25	19	28	11	39	29	12	4
Base: all establishments									
Unweighted	830	1189	592	597	769	420	462	416	311
Weighted	733	1267	424	843	604	663	1001	236	30

[1] See Note C.

more likely to be individual rather than collective. Committees covering health and safety matters at levels above the establishment were exclusively concerned with health and safety in three quarters of cases in the public sector as against one third of cases in the private cases.

Establishment-level health and safety committees, where they existed, had trade union representatives on them in three quarters of cases where there were union members present at the establishment. In the public sector this was universal, although even here not all worker representatives on the committees were union appointees. In private sector workplaces with union members a third of health and safety committees had all representatives appointed by the unions, a third had some of them and a third had none. The level of overall trade union density at the workplace was the strongest source of variation in these proportions. On health and safety committees above the establishment no equivalent question about trade union representation was asked, but it would be reasonable to assume that similar patterns existed, certainly in relation to ownership.

Communication with the workforce

So far this chapter has focused on institutional mechanisms for employee consultation and we have shown that such mechanisms are common, particularly in workplaces where other formal industrial relations structures exist. These formal mechanisms – committees in particular – provide not only a forum in which worker representatives can make their views, and those of the workers they represent, known to management; they also provide a formal channel for management to communicate to employees, although often on a restricted range of issues. These formal channels are by no means the only possible formal channels of communication between managers and other employees and we sought in the 1984 survey to explore what these other channels were and how commonly they were used.

Respondents were shown a card listing six specified methods, other than formal consultative committees, which managers might use to communicate with or consult employees. These were:

* Regular meetings (at least once a month) between junior managers or supervisors and all the workers for whom they are responsible.
* Regular meetings (at least once a year) between senior managers and all sections of the workforce (either all together or section by section).
* Systematic use of the management chain for communication with all employees.

Table 6.6 Methods other than consultative committees used by management to communicate with or consult employees, 1984

Percentages

	All establishments	Private manufacturing	Private services	Nationalised industries	Public services
Regular meetings – junior management	36	24	34	21	50
Regular meetings – senior management	34	37	33	25	34
Management chain	62	58	58	78	67
Suggestion scheme	25	15	25	60	26
Regular newsletters	34	24	33	71	36
Surveys or ballots	12	10	11	10	14
Other methods	8	8	8	9	8
None of these	12	17	15	6	7
Any of the named methods	80	75	77	85	85
Any of the named methods or a joint consultative committee	87	81	84	94	94
Base: all establishments					
Unweighted	2019	592	597	196	634
Weighted	2000	424	843	106	627

   * Suggestion schemes.
   * Regular newsletters distributed to all levels of employee.
   * Surveys or ballots of employees' views or opinions.

Interviewers recorded all methods mentioned or 'none of these' or 'other' methods not listed on the card. Table 6.6 shows the results separately for the different sectors of the economy.

Overall, the most frequently mentioned method of communication was *systematic use of the management chain*, which one might have expected to be endorsed by virtually all respondents. In fact, 62 per cent of managers reported it. Next most common were *regular meetings between junior managers and all the employees for whom they are responsible*, *regular meetings between senior managers and all sections of the workforce* and *regular newsletters*, each of which were reported by about a third of respondents. *Suggestion schemes* and *surveys or ballots of employees' views or opinions* were the least common and were reported by a quarter and an eighth of respondents respectively. Only eight per cent of managers added to our list of methods and most of them had already reported at least one of the listed methods. According to our respondents, who themselves were nearly always part of the management of the workplace being talked about and usually responsible for its personnel or industrial relations management, none of our suggested methods **or any other method** was used at their workplace in 12 per cent of cases.

Table 6.6 shows considerable variation between sectors of the economy in the use of these various methods of communication. Notable is the low use of regular management/employee meetings in the nationalised industries, where formal methods of communication – the formal chain of command, suggestions schemes and newsletters – are most commonly used. There was also considerable variation with size of organisation. Indeed, small establishments belonging to relatively small organisations were the least likely to use any of the specified methods, but particularly the more impersonal methods of *suggestions schemes*, *newsletters* and *surveys or ballots*. The use of none of our listed methods of communication in 17 per cent of private manufacturing plants and 15 per cent of private service establishments is also notable.

The most common combination of methods reported by respondents was *systematic use of the management chain* and *regular newsletters distributed to all levels of employee*, a combination which reflects the dominance of large-scale, bureaucratic organisations in the sample. This combination, however, was only reported by 28 per cent of establishments, employing roughly half of all employees. The least probable combination of methods appeared to be *suggestion schemes* and *surveys or ballots of employees' opinions*, reported in a mere six per cent of cases.

In some circumstances, small organisations are an obvious example, it might be thought that communication via the management chain, generally directly from manager to worker, would be a satisfactory and adequate method of communication, requiring no supplementation. If we leave it out of consideration for the moment (even though only 62 per cent of respondents actually reported it), then our respondents reported the existence of one of the **other** named methods **or** the existence of a joint consultative committee in 76 per cent of establishments, covering 85 per cent of employees in the sample.

So far we have reported what the survey results have told us about the channels of communication between management and the workforce, concentrating, naturally in a survey of this type, on the more formalised channels and methods. Does the use of these various methods, or combinations of them, make any difference to the amount of information actually given by management and received by the workforce? Again we had to rely on crude questioning to assess the amounts of information received by employees in the establishments in our sample: we were restricted to the reports of workers' representatives rather than samples of employees and we had to focus the questions on relatively specific issues which were likely to be recurrent in the great majority of workplaces. Even so it must be the case that the issues we specified could, across the whole range of workplaces, cover a wide variety of specific issues and items of information and it is likely that respondents interpreted our questions in relation to the specifics of their own circumstances. We would therefore expect responses to be on the generous side in evaluating the amount of information communicated to employees when the issues mentioned in our questions are given their most comprehensive interpretation. The issues we focused on were:

    terms and conditions of employment
    staffing or manpower plans
    major changes in working methods or work organisation
    investment plans
    the financial position of the establishment, and
    the financial position of the whole organisation.

Only two of the above issues had been the subject of identical questions in the 1980 survey, and for reasons of economy we simplified the response categories in 1984. Direct comparisons between the two surveys are therefore limited and even where they are possible there are problems of comparability. We concentrate in this analysis on the patterns evident in the 1984 results, only making brief reference to changes from the 1980 pattern where appropriate.

In Table 6.7 we summarise the responses to these questions by giving the proportion of worker representatives and managers who reported that the amount of information given by management was 'a lot'. It is evident from the first three columns that worker representatives are less likely to report receiving a lot of information on every issue than managers are to report that management gives a lot of information. But the pattern with respect to the six specified issues is very similar. *Terms and conditions of employment* and *major changes in working methods or work organisation* are the two issues that are the subject of most communication. *Staffing or manpower plans* is next. The two questions on the financial position of the establishment and of the organisation as a whole were close together and less commonly the subject of a lot of communication. *Investment plans* were least commonly reported as the subject of a lot of communication.

Given that the questions were framed in such a way as to elicit the responses, *a lot of information, a little information* or *no information*, it might be felt that our choice in Table 6.7 of the proportion of respondents reporting *a lot of information* would over-simplify the results. In fact, the inverse correlation between the proportions reporting *a lot* and the proportion reporting *none* was exact for all three types of respondent. Our summary measure is therefore adequate for reporting the patterns of variation, which again should be noted as being very similar for both managers and worker representatives. For this reason we feel it is legitimate to talk about 'the amount of information' as a shorthand for 'the proportion of establishments where respondents reported *a lot of information*'.

One of the basic patterns concerning the amount of information communicated by managements can be deduced from Table 6.7. Establishments with recognised trade unions roughly correspond to the first of the two columns reporting managers' responses, since worker representatives were only interviewed where there were recognised unions and there was little non-response among worker representatives. So it can be seen that managers in establishments with recognised unions reported giving more information on all six topics than the whole sample of managers and therefore substantially more than the subsample of managers in workplaces without recognised unions. Other patterns evident in the reports of managers (but not shown in tabular form) are as follows.

The amount of information on *terms and conditions of employment* was reported as being lowest in the public services, despite the almost universal recognition of trade unions in that sector, but was highest in the nationalised industries where recognition is as common. The lowest amounts were reported from establishments without any trade

Table 6.7 Information given to worker representatives by management, 1984

Percentages

Proportion of respondents reporting 'a lot of information' on:	Manual representatives' accounts	Non-manual representatives' accounts	Managers' accounts[1]	Managers' accounts[2]
Terms and conditions of employment	53	51	72	66
Staffing or manpower plans	32	35	50	40
Major changes in working methods or work organisation	46	55	77	70
Investment plans	10	7	15	12
The financial position of the establishment	21	25	32	30
The financial position of the whole organisation	23	24	34	32
Base: all respondents unless specified otherwise				
Unweighted	*910*	*949*	*1201*	*2019*
Weighted	*554*	*560*	*867*	*2000*

[1] Establishments where a worker representative was interviewed.
[2] All establishments.

union members (58 per cent stated *a lot of information*) and workplaces belonging to partnerships, self-proprietorships and cooperatives (55 per cent). On *staffing and manpower plans* public sector establishments communicated substantially more information than private sector workplaces, but this was not due to, for instance, differences in trade union recognition between the two sectors. However, the amount of information disclosed on manpower changes seemed to have little to do with their recent experience of manpower changes: establishments with shrinking, stable or growing workforces reported similar amounts of information on *staffing and manpower plans*. This was true whether we took changes in workforce size over the previous four years or over the previous twelve months as our measure.

Information on investment plans was more plentiful in the private sector than the public sector and particularly so in private manufacturing. Foreign-owned establishments were noticeably more forthcoming with information about *the financial position of the establishment*, a difference also evident in the 1980 survey.[6] However, it now seems likely that this is not a size effect, as it appeared to be on the basis of the 1980 data, but represents a fairly widespread difference between foreign-owned and indigenous workplaces.

A further notable feature of Table 6.7 is that the biggest difference between managers' and worker representatives' ratings of the amount of information given by management is on the issue of *major changes in working methods or work organisation*. Manual representatives are much less likely to say they receive a lot of information on this issue than managers are to say they give a lot of information. When the comparison is limited to managers where a manual worker representative was interviewed the difference remains very large. Of course, in some of these cases our management respondents may not have been thinking of manual workers in particular when they replied to the question, but this could not account for such a large difference. Manual worker representatives were also much more more likely to say that they received **no** information before such changes were introduced than managers in the same establishments. This adds further weight to the evidence reported in Daniel's companion volume, analysing the survey data on the introduction of new technology.[7] In Chapter 6 of that report, using responses to questions focused on the most recent major change, Daniel notes managements' lack of consultation with employees on major changes affecting manual workers. Using worker representatives' reports from these same questions, it appears nearly a third of manual stewards where a major technical change had taken place in the last three years reported that none of the six specified methods of discussion or consultation with manual workers was used to cover the issue of whether the

Table 6.8 Amount of information communicated to employees in relation to the comparative performance of the workplace (managers' reports), 1984

Percentages

Proportion of managers reporting that 'a lot of information' is given on:	Financial position compared with other plants in the same industry					
	Lots better	A little better	About average	A little below	A lot below	Can't say
Terms and conditions of employment	73	70	61	72	88	74
Staffing or manpower plans	41	33	24	41	47	41
Major changes in working methods or work organisation	76	66	60	70	75	69
Investment plans	21	10	9	20	6	14
The financial position of the establishment	33	25	28	34	46	25
The financial position of the whole organisation	41	28	34	31	45	43
Any of the six issues	88	84	80	81	88	86
Base: industrial and commercial establishments						
Unweighted	245	261	485	53	33	308
Weighted	275	256	534	42	34	232

change should be introduced or to discuss how it should be implemented. If the giving of information is regarded as a minimal first step in the consultation process – although it can, of course, be regarded as of value independent of any consultation process these results are consistent with the evidence reported here about a lack of information given to employees regarding changes in working methods or work organisation.[8]

A general pattern in respect of all of the topics of information was their variation, in industrial and commercial establishments, according to the financial performance of the establishment (as reported by management respondents). Table 6.8 shows the pattern. Most information was disclosed where comparative financial performance was either much better than average or below average. This was a clear and continuous curvilinear relationship with average performers providing the least amount of information generally on our six specified topics. In 1980 the pattern was different. Below average performers then disclosed less information than better performers on *pay and conditions* and on *manpower requirements* while on *the financial performance of the establishment* they were no different. This change in pattern might suggest that poor performing establishments have increased the amount of information they communicate to employees – or of course it may be that poor performers in 1980 were just a different type of establishment than poor performers in 1984.

An interesting feature of the 1980 results was the way in which the amount of information given by management to its employees correlated with the general industrial relations climate.[9] We were struck by how robust this correlation was, given that it existed irrespective of whether we took managers' or worker representatives' assessments of the industrial relations climate of their workplace. But the fact that it varied between information topics suggested that this was not just the 'halo effect' operating. It is therefore of further interest that the same correlation should exist in the 1984 results and that again it should vary by the topic in question.

Taking managers' reports for the present, the industrial relations climate was more favourably assessed when a lot of information was given to employees on *major changes in working methods or work organisation, investment plans* and the two items concerning the financial situation of the workplace and of the organisation as a whole. There was no such clear-cut relationship with information on *terms and conditions of employment* or with *staffing or manpower plans*. A similar pattern emerged when we looked at the result of another question on the general climate of industrial relations at the workplace, this time focusing it on relations with trade unions (where present) rather than with the workforce as a whole. But the relationship was only noticeable in respect of **manual** trade unions and was only apparent for information concerning *major changes in working methods or work organisation* and the two *financial position* items. With respect to relations with non-manual trade unions the correlation between good assessments of their relations with management and large amounts of information being communicated to employees was hardly apparent.

Returning to our earlier question as to whether the channels of communication actually used by management make any difference to the amount of information communicated to employees, the general answer is fairly clear. Establishments where none of the formal channels mentioned in our list was used were much less likely to be ones where managers said they communicated a lot of information to employees. This was also true when we used worker representatives' reports of the amount of information received and of the channels of communication used by management. These are cases where unions are recognised and we have no equivalent information from employees in situations without recognised trade unions. But, relying on managers' reports, the positive correlation between the existence of formal channels of communication and the quantity of information divulged to employees was still very evident when we examined only workplaces **without** recognised unions. In such workplaces, most of which were in the private services sector, the absence of formal channels of communication that we specified in our questions made a vary substantial difference to the amount of information communicated to employees. Of course, management in these workplaces may have adopted a conscious policy not to keep their employees informed on the issues we selected, in which case the lack of formal communication channels is hardly surprising.

It would be of interest to practitioners to be able to discern which of the six channels of communication mentioned in our questions were most effective in communicating with employees, but we cannot detect any clear pattern in the results which indicates this. Given that different sorts of information are likely to be communicated through different channels it would take more complicated and focused questioning than we had room for in our survey. However, the conclusion derived from our rather straightforward questioning, that the absence of formal channels of communication is associated with generally low amounts of information communicated to employees on the six important topics mentioned, is surely of some practical import.

Requests for disclosure of information
In workplaces with recognised trade unions there are provisions within the law for worker representatives to demand the disclosure of

certain types of information from management if it is not made available. In 1980 we found that quite substantial use was being made of these provisions – much more than was indicated by the number of references made to the legal appeal machinery where this right could be enforced.[10] We found that worker representatives were much more likely to report that they had used the statutory provision when there was a full-time shop steward or convenor at the workplace and where there were multiple negotiating groups. And we were struck by the greater use of the provisions by manual representatives where they said they received no information from management about pay and conditions of employment, suggesting that requests for disclosure of information were related to what trade union representatives at the workplace thought they needed to know for collective bargaining.

In the 1984 survey we omitted the question to managers about requests that they had received from worker representatives for disclosure of information because the 1980 results indicated that managers were sometimes unaware that requests were being made with statutory backing. We repeated the question to worker representatives as to whether or not they had made any requests for information under the legal provisions and we added a follow-up question, 'on the last occasion you requested information under the provision did you get the information you wanted?' The overall results of these two questions are shown in Table 6.9, with the 1980 figures for the first question set alongside for comparison.

The comparisons shown in Table 6.9 are not as direct as they might have been because the reference period for the question was altered for the second survey in line with our general preference for keeping the number of reference periods to a minimum and making four years, the interval between surveys, one of the principal reference periods. In 1980 the question had been asked with respect to the previous three years. So to evaluate whether there has been a change in the extent of requests for disclosure of information under the provisions of the Employment Protection Act we have to make a judgement about the effect of the changed reference period. It seems reasonable to assume that requests would be most likely to be recalled, and therefore reported, if they were recent. If this is so, adding a fourth year to the reporting period would add very few cases to the total, not only because of the lack of recall, but also because many of them would be likely to be in establishments where other, more recent, requests would be reported. On these assumptions it seems fair to assume that there may have been some slight reduction in requests from manual worker representatives between the late 1970s and the early 1980s, but little or no change in the case of non-manual worker representatives.

Again, this picture of the use of the disclosure provisions of the Act

Table 6.9   Requests[1] by worker representatives for information from management under the provisions of the Employment Protection Act and managements' response

Column percentages

	Manual worker representative		Non-manual worker representative	
	1980	1984	1980	1984
Request made	18	17	10	13
No request made	81	82	89	86
Not answered	1	1	1	1
Where request made, amount of information received				
All	..[2]	37	..	52[3]
Some	..	39	..	31
None	..	23	..	16
Not answered	..	1	..	2
Base: establishments with recognised trade unions and where worker representatives were interviewed				
Unweighted	*972*	*910*	*922*	*949*
Weighted	*643*	*554*	*585*	*560*

[1] Reference period for question on requests for disclosure was three years in 1980 and four years in 1984.
[2] See Note J.
[3] See Note C.

at workplace level is quite different from the picture of the use of the legal appeal machinery portrayed in the Annual Reports of the Central Arbitration Committee. These indicate a very steep decline in the number of complaints under the disclosure provisions from a peak of 62 complaints in 1978 to only 11 in 1984 with an average of 15 for the four years up to 1984. The Committee itself, commenting upon this decline, remarked, 'the very existence of the decided cases, and of a fall-back complaints mechanism, is likely to have a continuing influence on behaviour – which does not show up in casework'. It felt that 'union perceptions of the "usefulness" of, for example, the financial information likely to be available from companies in, or only just emerging from, a recession' was part of the explanation. It also posited 'an increasing awareness on the part of employers, not only of their obligations under the Act, but also, more generally, of the advantages to their enterprises of a better-informed and therefore more committed workforce.'[11] Our finding that the number of requests at workplace level has shown only a slight decline, if at all, supports at least the first of these suggestions, that in effect unions have learned how to use the provisions of the Act. But our findings do not square very well with the notion that unions have reduced their requests because of recessionary conditions facing employers. Moreover, although the nature of requests may indeed have changed, it is clear that the provisions are still used in a substantial minority of workplaces and that the decline in CAC references cannot be taken as a sound indicator of a decline in their use. Furthermore, the strong connection with plant-level pay bargaining – confirmed by correlating the same questions asked of both sets of worker representatives – indicates the continuing relevance of the provisions in this area of trade union activity.

The very small number of references to the CAC is also interesting in relation to the results of our question on how much of the information sought from management worker representatives actually received, or felt that they had received. Table 6.9 shows that less than a quarter of worker representatives said that they had received none of the information asked for. Nearly a half, taking manual and non-manual representatives together, received all they asked for. These figures suggest considerable realism on the part of union representatives in making requests, although perhaps somewhat less in the case of manual union representatives.

Initiatives by management to increase employee involvement

The last question in our survey interviews which touched upon the subject of consultation and communication was a broad question asking respondents if management had made any change in the last four years with the aim of increasing employees' involvement in the operation of their place of work. Apart from the change from a three-year to a four-year reference period (for reasons mentioned earlier) this question was asked identically in the two surveys and the responses were coded with the same twenty five codes. We summarised the 1980 results by combining the responses into three broad categories: *institutional innovations*, such as a new consultative committee; *other conventional participation initiatives*, such as moves to improve communications, or the introduction of a share ownership scheme; and *other initiatives*, not included in the first two groups, which did not fit into the more commonly held conceptions of 'participation' and 'employee involvement'. The 1980 results showed a very similar pattern, whether we took managers' or worker representatives' reports. We found that institutional innovations were more common in larger establishments and in the nationalised industries, irrespective of size. Managers in small establishments were just as likely to report changes that did not involve the creation of formal consultative machinery as their counterparts in larger workplaces. A rather different picture emerges in the 1984 results, both with respect to the types of innovation and the types of workplace

Table 6.10 Accounts of recent[1] changes made by management with the aim of increasing employee involvement

Percentages

	All establishments 1980	1984	Private manufacturing 1980	1984	Private services 1980	1984	Nationalised industries 1980	1984	Public services 1980	1984
Any initiative to increase involvement	24	35	23	35	24	33	26	37	24	36
New consultative committee	5	3	4	5	7	2	13	6	4	3
New health and safety committee	1	*	*	*	1	–	*	–	2	*
New joint meetings	3	5	4	6	6	4	3	6	4	5
Any structural innovation	9	8	8	11	13	6	16	12	9	8
Improvements to existing committee	*	1	*	1	6	2	*	2	*	1
More two-way communication	5	12	5	15	6	12	2	5	6	11
More information to employees	5	4	6	6	6	4	6	3	2	2
Participation scheme – unspecified	1	1	1	1	3	1	–	1	2	1
Suggestion or share scheme	1	1	2	2	2	1	–	*	1	*
Autonomous working groups	1	1	1	1	1	1		*	1	1
Management for employee participation	1	1	1	*	1	1	–	–	1	1
Any other conventional participation initiative	13	19	11	22	14	20	8	10	12	16
Other – specifically coded	4	5	5	2	4	5	4	4	5	6
Others – not coded elsewhere	*	7	*	4	*	5	–	14	*	9
Base: all establishments										
Unweighted	*2040*	*2019*	*743*	*592*	*587*	*597*	*134*	*196*	*576*	*634*
Weighted	*2000[2]*	*2000*	*503*	*424*	*859*	*843*	*69*	*106*	*567*	*627*

[1] Reference period for questions was previous **three years** in 1980, previous **four years** in 1984.
[2] See Note H.

where they occurred. Table 6.10 gives the overall picture for the main sectors of the economy.

Overall, the table shows that more initiatives were reported in 1984 than in 1980, even if we take the longer reporting period into account. If, on the other hand, we assume that the results will be dominated by more recent events and that developments four years prior to interview will not account for anywhere near a quarter of those reported, then it is evident that managers are reporting a significant increase in initiatives to increase employee involvement. This increase is apparent in each of the four main sectors of the economy shown in Table 6.10. But it is obvious from the detailed descriptions of the initiatives given to interviewers that the increase is not evenly spread, but confined to particular types of initiative.

Our first major subcategory, **structural innovations**, shows no increase overall. Indeed, a slight increase from eight per cent to 11 per cent in manufacturing was offset by a decrease in private services from 13 per cent to six per cent and in the nationalised industries from 16 per cent to 12 per cent. Most of the decrease in these latter sectors was accounted for by a substantial drop in the introduction of new joint consultative committees. Structural innovations, then, were not the type of initiative that made the early 1980s different from the late 1970s.

What stands out clearly as distinguishing the two periods is the very substantial increase in the number of managers reporting that in their workplace there had been an increase in *two-way communication*. In aggregate the proportion rose from five per cent in 1980 to 12 per cent in 1984 and roughly similar increases were shown in all main sectors of the economy. None of the *other conventional participation initiatives* shown separately in Table 6.10 shows any change over the same period, assuming we ignore the change in reporting period. Indeed, the increase in managers saying that two-way communication had been increased at their workplace accounts for the great majority of the increased reporting, between 1980 and 1984, of **any** initiative by management to increase employee involvement. It is also surely of some significance that while there was a substantial increase in those reporting more **two-way** communication there was no increase in those reporting that more information was being given to employees. The change was thus an important qualitative one, entailing more feedback from employees to management, some of this being at face-to-face meetings between managers and employees. But before reading too much into this finding we might reasonably ask whether it is sufficient to rely on managers' accounts of the changes that have occurred. More particularly, even if managers do say that there is more two-way communication between management and the work-

Percentages

Table 6.11 Managers' and worker representatives' accounts of management initiatives within the previous four years to increase employee involvement, 1984

	All managers	Managers where worker rep. interviewed	Manual or non-manual representative	Manual representative	Manager where manual rep. interviewed	Non-manual representative	Manager where non-manual rep. interviewed
Any initiative to increase involvement	35	39	22	18	36	18	42
New consultative committee	3	4	2	2	5	1	5
New health and safety committee	*	*	*	1	*	—	*
New joint meetings	5	5	2	2	5	2	7
Any structural innovation	8	9	4	4	9	3	12
Improvements to existing committee	1	1	*	*	1	*	1
More two-way communication	12	14	8	6	13	7	14
More information to employees	4	5	2	2	5	1	4
Participation scheme – unspecified	1	1	1	*	1	1	2
Suggestion or share scheme	1	1	*	*	1	*	1
Autonomous working groups	1	1	1	1	1	*	1
Management training for employee participation	1	1	*	*	1	*	1
Any other conventional participation initiative	19	22	10	9	19	8	23
Other – specifically coded	5	4	3	2	3	3	4
Others – not coded elsewhere	7	9	6	4	9	5	9
Base: all establishments where respondents at column heads were interviewed							
Unweighted	2019	1201	1201	910	910	949	949
Weighted	2000	867	867	554	554	560	560

force, is this also reported by worker representatives?

Three clear conclusions can be drawn from Table 6.11. The first is that worker representatives are less likely than managers to report that management has taken any initiative on employee involvement in the recent past. The second is that the relative frequency with which they report the various types of initiative is strikingly similar to the pattern of managers' responses. But thirdly, and to give a clear answer to our earlier question, they report an increase in two-way communication as the most common type of initiative, as indeed do managers. In fact, about a third of all types of respondent who reported any type of initiative reported an increase in two-way communication. Thus the qualitative change reported by managers is validated by the representatives of those affected, giving perhaps the clearest possible indication that there has been a change in the **type** of initiative that managements have been taking on employee involvement in the early 1980s as compared with the late 1970s.

A further notable feature of Table 6.10 is the increase in responses that did not fit into the 25 specific categories that we created on the basis of interviewers' records of respondents' answers in 1980. On further examination, some of the 1984 *other answers* could be allocated to some of these specific codes if we were prepared to widen slightly our definition of the category; but this would be to minimise the increase in **variety** shown in the comparisons of the two sets of responses. The 1984 *other answers* do contain a number of mentions of particular initiatives that were numerically insignificant in 1980 – 'quality of working life programmes' is an example – but which would have been put in a separate category if we had coded the 1984 responses without reference to the 1980 coding frame. This adds to the impression that initiatives to increase employee involvement have increased in variety in recent years.[12]

In reporting the patterns of variation in types of employee involvement initiative in the 1980 results we remarked upon the greater propensity of large establishments and nationalised industry plants and offices to introduce structural innovations and for large establishments to introduce any sort of innovation. In the 1984 data the relationships with size are still apparent. However, the differences between nationalised industry establishments and others had disappeared. What emerged from our analysis of the 1984 results in relation to size and ownership was that small firms were considerably less likely to have made employee involvement initiatives than other establishments in the private sector, even when we controlled for size of establishment in the analysis. This was also true when we looked at *increases in two-way communication* as a distinct type of initiative. On the other hand, foreign-owned establishments, again controlling for size, were more likely to have made initiatives.

Notes and references

1. For an introduction to the design and limitations of our panel sample the reader should refer to Chapter 1 and to the section in Chapter 3 which introduces the analysis of the panel data on trade union recognition. As in that analysis, we confine ourselves here to the 181 weighted (211 unweighted) cases where there were no queries about the definition of the establishment for the two sets of interviews.

2. Edwards P (1985) 'Managing Labour Relations through the Recession', *Employee Relations*, vol. 7, no. 2, pp.3-7.

3. McCarthy W E J (1966) *The Role of Shop Stewards in British Industrial Relations*, Royal Commission on Trade Unions and Employers' Associations, Research Paper No. 1, HMSO London; Joyce P and Woods A (1984) 'Joint Consultation in Britain: Towards an Explanation', *Employee Relations*, vol. 6, no. 2, pp. 2-8; MacInnes J (1985) 'Conjuring up Consultation: The Role and Extent of Joint Consultation in Post-war Private Manufacturing', *British Journal of Industrial Relations*, July, pp. 93-113. It might be noted that the title and some of the argument of the last of these references is based upon a misquotation from our report of the 1980 survey. On page 289 of our report we said, 'Overall, *our findings gave the impression* [emphasis added] that there have been substantial developments in Britain on a voluntary basis to promote worker involvement, in the absence of any general legislative framework to promote worker involvement in decision making, such as that which exists in many European countries.' This was selectively misquoted by MacInnes as, 'Daniel and Milward (*sic*) ... conclude that "there have been substantial developments in Britain on a voluntary basis to promote worker involvement in the absence of any legislative framework..."' and cited to support the assertion that 'The renaissance of consultation is said to *prove* [emphasis added] that without legislation industrial democracy in Britain is already developing.'

4. Daniel W W and Millward N (1983) *Workplace Industrial Relations in Britain: The DE/PSI/SSRC Survey*, Heinemann Educational Books, London, p.140.

5. *Ibid.* p.139-40.

6. *Ibid.* p.150.

7. Daniel W W (1986 forthcoming) *Workplace Industrial Relations and Technological Change*.

8. Future analysts of the survey data may wish to note that we have omitted presentation in this chapter of the data from a set of questions about whether consultation took place on the six issues covered by our questions on how much information employees were given by management. These additional questions on whether consultation occurred were inserted at the final stages of questionnaire development and were not piloted. The data from them seem of doubtful value since the replies indicating that no consultation occurred do not distinguish between circumstances where the issue had not arisen (and therefore no consultation was appropriate) and circumstances where the issue had arisen but there had been no consultation.

9. Daniel W W and Millward N (1983) *op. cit.* p.152.

10. *Ibid.* p.153.

11. Central Arbitration Committee (1984) *Annual Report*, p.15.

12. We intend to carry out some further coding of the 1984 *other answers* to this question, without destroying compatibility with the 1980 responses, and will deposit the results at the ESRC Data Archive for release with a new version of the dataset.

7   Industrial Relations Procedures

Since publication of the Donovan Commission's report almost twenty years ago, the development of rules and procedures about employment matters has been widely seen as being central to the promotion of fairness and consistency in the treatment of individuals and in the conduct of industrial relations.[1] The results from our first survey indicated that in 1980 formal procedures for dealing with the recurrent problems of management-employee relationships were widespread among workplaces in Britain. We asked similar and additional questions in the second survey and the results show that formal industrial relations procedures became even more widespread during the period between 1980 and 1984. In this chapter we explore that pattern of growth. For both 1980 and 1984 we look at the sources of variation in the presence of procedures, the importance of procedures in the resolution of disputes and how satisfied respondents were with the way they worked. Throughout the chapter, unless indicated otherwise, the responses of managers are used in the analysis presented.

The extent of the main types of procedure

In the 1980 survey we distinguished three main types of issue for which establishments might have procedures. These were; *issues concerning discipline and dismissal (excluding redundancies); disputes over pay and conditions of employment;* and *individual grievances.* In the 1984 survey we also asked about procedures for dealing with health and safety matters. Given our finding that industrial relations procedures figured so very prominently among the responsibilities of personnel managers in the 1984 survey (see Chapter 2), we would expect these procedures to have become more common among British workplaces, and this was indeed borne out by the data. Leaving aside procedures for health and safety issues, as this question was only asked in our second survey, between 1980 and 1984 the proportion of establishments where any of the other three procedures were reported increased from 85 per cent to 94 per cent, and the proportion with all three increased from just over a half (54 per cent) to two thirds.

It is clear from Table 7.1 that this overall increase is also manifested

Table 7.1 Changes in the extent of the main types of procedure in relation to ownership

Column percentages

Type of procedure	All establishments 1980	All establishments 1984	Public sector 1980	Public sector 1984	Private sector 1980	Private sector 1984
Pay and conditions	56[1]	68	55	74	57	65
Discipline and dismissals	81	90	83	94	81	88
Individual grievances	77	88	83	96	74	84
Health and safety	. .[2]	89	. .	95	. .	85
Any procedure[3]	85	94	87	99	84	91
All procedures[3]	54	66	54	73	55	63
Base: all establishments						
Unweighted	*2040*	*2019*	*710*	*830*	*1330*	*1189*
Weighted	*2000*	*2000*	*637*	*733*	*1363*	*1267*

[1] See Note E.
[2] See Note J.
[3] The 1984 figures exclude the results from the new question on health and safety procedures.

by each of the three types of procedure for which we have comparable data; substantially more managers reported each of them in 1984 than in 1980. The table also shows that, as in 1980, procedures for dealing with discipline and dismissals (excluding redundancies) and those for individual grievances were the most common, being reported in around 90 per cent of cases in 1984, compared with around 80 per cent in 1980. Indeed the 1980 survey showed that these two types of issue were dealt with under a single, general procedure in 51 per cent of establishments which had dismissal and disciplinary procedures. And in 1984 the great majority of workplaces with a procedure for discipline also tended to have one for individual grievances: managers in 85 per cent of cases reported both types of procedure.

   Procedures for health and safety issues were as common as both dismissals and individual grievance procedures in 1984 and in eight out of ten workplaces managers reported the **three** procedures concerning health and safety issues, dismissals and individual grievances.[2] It would seem likely that the extensiveness of both dismissals and health and safety procedures is in part due to the impact of legislation and the accompanying codes of practice in each of those areas.[3] The former emphasises the manner of dismissal for it to be considered 'fair' as well as the reason for it. The latter stresses the requirement for continual monitoring of working practices with regard to health and safety.

In 1984 almost two thirds (64 per cent) of managers reported all **four** types of procedure at their establishment. Procedures for dealing with disputes over pay and conditions were the least common of the four, being reported in about two thirds of establishments in 1984. However, this indicates a substantial increase since 1980 when they were reported in just over half of establishments. It should be emphasised that the questions used in our two surveys focused on collective disputes over pay and conditions, which in part explains the lower incidence of this type of procedure in 1980 and 1984 compared with the other types of procedure. For example, **individual** grievances over pay, which sometimes develop into collective disputes, may well have been conceived as falling within the general procedure for individual grievances. Moreover, as pay disputes most commonly arose in the context of collective bargaining, we would expect them to be more common among workplaces with recognised trade unions. We show later that this was indeed borne out by the data.

Table 7.1 shows that in 1984 each type of procedure was more common among establishments in the public sector than among those in the private sector, the difference in the figures being around ten percentage points, whereas in 1980 procedures for dismissals and for pay issues were as common in either sector. In other words, the bulk of the overall increase in the extent of procedures between 1980 and 1984 occurred in the public sector. However, Table 7.2 shows that the increases within each ownership sector occurred particularly among workplaces employing fewer than 200 people. This is unsurprising, given that those employing 200 or more were approaching saturation point in 1980 (see Table 7.2). The table also shows that in 1984, for establishments with 100 employees or more, the presence of formal procedures covering discipline and dismissals and those covering individual grievances were almost universal regardless of ownership, and even establishments employing between 25 and 49 employees in most cases reported procedures of each of these types in well over nine out of ten public sector workplaces and in around eight out of ten workplaces in the private sector. We can see from Table 7.3 and Table 7.4 that the absence of any recognised trade unions or the absence of any trade union members significantly reduces the likelihood that an establishment has formal procedures of any of the types mentioned. This is particularly the case within the private sector where trade unions are less commonly recognised and where union density is lower. Moreover, both these factors are characteristic of smaller workplaces where, as we have seen, procedures are less common.

The first survey established that small firms (single, independent

Table 7.2 Changes in the extent of the main types of procedure by broad sector in relation to size of establishment

Column percentages

	Number of employees at establishment											
	25–49		50–99		100–199		200–499		500–999		1000+	
	1980	1984	1980	1984	1980	1984	1980	1984	1980	1984	1980	1984
Public sector												
Type of procedure												
Pay and conditions	45[1]	76	61	66	59	69	78	81	77	80	81	93
Discipline and dismissals	76	93	84	92	87	97	96	99	99	100	100	100
Individual grievances	79[2]	96	81	93	89	97	95	98	97	97	99	100
Health and safety	:	94	:	94	:	99	:	99	:	99	:	100
Any procedure[3]	81	99	87	97	94	99	98	100	100	100	100	100
All procedures[3]	44	76	57	63	57	67	77	78	75	80	81	93
Base: all establishments												
Unweighted	*110*	*130*	*121*	*123*	*156*	*156*	*141*	*152*	*86*	*130*	*96*	*139*
Weighted	*299*	*376*	*148*	*156*	*104*	*104*	*60*	*65*	*18*	*20*	*9*	*13*
Private sector												
Type of procedure												
Pay and conditions	50	57	57	73	67	72	79	74	88	87	95	92
Discipline and dismissals	75	82	83	93	87	97	96	95	97	99	98	98
Individual grievances	66	76	78	90	87	97	95	90	98	100	99	98
Health and safety	:	80	:	88	:	91	:	92	:	98	:	97
Any procedure[3]	79	85	86	96	90	99	97	97	98	100	99	99
All procedures[3]	47	54	55	71	65	72	78	71	88	87	95	92
Base: all establishments												
Unweighted	*257*	*223*	*259*	*239*	*243*	*206*	*237*	*210*	*163*	*165*	*171*	*146*
Weighted	*707*	*663*	*358*	*338*	*164*	*156*	*93*	*80*	*25*	*20*	*17*	*10*

Table 7.3 The extent of each type of procedure in relation to union recognition

Column percentages

	None 1980	None 1984	One or more 1980	One or more 1984	Manual and non-manual 1980	Manual and non-manual 1984
Type of procedure						
Pay and conditions	41[1]	50	65	77	69	79
Discipline and dismissals	73	83	86	94	87	95
Individual grievances	64	77	85	94	89	97
Health and safety	. .[2]	79	. .	94	. .	95
Any procedure[3]	77	87	89	97	91	99
All procedures[3]	38	48	63	76	67	78

Base: all establishments with pattern of recognition specified in column heads according to managers

Unweighted	*465*	*426*	*1575*	*1593*	*1077*	*1209*
Weighted	*722*	*673*	*1278*	*1327*	*687*	*819*

Private sector only

	None 1980	None 1984	One or more 1980	One or more 1984	Manual and non-manual 1980	Manual and non-manual 1984
Type of procedure						
Pay and conditions	41	50	73	81	84	89
Discipline and dismissals	72	83	89	94	93	100
Individual grievances	63	77	86	91	94	98
Health and safety	. .	79	. .	91	. .	96
Any procedure[3]	76	86	92	96	96	100
All procedures[3]	38	48	71	79	84	88

Base: establishments with pattern of recognition specified in column heads according to managers

Unweighted	*436*	*420*	*894*	*769*	*548*	*504*
Weighted	*684*	*663*	*678*	*604*	*272*	*240*

[1] See Note E.
[2] See Note J.
[3] The 1984 figures exclude the results from the new question on health and safety procedures.

private sector establishments with between 25 and 49 employees) gave a relatively low figure for the presence of procedures.[4] Managers in these small firms reported discipline and dismissal procedures in 63 per cent of cases and individual grievance procedures in 45 per cent of cases. In 1984, however, the figures were 72 per cent and 57 per cent respectively, reflecting a substantial increase during the intervening period, although these types of procedure were still less common among these small firms than among other establishments. Clearly, this difference in the extent of these two types of procedure suggests

Table 7.4 The extent of each type of procedure in 1984[1] in relation to union membership

Column percentages

	No members	1–24%	25–49%	50–89%	90–99%	100%
		Union density among all workers				
Type of procedure						
Pay and conditions	50[2]	53	70	81	75	82
Discipline and dismissals	80	91	92	95	97	95
Individual grievances	75	84	90	94	97	95
Health and safety	77	89	88	96	95	93
Any of the four procedures	87	98	93	98	100	97
All four procedures	46	50	66	78	70	80
Base: all establishments						
Unweighted	*320*	*122*	*138*	*566*	*277*	*192*
Weighted	*536*	*163*	*176*	*460*	*182*	*215*
Private sector only						
Type of procedure						
Pay and conditions	50	52	71	88	79	90
Discipline and dismissals	80	90	89	97	98	93
Individual grievances	75	82	86	92	99	91
Health and safety	77	88	86	94	95	93
Any of the four procedures	87	98	90	98	100	93
All four procedures	46	48	66	83	74	90
Base: all establishments						
Unweighted	*313*	*114*	*100*	*294*	*130*	*57*
Weighted	*533*	*147*	*115*	*220*	*76*	*52*

[1] Only 1984 data are used as 1980 data on union density are not comparable (see Chapter 3).
[2] See Note E.

that small firms are an exception from the general finding reported above that the two procedures usually appeared together in the same establishment. However, Table 7.3 shows that in establishments with no recognised trade unions, individual grievance procedures were significantly less common than those for discipline and dismissal in both 1980 and 1984. It is to be expected, therefore, that this difference would be most marked in the small firms sector where trade unions are rarely recognised. As recent research indicates, the impact of the unfair dismissal legislation has probably stimulated development of the one type of procedure rather than the other here.[5] However, there was a slight (but not statistically significant) increase in the proportion of small firms reporting all three (comparable) procedures, from 38 per cent to 42 per cent. In 1984 procedures for health and safety issues were almost as common as those for discipline and dismissal, being reported in about two thirds (68 per cent) of these small firms.

We mentioned earlier that procedures for resolving disputes over pay issues were rather less common than the three other types in 1984 and that the results from the two surveys indicated that their extent varied with trade union recognition. Table 7.3 shows that in 1984 77 per cent of establishments with recognised unions had a disputes procedure for pay issues (79 per cent where both manual and non-manual unions were recognised), compared with 65 per cent in 1980 (69 per cent with manual and non-manual recognition). As in 1980, such procedures were slightly more common among private sector workplaces with recognised unions (81 per cent) than among those in the public sector, particularly where workplace-level pay bargaining for either manual or non-manual employees was predominant. In overall terms, since trade union recognition for even a minority of employees existed in about two thirds of establishments in both 1980 (64 per cent) and 1984 (66 per cent), the proportion of **all** establishments which had pay disputes procedures was naturally lower than the proportion with the other types of procedure. However the extent of pay procedures also increased among workplaces where unions were not recognised, from 41 per cent in 1980 to 50 per cent in 1984. As we might expect, and as Table 7.3 confirms, the bulk of the increase here was in the private sector where recognition is much less common than in the public sector. Procedures in these types of workplace were less structured, for example being less likely to be written down, presumably reflecting the ways in which management routinely dealt with informal pressures from the workforce concerning pay issues. In 1980, in both the public and private sectors, over 40 per cent of establishments appeared to have no formal procedure for resolving collective pay issues at establishment level, but the picture in 1984 was rather different, with just a quarter of public sector establishments reporting no procedure and around a third of those in the private sector doing so (see Table 7.1).

The growth of dismissals procedures – analysis of the panel data
We noted earlier that discipline and dismissals procedures had grown in extent from about 80 per cent of workplaces in 1980 to 90 per cent in 1984. This change is of sufficient size to suggest that there would be a predominance of workplaces acquiring this type of procedure in the interval between our two surveys – and possibly very few abandoning them. Our panel data confirm this in a quite unequivocal way. Of the 181 (weighted) cases used in the analysis,[6] only two reported having a dismissals procedure in 1980 but not having one in 1984. No less than 26 reported a procedure in 1984 but the absence of one in 1980. The

remaining 153 cases made no change – and, of course, most of them reported a procedure on both occasions. This picture of very substantial gross change in the direction of adoption of a procedure – coupled with the substantial net change shown by the cross-sectional sample – leaves us in nc doubt about the increased extent of discipline and dismissals procedures.

Characteristics of procedures

In both surveys we asked more detailed questions about two types of procedure: those for discipline and dismissals and those for pay and conditions. We turn now to examine some of the main characteristics of these procedures, as reported by managers, beginning with disciplinary procedures.

The nature of disciplinary procedures

In the great majority (90 per cent) of establishments that had a disciplinary and dismissals procedure in 1984 managers reported that substantially the same procedure applied to all employees covered (93 per cent gave this answer). In other words, 84 per cent of **all** establishments had a uniform disciplinary procedure, compared with 72 per cent in 1980. This suggests that disciplinary procedures have become not only more universal, but also more standardised in their application since 1980, probably under the impact of the unfair dismissals legislation. Of those cases where dismissals procedures were not uniform in 1984, 85 per cent did have uniform procedures for the manual workforce and around two thirds had uniform procedures for the non-manual workforce. Managers in more than half of cases said that a procedure was uniform for all manual workers and that a separate procedure was uniform for all non-manuals. A further 40 per cent said that a procedure was uniform for all manuals but that a separate procedure was non-uniform for different groups of white-collar staff. Technical and professional staff were the most frequently mentioned white-collar groups subject to non-uniform procedures for discipline and dismissal.

The growth of written disciplinary procedures

Without specifying the degree of precision, we also asked whether the discipline and dismissals procedure was set out in a written document. According to managers, disciplinary procedures were written down in 94 per cent of cases in 1984 (89 per cent in 1980). Table 7.5 contains the results. As in 1980 the most common exception was the small firm (25 to 49 employees) but, even so, written disciplinary procedures were reported in 75 per cent of these cases. In 1980 we found that the factors associated with the presence of a procedure, such as union recognition, union membership density, the size of the workplace, and public ownership, were also associated with the likelihood of that procedure being a written one. This was also true in 1984. Taking the sample as a whole, 85 per cent of **all** establishments had a written dismissals procedure in 1984 and they were more common among public sector establishments (94 per cent) than among those in the private sector (80 per cent).

Taking the results from the 1980 survey together with previous relevant surveys, we established in our earlier book that the introduction of written disciplinary procedures appeared to have been most common in the mid-1970s, but that by the late seventies the rate of introduction appeared to have slowed down.[7] In 1980 only 17 per cent of establishments with written disciplinary procedures had introduced them since mid-1977 and only 4 per cent since 1979. (These results have been unaffected by the revised 1980 weighting scheme.) The results from our second survey are clearly consistent with this pattern of a declining rate of introduction as saturation has been approached. Not surprisingly the trend is most marked in the public sector, where written procedures are much older and almost universal (Table 7.5).

In 1980 we also found that in almost all establishments with disciplinary procedures the procedure contained provision for a system of warnings prior to the ultimate sanction of dismissal. In the vast majority of cases this meant a sequence of oral then written warnings,[8] as recommended in the official code of practice.[9] As these systems were so widespread in 1980 we did not ask the question again in 1984. However, there is no reason to expect that they would be any less widespread in 1984, given the overall growth in procedural formality over the period.

For similar reasons we did not ask again about the extent of 'internal' and 'external' procedures. In the earlier book we reported that in the public sector procedures which applied more widely than the individual workplace were almost universal, while in the private sector procedures internal to the workplace were reported in around one quarter of cases. As we might expect, the proportion was even higher among single, independent establishments. In a further quarter of private sector establishments procedures applied at industry level and in the remaining half at enterprise level.[10] Although the growth in the extent of dismissals procedures among small, private sector establishments would suggest that internal procedures were more common in 1984, the parallel growth within the public sector points in the opposite direction, to an expansion of external procedures. It is difficult to say which tendency is dominant, but little change is likely.

Table 7.5 Characteristics of procedures for (a) discipline and dismissals and (b) pay and conditions disputes

Percentages

	All Establishments				Private Sector				Public Sector			
	Discipline and dismissal		Pay and conditions		Discipline and dismissal		Pay and conditions		Discipline and dismissal		Pay and conditions	
	1980	1984	1980	1984	1980	1984	1980	1984	1980	1984	1980	1984
Coverage												
Similar for all workers	88	93	86	89	93	97	88	91	79[1]	87	83	84
Different	9	7	11	11	3	3	8	9	19	13	18	15
Not answered	3	—	3	—	4	—	4	—	1	—	—	—
Set out in a written document	89	94	87	90	85	90	83	87	98	99	98	95
Union representation												
Employees covered also represented by trade unions	65	69	70	74	51	50	58	58	94	99	96	99
Procedure agreed between management and trade unions	59	62	65	70	44	42	52	53	90	94	92	95
Agreed procedure set out in a written document	40	48	61	66	31	34	48	48	59	71	81	92
Third-party intervention												
Provision made	66	74	70	79	58	62	63	69	83	94	85	93
No provision made	29	25	25	21	37	38	32	31	13	6	8	5
No information	4	*	6	1	5	*	5	*	4	1	6	2
In previous year:												
Provision used	12	13	13	17	11	12	12	17	14	14	15	18
Provision not used	85	86	84	82	85	87	84	83	84	85	85	81
No information	3	1	3	*	4	1	4	—	2	1	*	1
Base: establishments with procedure specified at column heads												
Unweighted	1829	1919	1430	1554	1188	1114	949	898	641	805	481	656
Weighted	1628	1808	1127	1361	1100	1117	773	821	528	691	394	541

Agreed procedures

The discussion of the extent and nature of disciplinary procedures so far has covered both those introduced unilaterally by management and those subject to agreement between management and worker representatives, most commonly through trade unions or staff associations. We now turn our attention specifically to the latter type. In 1984, 69 per cent of establishments with dismissals procedures reported that the employees covered by the procedure were also represented by trade unions or staff associations. If we take only these cases, in 1984 managers reported that the dismissals procedure had been agreed with those bodies in 89 per cent of cases (91 per cent in 1980) and the proportion was greater (at 93 per cent) among establishments where both manual and non-manual unions were recognised (96 per cent in 1980). Neither of these differences between 1980 and 1984 is large enough to suggest that there has been any falling off in the degree to which dismissals procedures are agreed with worker representative bodies. It remained true that procedures were more likely to be agreed in establishments with strong trade union organisation, at least as far as membership density is an indicator of union strength. As might be expected, therefore, agreed procedures were much more common among nationalised industries (97 per cent of workplaces in 1984) and public services (94 per cent) than in private manufacturing (83 per cent) and private services (83 per cent). In overall terms this suggests there was little change in either the public or the private sector in the extent of agreed procedures. Taking all establishments with procedures, however, there was a slight increase over the period from 59 per cent to 62 per cent in the extent to which they were agreed (Table 7.5).

As in 1980, in virtually all cases the agreed procedure was set out in a written document (99 per cent in 1984, 97 per cent in 1980) and this was true of both the public and private sectors. However, the increase in the overall extent of dismissals procedures over the period means that the overall extent of 'written and agreed' procedures also increased, from 40 per cent of those with procedures in 1980 to 48 per cent in 1984 (see Table 7.5). This represents an increase from 33 per cent to 43 per cent of **all** establishments. As Table 7.5 shows, in 1984 agreed procedures were much more likely to be written down among workplaces in the public sector (67 per cent of cases) than in the private sector (30 per cent).

In 1980 we also found that three quarters of **jointly signed** disciplinary procedures were agreed and signed at a higher level in the organisation than the individual establishment. This was so in 91 per cent of public sector establishments with jointly signed agreements (96 per cent in the nationalised industries) while in the private sector the figure was just over one half (55 per cent), clearly reflecting the existing patterns of bargaining within the two sectors.[11] The question about the level at which joint procedures were agreed was not repeated in 1984, but we have little reason to doubt that the pattern remained broadly the same.

Outside intervention – provision and use

Procedures at establishment level often contain a provision for referral of a case to a body or person 'external' to the establishment when the issue over dismissal or discipline cannot be resolved locally. Such provisions became more common between 1980 and 1984, being reported in almost three quarters of establishments with procedures in 1984, as against two thirds in 1980. In 1984 these provisions were almost universal in the public sector (94 per cent), showing a substantial increase on the 1980 figure (83 per cent); but they were much less common in the private sector (62 per cent), reflecting only a slight increase over the period (see Table 7.5). Table 7.6 shows that, in both 1980 and 1984, the third party most commonly specified within the procedure was higher-level management within the organisation. But the proportion of establishments reporting this increased very dramatically, from 39 per cent in 1980 to 60 per cent in 1984. Union officials or national union officers were also mentioned much more frequently in 1984 (24 per cent of cases compared with 7 per cent in 1980) and provisions for **joint** intervention by higher management and union officials also increased substantially over the period (see Table 7.6). The Advisory, Conciliation and Arbitration Service (ACAS) was mentioned in 18 per cent of cases in 1984, a substantial decline from the 1980 level (29 per cent), although a small part of this is accounted for by the drop in private sector workplaces between the two surveys. In 1984, private sector workplaces were more than three times as likely to specify ACAS within the procedure than those in the public sector and in over a third of single, independent workplaces in the private sector ACAS was the specified body. In overall terms, the proportion of **all** establishments where ACAS was specified in the procedure for discipline and dismissals declined slightly between 1980 and 1984 from 15 per cent to 12 per cent.

Of those respondents reporting provision for third-party intervention involving ACAS in 1984, over two thirds (68 per cent) said the type of ACAS referral envisaged within the procedure involved **both** conciliation and arbitration. This was particularly so within the private sector. A further 11 per cent reported *conciliation only* provisions and nine per cent said *arbitration only*. These figures indicate a decline since 1980 in the proportion of cases where both

Table 7.6 Provisions for and use of third-party intervention

Column percentages

	Discipline and dismissals		Pay and conditions	
	1980	1984	1980	1984
Person or organisation specified within the procedure				
ACAS	29[1]	18	35	27
Higher-level management	39	60	27	51
Union official	7	24	7	24
Employers' association	8	4	10	8
Joint: higher-level management/ union officials	5	16	5	14
Joint: employers' association/ union officials	6	9	10	11
Arbitrating body (not ACAS)	3	7	5	9
Other answers	5	16	5	13
No information	6	—	5	—
Base: establishments with procedures with third-party provisions				
Unweighted	*1253*	*1496*	*1118*	*1329*
Weighted	*1071*	*1341*	*789*	*1069*
Person or organisation used to settle dispute in previous year				
ACAS	17	11	11	19
Higher-level management	38	52	21	28
Union official	30	22	44	20
Employers' association	6	3	23	7
Joint: higher-level management/ union officials	..[2]	8	..	12
Joint: employers' association/ union officials	..	2	..	10
Arbitrating body (not ACAS)	..	6	..	6
Other answers	14	14	9	11
No information	4	—	6	—
Base: establishments making use of third-party provisions in previous year				
Unweighted	*322*	*457*	*360*	*410*
Weighted	*190*	*227*	*144*	*236*

[1] See Note E
[2] See Note J. This information was coded to the 'Other answers' category as the question was not precoded in 1980.

types of ACAS service were specified in the procedure (from 78 per cent), and a slight increase in those specifiying provisions for either *conciliation only* (nine per cent 1980) or *arbitration only* (seven per cent 1980).[12]

Table 7.7 Use of third-party intervention provisions in dismissals procedures by size of establishment

Percentages

	All establishments		25-49		50-99		100-199		200-499		500-999		1000 +	
	1980	1984	1980	1984	1980	1984	1980	1984	1980	1984	1980	1984	1980	1984
Provision for third-party intervention used last year	12	13	8	9	10	9	17	18	19	27	23	27	28	40
Base: establishments with dismissal and disciplinary procedures														
Unweighted	1829	1919	281	305	320	338	353	352	367	349	243	293	265	282
Weighted	1628[1]	1808	759	897	422	457	233	252	147	140	42	39	26	23
Public sector														
Provision for third-party intervention used last year	14	14	6	9	14	8	22	18	27	33	24	31	35	46
Base: establishments with dismissal and disciplinary procedures														
Unweighted	641	805	86	122	102	113	136	152	136	149	85	130	96	139
Weighted	528	691	229	350	125	143	90	101	57	64	18	20	9	13
Private sector														
Provision for third-party intervention used last year	11	12	9	9	9	9	14	19	13	21	22	24	24	31
Base: establishments with dismissal and disciplinary procedures														
Unweighted	1188	1114	195	183	218	225	217	200	231	200	158	163	169	143
Weighted	1100	1117	530	546	298	314	143	151	89	76	24	20	16	10

Number employed at establishment

[1] See Note H.

There was little change in the proportion of establishments making actual use of these third-party provisions. About one eighth of those with disciplinary procedures reported that an external person or body had been brought in to help settle a disciplinary dispute in the twelve months prior to interview in both 1980 and 1984. Although in 1984 it was still the case that larger establishments were more likely to make use of external bodies, it is clear from Table 7.7 that those employing 200 or more people, particularly within the public sector, made considerably more use of these provisions than they did in 1980. Smaller establishments made about the same amount of use overall, but interestingly, those in the public sector made considerably less (see Table 7.7). In 1984 referrals to outside bodies were more likely the higher the union membership density and in cases where trade unions were recognised. As we might expect, in workplaces where managers reported relations with white-collar trade unions as relatively bad, referrals were much more likely (21 per cent) than those where relations were better (12 per cent). Interestingly, the incidence of referrals was unrelated to the state of relations with blue-collar trade unions (15 per cent in both cases). As we have seen, however, not all procedures contained provisions for external interventions, but this did not mean that establishments without them did not make use of third parties in settling disputes. In fact, about half as many establishments with no formal provisions actually made use of third parties in 1984 (7 per cent) than those which had such provisions (15 per cent). The figures for 1980 were very similar to these. In the first survey we found that where an intervention during the year was reported it was usually a single occurrence, multiple occurrences being common only among large establishments[13] and we have no reason to expect this to have changed during the period between the two surveys.

Managers were asked the identity of the body or person brought in to settle the most recent disciplinary dispute during the twelve months prior to interview and in 1984 the pattern of use of third parties was identical to the pattern of provision (Table 7.6). As in 1980, management at a higher level were most frequently mentioned, but the proportion increased over the period from 38 per cent to 52 per cent of cases. Union officials were second most common (22 per cent) and third most frequently mentioned was ACAS (11 per cent), both of which appear to have declined in importance over the period. Joint interventions by higher-level management and union officials were reported in 8 per cent of cases in 1984 and, although we do not have comparable data for 1980 (see Table 7.6), this probably reflects an increase over the period, given the increase in use of each party separately, together with the more frequent **provision** for such joint

Table 7.8 Degree of satisfaction expressed by worker representatives at working of procedures by broad sector

Percentages[1]

Type of procedure	All establishments		Private manufacturing		Private services		Nationalised industries		Public services	
	1980	1984	1980	1984	1980	1984	1980	1984	1980	1984
Discipline and dismissals										
Very or quite satisfied	87	87	90[2]	95	87	91	76	86	86	83
Not very or not at all satisfied	13	13	13	8	8	12	24	17	13	15
Base: establishments with dismissals procedures where worker representatives from recognised trade unions were interviewed										
Unweighted	1128	1165	457	354	171	173	109	160	391	478
Weighed	775	810	227	161	168	165	56	88	324	396
Pay and conditions										
Very or quite satisfied	83	76	89	83	87	86	81	78	78	68
Not very or not at all satisfied	19	29	19	24	12	16	28	30	21	35
Base: establishments with pay procedures where worker representatives from recognised trade unions were interviewed										
Unweighted	1023	1065	455	346	155	160	94	141	319	418
Weighed	678	716[3]	217	150	147	146	43	67	271	352

[1] The percentages represent those establishments where either the manual or the non-manual worker representative reported satisfaction/dissatisfaction with procedure of type specified.

[2] See Note K.

[3] See Note H.

interventions than previously. In 1980, by contrast, it appeared that union officials were asked to help settle disputes much more commonly than they were mentioned in the formal procedure in this role. Therefore, it would appear that the ways in which the provisions for third-party interventions were **actually** operating in 1980 have in 1984 become incorporated into the procedures themselves.

Disciplinary procedures in use

In addition to the questioning about the extent and characteristics of dismissals procedures we also asked respondents, first, about the extent to which dismissal and disciplinary procedures were adhered to and, secondly, how satisfied they were with the way the procedures worked. In 1980 both managers and worker representatives were asked these questions, but in 1984 we restricted the questioning to worker representatives only. In order to maintain comparability between the results from both surveys, only the responses of worker representatives from recognised trade unions have been used in the analysis which follows: the few cases in 1980 where representatives from **unrecognised** trade unions were interviewed have been excluded.

In general terms it was more likely that disputes over discipline or dismissal actually found their way to the procedure in 1984 than in 1980. In 90 per cent of cases where there were procedures in 1984, manual worker representatives reported that most matters in respect of disputes over discipline and dismissals were dealt with under the procedure laid down (exactly the same proportion of non-manual representatives gave this answer), whereas the 1980 figures were 86 per cent and 82 per cent for manuals and non-manuals respectively.

We also asked our respondents how satisfied they were with the working of the disciplinary procedure at their establishment and, as in 1980, in the great majority of cases (87 per cent) either manual or non-manual representatives said they were 'very satisfied' or 'quite satisfied', while in 13 per cent of cases some form of dissatisfaction was expressed. As Table 7.8 shows there was again some variation by sector. As in 1980, worker representatives at workplaces within private manufacturing were most likely to express satisfaction (95 per cent) and dissatisfaction was expressed most frequently by those in the public sector. However, the high level of dissatisfaction within the nationalised industries in 1980 was no longer apparent in 1984 (see Table 7.8).

Dismissals for reasons other than redundancy

In addition to the series of questions on dismissals **procedures**, we also asked about the establishment's recent **experience** of dismissals.

In 1980 managers in about two fifths (41 per cent) of the surveyed establishments reported that an employee had been dismissed for reasons other than redundancy during the twelve months prior to interview, while in 1984 less than a third of establishments (31 per cent) reported dismissals. Where there had been a dismissal in 1984 it was more likely to be an isolated instance (43 per cent of cases) than was the case in 1980 (35 per cent of cases). The decline in the occurrence of any dismissals was evident in both the public sector (from 24 per cent to 15 per cent of workplaces) and the private sector (from 50 per cent to 40 per cent). It was less marked among manufacturing establishments (down from 55 per cent to 47 per cent) than in the service sector (from 37 per cent to 27 per cent). The proportion of small firms (single, independent workplaces employing between 25 and 49 people) reporting dismissals also declined slightly, from 37 per cent to 32 per cent over the period, and if we take **all establishments** employing between 25 and 49 people the proportion reporting dismissals declined from 32 per cent to 21 per cent over the period. In other words the incidence of reported dismissals among small **firms** in both 1980 and 1984 was above average for all workplaces in this size category and the difference was most marked in 1984. The reporting of substantial numbers of dismissals declined sharply; in just four per cent of establishments were five or more dismissals reported in 1984, compared with 11 per cent in 1980. During both study periods dismissals were much more likely to be reported among private sector establishments, particularly those concerned with manufacturing, but were less common among establishments with trade union recognition.

Although dismissals were less likely to be reported among establishments in the private services sector than in private manufacturing in 1980, their dismissal rate relative to the number of employees at that time was much higher. For every thousand people employed in the private services sector in 1980, 24 were dismissed in the twelve months prior to interview. The corresponding figure for private manufacturing was 14. However, although the incidence of reported dismissals was still lower in private services than in private manufacturing in 1984, their dismissal rates were about the same. Private manufacturing plants dismissed 14 per thousand in both 1980 and 1984, while in private services the figure dropped by over one third from 24 to 15 per thousand. Clearly, the decline[14] in the rate of dismissals within manufacturing during the late 1970s appears to have levelled off during the early 1980s. In fact, the figures show an increase among small manufacturing plants and a decrease or no change among larger ones.

Dismissal rates were still much lower in the public sector in 1984, but they had also declined over the period. The nationalised industries dismissed four per thousand in 1984 (seven in 1980) and the public services dismissed three per thousand (five in 1980). In the sample as a whole, the overall dismissal rate fell from 14 per thousand in 1980 to nine per thousand in 1984, but it was still the case that, although larger establishments reported more dismissals than smaller establishments, their dismissal rate was lower. Establishments with less than 50 employees dismissed 17 employees per thousand in 1984 (25 in 1980), while the corresponding figure for establishments of 1000 or more was three per thousand (four in 1980). Small firms (25-49 employees) dismissed 15 per thousand in 1984, substantially less than in 1980 (39 per thousand) and slightly less than the average for **all establishments** employing between 25 and 49 people.

Among workplaces which used various types of 'non-core' workers (see Chapter 8) in 1984, the dismissal rate was seven per thousand, almost half that for workplaces where such workers were not present (12 per thousand). Part of the explanation for such a relatively low dismissal rate may be that it is precisely the flexibility of labour utilisation provided by the non-core workforce which lessens the requirement for dismissals among core employees.

Table 7.9 Extent of dismissals[1] in 1984 in relation to employees' length of service by broad sector

Column percentages

	All establishments	Private manufacturing	Private services	Nationalised industries	Public services
Length of service of dismissed employees					
Less than one year	56[2]	61	57	37	40
1–2 years	21	20	23	12	20
2–3 years	16	17	17	10	13
3 years or more	41	45	34	67	43
Base: establishments where dismissals were reported in last year					
Unweighted	*624*	*198*	*313*	*27*	*87*
Weighted	*1029*	*384*	*297*	*102*	*246*

[1] Dismissals for reasons other than redundancy.
[2] See Note E.

In our second survey we also asked about the length of service of those employees who had been dismissed during the previous year and Table 7.9 gives the overall results in relation to broad industry and ownership categories. The results indicate that dismissals for reasons other than redundancy among new employees, particularly those with less than twelve months' service were fairly widespread among British workplaces in 1984. Establishments dismissing such short-service employees were more likely to be located in the private sector than the public sector, but regardless of sector it would appear that establishments were less likely to dismiss employees with more than one year, but less than three years' service than those with less than a year or those with more than three years' service. Dismissals of employees with three or more years' service occurred in over 40 per cent of cases where dismissals were reported, and they were particularly common among the nationalised industries (see Table 7.9).

A further aspect of the experience of dismissals we explored was whether they lead on to actions by the employee at industrial tribunals for alledged unfair dismissal or other grounds. In seven per cent of establishments in 1984 management respondents said that, in the previous year, they had received notification that an employee (or ex-employee) had started an official tribunal action against the employer. Such notifications were particularly common in the private manufacturing sector (13 per cent of establishments). In overall terms, however, very few establishments (less than five per cent) reported more than **four** such actions and in three quarters of cases just one action was reported. If we take those workplaces with just one tribunal action, managers in 82 per cent of cases said the action had been on grounds of unfair dismissal, which is broadly in line with the official statistics on unfair dismissal applications.[15]

Procedures for disputes over pay and conditions

Earlier in this chapter we reported the overall findings on the extent of procedures for dealing with disputes over pay and conditions of employment. In general, we noted that these procedures were rather less common than the other types in both 1980 and 1984, although there had been an increase in their overall extent between the two study periods. In the two surveys we asked the same sequence of detailed questions about procedures for pay and conditions that we asked about those for discipline and dismissal and so we now turn to an analysis of some of the characteristics of these procedures and the sources of variation. The analysis is briefer than that given above for dismissals procedures and highlights differences between the two types of procedure. For much of the discussion we shall again be making reference to Table 7.5 which shows the characteristics of both dismissals and pay procedures in relation to ownership, and to Table 7.6 which shows the provisions for, and use of, third-party intervention.

As Table 7.5 shows, whereas in 1980 the same pay and conditions procedure applied to all employees in establishments to about the same extent that dismissals procedures had applied to all, in 1984 dismissals procedures were slightly more likely than pay procedures to apply to all. Within the private sector, in both 1980 and 1984, pay procedures were more likely to be different for different groups than were dismissals procedures, while there was little difference in this respect between the two types of procedure among public sector workplaces in both 1980 and 1984. Regardless of sector, however, pay procedures were almost as likely to be written down as were disciplinary procedures in both study periods and the overall extent to which pay procedures were written down increased slightly (from 87 per cent to 90 per cent of cases) over the period. Taking the sample as a whole, written pay procedures were rather less common than written dismissals procedures in 1984, with 61 per cent of all establishments reporting them (compared with 85 per cent having written dismissals procedures). As with dismissals procedures, however, written pay procedures were more common among workplaces in the public sector (70 per cent of all establishments) than in the private sector (56 per cent) in 1984. In the first survey we found that written pay procedures had existed for longer than those for dismissals. In the three years prior to 1980, for example, six per cent of all establishments had introduced a written pay procedure, while 12 per cent had introduced a written procedure for discipline and dismissals. While the data from our two surveys clearly confirm an overall expansion of procedural formality between 1980 and 1984, the growth in the extent of written **dismissals** procedures (from 89 per cent to 94 per cent of establishments with those procedures) relative to those for pay and conditions (from 87 per cent to 90 per cent) suggests that new written dismissals procedures were still twice as common as new written pay procedures. Clearly, the absence of a legislative catalyst for the development of pay procedures may be part of the explanation here.

In both 1980 and 1984 pay procedures were more likely to be agreed between management and unions than were dismissals procedures. In overall terms 70 per cent of establishments with pay procedures in 1984 said they were agreed with trade unions (65 per cent in 1980). If we take those establishments with recognised unions, however, these 'negotiating procedures' were present in 71 per cent of cases compared with 57 per cent in 1980. As in 1980, in 94 per cent of cases where pay disputes procedures were agreed with trade unions, they were also set out in a written document. In 1980 we found that agreed pay procedures were more likely to be written down in the public than the private sector and this was also true in 1984. Taking all establishments with procedures, written and agreed pay procedures were still more common than written and agreed dismissals procedures and increased from 61 per cent to 66 per cent of cases over the period (see Table

7.5). Taking the sample as a whole, however, written and agreed pay procedures were about as common as written and agreed dismissals procedures in 1984 (just over two fifths of workplaces). This was true in both the public sector, where about two thirds of workplaces had them and in the private sector where just one third of workplaces had them. We found in the first survey that, as with dismissals procedures, the vast majority of agreed pay procedures were agreed above establishment level and in only a minority of cases were written and agreed pay procedures not jointly signed by management and unions.[16]

In 1980 managers reported provisions within pay procedures for third-party intervention in 70 per cent of cases. By 1984 that figure had increased to 79 per cent. As Table 7.5 shows, such provisions were reported less frequently in relation to dismissals procedures in both 1980 and 1984, particularly within the private sector. In the public sector there was little difference in the extent of such provisions between the two types of procedure. As in 1980, however, the third parties most frequently mentioned varied between the two types of procedure. These results are given in Table 7.6. Broadly, provisions for intervention by ACAS and employers' associations were more frequently mentioned in pay procedures than dismissals procedures, while higher-level management featured less often. Union officials were as frequently mentioned for both types of procedure in 1984. Higher-level management probably figured less often because pay procedures tended to be concentrated in establishments with recognised unions and thus pay was more often a negotiated issue than were disciplinary cases. However, it is also interesting to note that between our two study periods the provision for intervention by higher-level management in pay disputes almost **doubled**, regardless of ownership sector. By contrast, provision for intervention by ACAS declined by almost a quarter (from 35 per cent to 27 per cent). Provision for intervention by union officials almost quadrupled over the same period. In overall terms, however, the proportion of **all** establishments where ACAS was specified in a pay procedure remained the same between 1980 and 1984 at 14 per cent, owing to the growth in the overall numbers of establishments with a procedure. As with dismissals procedures, respondents in about two thirds of cases (64 per cent) where intervention provisions involved ACAS said the type of ACAS referral envisaged involved **both** conciliation and arbitration (71 per cent in 1980). Provisions for *arbitration only* were more common for pay procedures (14 per cent) than dismissals procedures (nine per cent), and had increased slightly since 1980 (11 per cent). Provisions for *conciliation only* were equally common for both types of procedure in 1984 (around one tenth of cases), and for pay procedures the same proportion reported this in 1980.

There were changes in the extent to which third-party provisions for pay issues were used between 1980 and 1984. Whereas about the same proportion of establishments reported making use of the referral provisions in pay disputes in 1980 as in disputes over discipline and dismissal (about one eighth), in 1984 external interventions in disputes over pay issues were more common than for cases of dismissal (17 per cent as against 13 per cent). The increase in the use of third-party provisions in pay disputes since 1980 occurred in both public and private sectors (see Table 7.5). In overall terms this reflects an increase in the use of such provisons in pay cases since 1980, while their use in disciplinary cases remained at the same level.

In 1984, as with dismissals procedures, the identity of the person or organisation brought in to settle pay disputes was broadly similar to the pattern of provision (see Table 7.6). By contrast, in 1980 employers' associations and union officials were used much more often, and ACAS was used much less often, than they were specified. ACAS was used much more often to help to resolve pay disputes in 1984 (19 per cent of cases) than they were in 1980 (11 per cent). In 1984 ACAS intervened in pay disputes in almost half (46 per cent) of cases in the private services sector, an increase of over half on the 1980 figure, while interventions in the private manufacturing sector declined by a third (from 12 per cent to eight per cent of cases). Union officials were used half as much in 1984 than in 1980 (down from 44 per cent to 20 per cent of cases) and, while the decline was evident in all sectors, it was less marked in the private manufacturing sector where almost half (47 per cent) of affected workplaces reported them (55 per cent in 1980). Employers' associations were used one third as much in 1984 (7 per cent of cases) than in 1980 (23 per cent) and higher-level management were used slightly more often than previously (up from 21 per cent to 28 per cent).

As in 1980, respondents reported that most disputes about pay and conditions were actually dealt with under the procedure. Manual worker representatives in 90 per cent of cases said this was so (86 per cent in 1980) and exactly the same proportion of non-manual representatives gave this answer. However, within the public sector rather more manual worker representatives said this in 1984 (91 per cent) than in 1980 (82 per cent).

The pattern of evaluation changed substantially over the period, with the proportion of stewards (either manual or non-manual) who said they were 'very satisfied' or 'quite satisfied' declining overall (from 83 per cent to 76 per cent). The decline was particularly marked within the public services sector where representatives in two thirds of workplaces expressed satisfaction in 1984, whereas in 1980 the figure was three quarters (see Table 7.8). We show in Chapter 10 that the bulk of the strike action in 1983/84 was among white-collar workers in the public services sector and was related to pay issues, which suggests that the decline in satisfaction with pay procedures and the willingness to take strike action may have been related.[17] Overall, in 1984 substantially fewer respondents expressed satisfaction with their pay procedure than expressed satisfaction with their dismissals procedure, whereas in 1980 pay procedures were almost as favourably evaluated as dismissals procedures.

Notes and references

1. Royal Commission on Trade Unions and Employers' Associations (1968), *Report*, Cmnd. 3623, HMSO, London, p.45; Advisory, Conciliation and Arbitration Service (ACAS) (1985), *Disciplinary and Other Procedures in Employment: Consultative Document on a Draft Code of Practice*.

2. Rejecting the possibility that respondents were trying to 'please the sponsors' by saying they had procedures.

3. Advisory, Conciliation and Arbitration Service (ACAS) (1977) *Disciplinary Practice and Procedures in Employment*; ACAS (1985) *op. cit.*

4. Daniel W W and Millward N (1983) *Workplace Industrial Relations in Britain: The DE/PSI/SSRC Survey*, Heinemann Educational Books, London, p.161.

5. Evans S, Goodman J and Hargreaves L (1985) *Unfair Dismissal Law and Employment Practice in the 1980s*, Research Paper No. 53, Department of Employment, London.

6. Here again our analysis is restricted to the 181 weighted (211 unweighted) cases where there were no queries about the definition of the establishment for the two sets of interviews. The design and limitations of the panel sample are set out in Chapter 1 and the analysis of the panel data on trade union recognition in Chapter 3 includes some further introductory remarks.

7. Daniel W W and Millward N (1983) *op. cit.* p.163.

8. *Ibid.* p.165.

9. ACAS (1977) *op. cit.*

10. Daniel W W and Millward N (1983) *op. cit.* p.165.

11. *Ibid.* p.167.

12. The comparision is not absolutely strict because in 1980 we asked about '*conciliation/mediation*' whereas in 1984 we asked about '*conciliation only*'.

13. Daniel W W and Millward N (1983) *op. cit.* p.168.

14. Daniel W W and Stilgoe E (1978) *The Impact of Employment Protection Laws*, Policy Studies Institute No. 577, London; Brown W (ed) (1981) *The Changing Contours of British Industrial Relations*, Blackwell, Oxford.

15. Department of Employment (1984) *Employment Gazette*, November, p.488; Department of Employment (1986) *Employment Gazette*, February, p.49.

16. Daniel W W and Millward N (1983) *op. cit.* p.174.

17. However, in Chapter 10 we also show that there was no tendency for establishments with written and agreed procedures for either dismissals or pay issues to be less prone to strike action than those without them.

8 Employment Practices

In this chapter we bring together a variety of information from the 1984 survey on the employment practices of our sample of workplaces. These include the methods by which employees are recruited, the composition and working arrangements of the current workforce and methods of reducing the workforce or its level of input. Our analysis of these data is briefer than for many other topic areas covered by the surveys. There are several reasons for this. To begin with, most of the questions were new in the 1984 survey; as the emphasis of this report has been on change we have much less relevant material in this topic area than in most of the others covered.[1] Secondly, the topic was singled out by the Economic and Social Research Council as one for separately funded further analysis of the 1984 survey data.[2] Thirdly, the new questions in our 1984 survey were of a rather general nature and only begin to capture the variety and complexity of the phenomena; additional, large-scale survey work on the topic is already being planned. Finally, some of the questions on employment practices, those concerning labour flexibility, were only asked of works managers in manufacturing industry as part of the background information on the introduction of change; the analysis of those results may be found in Daniel's companion volume.[3] For these reasons we have confined ourselves in this chapter to a brief presentation of the results – pointing out any associations between employment practices and the industrial relations characteristics of workplaces, this being the aspect of employment practices on which our survey can perhaps make the most distinctive contribution.

Recruitment practices

Our questioning on recruitment practices was divided into two broad sections dealing with the two complementary components of the recruitment process. The first dealt with what we term *external recruitment*, where new employees from **outside** the establishment are taken on for permanent posts. We asked whether any external recruitment had taken place in the last year and, if so, at which skill and occupational levels. As the possibilities for recruitment depend partly on the opportunities employers and potential employees have to make contact with each other, we also asked about the various channels which employers typically used for recruiting workers at particular skill and, occupational levels. The second section of questioning covered *internal recruitment*, that which takes place among the establishment's existing workforce via transfers and promotions. Again, we asked to which level employees had been transferred or promoted but, in addition, we asked whether any formal training was involved in these internal job movements. We now present the results on these two components of the recruitment process, beginning with external recruitment.

External recruitment
Managers in the 1984 survey were asked whether any new employees from outside the establishment had been taken on for permanent posts in the year prior to interview. Taking the sample as a whole, 85 per cent of managers said they had taken on some new employees in the last year. Obviously, this figure may not relate to a net increase in employment because workplaces which recruited labour may also have shed it during the same period. This is borne out by our data – around three quarters of workplaces which reported a decline in the overall size of the workforce in the last year also reported recruitment. But, as we might expect, establishments with expanding workforces were more likely to report that they had taken on additional employees in the last year. Indeed, establishments that were performing better than average on a variety of measures were also more likely to report recruitment. Of those cases where managers assessed the establishment's financial performance as *a lot better than average*, 92 per cent said they had recruited additional labour; this compares with 76 per cent of cases where financial performance was reported as *a lot below average*. Similarly, recruitment was much more likely where output[4] was expanding (being reported in 90 per cent of cases) than where it was either stable (82 per cent) or falling (77 per cent). And the pattern was virtually identical for establishments that were working at *full capacity* (92 per cent) compared with those working *somewhat below capacity* (83 per cent), or *considerably below capacity* (75 per cent).

New employees were more likely to have been taken on the larger the size of either the manual or the non-manual workforce at the establishment. But there was very little variation in relation to industrial sector, although recruitment was particularly common among establishments in the following sectors: engineering, construction, retailing, hotels and catering, and banking. Recruitment was also more frequently reported in workplaces where union membership was either low or absent, where trade unions were not recognised for collective bargaining purposes and where an 'open shop' was in operation. Managers who assessed relations with either their work-force or the recognised trade unions at the establishment as relatively poor were less likely to report that new employees had been taken on in the last year.

Of those managers that said they had recruited new employees, we also asked at which skill or occupational levels the people were taken on. Interviewers presented respondents with a card on which were printed eight categories of employee, ranging from *unskilled manuals* through to *middle and senior management*. Answers were multi-coded. In Table 8.1 we show the proportion of workplaces with existing employees in each specific occupational category where the recruit-ment of additional employees in that category was reported. In general terms the table shows that employers were more likely to recruit externally for the lower levels of each broad occupational grouping. For example, almost half of all workplaces with unskilled manuals recruited additional employees in this category from outside the workplace, while just over a third of all workplaces with skilled manuals reported external recruitment in the skilled manual category. The difference is even more marked between either skilled manuals or clerical employees and the supervisory grades (see Table 8.1). (We have no way of distinguishing supervisors of manual employees from supervisors of non-manual employees in the dataset.) A similar pattern is evident for junior and senior technical or professional staff. This general picture was also evident within each of the four broad industry and ownership sectors (Table 8.1). The exception was among the nationalised industries, where 60 per cent of managers reported recruiting externally for semi-skilled manuals, compared to a third for unskilled manuals and 29 per cent for skilled manuals. Clearly, to the extent that 'internal labour markets' exist, we would expect that establishments would be more likely to recruit from among their **existing** workforce to the higher-level positions in each broad category and we show later that the pattern for internal transfers and promotions confirms this hypothesis.

With the exception of semi-skilled recruitment in the nationalised industries, recruitment of manual employees was more commonly reported at workplaces in the private sector, both manufacturing and services. New clerical and secretarial employees were most likely to have been taken on in the private services sector, but otherwise there was little sectoral variation. External recruitment of either junior or senior technical and professional staff also showed little sectoral variation with the exception of the nationalised industries where it was relatively infrequently reported. However, we show below that **internal** recruitment of these types of employee was more common

Percentages

Table 8.1   Level of jobs filled by external recruitment, 1984

	Unskilled manual	Semi-skilled manual	Skilled manual	Clerical, secretarial, administrative	Supervisors or foremen	Junior technical or professional	Senior technical or professional	Middle or senior management
All establishments	46	42	37	46	15	49	30	21
Base: establishments with any of types of employees specified in column heads								
Unweighted	*1667*	*1347*	*1472*	*1960*	*1611*	*1443*	*1472*	*1906*
Weighted	*1494*	*1117*	*1220*	*1876*	*1298*	*1153*	*1225*	*1794*
Private manufacturing[1]	50	50	45	43	17	48	26	24
Private services	50	40	41	51	12	49	30	19
Nationalised industries	33	60	29	41	8	30	11	20
Public services	42	31	22	42	19	51	33	21

[1] Bases for the subcategories in the variable were calculated in the same way as for the total but have been excluded from the table for presentational reasons.

among the nationalised industries than in other sectors.

In the companion volume to this report, Daniel shows that the use of advanced technology had a significant effect on the **categories** of employee recruited in 1984. Workplaces that used advanced technology affecting manual grades were much more likely to recruit additional employees in the skilled manual and semi-skilled manual categories than those that did not. Similarly, workplaces using computers or word processors were twice as likely as others to have recruited not only clerical, secretarial and administrative staff, but also staff at supervisory, technical, professional and managerial levels.[5]

We asked about the various methods that employers used for finding employees in the year prior to interview. The question was only asked if managers had said they had recruited in each of the four categories of employment shown in Table 8.2. Answers were multi-coded to allow for the fact that employers may use several channels of recruitment. There are a number of striking features about these results. Employers were more likely to use Job Centres, PER, Careers Offices or local employment offices if they were recruiting for jobs lower down the occupational hierarchy. Almost two thirds of those recruiting semi-skilled manual workers in 1984 had used these channels, while just a quarter of those recruiting junior or senior technical and professional staff had done so. Recruitment of the latter category was much more likely to be conducted through the more expensive media of newspaper or journal advertisements, this being reported in two thirds of cases, compared with two fifths of cases of semi-skilled manual recruitment. Personal contacts of existing staff and off-chance enquiries from potential employees were used more frequently for recruitment to lower-level occupations. Among the manual grades this channel was mentioned in two fifths of cases of semi-skilled recruitment, and in a third of cases of skilled recruitment. By contrast, it was used in the recruitment of clerical staff in a quarter of cases and in a fifth of cases of junior or senior technical or professional recruitment. Private employment agencies or recruitment consultants were mentioned more frequently for non-manual jobs than for manual jobs, as was recruitment from another part of the same organisation. Indeed, recruitment at a higher level in the organisation was more likely to be reported in relation to non-manual jobs than to manual jobs (see Table 8.2). Trade union channels were infrequently used to recruit additional employees, being mentioned very rarely in the context of non-manual jobs. They were used in two per cent of cases where there was skilled manual recruitment, and in one per cent of semi-skilled; most of these cases had 100 per cent manual union density or were closed shops.

Table 8.2 Methods used for finding new employees, 1984

Column percentages

Method used	Semi-skilled manual	Skilled manual	Clerical, secretarial, administrative	Junior or senior technical or professional
Recruitment carried out elsewhere in organisation	2[1]	2	8	7
Advertise in newspapers, journals or magazines	40	57	53	67
Personal contacts of existing staff	42	34	24	19
Temporary or casual staff	12	9	15	5
Off-chances enquiries	24	18	15	5
Notify Job Centre, PER, Careers Office or local employment office	64	58	54	24
Contact ex-employees	7	5	5	2
Private employment agency, recruitment consultant	2	3	15	12
Nominations from trade unions	1	2	*	*
Notify head office or other estab. in organisation for internal transfer	13	11	21	26
Other methods	4	6	6	9
YOP or YTS kept on	2	—	3	1
Not answered	*	*	*	3
Base: establishments which recruited any of types of employee at column heads				
Unweighted	647	624	1183	985
Weighted	469	448	862	705

[1] See Note E.

Although we did not ask about channels of recruitment in our 1980 survey, some data on this are available from the Warwick survey[6] of manufacturing establishments with 50 or more full-time employees, conducted in 1977/78. However, the question on recruitment channels in that survey was asked of **all** respondents, irrespective of whether they had any recent experience of recruitment. It was also asked in a general way with no specific time-period given. By contrast our question was only addressed to those managers that had reported recruitment in the relevant category in the year prior to interview. We would expect that the likely effect of the vaguer question in the Warwick survey would be to decrease the proportions slightly for each category of response. The categories of recruitment channels used in the two surveys were also slightly different. However, bearing these points in mind it is possible to compare the findings from the two surveys for the two comparable categories of employee[7] if we take manufacturing establishments with 50 or more full-time employees in the 1984 survey. The results of this analysis are given in Table 8.3. The actual categories used to code responses in the Warwick survey are also given to show the assumptions we have made about the comparability of the two sources.

There are two particularly striking aspects to the table. The first of these is the almost universal decline in the use of each (broadly similar) channel of recruitment between 1978 and 1984. The second is the only exception to this – that the use of informal methods of recruitment for semi-skilled manual employees remained at about the same level over the six-year period. (Sampling error, the difference in the bases for calculating percentages, and the differences in question format across the two surveys mean that we cannot assume that the **increase** shown in the table is a real one. However, we can be more confident that there was no decline over the period.) In 1984, therefore, these informal methods of recruitment were relatively more important than they were in 1978. It seems likely that the tighter labour market in 1977/78 encouraged employers in manufacturing to use a larger number of channels of recruitment at that time, both formal and informal, the average being 3.0 for skilled workers and 2.7 for semi-skilled.[8] In 1984 the figures were 2.1 in both cases.[9] This, together with the increase in the relative importance of informal methods, probably reflects the ease of recruitment in times of higher unemployment.

Internal recruitment

In addition to the questions about recruitment of people from outside the workplace, we also asked about transfers and promotions within the workplace. Taking the 1984 sample as a whole, 53 per cent of managers reported transfers or promotions in the year prior to interview. As we might expect given the foregoing discussion, within the nationalised industries the proportion was much higher than elsewhere, at 69 per cent. As internal labour markets are more likely to develop in larger workplaces, we would expect transfers and promotions to be reported more frequently in larger workplaces, and this was, indeed, borne out by the data. Two fifths of workplaces employing between 25 and 49 people reported transfers or promotions in 1984, compared with 92 per cent of those with 500 or more employees. Obviously, part of this is a size effect: where there are more jobs, there are likely to be more job changes. Internal recruitment was also more likely in cases where managers said the market for their products was dominated by their own organisation. Again, this points to a size effect: workplaces belonging to a monopoly are likely to be larger than average and, therefore, more likely to

Table 8.3   Methods used for finding new employees in manufacturing,[1] 1978 and 1984

Column percentages

Method used	Semi-skilled manual 1978	Semi-skilled manual 1984	Skilled manual 1978	Skilled manual 1984
Recruitment carried out elsewhere in organisation (1984)	..[2]	1	..	3
Advertise in newspaper, journals, magazines (1984); Newspaper advertisements (1978)	69	45	87	57
Personal contacts of existing staff or off-chance enquiries (1984); Applicants just apply or existing employees recommend people (1978)	57	64	54	45
Use temporary or casual staff (1984)	..	16	..	10
Notice boards inside or outside (1978)	36	..	35	..
Notify Job Centre, PER, Careers Office or local employment office (1984); Official employment exchange (1978)	81	68	77	63
Contact ex-employees (1984)	..	10	..	8
Private employment agency, recruitment consultant (1984); commercial employment exchange (1978)	10	1	18	6
Nominations from trade unions (1984); Trade union offices (1978)	9	4	14	4
Notify head office or other estab. in organisation for internal transfer (1984)	..	3	..	3
Radio & TV advertising (1978)	2	..	4	..
Other methods (1978, 1984)	5	3	10	8
YOP or YTS kept on (1984)	..	4	..	..
Not answered (1984)	..	—	..	1

Base: 1978 – establishments with any of the types of employee at column heads;
1984 – establishments which had recruited any of the types of employees at column heads in last year

	Semi-skilled manual 1978	Semi-skilled manual 1984	Skilled manual 1978	Skilled manual 1984
Unweighted	*248*	*..*	*251*	*..*
Weighted	*109*	*..*	*110*	*..*

develop internal labour markets. As with external recruitment, internal job changes were more likely to be reported at workplaces that were working at *full capacity* (59 per cent of cases) than those that were working *somewhat below capacity* (53 per cent) or *considerably below capacity* (41 per cent). Interestingly, internal transfers were more likely at workplaces where managers assessed relations with either the workforce or the recognised trade unions as relatively poor, but this again could be a size effect.

We asked more detailed information about the **levels** of jobs filled by internal transfers or promotions. Table 8.4 shows that recruitment to higher-level jobs within each broad occupational group was more likely to be achieved by internal recruitment than to lower-level jobs. For example, just five per cent of workplaces with unskilled manuals reported internal recruitment of further unskilled manuals in 1984 while around an eighth of workplaces with semi-skilled manuals reported internal recruitment to the semi-skilled category. (A similar proportion of those with skilled manuals reported recruitment at the skilled level.) Moreover, in almost a third of workplaces with supervisors or foremen internal recruitment at that level was reported. Although we have no way of distinguishing supervisors of manual employees from supervisors of non-manual employees in the dataset, the fact that the figure of almost a third is significantly larger than the 12 per cent and 19 per cent for internal recruitment of skilled manuals and clerical employees respectively is of particular interest. There was just a slight difference in the internal recruitment of senior from junior technical or professional employees. Moves to the senior level were reported in 20 per cent of cases, moves to the junior level in 18 per cent of cases. We noted earlier, however, that external recruitment at the junior level was much more likely than at the senior level. Internal recruitment of managers at middle or senior level was reported in 17 per cent of cases.

In cases where managers reported transfers or promotions, we also asked whether the moves had involved any formal training of the staff concerned. Managers in 52 per cent of cases reported formal training of staff and there was little sectoral variation in this respect. As we would expect, however, formal training of staff on transfer or promotion was more likely to be reported in larger workplaces. It was also more likely in cases where output was reported to be rising (59 per cent of cases) than where it was either stable (46 per cent) or falling (39 per cent).

It is often argued that the provision of formal training is an 'adjustment cost' to be added to the normal costs an employer must bear when recruiting labour.[10] We might expect, therefore, that in cases where labour costs form a substantial proportion of total costs

Table 8.4 Level of jobs filled by internal transfers or promotions, 1984

Percentages

	Unskilled manual	Semi-skilled manual	Skilled manual	Clerical, secretarial, administrative	Supervisors or foremen	Junior technical or professional	Senior technical or professional	Middle or senior management
All establishments	5	14	12	19	31	18	20	17
Base: establishments with any of types of employees specified in column heads								
Unweighted	*1667*	*1347*	*1472*	*1960*	*1611*	*1443*	*1472*	*1906*
Weighted	*1494*	*1117*	*1220*	*1876*	*1298*	*1153*	*1225*	*1794*
Private manufacturing[1]	6	23	13	12	35	20	13	18
Private services	5	10	11	20	35	20	20	14
Nationalised industries	7	20	29	26	30	32	30	33
Public services	4	7	10	20	22	14	25	20

[1] Bases for the subcategories in the variable were calculated in the same way as for the total but have been excluded from the table for presentational reasons.

the additional costs of providing formal training for employees who transfer to another job would be considerable and less likely to be incurred. When we looked at the occurrence of formal training for internal job moves in relation to the workplace's labour cost ratio, we found that such training was more likely to be reported where labour costs formed a smaller proportion of total costs. In cases where labour costs formed up to 24 per cent of total costs, 60 per cent of managers reported training for internal transfers. That figure dropped to 55 per cent of those with a 25 to 49 per cent labour cost ratio and was down to 43 per cent where the labour cost ratio was 50 per cent or more.

Table 8.5 shows that formal training was much less likely to be provided for employees making internal moves to both senior technical or professional jobs and middle or senior management level, than for job moves to other levels. Formal training was mentioned in the majority of cases for moves to each of the manual grades and for moves to supervisory level (around three fifths of cases). Similarly, in 62 per cent of cases transfers to junior technical or professional level had involved formal training. The figure for the clerical, secretarial and administrative grades was just over half. The occurrence of formal training for transfers to semi-skilled manual grades was particularly common in the nationalised industries and in the private services sector. For moves to skilled manual jobs, formal training was more likely in the private manufacturing sector and in the nationalised industries than in the non-manufacturing sector. As far as training for moves to the clerical, secretarial and administrative grades was concerned, it was least likely to be reported in the nationalised industries than elsewhere. Transfers to supervisory level were more likely to involve training in non-manufacturing workplaces, public sector or private sector. For job moves to the technical or professional grades, particularly at the junior level, formal training was more common in the private sector, manufacturing or services. And it was in a minority of cases that transfers to jobs at middle or senior management level involved any formal training. This was so in all sectors of the economy, but was particularly so in the nationalised industries (Table 8.5).

Workforce composition
The bulk of the detailed questioning concerning the composition of the workforce at our sample of establishments was contained in the *Basic Workforce Data Sheet (BWDS)*, a self-completion questionnaire sent to managers several days before the main management interview. A broadly similar questionnaire was used in both our surveys. In the 1984 survey, however, we also included some additional questions on workforce composition in the *employment practices* section of the

Table 8.5 Level of jobs filled by internal transfers or promotions for which formal training was given, 1984

Percentages

	Unskilled manual	Semi-skilled manual	Skilled manual	Clerical, secretarial, administrative	Supervisors or foremen	Junior technical or professional	Senior technical or professional	Middle or senior management
All establishments	59	58	59	52	58	62	40	41
Base: establishments reporting transfers to grades specified in column heads								
Unweighted	*182*	*351*	*332*	*669*	*720*	*468*	*521*	*655*
Weighted	*70*	*154*	*149*	*347*	*406*	*208*	*250*	*311*
Private manufacturing[1]	§	54	76	57	54	79	65	47
Private services	§	61	53	49	62	62	40	40
Nationalised industries	§	80	61	35	48	40	36	33
Public services	§	50	45	56	58	54	34	40

[1] Bases for the subcategories in the variable were calculated in the same way as for the total but have been excluded from the table for presentational reasons.

interview. The first of these concerned changes in the proportion of part-time employees in the year prior to interview; the second was about the use of various types of non-core employee. Most of the *BWDS* data have been used in summary form in previous chapters where we have related industrial relations characteristics to broad categories of workforce composition (for example, three broad bands of the proportion of part-time workers at the establishment).[11] However, given that the prime source of employment growth in the near future is expected to come from part-time jobs,[12] we begin this section by focusing on recent developments in part-time working using the 1984 questions on changes from mid-1983 to mid-1984, commenting only briefly on the changes between 1980 and 1984. In particular we look at these new questions in relation to industrial relations variables, the area where our survey can make its most distinctive contribution. This will provide a pointer to likely developments on the industrial relations front in relation to the recent trend towards part-time employment. We then go on to present the results on the extent of non-core employment, based mainly on the 1984 survey.

Recent changes in the extent of part-time working

As in 1980, we defined *part-time* employees as employees with a contract of employment to work fewer than 30 hours per week.[13] In overall terms, 16 per cent of the total workforce in the 1984 sample consisted of part-time employees (either manual or non-manual). This reflects a small but significant increase since 1980 when the proportion was almost 14 per cent. The 1984 survey showed that part-time employment was concentrated in non-manufacturing and in the public sector of the economy, as it had been in 1980. Indeed, as a proportion of total employment within the non-manufacturing sector, part-time employment increased between 1980 and 1984 from 18 per cent to 22 per cent. By contrast, a smaller proportion of the workforce in the manufacturing sector consisted of part-time employees in 1984 than in 1980. The proportion dropped from seven per cent to five per cent over the four-year period.

Before presenting the analysis of recent changes in part-time working between mid-1983 and mid-1984, it is appropriate to sketch briefly the general picture of part-time working in 1984. A fifth of the total manual workforce and 13 per cent of the total non-manual workforce in our sample of workplaces consisted of part-time workers in 1984. Within non-manufacturing employment, the distribution of non-manual part-time workers was fairly evenly divided between the public sector (15 per cent of total employment) and the private sector (17 per cent). However, manual part-time workers in non-

Table 8.6 Change in proportion of part-time workers in last year by broad sector, 1984

Column percentages

	All establishments		Private manufacturing		Private services		Nationalised industries		Public services	
	Manual	Non-manual	Manual	Non-manual	Manual	Non-manual	Manual	Non-manual	Manual	Non-manual
Change in proportion of part-time workers in last year										
Much higher	1[1]	2	2	1	1	2	*	*	1	1
A bit higher	8	10	6	5	9	9	6	28	8	12
Same	81	79	78	86	82	79	85	67	81	76
A bit lower	7	8	11	6	4	8	8	4	8	8
Much lower	2	1	3	1	1	—	*	1	1	1
Base: establishments with manual or non-manual part-time workers respectively										
Unweighted	1333	1347	387	363	354	417	107	77	485	490
Weighted	1249	1256	254	249	463	543	59	27	473	437

[1] See Note C.

manufacturing employment were particularly common in the public sector. Two fifths of the manual workforce in the public services sector consisted of part-time workers in 1984, compared with just over a quarter in the private services sector. Within production industries generally, part-time workers (either manual or non-manual) formed a larger proportion of the workforce in the private sector than the public sector. But the proportions were much smaller than in non-manufacturing: only six per cent of the total workforce in the private manufacturing sector and three per cent of the total workforce in the nationalised industries consisted of part-time employees.[14]

The questions on changes in the use of part-time workers in the year prior to interview were asked in relation to manual and non-manual workers separately. Table 8.6 gives the overall results in relation to the four broad industry and ownership categories. Although the great majority of workplaces which had part-time workers in 1984 had about the same proportion as a year prior to interview, there was also a fairly mixed pattern of change. We describe the results on changes in part-time working among **manual** employees first of all.

Overall, in nine per cent of workplaces an **increase** in the proportion of manual part-timers was reported, but a further nine per cent reported a **decrease** over the period. Increases in the proportion of manual part-time workers were more likely to be reported in the private services sector than elsewhere (10 per cent of cases). Decreases were more likely among private manufacturing plants (14 per cent). (Changes in the nationalised industries and public services counterbalanced each other.) There was no relationship between the size of the establishment and changes in the proportion of the manual workforce that was working part-time, although those employing 2000 or more people, particularly those in the public services sector, were much more likely to report increases (27 per cent of cases) than decreases (13 per cent) in the year prior to interview.

We also looked at changes in part-time working in relation to trade union recognition, trade union membership and the closed shop. This analysis produced no clear pattern and we concluded that neither increases nor decreases in the use of manual part-timers among those that had them in 1984 were related to the level of trade union organisation, in so far as the above-mentioned categories provide an index of it.

Changes in the proportion of **non-manual** part-time workers were more pronounced, in that increases were more frequently reported (12 per cent of cases) than were decreases (nine per cent). Among the nationalised industries 28 per cent of workplaces with part-time non-manuals in 1984 reported increases (five per cent reported

Table 8.7   Proportion of establishments using non-core workers by broad sector, 1984

	All establishments	Private manufacturing	Private services	Nationalised industries	Public services
					Percentages
Any non-core workers used	45	52	43	22	47
Types of non-core workers used					
Short, fixed-term contract	19[1]	11	11	13	39
Temps	18	22	23	10	9
Freelancers	14	20	18	2	6
Homeworkers, outworkers	4	12	3	*	*
					Numbers
Numbers of non-core workers used					
Short, fixed-term contract	174,000	23,000	43,000	5,000	102,000
Temps	161,000	51,000	75,000	4,000	32,000
Freelancers	208,000	31,000	108,000	—	69,000
Homeworkers, outworkers	23,000	17,000	7,000	—	—
Base: all establishments					
Unweighted	2019	595	597	196	634
Weighted	2000	424	843	106	627

[1] See Note F.

decreases). Non-manufacturing establishments in both the public sector and the private sector were more likely to report increases than decreases over the period, but there was little overall change within the private manufacturing sector. As with manuals, there was no overall relationship to establishment size but, again, those employing 2000 or more people were much more likely to report increases (27 per cent) than decreases (four per cent) in the year prior to interview. Again, this was particularly the case in the public services sector. Further analysis of the material from the *Basic Workforce Data Sheet* from both surveys may well show that the growth in part-time employment amongst these largest workplaces in the public services sector accounts for much of the net increase in part-time employment between 1980 and 1984. From the results presented here any more recent growth does not appear to be widespread.

In contrast to the picture for manuals, increases in the proportion of non-manual part-timers were more likely to be reported where non-manual trade unions were recognised. Increases were also more likely where union membership among non-manual workers was high, but less than comprehensive. This clearly reflects the concentration of non-manual unionism in the public sector.

Not all workplaces were using part-time workers in 1984 and we were interested to see whether those that were not using them had used them in the recent past. For those **without** any part-timers at the time of our survey, therefore, we asked whether they had had any in the year previously and, if so, how many. In the great majority of cases (84 per cent manual, 87 per cent non-manual) those without part-timers in 1984 did **not** have them in the year previously. Of those cases where managers said they **did** have part-timers in the year previously, less than five were typically reported in each case (manual or non-manual).

The extent of non-core employment

We now turn to the results on the use made of various types of 'non-core' workers among our sample of workplaces. In 1984 managers were asked whether various types of non-core workers had been used in the year prior to interview. Some questions in this area were also asked in 1980, but differences in question wording and particularly in the reference periods in the two surveys mean that in most cases the results are not comparable. We therefore concentrate on the 1984 results and make reference to 1980 data in only those cases where reasonable comparisons can be made. The categories of employees we refer to as *non-core workers* were those working short, fixed-term contracts, temporary workers from private employment agencies, freelancers and homeworkers or outworkers.[15] Table 8.7

shows that 45 per cent of all establishments had made use of one or more of these categories of non-core worker in the year prior to interview. They were more commonly used in the private sector than the public sector. Over half of private manufacturing plants reported them and 43 per cent of workplaces in the private services sector did so. Almost a half of workplaces in the public services sector reported non-core workers, but the nationalised industries made least use of them (22 per cent of cases).

There was a marked relationship between the use of non-core workers and capacity utilisation. Of those establishments working at *full capacity* in 1984, 46 per cent had used or were using at least one of the four types of non-core employee that we asked about. This compares with 44 per cent of those working *somewhat below capacity* and 36 per cent of those working *considerably below capacity*. The relationship adds some weight to the view that non-core or 'peripheral' workers are, perhaps increasingly, being used by employers to make a closer connection between output and employment.[16]

The concentration of the non-core workforce in establishments with a relatively low level of trade union organisation is evident from our survey. In 51 per cent of workplaces where trade unions were not recognised for collective bargaining, managers reported the use of non-core workers in the year prior to interview. Among those that did recognise trade unions the figure was 42 per cent. There was also a striking, linear relationship with the level of trade union membership. This ranged from 51 per cent of workplaces where less than a quarter of the workforce were union members, down to 25 per cent of workplaces with comprehensive union membership.

Employees on a *short, fixed-term contract* were the one category where the questions in the two surveys were directly comparable. These employees were reported in 19 per cent of workplaces in both surveys. As in 1980, they were much more common in the public services sector than elsewhere, being reported in 39 per cent of cases (40 per cent 1980), and in larger establishments than in smaller ones. In both surveys a follow-up question asked for the number of such workers currently employed: less than five employees of this type were reported in the great majority of cases. The numeric results can be grossed up to give a national estimate of the total number of employees of this type being used by workplaces employing 25 or more people. As the second half of Table 8.7 shows, that figure was in the order of 174,000 in 1984. As we might expect from the foregoing analysis and as the table shows, the majority of these employees were being used by establishments in the public services sector. Nearly half of them were employed in the education sector.[17]

Employees working on a *temporary assignment from a private employment agency* were reported in 18 per cent of workplaces in 1984. As Table 8.7 shows, they were concentrated in the private sector, being reported in over a fifth of workplaces in both the private manufacturing and the private services sectors. Around a tenth of workplaces in the public sector used them. As we might expect, 'temps' were more frequently reported in larger workplaces. We estimate that around 161,000 employees working on a temporary assignment from a private employment agency were used by establishments employing 25 or more employees between mid-1983 and mid-1984. The concentration of these employees[18] in the private sector is evident from Table 8.7.

The third type of non-core worker we asked about was those working on a *freelance* basis. Again, strictly speaking, there was a change to the wording of the question, but its effect, if any, would probably be to understate the use of freelance workers in 1980 compared to 1984.[19] Between 1980 and 1984 the proportion of managers who said they had used the services of freelancers in the year prior to interview declined from 22 per cent to 14 per cent. As in 1980, the use of freelancers was much more common in the private sector than the public sector. Around a fifth of workplaces in both the private manufacturing and the private services sectors used freelancers in 1983/84. This represents a decline since 1980, particularly in the private manufacturing sector from 30 per cent to 20 per cent of plants. There was also a substantial decline in the use of freelancers in the nationalised industries from 13 per cent to just two per cent of workplaces between 1980 and 1984. In the public services sector the proportion of workplaces using freelancers declined from 11 per cent to six per cent over the four-year period. In both years there was a greater tendency to use freelancers in larger workplaces. In the year up to mid-1984, just over 200,000 employees working on a freelance basis were used by establishments employing 25 or more people. (This includes the small number of cases where the respondent could not distinguish between freelancers and outworkers. Over half of the total were in the private services sector (see Table 8.7)).

In 1984 we also asked managers whether they had used any *outworkers* or *homeworkers* in the year prior to interview. In overall terms the use of this type of worker was reported in four per cent of workplaces in 1984. (The proportion of establishments where the respondent made no distinction between freelancers and outworkers was less than half of one per cent.) As we might expect, establishments using outworkers were predominantly in the private manufacturing sector, where they were reported in 12 per cent of cases. Taking workplaces within that sector only, the use of outworkers or homeworkers was independent of the size of the establishment. We estimate that the number of outworkers used by establishments employing 25 or more people between 1983 and 1984 was 23,000. This represents a substantial decline since 1980.[20] As in 1980, however, the great majority of these workers were used by private manufacturing plants, the rest by workplaces in the private services sector. Some of the difference between 1979/80 and 1983/84 could be a result of the change in question format, but a real decline in numbers seems likely in view of the contraction in manufacturing, where outworkers are mostly used. Of course, their employment by smaller establishments (less than 25 employees) and individual entrepreneurs may have changed in a different direction, but such employers are not covered by our survey series.

Working practices

Shiftworking

In both surveys we asked whether there was any shiftworking at the establishment and, if so, which system or systems of shiftwork were in operation. In the first survey we also asked how many employees worked under each shift system, taking full-time and part-time workers separately, but in 1984 we asked only about the types of shift system being worked, irrespective of either the status or the number of employees working under them.

The results show no change in the proportion of establishments reporting shiftworking between 1980 and 1984. In both surveys 37 per cent of managers gave this answer. It was still the case that shiftwork was much more common the larger the establishment,[21] in both surveys around a third of workplaces employing between 25 and 49 people reported shiftworking, compared to more than nine out of ten employing 1000 or more.

Despite the lack of overall change in the extent of shiftworking, there were changes in certain sectors. In broad terms shiftworking was more common among the nationalised industries than previously, being reported in almost two thirds of cases in 1984, compared to just over half in 1980. There was a slight increase among private manufacturing plants, from 37 per cent to 41 per cent of cases, but no detectable change within private services (around 30 per cent). Shiftworking in public service workplaces declined slightly over the period, from 45 per cent to 41 per cent of cases.

In 1980, shiftworking was most common in the medical services sector. This was also true in 1984, being reported in almost nine out of ten cases. Elsewhere in the service sector, as in 1980, shiftworking was reported in the majority of cases within the following sub-sectors: hotels, catering and repairs; transport and communication; and other

services. There were substantial increases in the extent of shiftworking in the *postal services and telecommunications*[22] sector (from 48 to 67
per cent) and in the *energy and water supply industries* (from 48 to 62
per cent) over the four-year period.

There was a substantial increase in reported shiftworking in vehicle
manufacturing, from 42 per cent to 65 per cent of cases, but a decline,
from around half to a third of cases, within electrical and instrument
engineering. However, a majority of workplaces in the following
sub-sectors of manufacturing industry reported shiftworking in both
1980 and 1984: chemicals; textiles; food, drink and tobacco; and
metals and mineral products.

In 1980 there was little variation in the incidence of shiftworking in
relation to the comparative financial performance of the establishment. In 1984, however, workplaces with below average financial
performance were more likely to report shiftworking. Obviously, it is
difficult to suggest the direction of causality here. The incidence of
shiftworking was also associated with product specialisation. Workplaces where a single product was manufactured in 1984 were more
likely to report shiftworking (41 per cent of cases) than those where
one main product (35 per cent) or multiple products (28 per cent)
were manufactured.

In both our surveys, and as we might expect, shiftworking was
more commonly reported where trade unions were recognised. As in
1980, this was so in 40 per cent of cases where trade unions were
recognised in 1984 compared to 30 per cent of cases where they were
not recognised (31 per cent in 1980). Where both manual and
non-manual trade unions were recognised the proportion reporting
shiftworking in both 1980 and 1984 increased to a half. Indeed, this
relationship still holds if we take only workplaces in the private sector
in both surveys, although the percentages are one or two points lower.
Given the finding in relation to establishment size, we would expect
that shiftworking would be more common where trade union
membership was high. This was borne out by the 1984 data for both
manual and non-manual workers.[23] In 1984 we found that in cases
where relations between management and recognised unions were
relatively poor, some form of shift system was more likely to be in
operation.

We now turn, briefly, to the types of shift system in operation,
bearing in mind that our respondents may have reported more than
one type of system being worked at their establishment. As the
questions were substantially different in the two surveys we report
only the 1984 results. The most common type of shift system worked
in 1984 was the *double day-shift*. Managers in over a third of cases
overall gave this answer and over half in private manufacturing did so.

Three or four shift continuous working was reported in around a quarter of cases although, as might be expected, this system was relatively uncommon in private services. A permanent night shift was reported in a quarter of cases, but this was relatively uncommon in the nationalised industries.

Overtime

In the 1984 survey we included a question concerning changes in the balance of paid overtime[24] working in the year prior to interview where there were categories of workers eligible for it. The question asked whether the amount of paid overtime worked was more, the same or less than in the year previously. In the majority of cases (59 per cent) the amount of overtime worked was the same as a year prior to interview. However, in 18 per cent of cases it had increased and in 15 per cent it had decreased. In five per cent of the sample no paid overtime was worked; as we might expect, these cases were concentrated in the non-manufacturing sector of the economy, particularly in the business services sector and in the hotel, catering and repairs sector. Increases in overtime were more likely to be reported where the proportion of either female or part-time employees was low. Where non-core workers were present at the establishment increases in overtime working were also more frequently reported. Interestingly, managers in workplaces where union membership was low or where trade unions were not recognised were also more likely to report increases. There was no relationship to the size of the establishment, but increases were more likely at establishments manufacturing multiple products (34 per cent) than at those making one main product (20 per cent) or just a single product (15 per cent). The same was also true in cases where output was rising (24 per cent) than where it was either stable (10 per cent) or falling (10 per cent). And a similar pattern was evident in relation to capacity utilisation. In 22 per cent of cases where the establishment was working at *full capacity* increases in overtime working were reported. This compares with 18 per cent of those working *somewhat below capacity* and 16 per cent of those working *considerably below capacity*. Clearly, as these performance measures relate to the same time period as the increases in overtime working, the case for inferring a causal connection between them is strong.

Overtime working is traditionally a feature of manufacturing industry. In 1984 two per cent of manufacturing plants reported **no** paid overtime, compared to five per cent of workplaces in the service sector. From this we might expect that overtime working would be more likely to have increased in the manufacturing sector, and this was, indeed, borne out by the data. Managers in over a third of workplaces in manufacturing reported an increase in overtime, compared to 13 per cent in services. The increase was most marked in the engineering industry. Managers in around half of plants in both vehicle manufacture and electrical and instrument engineering reported an increase in overtime working in the year prior to interview and two fifths of managers in the metal goods sector did so. Overtime working also increased in around a third of workplaces in both metals and mineral products and chemicals and manufactured fibres, but a quarter of workplaces in each of these sectors reported a **decrease** in the year prior to interview. Among the nationalised industries, managers in two fifths of cases reported a decrease in overtime working and a further half said it had remained at the same level.

In overall terms two thirds of workplaces in the service sector worked the same amount of overtime as they did a year earlier. Well over a third of workplaces in both the *energy and water supply industries* and the *posts and telecommunications* sector reported a decrease. The increases were most marked in wholesale distribution (20 per cent of workplaces) and in the banking sector (20 per cent). There were also substantial increases in the business services sector (18 per cent of cases), although that sector is characterised by a relative **lack** of paid overtime, and in transport (17 per cent).

Reductions in the workforce
In this final section of the chapter we present the results from our surveys on workforce reductions. Again much of the material presented relates to the 1984 survey, but we do have a limited amount of data that is comparable from 1980. The questioning was divided into two sections. First, we asked whether there had been any reductions in a section or sections of the workforce in the year prior to interview. The questioning also covered the main reasons for the reductions and the methods by which they were achieved. Where compulsory redundancies were used we asked a further question about the basis of selection. Finally, managers were asked about the locus of decision-making about both the workforce reductions themselves and the methods by which they were achieved: whether decisions were taken at the workplace or at a higher level in the organisation. The second broad area of questioning covered more temporary reductions in manpower, by various methods of short-time working. Again we asked about the main reasons for reducing the level of input from the workforce in this way. Finally, managers were asked the length of the longest spell of short-time working and the proportion of the total workforce that was involved. We begin by briefly outlining these results on the extent of short-time working. Workforce reductions are covered in the subsequent section.

The extent of short-time working

In 1984 seven per cent of establishments were affected by short-time working – about the same proportion as were affected in 1980 (eight per cent). And as in 1980, the bulk of short-time working occurred in the private manufacturing sector, although there was a slight decline over the period (from 18 to 15 per cent). In the other three broad sectors of the economy around a twentieth of establishments were affected in both 1980 and 1984. In the great majority of cases in private manufacturing, the main reason for short-time working in 1984 (and in 1980) was *lack of demand* for the establishment's products; when we looked at the performance data from our 1984 survey we found a similar pattern. Establishments where either output or capacity utilisation was below average were more likely to have resorted to short-time working arrangements in the year prior to interview. But there was no relationship between the level of trade union organisation, as measured by either recognition or density, and short-time working in 1984.

Taking those workplaces in private manufacturing where short-time working was reported in 1984, the arrangement was still in operation at the time of interview in about a fifth of cases. A further third of managers said that the longest spell of short-time working had been up to a month and 38 per cent said it had lasted longer than a month. On average, two thirds of the workforce had been affected by short-time working in the workplaces where it was reported. In grossing up from these figures, we estimate that 150,000 of those employees working at plants with 25 or more people were affected by some form of short-time working arrangement in 1983/84.

In the 1984 survey the questioning on short-time working was more detailed than previously and included the particular types of arrangement that had been in operation. Answers were multi-coded. The type of arrangement most frequently mentioned was a temporary lay-off of employees. This was reported in over a quarter of cases and occurred in two per cent of all establishments in the sample in 1984. A similar proportion of managers reported a reduction in the number of shifts worked. Short-time working that was partly financed by a government subsidy was reported in 17 per cent of establishments, or one per cent of all establishments in the sample. Instances of short-time working that were not financed by a government subsidy were reported in 23 per cent of cases, or two per cent of all establishments.

Workforce reductions

In both surveys we asked managers whether there had been any reductions in the workforce at the establishment in the year prior to interview.[25] In 1980 managers in 45 per cent of workplaces said there had been workforce reductions. By 1984 that figure had declined slightly to 41 per cent. But changes were more pronounced in certain sectors. In broad terms workforce reductions were less likely to be reported among workplaces in the private sector in 1984 than they were in 1980. The opposite was the case in the public sector. Table 8.8 gives the results. Managers in two fifths of private manufacturing plants reported workforce reductions in 1984 compared to almost half in 1980. The decline was even more pronounced in the private services sector where the proportion of managers reporting workforce reductions dropped from two fifths to a third over the four-year period. By contrast, workforce reductions in the nationalised industries were considerably more common than previously; they were reported in half of workplaces in 1984 compared to a third in 1980; there was little detectable change in the public services sector (around half of workplaces).[26]

The 1980 results showed that workforce reductions were more commonly reported in larger workplaces. This was also true in 1984, although establishments employing 500 or more employees in 1984 were **more** likely to report workforce reductions than previously. For those employing 1000 or more, the proportions increased from three fifths to four fifths over the four-year period. Naturally the strength of the relationship is somewhat understated because our measure of size is **net** of the changes in size.

We would have expected workforce reductions to be inversely related to the economic performance of the establishment and this was indeed borne out by our data. Workplaces that were performing below average were much more likely to have reduced their workforce in the year prior to interview than those performing better. Managers in 30 per cent of establishments that were working at *full capacity* in 1984 said they had reduced their workforce. This compares with 41 per cent of those working *somewhat below capacity* and 55 per cent of those working *considerably below capacity*. A similar pattern was evident in relation to the trend in output in the year prior to interview. Taking those cases where output was *rising*, 33 per cent had experienced workforce reductions over the same period. Managers in 44 per cent of workplaces where the trend in output had been *stable* reported workforce reductions and 64 per cent of those with *falling* output did so.

As workforce reductions were related to the size of the establishment affected, we would also expect there to be a relationship with the level of trade union organisation at the establishment. Our data confirm this expectation. Around half of workplaces where either manual or non-manual trade unions were recognised experienced workforce reductions, compared to around a third of those with no recognised trade unions. In general terms workforce reductions were also strongly associated with the level of union membership among non-manual workers. This was so in workplaces with up to 99 per cent non-manual union membership, where reductions were reported in over half of cases, but, interestingly, in workplaces with comprehensive non-manual union membership the proportion fell to just over a third. The relationship to union density among manual workers was less clear-cut, but reductions in the workforce were more commonly reported in cases where over half of the manual workforce were trade union members. Reductions were also more likely to be reported at workplaces with a closed shop (48 per cent of cases) than at those with an 'open shop' (40 per cent).

Reasons given for workforce reductions

In cases where managers reported workforce reductions in the year prior to interview we also asked what the main reasons were for the reduction. As this was a new question in the 1984 survey we do not have comparable data for 1980. Answers were multi-coded. Within manufacturing industry the main reasons given were *lack of demand* (48 per cent), *reorganised working methods* (43 per cent) and *improved competitiveness* (28 per cent). Workforce reductions at workplaces in the metal goods sector were most likely to have arisen from a *lack of demand*. Managers in 59 per cent of cases gave this answer. In the electrical and instrument engineering sector the main reasons given were *lack of demand* and *automation*. Managers at workplaces in the food, drink and tobacco sector were most likely to give *reorganised working methods* as the main reason, mentioned in two thirds of cases, but *lack of demand* was also mentioned in a third of cases. *Automation* and other forms of new technology were relatively rare as reasons cited for reductions in the workforce, but the relationship between technical change and manpower changes is complex and is discussed in detail in Daniel's companion volume.[27]

In the non-manufacturing sector there were four main reasons given for workforce reductions in 1984. These were: *cash limits* (34 per cent of cases); *reorganised working methods* (34 per cent); *lack of demand* (31 per cent); and *improved competitiveness* (24 per cent). As we might expect, workforce reductions at workplaces in the public sector were most likely to have arisen from *cash limits*. This was mentioned by over half of managers in both the public administration and the medical services sectors and by 43 per cent of managers in the education sector. A further 43 per cent of managers in the education sector gave *lack of demand* as one of the main reasons for contracting the workforce. This is likely to reflect falling school rolls resulting in less demand for teachers and ancilliary workers in that sector. Over half of managers in the transport sector gave *lack of demand* as one of the main reasons for job losses. In public administration, about as many managers mentioned *reorganised working methods* (51 per cent) as *cash limits*, suggesting that there may have been a relationship between the two. Reorganisations of this kind were also mentioned by over half of managers in the *energy and water supply industries*, and 40 per cent of those in retailing. The main reason given for job loss in the retailing sector, however, was *improved competitiveness* (51 per cent of cases).

Methods used to reduce the workforce
In both surveys we asked managers that had reported reductions in manpower which methods they had used. Interviewers read out a list of methods and recorded all those that applied. We give the results[28] for each broad sector of the economy in Table 8.8. In overall terms, fewer workplaces were reducing their workforce by means of natural wastage in 1984 than in 1980, but more were using early retirement. There was no change overall in the proportion of workplaces reporting either voluntary or compulsory redundancies (eight per cent and 10 per cent respectively in 1984), although our figures for redundancies are, obviously, net of those arising from total workplace closure. The decline in the use of natural wastage occurred exclusively in the private sector of the economy and particularly in manufacturing. Clearly, the very large job losses in that sector during the late 1970s and early 1980s suggests that there would be very little scope for natural wastage in 1984. There was no change in the extent of either voluntary or compulsory redundancy in this sector over the four-year period, although compulsory redundancies were still much more common than in other sectors (see Table 8.8). The use of early retirement increased slightly and was reported in 16 per cent of workplaces in 1984. Redeployment within the establishment was fairly widespread in 1984, being reported in almost a fifth of cases. In our two surveys the pattern of use of each method was very similar in the private services sector, although each method was mentioned much less frequently than in private manufacturing.

The sector that exhibited most change between 1980 and 1984 was the nationalised industries. In contrast to workplaces in the private sector, natural wastage was being used more frequently than in 1980. The proportion of workplaces using early retirement doubled over the period and redundancies were much more common. Reporting of voluntary redundancies increased from 12 per cent to 16 per cent of workplaces and compulsory redundancies were reported in five per cent of workplaces, compared to one per cent in 1980. In 1984 there was also greater use of redeployment within workplaces in this sector

Table 8.8 Proportion of establishments reporting workforce reductions and methods used by broad sector

Percentages

	All establishments		Private manufacturing		Private services		Nationalised industries		Public services	
	1980	1984	1980	1984	1980	1984	1980	1984	1980	1984
Reductions in any section or sections of the workforce reported in last year	45	41	49	41	42	32	35	51	46	52
Methods used to reduce a section or sections of the workforce										
Redeployment within workplace[1]	..[2]	16	..	18	..	13	..	21	..	17
Natural wastage	36	29	42	28	33	20	29	41	36	40
Early retirement	9	14	14	16	4	7	12	25	13	21
Voluntary redundancies	9	8	14	15	7	5	12	16	7	6
Compulsory redundancies	11	10	21	21	12	11	1	5	3	3
Other methods	1	5	1	3	1	4	—	7	1	10
Not answered	—	—	—	—	—	—	—	—	—	—
Base: all establishments										
Unweighted	2040	2019	743	595	587	597	134	196	576	634
Weighted	2000	2000	503	424	859	843	69	106	569	627

[1] See text.
[2] See Notes E and J.

than in other sectors. Clearly, as workforce reductions in this sector were much more commonly reported in 1984 than in 1980 we would expect increases in the methods used to bring these about. The substantial increases in both natural wastage and early retirement suggests the beginnings of a process that has been in operation in the private manufacturing sector for much longer. In the public services sector the pattern of change in the use of early retirement and natural wastage was very similar, although the increases were less marked. Redundancies were reported as frequently as they were in 1980 in this sector. The use of methods of workforce reduction not included in the list that interviewers read out to respondents were much more common in the public sector than the private sector in 1984 and had increased substantially since 1980. These were predominantly cases where sections of employees had been moved to other establishments of the same organisation.

With the exception of compulsory redundancies, all methods of workforce reduction were strongly associated with the size of the establishment. In consequence they were also strongly associated with other size-related factors such as union recognition and higher union membership density. Compulsory redundancies in 1984 were unrelated to the size of the establishment where they were reported and were much more likely to be reported the **lower** the level of trade union membership. Moreover, of those workplaces reporting workforce reductions, 45 per cent of those where trade unions were not recognised reported compulsory redundancies in 1984. This compares with 19 per cent of cases where trade unions were recognised.

In almost half of cases where compulsory redundancies were reported in 1984, the basis for selecting those to be made redundant was *last-in/first-out*. The same proportion reported this method in the private sector, manufacturing or services. Taking those cases in the private sector only where redundancies were reported, a further third of managers reported that a particular job had been abolished and the particular job-holder was dismissed; in a fifth of cases redundancies were decided on the basis of the skill levels. There was little variation between the private manufacturing and the private services sectors in these respects. However, a poor performance record and a poor disciplinary or attendance record were much more likely to be used as the basis for selection in the private manufacturing than the private services sector. There were too few cases of compulsory redundancy in the public sector for separate analysis.

In those cases where workforce reductions were reported in workplaces that were part of a multi-establishment group, we also asked at which level of the organisation the decision to reduce the workforce was taken. In the private sector, either manufacturing or services, the decision was taken at establishment-level in around a half of cases and at **both** establishment-level and at a higher level in a further fifth of cases in 1984. Decisions were most likely to have been taken at a higher level in the public sector. This was so in half of workplaces in the nationalised industries and two thirds of workplaces in the public services.

We also asked a question about the level of decision-making in relation to the **method** used to reduce the workforce. In two thirds of manufacturing plants the decision on methods was taken at establishment-level in 1984 and in a further 12 per cent of cases it was taken at both levels. In private services 53 per cent of managers said methods were decided at the establishment and a further fifth said both levels. In the public sector the methods of workforce reduction were decided at a higher level in around a half of cases.

Notes and references

1. In addition, although certain topics were covered in both surveys, the questions were, in some cases, sufficiently different to make comparisons between the two surveys of doubtful validity.

2. This is being carried out at the Work and Employment Research Unit, Department of Sociology and Social Policy, University of Durham, under the direction of Professor R K Brown.

3. Daniel W W (1986 forthcoming) *Workplace Industrial Relations and Technical Change.*

4. For industrial and commercial establishments we defined *output* as the *value of sales of the main products or services at the establishment*. For public sector, non-trading establishments we defined *output* as the *operating budget for the establishment*. In the text we use the single term *output* to cover both cases.

5. Daniel W W (1987 forthcoming) *op.cit.*, Chapter IX.

6. Brown W (ed.) (1981) *The Changing Contours of British Industrial Relations*, Blackwell, Oxford.

7. We restricted the questioning about manual recruitment channels to those grades where difficulties of recruitment are often expressed – at the semi-skilled and skilled levels. As the Warwick survey did not include questions about recruitment channels for non-manual employees, we must restrict the comparisons to these two types of manual employee.

8. Brown W (1981) *op.cit.*, pp.102-3.

9. Although the number of categories differed between the two surveys (ten in 1984, eight in 1978 plus a residual in each case), including two each that were not comparable, the effect would probably be to spread the available response, rather than invalidate the comparison as such.

10. Bowers J, Deaton D, and Turk J (1982) *Labour Hoarding in British Industry*, Blackwell, Oxford, p.32.

11. More detailed analysis of the 1980 (*BWDS*) data on part-time employment has already been carried out: Blanchflower D and Corry B (1986 forthcoming) *Part-Time Employment in Great Britain: An Analysis Using Establishment Data*, Research Paper, Department of Employment, London.

12. *Ibid.*, Chapter 9.

13. This is slightly different from the definition used in the *Census of Employment*, where a part-time employee is defined as working 30 hours or less.

14. Even if we used our three other measures: whether establishments had *any* part-timers, *five or more* part-timers, or the *average number* of part-timers at the establishment, the contrast between the four sectors is the same.

15. Questioning on the different types of 'non-core' workers is complicated by problems of terminology, particularly with respect to freelancers and homeworkers or outworkers. This issue is extensively discussed in Hakim C (1985) *Employers' Use of Outwork: A Study Using the 1980 Workplace Industrial Relations Survey and the 1981 National Survey of Homeworking*, Research Paper No. 44, Department of Employment, London, *passim*.

16. Institute of Manpower Studies (1986) *Changing Work Patterns: how companies achieve flexibility to meet new needs*, National Economic Development Office, London, p.81; Hakim C (1985) *op.cit.*, p.57.

17. However, this is still likely to be an understatement as the question asked about *current* usage and some of our interviews at establishments in this sector were conducted during the 1984 summer holidays.

18. In the great majority of cases (77 per cent) these employees received their pay from the agency concerned, and a further 12 per cent were paid directly from the host workplace. In the remainder of cases, some were paid by the agency and some by the host workplace.

19. The change was essentially in the introduction to the question. In 1980 the question asked '*Apart from homeworkers* . . .' thus putting freelancers into a residual category. The 1984 question combined the two categories of worker but mentioned freelancers first ('. . . *has this establishment paid any individuals on a freelance basis or as homeworkers or outworkers?*'). However, the combination of the two types of worker in the 1984 question may have also led to some understatement of the extent of freelancers.

20. Precise comparisons are not possible because the reference period of the question in 1980 was the previous *month*, whereas in 1984 it was the previous year. The seasonality of outwork usage suggests that the 1980 data under-represent their employment throughout the year (see Hakim (1985) *op.cit.*, p.34). Any comparison between the two results would therefore be likely to understate the decline in outworking among establishments covered by our survey series.

21. This has been confirmed by multi-variate analysis of 1980 data by Blanchflower D and Bosworth D (1986) 'The Determinants of Shiftworking at Establishment Level', mimeo., Institute of Employment Research, University of Warwick. The relationship to establishment size was the strongest revealed by their analysis.

22. We use italics to distinguish the actual categories (Divisions or Classes) used in the *Standard Industrial Classification*. Industry names not italicised are groupings of *SIC* Divisions and Classes.

23. It should be emphasised that the 1980 density figures relate to union membership among full-time employees only.

24. The 1984 survey also includes information on hours of work and hours of paid overtime for typical employees in five occupational groups.

25. In the 1984 survey we extended the question to cover reductions '. . . *in any section or sections of the workforce*'. The likely effect of the change in question wording is to increase the proportions in 1984, so we can be more confident about **decreases** over the period. Workforce reductions may not mean a decline in employment as the reduction in a particular section of the workforce may have been achieved by redeployment within the establishment.

26. Although the table shows a slight increase, the slight change in question wording could mean that this is a methodological artefact.

27. Daniel W W (1986 forthcoming) *op.cit.*

28. As the 1980 figures understate the extent of redeployment, they have been excluded from the table.

9 Pay Determination*

Historically, the study of systems of pay and of pay determination in Britain has essentially been the study of the pay of manual workers in manufacturing industry in general, and in the engineering industry in particular. In contrast to that tradition, the first survey in our present series demonstrated the range and diversity of arrangements for determining pay in Britain.[1] We covered all sectors of activity and all levels of employment. We showed that there were major differences between private manufacturing industry and private services and between public administration and nationalised industries. Indeed, the contrasts between the four different broad sectors were so great, that it made little sense to analyse them together. Moreover, within the private sector there were further major differences in relation to the size and the other characteristics of workplaces. Overall, as would be expected, these broad patterns persisted into our second survey. In consequence, we tend to analyse our information on pay determination in the following way. First, we establish the overall pattern of variation between the four main sectors. Secondly, we explore more detailed sources of variation in private manufacturing and private services. These were the two sectors where diversity was most common. In nationalised industries and public services, systems of pay determination were more centralised and less variable among different types of workplace. Initially, however, we looked to see if there were any signs of aggregate **change** between 1980 and 1984.

It did appear that there were significant shifts in the overall pattern of pay determination during the four years, but those arose much more as a result of structural change in the economy than as a result of change in particular types of workplace. That is to say, the shifts occurred chiefly because there were changes in the balance between the broad sectors of employment and the different sizes of workplace. As Table 9.1 shows, there was between 1980 and 1984 an increase in the proportion of workplaces where rates of pay were determined by collective bargaining. That was true in relation to the overall pattern of pay determination for both the largest group of manual workers and

* W W Daniel is principal author of this chapter.

Table 9.1   Basis for most recent pay increase

Percentages

	Manual workers 1980	Manual workers 1984	Non-manual workers 1980	Non-manual workers 1984
Result of collective bargaining	55	62	47	54
Most important level:				
National/regional	32[1]	40	29	36
Company/divisional	12	13	11	13
Plant/establishment	9	7	4	4
Other answer	1	1	2	1
Not result of collective bargaining	44	38	53	46
Locus of decision about increase:				
Management at establishment	..[2]	20	..	30
Management at higher level	..	11	..	15
National joint body	..	5	..	2
Wages council	..	3	..	1
Not stated	..	1	..	★
Base: establishments employing the relevant category of workers in 1980 and 1984				
Unweighted	*1899*	*1853*	*2034*	*2010*
Weighted	*1823*	*1749*	*1988*	*1985*

[1] See Note D.
[2] See Note J.

the largest group of non-manual workers.[2] In particular, there was an increase in the proportion of workplaces where pay was regulated by national or industry-wide agreements. The increase arose, principally, because of a movement in the balance between our four broad sectors of the economy. Within each sector the pattern of change tended to be different.

There was little change in the overall system of pay determination in the nationalised industries and public services during the early 1980s. In 1980, very nearly all nationalised industries reported that pay was determined by collective bargaining and that bargaining at the national, industry-wide or **company** (which in the case of nationalised industries tended to be industry-wide) levels was most important so far as increases in rates at their establishments were concerned. In 1984 the pattern remained very similar. So far as public services were concerned, there did appear from our findings to be an increase in the proportion of managers who reported that pay at their establishments was determined by collective bargaining, but, essentially, that increase was a consequence of a tendency for managers in

Table 9.2 **Basis for most recent pay increase in private manufacturing industry**

Percentages

	Manual workers		Non-manual workers	
	1980	1984	1980	1984
Result of collective bargaining	65	55	27	26
Most important level:				
National/regional	27[1]	22	5	5
Company/divisional	10	11	8	9
Plant/establishment	26	21	13	11
Other answer	1	1	★	1
Not result of collective bargaining	35	45	73	74
Locus of decision about increase:				
Management at establishment	. .[2]	33	. .	53
Management at higher level	. .	10	. .	21
National joint body	. .	2	. .	1
Wages council	. .	1	. .	★
Not stated	. .	★	. .	★
Base: private manufacturing establishments employing relevant category of workers in 1980 and 1984				
Unweighted	*734*	*580*	*743*	*592*
Weighted	*498*	*412*	*503*	*424*

[1] See Note D.
[2] See Note J.

public services to be less likely to say that pay was determined by national joint bodies and more likely to attribute it to collective bargaining. As we noted in our analysis of union recognition in Chapter 3, that change was as likely to have occurred as a result of better interviewing and coding as to have been the result of any real change on the ground. But we stressed in Chapter 1, and have noted frequently throughout our analysis, that there was a substantial shift in the balance between private manufacturing and public services establishments between 1980 and 1984. The proportion of manufacturing workplaces declined very substantially while there was an increase in the proportion of workplaces engaged in public services. That was the chief reason for the change that we found in the overall pattern of pay determination. In many ways it was the changes that occurred within private manufacture and private services, where, as we emphasised, there was more diversity and choice, that were of more interest. It is those that we go on to consider now.

Table 9.3 Collective bargaining over rates of pay for manual workers in private manufacturing industry

Percentages

	All establishments	Number of manual workers at establishment						All manual employees
		1–24	25–49	50–99	100–199	200–499	500 or more	
1980								
Pay determined by collective bargaining	65	(47)	54	66	84	92	96	84[1]
Plant-level bargaining most important	26	(23)	17	27	32	46	53	41
Unweighted base	734	36	83	121	143	163	188	734
Weighed base	498[2]	79	168	119	69	43	21	498
1984								
Pay determined by collective bargaining	55	(36)	45	64	83	83	99	79
Plant-level bargaining most important	21	(5)	20	22	38	41	48	35
Base: private manufacturing establishments employing manual workers								
Unweighted	580	42	75	89	100	132	142	580
Weighed	412	91	142	97	45	27	11	412

[1] The percentage represents the number of manual employees in establishments of this type as a percentage of the number of employees in all establishments in the base.
[2] See Note H.

Pay determination in private manufacturing industry
Within private manufacturing industry there was a tendency for the coverage of collective bargaining to decline (see Table 9.2). That was certainly the case for pay determination for manual workers. So far as non-manual workers in private manufacturing industry were concerned, there was no significant change in the extent of joint regulation over pay. In 1980, two thirds of managers reported that rates of pay for manual workers were determined by collective bargaining. By 1984, that proportion dropped to a little over half. There was a particular decline in the influence of both national agreements and workplace or plant agreements.

The decline in the influence of collective bargaining over the pay of manual workers in private manufacturing industry did not come about only because larger workplaces became less common in that sector. Among smaller workplaces there was also an indication that plants of similar size were less likely to operate negotiated rates for manual workers (see Table 9.3). The table also shows the familiar tendency for the rates of pay of manual workers to be more frequently subject to collective bargaining the larger the size of the plant where they worked, as measured by the number of manual workers employed there. In consequence, although the proportion of workplaces in private manufacturing industry where the pay of most manual workers was determined by collective bargaining fell to 55 per cent, 79 per cent of manual workers in the sector worked at places where increases in rates were collectively bargained for most manual workers there. Indeed, the difference between the proportion of workers covered by collective bargaining in 1980 and 1984 was less than the contrast between the proportion of workplaces covered. The tendency persisted for collective bargaining over rates of pay to be more common the larger the total enterprise of which the plant was part, independently of the size of the workplace.

For non-manual workers in manufacturing, there was little sign of equivalent change in the extent to which pay increases were collectively bargained, as we noted earlier. That appeared to be as true for workplaces of different sizes as it was overall (see Table 9.4). The table also shows that the extent to which the coverage of collective bargaining was associated with the size of the workforce was even more marked for non-manual workers than it was for manual employees. In consequence, there was a very marked contrast in manufacturing industry between the proportion of workplaces where the pay of most non-manual workers was subject to collective bargaining (26 per cent) and the proportion of non-manual employees in such establishments (59 per cent). Indeed, the contrast between manual and non-manual workers in manufacturing industry became

Table 9.4   Collective bargaining over rates of pay for non-manual workers in private manufacturing industry

Percentages

	All establishments	Number of non-manual workers at establishment						All non-manual employees[1]
		1–24	25–49	50–99	100–199	200–499	500 or more	
1980								
Pay determined by collective bargaining	27	12	32	46	60	80	89	63
Plant-level bargaining most important	13	6	13	25	27	42	56	36
Unweighted	*743*	*172*	*124*	*120*	*102*	*134*	*91*	*743*
Weighted	*503*	*288*	*99*	*61*	*26*	*20*	*9*	*503*
1984								
Pay determined by collective bargaining	26	13	28	54	62	81	93	79
Plant-level bargaining most important	21	3	16	29	25	47	53	35
Base: private manufacturing establishments employing non-manual workers								
Unweighted	*592*	*139*	*81*	*95*	*111*	*102*	*64*	*743*
Weighted	*424[2]*	*263*	*69*	*46*	*29*	*12*	*5*	*503*

[1] See Note 1 to Table 9.3
[2] See Note H.

very much less marked when the focus was employees rather than workplaces. So far as the impact of collective bargaining upon non-manual workers was concerned, not only was there an independent association with the total size of the enterprise, there was also an independent association with the number of **manual** workers employed on site. That is to say, the position of manual workers at the workplace appeared to have an influence upon the way in which non-manual workers were managed. The opposite was not so apparently true.

Levels of bargaining

In order to focus upon any changes that had occurred in the level at which bargaining over pay increases was conducted, it is appropriate to confine analysis to those places where there was bargaining over pay increases. Table 9.5 shows managers' accounts of the different levels at which there was bargaining over the rates of pay applying to the largest groups. Table 9.6 summarises their judgements as to which of these levels was most important. The patterns for manual and non-manual groups are shown separately. The analysis suggests, first, that there was a general decline in the rate of bargaining activity for both manual and non-manual grades. That is to say, there was a fall in the number of cases where managers reported that pay increases were the result of multiple stages of bargaining. In 1980, the pay of manual workers was subject to 1.4 stages, on average, while in 1984 it was subject to 1.2 stages. The reduction in the number of stages involved in bargaining over the pay of non-manual workers appeared slightly less. Multi-stage bargaining over the pay of non-manual workers was less common initially and became rare by 1984. Secondly, it appeared to be the case that company or divisional bargaining over rates of pay was of growing importance in private manufacturing industry during the early 1980s. That tendency was most apparent when the focus was the most important level of bargaining, according to the assessments of managers (see Table 9.6). The balance between plant bargaining and bargaining at a higher level in the organisation appeared to shift to the higher level for both manual and non-manual workers. But the change was significant only in relation to bargaining over increases for non-manual workers. Managers were less likely to report that national or industry-wide bargaining played any part in determining the pay of both manual and non-manual workers, but there was little change in their accounts of the extent to which national bargaining was the most important level. The chief feature revealed by any focus upon collective bargaining at the national level was how much less important it was for non-manual workers in manufacturing industry than for manual workers. But that feature was as true in 1980 as it was in 1984.

Table 9.5   Levels of bargaining that influenced pay increases in private manufacturing industry

	Manual workers 1980	Manual workers 1984	Non-manual workers 1980	Non-manual workers 1984
				Column percentages
National/regional	61[1]	50	29	22
Company/divisional	20	21	32	38
Plant-establishment	53	49	57	43
Other answer	2	2	3	5
Not stated	★	1	1	★
Average				Means
where levels stated	1.4	1.2	1.2	1.1
Base: private manufacturing establishments employing the relevant category of workers in 1980 and 1984				
Unweighted	*589*	*462*	*404*	*351*
Weighted	*322*	*228*	*134*	*109*

[1] See Note E.

Table 9.6   Most important levels of bargaining influencing pay increases in private manufacturing industry

Column percentages

	Manual workers 1980	Manual workers 1984	Non-manual workers 1980	Non-manual workers 1984
National/regional	41	40	18	19[1]
Company/divisional	15	20	29	36
Plant-establishment	41	38	49	42
Other answer	1	1	3	2
Not stated	2	1	1	★
Base: private manufacturing establishments employing the relevant category of workers in 1980 and 1984				
Unweighted	*589*	*462*	*404*	*351*
Weighted	*322*	*228*	*134*	*109*

[1] See Note C.

As in 1980, there were tendencies for plant bargaining, and to a lesser extent company bargaining, to assume greater importance for both manual and non-manual workers the greater the number of people employed on site. In consequence, the proportion of workers in establishments where plant and company bargaining had most significance was larger than the proportion of workplaces where those levels were judged to be most important (see Table 9.7).

Apart from size, there were two further characteristics of workplaces in manufacturing that were very strongly associated with the level of collective bargaining that was judged to be important in determining the pay increases of both manual and non-manual workers. These were, first, the nationality of the company to which the workplace belonged and, secondly, the industrial sector in which it operated. Plant bargaining was very much more important in establishments belonging to overseas companies than in domestic counterparts. That was true at both manual and non-manual levels, but the contrast was especially strong in relation to non-manual employees. In relation to industrial sector within manufacturing, the engineering industries and vehicle manufacture, as always, stood out as industries where plant bargaining was especially important. The most striking feature of our analysis, when compared with much earlier research on pay determination, however, was that while it revealed that over 60 per cent of managers in engineering workplaces that recognised manual trade unions reported that the plant was the most important level at which bargaining over periodic pay increases took place, the same was true for only 38 per cent of all workplaces in manufacturing, and 11 per cent of workplaces from all sectors that recognised manual trade unions.

Pay determination in private services
While in private manufacturing we have indicated a slight decline in the coverage of collective bargaining, there was in private services, if anything, a slight increase (see Table 9.8). As in manufacturing, though, any change was more marked for manual workers. When we analysed any change in the extent to which the pay increases of manual workers in private services were collectively bargained in relation to size, we found the pattern in Table 9.9. There remained a strong tendency for collective bargaining to be more common in larger establishments. In consequence, the proportion of manual workers in workplaces in private services where pay increases for most were the result of collective bargaining remained much the same as in 1980. On the other hand, the 'gearing' of workplace size to collective bargaining was not as great as it was in the case of private manufacturing industry. Indeed, it appeared that the overall size of the enterprise of which the workplace was part was more strongly associated with the coverage of collective bargaining in private services.

So far as non-manual workers in private services were concerned, there appeared to be no consistent pattern of change in relation to the size of establishments. In consequence, the relationship between the

Table 9.7 Most important levels of bargaining in private manufacturing industry in relation to numbers employed, 1984

Column percentages

Manual workers	All establishments	Number of manual workers at establishment					All manual employees[1]
		1–49	50–99	100–199	200–499	500 or more	
National/industry	40	46[2]	43	30	27	21	30
Company/division	20	16	22	23	22	29	24
Plant/establishment	38	34	34	46	49	49	45
Other answer	1	3	—	—	2	1	1
Not stated	1	2	1	1	—	—	1
Unweighted base	*462*	*56*	*62*	*87*	*117*	*140*	*462*
Weighted base	*228[3]*	*97*	*99*	*37*	*22*	*11*	*228*

Non-manual workers	All establishments	Number of non-manual workers at establishment					All non-manual employees
		1–49	50–99	100–199	200–499	500 or more	
National/industry	19	22	11	28	5	8	13
Company/division	36	39	35	31	35	33	33
Plant/establishment	42	33	53	41	58	59	53
Other answer	2	5	—	—	1	—	*
Not stated	*	—	—	—	1	—	*
Unweighted	*351*	*55*	*62*	*86*	*88*	*60*	*351*
Weighted	*109*	*52*	*25*	*18*	*94*	*4*	*109*

Bases: establishments in private manufacturing where manual and non-manual workers, respectively, were employed and trade unions were recognised

[1] See Note 1 to Table 9.3.   [2] See Note C.   [3] See Note H.

Table 9.8   Basis for most recent pay increase in private services

Percentages

	Manual workers 1980	Manual workers 1984	Non-manual workers 1980	Non-manual workers 1984
Result of collective bargaining	34	38	28	30
Most important level				
National/regional	19	20	12	11
Company/divisional	10	12	10	15
Establishment	3	4	2	3
Other answer	*	2	5	*
Not result of collective bargaining	66	62	72	70
Locus of decision about increase:				
Management at establishment	..	30	..	45
Management at higher level	..	21	..	24
National joint body	..	9	..	3
Wages council	..	5	..	2
Not stated	..	1	..	1
Base: establishments employing the relevant category of workers in 1980 and 1984				
Unweighted	*521*	*515*	*585*	*593*
Weighted	*733*	*689*	*854*	*836*

proportion of non-manual workers covered by collective bargaining in 1980 compared with 1984 was similar to the relationship between the proportion of workplaces covered in the two years (see Table 9.10). The association between collective bargaining over pay increases for non-manual workers in private services and **total enterprise size** was particularly strong in relation to smaller workplaces.

Levels of bargaining
Focusing upon levels of bargaining in parts of private services where pay increases were subject to collective bargaining revealed the picture shown in Tables 9.11 and 9.12. The analysis reflects again the two features that were apparent in the parallel tables for manufacturing industry. First, there appeared to be a slight decline in the extent of multi-stage bargaining. Secondly, company bargaining appeared to be of growing importance for non-manual workers. Workplace bargaining was, and remained, relatively infrequent in private services and the increasing importance of company bargaining was at the expense of national or industry-wide bargaining.

In contrast to manufacturing industry, levels of bargaining in

Percentages

Table 9.9 Collective bargaining over rates of pay for manual workers in private services

	All estab-lishments	Number of manual workers at establishment					All manual employees[1]
		1–24	25–49	50–99	100–199	200 or more	
1980							
Pay determined by collective bargaining	34	20	38	58	68	74	53
Establishment-level bargaining most important	3	2	3	1	8	26	6
Unweighted	*521*	*179*	*137*	*75*	*69*	*61*	—
Weighted	*755*	*359*	*270*	*70*	*41*	*15*	—
1984							
Pay determined by collective bargaining	38	24	46	50	68	73	53
Establishment-level bargaining most important	4	5	5	7	7	16	8
Base: all private service establishments employing manual workers							
Unweighted	*515*	*182*	*143*	*76*	*54*	*60*	*515*
Weighted	*689*	*322*	*252*	*75*	*30*	*10*	*689*

[1] See Note 1 to Table 9.3.

Table 9.10 Collective bargaining over rates of pay for non-manual workers in private services

Percentages

| | All estab-lishments | Number of non-manual workers at establishment | | | | | All non-manual employees[1] |
		1–24	25–49	50–99	100–199	200 or more	
1980							
Pay determined by collective bargaining	28	21	33	43	25	52	37
Establishment-level bargaining most important	2	1	1	6	5	12	5
Unweighted base	585	219	139	91	57	79	—
Weighted base	854	455	259	89	33	18	—
1984							
Pay determined by collective bargaining	30	21	36	37	42	34	40
Establishment-level bargaining most important	3	2	4	4	8	5	6
Base: all private service establishments employing non-manual workers							
Unweighted	593	168	134	99	85	107	593
Weighted	836	383	271	114	48	20	836

[1] See Note 1 to Table 9.3.

Table 9.11   Levels of bargaining that influenced pay increases in private services

Column percentages

	Manual workers		Non-manual workers	
	1980	1984	1980	1984
National/regional	62[1]	58	46	37
Company/divisional	40	38	50	59
Establishment	14	14	8	12
Other answer	7	2	11	2
Not stated	1	1	4	⋆

Base: private services establishments employing the relevant category of worker in 1980 and 1984 and recognising trade unions for the category

	Manual workers		Non-manual workers	
Unweighted	227	231	207	229
Weighted	253	260	236	247

[1] See Note E.

Table 9.12   Most important levels of bargaining influencing pay increases in private services

Column percentages

	Manual workers		Non-manual workers	
	1980	1984	1980	1984
National/regional	57[1]	54	43	36
Company/divisional	28	33	36	52
Establishment	9	11	7	11
Other answer	3	3	10	⋆
	2	—	4	⋆

Base: private service establishments employing the relevant category of workers in 1980 and 1984 and recognising trade unions for the category

	Manual workers		Non-manual workers	
Unweighted	227	231	207	229
Weighted	253	260	236	247

[1] See Note C.

private services were not associated with workplace size. Consequently, the proportions of both manual and non-manual workers employed at workplaces practising the different levels of bargaining were close to the proportions of workplaces doing so. So far as private services were concerned the size of the total enterprise of which the establishment was part was a more important source of variation than workplace size (see Table 9.13). The number of foreign-owned

Table 9.13 Most important levels of bargaining in private services in relation to numbers employed

Column percentages

	All establishments	Number of manual workers at establishment				All manual employees[1]
		1–49	50–99	100–199	200 or more	
Manual workers						
National/industry	54	53	(56)	(57)	37[2]	50
Company/division	33	35	(19)	(33)	44	33
Establishment	11	10	(13)	(10)	20	15
Other answer	2	2	(11)	(—)	1	2
Not stated	—	—	—	—	—	—
Unweighted base	231	107	42	38	45	231
Weighted base	260	194	37	20	7	260

	All establishments	Number of non-manual workers at establishment				All non-manual employees
		1–49	50–99	100–199	200 or more	
Non-manual workers						
National/industry	36	34	(44)	(38)	30	40
Company/division	52	55	(45)	(41)	47	45
Establishment	11	10	(11)	(19)	16	14
Other answer	*	—	(—)	(—)	7	1
Not stated	*	—	(—)	(2)	—	*
Unweighted	229	92	42	38	57	229
Weighted	247	178	42	20	7	247

Bases: private service establishments where manual workers and non-manual workers, respectively, were employed and trade unions were recognised

workplaces recognising trade unions was too few to sustain serious analysis in private services.

Beyond that the chief feature of interest in variations in levels of bargaining in the private service sector related to the use of advanced technology. The greater the use of advanced technology the more likely was pay bargaining at the workplace level judged to be most important. That association may provide a hint that the growth in the importance of new technology in private services may encourage a pattern of collective bargaining over pay increases more akin to the pattern in private manufacturing.

Constraints on local management autonomy
Studies such as our own, based upon interviews with people at workplace level have been subject to some criticism on the grounds that they create an exaggerated impression of local autonomy.[3] For instance, where collective bargaining over pay increases takes place at a number of different levels including the workplace level and we ask local managers and shop stewards which of the levels is most important, there may be an understandable tendency for them to feel that the level in which they are engaged is most important. Employer representatives and union officers involved in bargaining at company or industry level might take a different view and be similarly inclined to emphasise the importance of the bargaining in which they themselves are engaged. In order to fill out our picture of influences at different levels upon pay settlements, we first asked local managers in cases where there was collective bargaining over pay increases whether their most recent settlement was the result of or was influenced by any national or regional agreement. If it was, we asked in what ways the pay of workers at the establishment was affected by that agreement. Secondly, in cases where local managers reported that the local plant level was the most important for bargaining over pay increases, we asked about any consultations that they had had with managers at a level higher than the establishment.

The influence of national or regional agreements upon pay increases
Even interviewing at workplace level showed clearly that levels of bargaining over pay increases were heavily centralised in the public sector. Consequently, our supplementary question asking managers whether their most recent settlement was the result of or influenced by a national or regional agreement involving more than one employer (a *multi-employer agreement*) was most relevant to the private sector and especially those parts of the private sector where managers reported that plant or company bargaining was most important for their workplace. The answers did not suggest a very much more centralised

pattern of pay determination than our earlier questioning. Table 9.14 gives the results for manual and non-manual workers separately. The table also includes the proportion who, in answer to the earlier question, reported that bargaining over their most recent pay increase took place at national, industry or regional levels. The first line differs from the second by including cases where managers and trade unions were influenced by a multi-employer agreement although they were not formally party to it. It is clear that in private services the supplementary question checking on how far company and workplace agreements were influenced by multi-employer agreements even though company and workplace negotiators were not party to them increased the role attributed to multi-employer agreements by only a very few percentage points. That was true for both manual and non-manual pay increases. In private manufacturing industry, the role of multi-employer bargaining was enhanced a little more when weight was attached to its indirect influence as well as its direct impact. On the other hand, the increase remained modest.

A second way of looking at the role and influence of multi-employer agreements was to analyse the extent to which managers reported that

Table 9.14 **Extent to which most recent pay settlements were influenced by multi-employer (national or regional) agreements compared with the extent with which they were subject to bargaining at the national, industry or regional levels**

Percentages

| | Manual workers | | Non-manual workers | |
	Private manufact-uring	Private services	Private manufact-uring	Private services
Most recent pay settlement influenced by national/regional agreement (multi-employer)	58	60	29	40
Bargaining over most recent pay settlement at workplace took place at national industry or regional levels	50	58	22	37
Base: establishments where rates of pay were determined by collective bargaining				
Unweighted	*462*	*231*	*351*	*229*
Weighted	*228*	*260*	*109*	*247*

Table 9.15   **Influence of multi-employer agreements upon pay settlements in cases where managers attributed most importance to company or workplace negotiations**

| | Most important level of negotiations | | | |
| | Manual workers | | Non-manual workers | |
	Company	Workplace	Company	Workplace
Most recent settlement influenced by national or regional agreement				Column percentages
	26	28	16[1]	14
Independent settlement	72	72	83	86
Not stated	2	—	★	★
Nature of influence				Percentages
Precise application of basic rates	7[2]	8	4	2
Basic pay increased where new minimum was higher	2	4	★	—
Applied in money terms	5	3	2	2
Applied in percentage terms	9	8	7	6
Basis for further negotiation/ consultation	6	14	2	7
Other answer	1	★	1	3
Base: most recent pay increase for relevant workers determined by collective bargaining				
Unweighted	*332*	*271*	*369*	*222*
Weighted	*231*	*120*	*262*	*78*

[1] See Note C.
[2] See Note F.

these agreements played any part in their most recent pay increases in cases where they said that company or workplace negotiations represented the most important level of bargaining (see Table 9.15). It is clear that even in response to direct questioning on the matter, only minorities of those who said that the company level and the workplace level were most important in their systems of pay determination attributed any influence to multi-employer agreements. In the case of settlements affecting manual workers the minority was in the order of a quarter. Multi-employer agreements had even less influence so far as non-manual workers were concerned.

Consultation with central management
Our questioning on the extent to which local managers consulted central management (in cases where the establishment was part of a group) but workplace bargaining was judged to be the most important level in the process suggested that managements at a level higher than the plant did have substantial influence over plant bargaining. We distinguished between consultations at two stages. First, we asked whether local managers consulted higher-level managers in the

Table 9.16 **Consultations by local managements with head or divisional offices over their most recent establishment-level pay settlement**

Percentages

	Manual workers Private manufacturing	Manual workers Private services	Non-manual workers Private manufacturing
Consultations with higher level before start of most recent negotiations	66	(64)	51
Level of consultations:			
Head office	66[1]	(83)	61
Consultations after start of negotiations but before settlement	49	(56)	43
Level of consultations:			
Head office	64[2]	(80)	55
Consultations at both stages	39	(55)	37
No consultations at either stage	24	(33)	39
Base: establishments where managers reported that the most important level of bargaining over the most recent pay increase was at the establishment level			
Unweighted	204	30	167
Weighted	62	18	39

[1] Base is cases where consultations before start of negotiations are reported.
[2] Base is cases where consultations during negotiations were reported.

enterprise before the start of negotiations over their most recent pay settlement. Secondly, we asked them whether there were consultations after the start of negotiations but before the conclusion of the settlement. Table 9.16 summarises the details. In private manufacturing industry, where plant bargaining was most common, local managers reported that they consulted senior management before the start of their most recent plant level negotiations with manual workers in two thirds of cases. In a half of cases there were consultations after the start of negotiations but before their completion. Mostly local managers were consulting their seniors for the second time in those instances, for in 39 per cent of cases local managers referred up the chain both before the start of negotiations and subsequently. There was full local autonomy for managers in about a quarter of cases. Generally, local managers consulted senior management at head office level when they were taking soundings up the line.

Workplace bargaining over the pay of either of the two main groups of workers was too infrequent in private services for us to make much of the distinctive pattern in that sector. Private manufacturing was the only sector which provided a substantial number of cases of plant bargaining over non-manual pay. It appeared that local managers in manufacturing had more autonomy when negotiating the pay of non-manual workers than when dealing with manual employees. That reflected a common tendency in our analysis of the manufacturing sector for decisions affecting the non-manual workforce more often to be taken locally than decisions affecting manual workers. But it should be remembered here that non-manual workers in manufacturing were normally a minority and that our data on pay determination refer to the most numerous group represented by recognised unions.

There was surprisingly little association between the size of either workplaces or the organisations of which they were part in the extent to which local managers referred up the line about negotiations over the pay of either manual or non-manual workers. We showed earlier that plant bargaining was very much more common in manufacturing industry the larger the number of workers employed. But, if anything, there appeared to be less local management autonomy in larger workplaces when it came to the conduct of negotiations. That may be because settlements in their larger establishments have major implications for many other establishments in enterprises that decentralise the process of pay determination. A final source of variation, of particular strength and interest, in the extent to which local managers referred up the line over pay negotiations was the nationality of the enterprise of which the workplace was part. Previous research on plant bargaining in places belonging to large organisations has suggested that the optimum arrangement is for local managers to have a high level of local autonomy within the framework of clear and agreed guidelines from the centre.[4] Our present findings suggested that workplaces belonging to overseas companies approximated much more closely to that pattern than British counterparts. They were much more likely to consult with managers at the centre before the start of negotiations but much less likely to refer back to senior managers after the start of negotiations but before agreeing upon a settlement.

Local consultations by union negotiators on pay settlements

On the trade union side of pay negotiations there may also be various levels of consultation between negotiators and those that they represent at workplace level. As with management, our question in 1980 simply asked about consultations before the final settlement was reached. We found that in about three quarters of cases manual worker representatives, representing the largest or sole negotiating group at their workplace, reported that local stewards or members or both were consulted over their most recent pay settlement.[5] In about two thirds of cases rank-and-file members were consulted. Consultation was more common in larger establishments and where the settlement was local. When consulted, manual workers most commonly made their views known by a *show of hands at a meeting*. Non-manual representatives were less likely to report consultation on pay offers than manual representatives, but where consultations did take place *workplace ballots* were the most common medium for expressing their views. *Postal ballots* were reported by roughly a tenth of representatives.

In our 1984 survey these questions were repeated, but with a different set of pre-coded responses for the form of consultation. As we explain in Chapter 5, where a similar change was made in relation to the method of appointment of worker representatives, this change in coding makes it rather difficult to make comparisons between the two sets of results. Our general impression is that for manual workers the predominant method of consultation before a final pay settlement was reached was still *a show of hands at a meeting*. This was reported by 62 per cent of manual representatives where consultations took place. *A general feeling of a meeting without a show of hands* was reported in 19 per cent of relevant cases, while *voting-slips* and *postal ballots* were reported in 14 per cent and five per cent of cases respectively. Non-manual representatives reported the use of *voting slips* in 18 per cent of cases and *postal ballots* in 12 per cent. Because of the change of coding it is not possible to say whether ballots and other more formal methods of expressing a view about prospective pay settlements have become more or less common in the early 1980s, but the results indicate that informal methods are still the more common.

Influences upon pay settlements
We asked managers what factors influenced the level of pay decided upon at their most recent pay settlement. In cases where the agreement was the subject of collective bargaining, we asked the question of all managers, independently of whether the agreement was made at the national level, the level of the organisation or the workplace level. We also asked a similar question in circumstances where the most recent pay increase was **not** a result of collective bargaining. The question was asked whether the increase was determined by local managers, managers at a higher level in the organisation, a wages council or an employers' association or national joint negotiating body. The full set of questions was asked in relation to pay increases for both manual and non-manual workers.

As would be expected, local managers were sometimes not able to answer the question or were not able to give a very full answer. That tendency is reflected in the unusually high proportions in Tables 9.17 and 9.18 where our respondent was recorded as giving no answer.

Such cases were especially common where pay was not agreed or decided at the workplace. In places where pay was locally determined, then managers had no difficulty in answering the question. The analysis reveals, first, that although our survey was carried out when the rate of inflation had fallen to a low level, nevertheless the increase in the cost of living or inflation remained the most frequently cited influence upon pay settlements. Secondly, in general terms, the influences upon the pay settlements that were jointly regulated were not very different from those that were unilaterally determined by managers. It was true that more weight was attached to managerial definitions of individual merit or performance in places where trade unions were not recognised and especially where pay reviews were undertaken by local managers, unilaterally. But it is worth noting in passing that such arrangements covered only 14 per cent of manual workers in manufacturing industry. Even among non-manual workers

Table 9.17 **Managers' accounts of influences upon the most recent pay settlement affecting manual workers**

Column percentages

	All estab- lishments	Pay collectively determined and most important level of bargaining was:			No manual union recognised	
		National	Company	Workplace	All not recognised	Pay decided by local managers
Cost of living/ inflation	29[1]	26	45	26	27	37
Productivity/ profitability	23	8	32	48	31	21
Market rates/rate for the job	14	7	18	14	21	23
Geared to other (external) settlements	12	11	8	16	14	16
Geared to other (internal) settlement	2	*	3	2	3	2
Ability to pay/ 'all we could afford'	9	8	18	16	4	7
Merit/settled person- by-person	8	1	1	8	18	35
Recession/economic climate	4	7	3	7	2	2
Published norms/ salary clubs	2	2	2	2	3	2
Other answers	10	10	18	10	8	5
Not stated	18	17	10	1	24	1
Base: establishments employing manual workers						
Unweighted	1853[2]	778	332	271	448	81
Weighted	1749	696	231	120	672	105

[1] See Note E.
[2] See Note G.

in private services, the largest group of unrepresented non-manual employees, the arrangement covered only 39 per cent. Generally, however, the considerations taken into account in determining the pay of unionised workers applied also to unorganised workers. The difference lay not in the considerations but in who considered them and how the decision was taken as to what weight should be attached to each. Thirdly, influences upon the pay increases of non-manual workers (see Table 9.18) were broadly in line with those affecting manual employees. At the workplace level, manual increases were more likely to be geared to external settlements while those of non-manual workers were more likely to be linked to internal settlements, presumably of manual workers.

When it came to exploring further sources of variation in influences upon pay settlements, we confined analysis to places where they were determined locally, because it was in relation to such increases that we had the fullest accounts of how they came about. That analysis,

Table 9.18   Managers' accounts of influences upon the most recent pay settlement affecting non-manual workers

	All estab-lishments	Pay collectively determined and most important level of bargaining was:			No non-manual union recognised
		National	Company	Workplace	
Cost of living/ inflation	30[1]	26	46	22	32
Productivity/ profitability	25	5	31	41	37
Market rates/rate for the job	12	5	9	19	19
Geared to other (external) settlements	8	6	6	9	14
Geared to other (internal) settlement	9	2	5	10	3
Ability to pay/ 'all we could afford'	9	8	16	11	7
Merit/settled person-by-person	16	1	3	13	11
Recession/economic climate	5	5	14	6	2
Published norms/ salary clubs	3	1	*	5	5
Other answers	10	10	27	4	6
Not stated	10	12	11	6	7
Base: establishments employing non-manual workers					
Unweighted	2010[2]	789	369	222	613
Weighted	1985	712	262	78	917

[1] See Note E.
[2] See Note G.

Table 9.19 Managers' accounts of the extent of joint regulation with manual trade unions over a number of specified non-pay issues

Percentages

	All establishments 1980	All establishments 1984	Private manufacturing 1980	Private manufacturing 1984	Private services 1980	Private services 1984	Nationalised industries 1980	Nationalised industries 1984	Public services 1980	Public services 1984
Negotiated at some level										
Physical working conditions	92	78	91	75	90	69	97	87	94	82
Redeployment within establishment	79	62	77	63	72	43	92	85	84	66
Staffing/manning levels	76	55	72	47	68	40	81	77	85	62
Redundancy (1980) Size of redundancy payments (1984)	88	46	85	51	85	44	99	37	90	48
Recruitment	69	38	60	31	64	21	62	41	83	49
Negotiated at establishment level										
Physical working conditions	63	37	83	62	57	30	72	63	47	24
Redeployment within establishment	61	32	72	53	63	25	70	69	48	19
Staffing/manning levels	46	24	63	40	52	22	45	63	26	8
Redundancy (1980) Size of redundancy payments (1984)	45	9	73	31	46	7	42	5	19	1
Recruitment	42	15	54	26	47	14	34	29	29	7
Base: establishments where trade unions were recognised for manual workers										
Unweighted	1344	1405	589	462	227	231	128	191	400	521
Weighted	998	1077	322	228	253	260	65	103	358	486

however, full and thorough though we made it, proved to be disappointing. We looked at accounts of influences upon both manual and non-manual settlements in relation to our information on the extent to which the workplace had been running down or increasing its workforce; on the trend in relation to its output or turnover; on its financial performance and the sensitivity of sales to changes in prices; and on its use of advanced technology. We carried out the analysis separately for places where pay increases were unilaterally determined by managers and for places where pay increases were settled by collective bargaining at the workplace level. We found very little evidence of systematic variation in managers' accounts of the influences upon pay settlements. That negative result was particularly surprising as it came after a period when the whole emphasis in public policy towards private sector pay settlements was to encourage managers to attach more attention to the ability of enterprises and establishments to pay and less to such **social** considerations as equity in relation to the increases received by other groups of workers and in relation to the rise in the cost of living. And yet we found little sign of any association between the financial circumstances of workplaces and managers' accounts of the considerations that influenced their most recent settlement, even in places where managers were unconstrained by any trade union representation.[6]

The joint regulation of non-pay issues

In 1980 we asked both managers and shop stewards whether a number of issues other than pay, such as those listed in Table 9.19, were negotiated at the establishment, or were negotiated but not at the establishment or were not negotiated. At that time very surprisingly high levels of negotiation were reported by both managers and shop stewards. For instance, in workplaces where manual unions were recognised, 79 per cent of managers reported that redeployment within the establishment was negotiated and 69 per cent reported that the number of people recruited was negotiated. The accounts of the extent of negotiation over non-pay issues by managers were particularly surprising as managers might have been expected to be reluctant to concede the principle of joint regulation on issues other than pay. We concluded that the most reasonable explanation of the answers we received was that managers and shop stewards were reporting whether any negotiations ever took place over any issue relating to the subject matter about which we asked. That explanation certainly appears even more likely in the light of the more detailed analysis of the extent of consultation and negotiation over the introduction of major technical and other changes in the present survey. As Daniel reports in the companion volume to this book,[7] the extent of negotiations over

Table 9.20 Managers' accounts of the extent of joint regulation with non-manual trade unions over a number of specified non-pay issues

Percentages

	All establishments 1980	All establishments 1984	Private manufacturing 1980	Private manufacturing 1984	Private services 1980	Private services 1984	Nationalised industries 1980	Nationalised industries 1984	Public services 1980	Public services 1984
Negotiated at some level										
Physical working conditions	88	76	91	60	76	69	98	81	91	81
Redeployment within establishment	78	61	80	61	55	44	94	80	87	65
Staffing/manning levels	74	55	64	42	56	32	76	77	84	62
Redundancy (1980)	84		86		74		96		87	
Size of redundancy payments (1984)		49		51		53		38		48
Recruitment	69	39	57	26	51	25	68	38	81	48
Negotiated at establishment level										
Physical working conditions	54	29	84	47	47	17	68	50	47	27
Redeployment within establishment	53	25	75	51	42	17	60	52	51	20
Staffing/manning levels	31	17	55	31	33	9	37	52	23	11
Redundancy (1980)	32		71		31		42		21	
Size of redundancy payments (1984)		5		30		5		5		1
Recruitment	32	11	51	19	34	9	32	21	26	9
Base: establishments where trade unions were recognised for non-manual workers										
Unweighted	*1250*	*1397*	*404*	*351*	*207*	*229*	*130*	*194*	*509*	*623*
Weighted	*932[1]*	*1069*	*134*	*109*	*236*	*247*	*63*	*105*	*498*	*608*

specific, identified changes was low, according to the accounts of both managers and stewards. They were certainly very much lower than would have been expected according to the answers to our general questions asking whether there were negotiations over nominated issues. It is accepted in survey research that people's accounts of how they behaved in specific instances are a better guide to their normal behaviour than general questions about how they do things. In consequence, we concluded that the answers to our questions about negotiations over non-pay issues are best interpreted as reflecting the extent to which there are ever negotiations over some matter relating to the issues, rather than showing the extent to which there are normally full negotiations over all matters concerned with the issues. Accordingly, the answers are most useful for what they tell us about **variation** in patterns of negotiation as between different types of workplace rather than what they have to say about absolute levels of negotiation in any particular type of establishment. That should mean that they were of value to us in determining how far there was change in the extent of collective bargaining over non-pay issues in the period following 1980. Making such comparisons, however, was further complicated by the fact that we modified our questioning about negotiations over non-pay issues in 1984 so that it became no longer possible to make strict comparisons with many of the 1980 results. In 1984 we reduced the number of topics in our list and we asked, first, whether negotiations took place with the unions about the topic and, secondly, in cases where there were negotiations, at what level they took place. We found, as Table 9.19 shows, that, so far as manual workers were concerned, there appeared to be substantially less negotiation over non-pay issues in 1984 and the contrast was particularly marked at the workplace level. The decline in joint regulation appeared to be most marked in private services while nationalised industries seemed to be most immune from the trend. It was also very marked within manufacturing.[8]

The pattern of change in relation to negotiations with non-manual trade unions was very similar to that for manual groups (see Table 9.20). There were, again, strong indications of a general decline in the joint regulation of non-pay issues. The indications were stronger at the workplace level, most apparent in private services and least marked in nationalised industries. In consequence, the pattern of contrast between the four broad sectors was even more pronounced in 1984 than it was in 1980. The contrasts were most clear at the workplace level where joint regulation was most frequently reported in nationalised industries and private manufacturing industry and least frequently reported in private services. Public administration occupied an intermediate position. Here, though, there was a

Table 9.21 Distribution and nature of job evaluation

	All establishments		Private manufacturing		Private services		Nationalised industries		Public services	
	1980	1984	1980	1984	1980	1984	1980	1984	1980	1984
Whether job evaluation exists										
Formal job evaluation							Column percentages			
scheme present	21[1]	21	28	24	20	23	24	34	14	15
No scheme	78	78	72	76	79	77	76	65	84	84
Not stated	*	1	*	*	1	*	*	1	*	*
Base: all establishments										
Weighted	2040	2019	743	592	587	597	134	128	576	400
Unweighted	2000[2]	2000	503	424	859	843	69	65	568	358
Number of schemes									Percentages	
Two or more	22	34	31	48	15	35	29	29	20	19
Basis of largest scheme									Column percentages	
Points system	46	46	45	34	45	45	48	64	50	52
Grading	27	27	25	32	28	32	38	14	27	18
Ranking	13	10	19	12	11	11	9	7	9	5
Factor comparison	9	7	8	6	10	4	1	10	8	13
Other/not stated	5	10	3	15	5	9	4	4	6	11

Base: establishments with formal job evaluation schemes

[1] See Note C.
[2] See Note H.

difference between the non-manual and the manual pattern. Public administration was the only sector in which there was a higher level of joint regulation over issues affecting non-manual workers than over matters affecting manual groups. In evaluating the pattern revealed by Tables 9.19 and 9.20, it should be remembered that the percentages in them are based upon those workplaces that recognised trade unions for the respective categories of worker. When differences in the extent to which trade unions were recognised in the four sectors are added to the picture then they further accentuate the contrasts in the extent of joint regulation in the four sectors.

Variations in negotiations over non-pay issues in manufacturing industry
Within private manufacturing there was a strong tendency for negotiations with manual unions over physical working conditions and redeployment to be more frequently reported at the workplace level the larger the number of manual workers employed at the workplace. But a similar pattern was not apparent in relation to manning levels and recruitment. Independently of size, managers in workplaces belonging to overseas companies were substantially more likely to report that there were negotiations with manual trade unions over non-pay issues. There was also a very marked tendency for negotiations to be reported more frequently the higher the level of manual trade union density at the workplace. The most striking feature of the non-manual analysis in private manufacturing industry, relative to the manual analysis, concerned the contrasting patterns for workplaces belonging to overseas companies. While managers in such places were much more likely than British counterparts to report bargaining with manual unions over non-pay issues, they were very much less likely to report bargaining with non-manual unions over similar matters.

Job evaluation
Over the twenty years or so leading up to our 1980 survey, the use of job evaluation as a basis for systematically determining pay differentials within workplaces and enterprises became much more common. It appears that there may have been further growth over the four years leading up to our 1984 survey. The nature of that growth, however, was a little complex. There was no change, overall, in the proportion of workplaces that practised job evaluation. But those workplaces that did have schemes tended to have more of them. The implication was that there was a marked tendency for workplaces with experience of job evaluation for particular categories of worker to add further schemes over the period for other categories of worker.

So far as the overall distribution was concerned, about a fifth of all

Table 9.22 Distribution of job evaluation in private manufacturing and services, in relation to size, 1984

	All establishments	Number of employees at establishment					All employees[1]
		25–49	50–99	100–199	200–499	500 or more	
Private manufacturing							
1980							
Any formal job evaluation scheme present	28	12	21	34	53	75	55
Two or more schemes	9	5	3	8	16	44	28
Unweighted base	*743*	*63*	*113*	*127*	*164*	*276*	*743*
Weighted base	*503[2]*	*171*	*151*	*86*	*62*	*34*	*503*
1984							
Any formal job evaluation scheme present	24	14	24	21	43	71	48
Two or more schemes	11	7	8	9	23	52	32
Unweighted base	*592*	*61*	*87*	*86*	*134*	*225*	*592*
Weighted base	*424*	*173*	*119*	*63*	*48*	*21*	*424*
Private services							
1980							
Any formal job evaluation scheme present	20	17	23	23	42	46	29
Two or more schemes	3	1	6	4	12	24	9
Unweighted base	*587*	*194*	*146*	*116*	*73*	*58*	*587*
Weighted base	*859*	*536*	*206*	*78*	*31*	*8*	*859*
1984							
Any formal job evaluation scheme present	23	18	29	31	30	52	32
Two or more schemes	8	6	9	13	17	25	15
Unweighted base	*597*	*162*	*152*	*120*	*76*	*87*	*597*
Weighted base	*843*	*490*	*219*	*93*	*32*	*9*	*843*

Bases: establishments in private manufacturing and private services, respectively

workplaces had at least one job evaluation scheme in 1980 and about a fifth also had at least one scheme in 1984 (see Table 9.21). That lack of overall change, however, may have concealed countervailing patterns of change within different sectors. In private manufacturing, there was if anything a decline in the proportion of workplaces operating job evaluation. But, at the same time, there was very substantial growth in the proportion of places with job evaluation that operated two or more schemes. In private services there appeared to be growth in both the proportion of places having any scheme and the proportion having two or more schemes. In the public sector there was less change. Public administration remained very much as it had been. The nationalised industries seemed slightly more likely to have schemes but in cases where they operated job evaluation they were no more likely to have two or more schemes. This pattern was further complicated by differential patterns of change in workplaces of different sizes which had implications for the proportion of workers who worked in places operating job evaluation schemes. Those complications we consider when discussing later in this section the patterns of variation in the use of job evaluation in the different sectors.

While there was no evidence of overall growth in the proportion of workplaces operating job evaluation, there was evidence of very substantial proliferation of job evaluation schemes within workplaces. In 1980, just over a fifth of workplaces with job evaluation had two or more schemes in operation. By 1984, that proportion rose to just over a third (see Table 9.21). Of course, an alternative explanation of the increase in the number of schemes could be that schemes became more fragmented without their coverage having increased. According to that explanation, a group of workers which was covered by just one scheme in 1980 would have become covered by two or more schemes by 1984. We were able to carry out a rough check on these competing explanations because in 1980 we collected information on the number of employees covered by the most recently introduced scheme, while in 1984 we had data on the numbers covered by the largest scheme. We found that these two figures were of a similar order, which suggested that, as there were more schemes in 1984, the coverage of job evaluation had grown. The growth in job evaluation within workplaces was especially marked in private services but it was also very substantial in private manufacturing.

There appeared to be very little difference in the popularity of the different types of scheme over the four years. Points systems remained most popular and grading systems had a good following, while both ranking and factor comparison systems were favoured by only a few. Points systems were especially common in the public sector while

Table 9.3 Distribution of job evaluation in public services and nationalised industries, in relation to size, 1984

	All estab-lishments	Number of employees at establishment				All employees[1]
		25–99	100–199	200–499	500 or more	
Public services						
1980						
Any formal job evaluation scheme present	14	11	17	26	28	22
Two or more schemes	3	3	2	3	7	4
Unweighted base	*576*	*206*	*130*	*113*	*127*	*576*
Weighted base	*568*[2]	*410*	*87*	*50*	*23*	*568*
1984						
Any formal job evaluation scheme present	15	12	22	30	21	20
Two or more schemes	3	3	1	7	3	3
Unweighted base	*634*	*224*	*121*	*109*	*190*	*634*
Weighted base	*627*	*368*	*85*	*49*	*25*	*627*
Nationalised industries						
1980						
Any formal job evaluation scheme present	24	24	23	20	46	46
Two or more schemes	7	11	—	8	22	27
Unweighted base	*134*	*25*	*26*	*28*	*55*	*134*
Weighted base	*69*	*37*	*17*	*9*	*5*	*69*
1984						
Any formal job evaluation scheme present	34	31	30	46	48	43
Two or more schemes	10	4	8	26	30	21
Unweighted base	*196*	*39*	*35*	*43*	*79*	*196*
Weighted base	*106*	*64*	*20*	*15*	*8*	*106*

Bases: establishments in public services and nationalised industries, respectively

[1] See Note 1 to Table 9.3.   [2] See Note H.

grading schemes were more widely used in the private sector. These results referred to the largest scheme if there was more than one. In instances where workplaces operated more than one scheme, we also asked about the system used in the scheme that covered the second largest group of workers at the establishment. We wanted to see whether there was one system that was most commonly used for one category of employee but yet another most commonly used for a second category. We found that, in practice, the systems used in secondary schemes very closely mirrored those used in the schemes which covered the largest group of workers at the establishment. As a consequence, the picture presented by our data on the largest schemes can be taken as a broad indicator of the underlying pattern when all schemes are taken into account.

Tables 9.22 and 9.23 show the pattern of variation in 1984 within our four broad sectors in relation to size. It is apparent that the tendency for job evaluation to be more common the larger the number of people employed was strongest in manufacturing industry. In public services, by contrast, any association between the use of job evaluation and establishment size was much less marked. This was because, as our 1980 data showed, job evaluation schemes in the public sector almost never covered just a single establishment. As there was generally more variation in the use of job evaluation in private manufacture and private services, our analysis in the next section of patterns of variation in the use of systematic job evaluation is concentrated in those sectors.

Job evaluation in private manufacturing
As one of the strongest influences upon the extent to which workplaces in the private sector operated job evaluation was the number of people employed at the establishment, the proportion of workers employed at places that used such systems was very substantially higher than the proportion of workplaces using schemes (see Table 9.22). For example, only about a quarter of workplaces in private manufacturing used job evaluation, larger workplaces were so much more likely to do so that very nearly a half of all employees were employed at places where the rates of pay for at least some group of workers were determined by job evaluation.[9] A third of employees in manufacturing were employed at places with two or more schemes in operation. A fifth worked where there were three or more schemes. The use of job evaluation appeared to be very slightly more highly geared to the number of non-manual workers employed than to the number of manual workers.

Apart from size there were two further characteristics of workplaces in manufacturing that were very strongly associated with the extent to which they used systematic job evaluation. The first was the nationality of the company to which they belonged and the second was arrangements for trade union recognition at workplaces. First, workplaces belonging to overseas companies were very much more likely, independently of size, both to use job evaluation and to have more than one scheme. Secondly, workplaces that recognised trade unions were three times as likely to use job evaluation than places that did not. That was partly a consequence of size, but even when places of similar size were compared it remained true that workplaces where trade unions were recognised were very much more likely to use job evaluation. The contrast was especially marked so far as smaller workplaces were concerned. In smaller workplaces where trade unions were not recognised then job evaluation was rare. In places of similar size where unions were recognised then job evaluation was common. The patterns were similar for both manual and non-manual trade union recognition. They provided very strong evidence that the need to justify pay differentials to trade union representatives encouraged the use of systematic methods for determining differentials.

Job evaluation in private services
The 'gearing' of job evaluation to the size of workplaces was not as strong in private services as it was in private manufacturing. In consequence there was not such a large difference between the proportion of private service establishments that operated job evaluation and the proportion of workers that were employed at them (see Table 9.23). Twenty three per cent of service units had job evaluation while 32 per cent of service workers were employed at them. Eight per cent had two or more schemes while 15 per cent of service workers worked at places with two or more schemes. So far as services were concerned, the number of non-manual workers employed at the establishment had substantially more influence upon the extent to which job evaluation was used than the number of manual workers employed. Moreover, the overall size of the enterprise of which the workplace was part tended to be a more important independent influence than in manufacturing upon the use of job evaluation.

Apart from size, the nationality of the company to which the workplace belonged and the pattern of trade union recognition proved to be major sources of variation in the use of job evaluation in private services – as they were in manufacturing. Workplaces belonging to overseas companies were less common in service industry than in manufacturing, but it remained the case that they were more likely to use job evaluation. The contrast between them and UK-owned workplaces was not, however, as marked as in manufacturing. Similarly, job evaluation was very much more common in service workplaces where trade unions were recognised, independently of workplace size. In services, though, it was the pattern of white-collar trade union recognition that had substantially greater impact upon the extent to which there was systematic job evaluation. This reflected a general tendency for the pattern of white-collar employment to be more important for industrial relations arrangements in private services, probably reflecting the predominance of white-collar employment in that sector.

Share-ownership schemes

A feature of systems of pay that has been attracting increasing attention over the past decade has been the share-ownership scheme, including share option schemes, often designed to encourage wider ownership of shares among the employees of enterprises. We found in 1980 that there was evidence of rapid growth in such schemes towards the end of the 1970s. It seemed that that growth was encouraged by the fiscal benefits that some schemes were given in 1978, although the growth was apparent before that date. In 1980, schemes were heavily concentrated in the financial services sector and their introduction tended to be strongly associated with a favourable financial performance on the part of the establishment. [10]

By 1984, the proportion of workplaces in industry and commerce whose parent company operated a share-ownership scheme rose from 13 per cent to 23 per cent. Schemes remained most common in financial services (69 per cent), although they were already so well established in that sector in 1980 that the rate of increase there was less marked than elsewhere. In retail distribution, which was the next most favoured sector, the proportion rose from 19 per cent to 34 per cent over the four-year period. In 1980, schemes were comparatively rare in manufacturing industry but there has subsequently been growth in that sector too. It was most marked in electrical and instrument engineering, where the incidence had doubled, rising to 32 per cent.

Not only had the number of schemes grown over the period but so also had the coverage of the schemes. Only 15 per cent were for management level only. The proportion of schemes with 100 per cent eligibility rose from 16 per cent to 35 per cent. That doubtless reflected the way in which the new tax exemptions in the 1980 legislation encouraged schemes to be comprehensive in their criteria for eligibility. On the other hand, there was also some growth in schemes that excluded such a high proportion of employees that they were very unlikely to qualify for approval under the 1980 Finance

Act. These were presumably schemes confined to senior staff. Typically, though, about 85 per cent of the employees at a workplace which was part of a scheme were eligible for it. Many fewer actually participated, however. The most common level of participation in 1984 was 15 per cent, a proportion very similar to the level in 1980. On the other hand, because the number of schemes increased over the period[11] there was also some increase in the number of employees participating in share-ownership schemes. The proportion rose from five per cent to seven per cent of all employees in the industrial and commercial sector. It is clear that despite the spread in the number of schemes and their coverage, only a small proportion of employees yet enjoy the benefit of share ownership as part of their package of remuneration from work.

Notes and references

1. Daniel W W and Millward N (1983) *Workplace Industrial Relations in Britain: The DE/PSI/SSRC Survey*, Heinemann Educational Books, London, pp.177-213.

2. Our detailed questions about levels of bargaining over pay increases focused upon the bargaining group covering the largest group of manual workers or non-manual workers as the case might be. So far as manual workers were concerned, 71 per cent were covered by the largest or only bargaining group for manual workers in places that recognised manual unions. The comparable figure for non-manual groups was 73 per cent. In the 1980 survey, we asked the questions about bargaining levels of the second largest bargaining groups as well as the largest groups. We found little difference between the overall patterns reported for largest groups compared with those for second largest groups.

3. This theme was apparent in the comments of industrial relations researchers who attended a conference organised by the ESRC to discuss the first survey in our series. Subsequent support for the theme led the ESRC to establish a separate company-level survey. The preliminary findings indicate that there is no systematic over-statement by managers at workplace level of their role in pay negotiations.

4. Daniel W W (1976) *Wage Determination in Industry*, Political and Economic Planning No.563, London.

5. Daniel W W and Millward N (1983) *op. cit.*, pp.193-4.

6. The pattern is consistent with our analysis of pay levels in the 1980 survey, which showed them to be largely independent of the financial circumstances of workplaces (see Daniel and Millward (1983) *op. cit.*, pp.260-75). Our analysis of that material has been largely confirmed by extensive multivariate analysis of the determinates of pay levels by other researchers. See Blanchflower D (1985) *Union Relative Wage Effects: A Cross-Section Analysis Using Establishment Data from the 1980 Workplace Industrial Relations Survey*, Doctoral thesis, University of London; Blanchflower D (1984) 'Union relative wage effects: a cross-section analysis using establishment data', *British Journal of Industrial Relations*, November, pp.311-32.

7. Daniel W W (1986 forthcoming) *Workplace Industrial Relations and Technical Change*.

8. This is in stark contrast with Batstone's findings, comparing his results from a small postal survey in 1983 with those of the 1978 Warwick survey. (But see also note 1 at end of Chapter 1.) Batstone E (1984) *Working Order: Workplace Industrial Relations Over Two Decades*, Blackwell, Oxford, pp.274-9.

9. The survey results contain precise estimates from management respondents of the numbers of male and female employees covered by the largest and second largest schemes. So far no analysis of these data from the 1984 survey has been made.

10. Daniel and Millward (1983) *op. cit.*, pp.210-12.

11. Share ownership schemes are the subject of a current research project, funded by the Department of Employment, involving both survey and case-study methods; for a summary of the results see Smith G R (1986) 'Profit sharing and employee share ownership in Britain', *Employment Gazette*, September, pp.380-5.

10 Industrial Action

In this chapter we report the findings on the form and extent of industrial action among our sampled establishments. We show that the extent and nature of industrial action in 1984 was very different from that recorded in 1980, the intervening period being one of rapid economic change and one in which important legislative provisions relating to industrial disputes were either enacted or had come into practical effect. In particular, the results show a substantial increase in the proportion of establishments affected by very short strikes over the period, mainly among white-collar employees within the public services sector, and a decline in the proportion affected by blue-collar strike action, mainly within the private manufacturing sector. It is important to emphasise that our measures of the **extent** of industrial action relate to the *proportion of workplaces affected* and are, therefore, different from, though not inconsistent with, the official Department of Employment figures for the number of stoppages of work due to industrial disputes, which record stoppages with a common 'cause' as a **single** stoppage, regardless of the number of workplaces affected.

As in 1980, the survey questions covered all manifestations of collective conflict behaviour, such as strikes, picketing, overtime bans and go-slows, but individual withdrawals such as absenteeism or accidents were again excluded. In both surveys the questioning referred to the twelve months prior to interview and thus typically covered the periods from mid-1979 to mid-1980, and mid-1983 to mid-1984 respectively. The questions covered the manual and the non-manual workforces separately, and the findings are generally reported as such in this chapter. Although coal mining was excluded from the samples for both surveys, it is still likely that the 1984 survey results will reflect the indirect effects of the 1984/85 dispute within that industry.

To lessen the burden on respondents in smaller workplaces, questioning in our second survey was restricted to those establishments with either five or more manual workers, or five or more non-manuals, given that the 1980 results showed that it was very rare for those with less than five of either type to report **any** industrial action. The 1984 survey results reported here, therefore, have been adjusted to make the results from the two surveys comparable by making a similar exclusion. Similarly, although all respondents were asked questions about the forms and extent of industrial action in both surveys, in 1980 these included a small number of representatives of **unrecognised** unions whereas in 1984 only representatives of **recognised** trade unions were interviewed. Therefore, to maintain comparability, those few cases in the 1980 survey where representatives from unrecognised unions were interviewed have also been excluded from the analysis presented here.

Where possible, the figures presented refer to the **combined** responses of managers and worker representatives. As in 1980, the 1984 results suggest that there is some variation in the reporting of forms of industrial action across the main respondents, and for the reasons that were spelled out in our earlier book,[1] it is clear that taking the combined responses provides the best possible measurement of the **extent** of industrial action in the majority of cases. However, later in the chapter, where the focus of attention is the relationship between the various **characteristics** of industrial action rather than the overall extent, we shall use the responses from a single type of respondent, namely worker representatives, as our management respondents were not asked these more detailed questions in 1984.

Changes in the form and extent of industrial action

Table 10.1 shows that, in overall terms, the proportion of establishments affected by any form of industrial action among either the manual or the non-manual workforce increased slightly between 1980 and 1984, from 22 per cent to 25 per cent of establishments. However, the proportion experiencing a strike increased by about half, from 13 per cent to 19 per cent of establishments, reflecting a substantial increase among establishments in the public services sector (from 17 per cent to 41 per cent) and a large decline among private manufacturing establishments (from 22 per cent to 10 per cent). The proportion of strike-affected establishments within the nationalised industries (outside coal mining) remained the same at about one third, and strikes among establishments within private services were still very rare (five per cent of establishments). More specifically, the **increase** occurred mainly within Public Administration (from 17 per cent to 50 per cent of establishments) and Education (12 per cent to 46 per cent). To a lesser extent there was also an increase within the Energy and Water Supply Industries (20 per cent to 36 per cent), even though the strike within the coal mining industry is excluded from the 1984 figure. The decline in manufacturing occurred within vehicle manufacturing (from 67 per cent to 23 per cent) and other engineering sectors (such as metal goods and mechanical engineering which

Table 10.1   The extent to which establishments were affected by industrial action, as reported by any respondent[1]

Percentages

	Manual or Non-manual		Manual		Non-manual	
	1980	1984	1980	1984	1980	1984
Strike action	13	19	11[2]	8	4	14
Non-strike action	16	18	10	8	8	12
Strike or non-strike action	22	25	16	13	11	18
Strike action lasting:						
less than 1 day	6	14	4	5	2	10
1 day or more	9	12	7	5	3	9
1 day but less than a week	..	11	..[3]	5	..	9
1 week or more	..	1	..	1	..	★
Non-strike action:						
Overtime bans/restriction	10	11	7	6	5	6
Work to rule	7	8	4	2	4	6
Blacking of work	5	3	2	2	3	2
Lockout	1	★	1	★	★	★
Go-slow	1	★	1	★	★	★
Other pressure[4]	1	2	1	1	1	2
Base: establishments with any of types of workers at column heads						
Unweighted	*2040*	*2019*	*1899*	*1853*	*2034*	*2010*
Weighted	*2000*	*2000*	*1823*	*1749*	*1981*	*1985*

[1] The percentages represent those establishments where either the manager or the relevant worker representative reported industrial action of the type specified.
[2] See Note F.
[3] See Note J.
[4] 'Work-ins' and 'sit-ins' are included with the more general 'other pressure' category as so few cases were reported.

declined from 33 per cent to 11 per cent). Clearly, whereas the 1980 figures tend to reflect the disputes within the steel and engineering industries, the 1984 figures reflect those within Education and Public Administration (given the absence of coal mining from both the survey samples).

In the 1984 survey we used more precise measures of the duration of strikes than the *less than one day* and *more than one day* categories used in 1980, and from these data it is clear that in cases where strikes of one day or more were reported, the vast majority were less than one week in length (Table 10.1). Indeed, the table shows that the proportion of workplaces where very short strikes (less than one day) were reported more than doubled between 1980 and 1984, from six per cent to 14 per cent. We pointed out earlier that there is no inconsistency between our figures for the number of strike-affected workplaces and the official Department of Employment figures for the number of stoppages of work due to industrial disputes, even though the latter showed an overall **decline** of one quarter between our two study periods.[2] Besides the exclusion of small and 'political' strikes from the Department's figures, the two sources are clearly measuring different aspects of strikes and there need be no necessary correlation between them. While the Department's figures are a measure of strike **frequency**, the results from our survey series are a measure of the **extensiveness** strikes. In general terms then, our results suggest that in 1984 strikes were shorter but affected a larger proportion of workplaces than in 1980.

It is also clear from Table 10.1 that overtime bans among either the manual or the non-manual workforce were as widespread as strikes of one day or more in both 1980 and 1984, around one tenth of workplaces being affected. Working to rule was reported in eight per cent of workplaces, about the same as previously, but blackings were down from five per cent to three per cent. Other types of non-strike action were rarely reported in either 1980 or 1984.

In overall terms the proportion of establishments reporting some form of industrial action among the **manual** workforce declined slightly between the two study periods, from 16 per cent to 13 per cent of establishments, while the figure for **non-manuals** increased by over a half from 11 per cent to 18 per cent. In 1984 non-manual workers were much more likely than manuals to take strike and non-strike action, a reversal of the position in 1980. In addition, whereas overtime bans were the most common form of non-strike action among both groups in 1980, in 1984 this remained so for manuals but for non-manuals working to rule was as common as the overtime ban (see Table 10.1).

Industrial action among the manual workforce
Between 1980 and 1984 strike action among the manual workforce fell from 11 per cent to eight per cent of establishments with manual workers, and non-strike action declined by a similar amount (from ten per cent to eight per cent). It is also clear from Table 10.1 that, in 1984, strikes of less than a day were as common as those lasting a day or more, whereas in 1980 the longer strikes were twice as common. However, in 1984 one per cent of establishments were affected by strikes of one week or more (these data are not available for 1980).

As Table 10.2 shows, and as we might expect given the general pattern reported above, there was a substantial decline in manual strike action among establishments in the private manufacturing sector. There was a slight increase among the nationalised industries but virtually no change in the public services sector. In other words,

Table 10.2   Changes in manual and non-manual industrial action by broad sector, as reported by managers or worker representatives

Percentages

	Private manufacturing 1980	1984	Private services 1980	1984	Nationalised industries 1980	1984	Public services 1980	1984
Manual industrial action								
Strike action	21[1]	10	3	4	24	30	10	9
Non-strike action	20	13	3	4	25	20	8	7
Strike or non-strike action	31	19	5	6	41	38	15	13
Base: establishments with manual workers								
Unweighted	734	580	521	515	130	191	514	567
Weighted	498	412	755	689	66	103	504	545
Non-manual industrial action								
Strike action	3	1	1	4	16	9	9	38
Non-strike action	3	4	2	2	10	11	22	31
Strike or non-strike action	5	5	4	5	27	19	28	44
Base: establishments with non-manual workers								
Unweighted	743	592	585	593	133	194	573	631
Weighted	503	424	854	836	68	105	562	621

[1] See Note F.

the bulk of the decline in strike action within manufacturing is accounted for by a large decline in **manual** strike action. Similarly, the decline was most marked within vehicle manufacturing (from 66 per cent to 23 per cent of establishments with manual workers) and among workplaces in the metal goods and mechanical engineering sectors (from 33 per cent to 10 per cent); but there was also a large decline within electrical and instrument engineering (from 21 per cent to 14 per cent) and rubber and plastics, and other manufacturing (from 20 per cent to 11 per cent). It was still the case, however, that strike or non-strike action among the manual workforce was much more likely the larger the establishment, the larger the manual workforce, where trade unions were recognised, where union membership was high and where managers assessed the state of relations with the workforce[3] as generally poor. In 1980 manual workers were more likely to take both strike and non-strike action where they negotiated at workplace level, and although industrial action was still unlikely in cases where multi-employer bargaining was predominant in 1984, it was as likely among workplaces with either workplace or single-employer bargaining. In our earlier book we concluded that in 1980 there was no tendency for establishments with agreed procedures for dealing with disputes to be less prone to industrial action,[4] a finding recently confirmed by other researchers using more sophisticated, multivariate techniques.[5] Cross-tabulation of the results from our second survey shows that this was also true in 1984.[6]

As in 1980, the most widespread forms of non-strike action among blue-collar workers were overtime bans, working to rule and blackings, although overtime bans and working to rule were slightly less common than previously. The other forms of non-strike action we classified (go-slows, lockouts, work-ins/sit-ins) were reported only rarely in both surveys (see Table 10.1). The decline in the extent of overtime bans occurred exclusively within the private manufacturing sector, again a reflection of the 1979/80 engineering dispute. The bulk of the decline in the extent of working to rule occurred within this sector and within the public services sector.

The comparative pattern for the non-manual workforce
The pattern of industrial action among non-manuals changed substantially between 1980 and 1984 with strikes increasing from four per cent to 14 per cent of establishments with non-manual workers, and non-strike action increasing by a half, from eight per cent to 12 per cent. Strike action lasting both less than a day and a day or more increased substantially between 1980 and 1984 (Table 10.1), but the more precise measures of strike duration used in our second survey enable us to say that very few cases of white-collar strike action lasted longer than a week in 1984. As with manuals, overtime bans and working to rule were the most widespread forms of non-strike action among white-collar staff, with both increasing slightly over the period, followed by blackings, which were less widespread than in 1980.

Table 10.2 shows that there was a substantial increase in white-collar strike action within the public services sector, from nine per cent to 38 per cent of establishments. As we might expect, much of the increase in strike action in the Education and Public Administration sectors reported above is accounted for by strike action among the white-collar workforce. In Public Administration, a half of workplaces with white-collar workers reported white-collar strike action in 1984, compared with only 13 per cent in 1980, and within the Education sector the proportion reporting strikes increased from seven per cent in 1980 to 45 per cent in 1984. There were also substantial increases in the Energy and Water Supply Industries (from one per cent to 17 per cent) and among establishments within the Banking sector (from zero to 14 per cent). Though still rare, strikes among establishments within the private services sector also showed a slight increase over the period. However, there was a decline of about a half among the nationalised industries (from 16 per cent to nine per cent of workplaces) and a small decline among private manufacturing establishments.

Non-strike action among white-collar staff remained fairly uncommon among workplaces in the private manufacturing and private services sectors, but among the nationalised industries, as in 1980, about one tenth of workplaces were affected. However, it was again in the public services sector that the bulk of the overall increase occurred, from 22 per cent of establishments in 1980 to almost one third in 1984 (see Table 10.2). Within that sector there was a slight increase in overtime bans, but much of the increase is accounted for by a doubling of the proportion of workplaces affected by working to rule, from 10 per cent in 1980 to 19 per cent in 1984. Interestingly, however, it was mainly within the Education sector that the increase occurred (from 18 per cent to 43 per cent of workplaces), non-strike action within Public Administration **declining** between the two study periods (from 41 per cent to 30 per cent of establishments). Among educational establishments there was a substantial increase in instances of working to rule (from 12 per cent to 35 per cent of workplaces) and in overtime bans (from three per cent to 17 per cent), which probably reflects the teachers boycott of lunch-time supervision and extra-curricular activities during their pay dispute of that year.

The sources of variation in industrial action by manual workers, outlined above, tend to apply equally for non-manuals, but with strike action being particularly common in very large establishments. Interestingly, however, the better union density measures used in our second survey (see Chapter 3) indicate that in 1984 this particular relationship only holds for establishments with up to 99 per cent white-collar union membership, the tendency to take action being substantially less among those with comprehensive union membership. These results are given in Table 10.3. The pattern is very similar in both the private and the public sectors and the relationship remained when we controlled for establishment size. If there was any hint of an exception here it was among workplaces employing between 500 and 999 people, but the number of cases in this particular category is too small to contradict the general pattern. As in 1980, however, and in contrast to the pattern for manual workers, non-manuals were much more likely to take industrial action where the locus of pay bargaining was at the multi-employer level, obviously reflecting the public sector concentration of white-collar employees.

The characteristics of reported industrial action
Although all respondents in both surveys were questioned in general about the forms of industrial action which had occurred during the twelve months prior to interview, in the 1984 survey only worker representatives were asked the more detailed questions about the

Table 10.3   Non-manual industrial action in 1984 in relation to union membership

Percentages

| | Union density among non-manual workers | | | | | |
	No members	1–24%	25–49%	50–89%	90–99%	100%
Strike action	★	1	16[1]	35	45	15
Non-strike action	★	5	2	30	45	14
Strike or non-strike action	★	6	17	42	58	19
Base: establishments with non-manual workers						
Unweighted	*542*	*97*	*153*	*482*	*161*	*251*
Weighted	*830*	*88*	*122*	*331*	*136*	*299*

[1] See Note F.

most recent strike or non-strike action. During the design of the second survey it was decided to restrict the more detailed questioning to worker representatives for two main reasons. First, by allocating this section to worker representatives only, space could be made available on the main management questionnaire for new topic areas, such as the sections on new technology. Secondly, it seemed reasonable to assume that worker representatives would be particularly well placed to provide detailed information about the industrial action in which they are likely to have played a part. Obviously, to make the results from the two surveys comparable, the few cases in the 1980 survey where worker representatives from unrecognised unions were interviewed have been excluded from the analysis presented below.

The questioning in both surveys was broadly the same. Taking the most recent strike and non-strike action separately, we asked about the duration of the action, the number of employees from the establishment taking part, the groups of employees involved, whether it was the first time that these employees had taken action, whether employees from other establishments were involved and the main reasons for the action. A feature of the 1984 survey was the inclusion of a question about whether the reported action had at any time been made 'official' by the union or unions concerned, but as there was no comparable question asked in the first survey, we report these results in a separate section.

Although the findings refer only to the **most recent** dispute, they can be regarded as typical of all the disputes that affected our sampled establishments during the years in question because in both surveys only a small proportion of establishments were reported as having more than one instance of each of the types of action we specified among either section of the workforce. However, it should be emphasised that the findings on recent strikes refer only to those lasting one day or more: cases with only recent strikes of less than one day were excluded from the more detailed questioning. The series of questions covered the manual and the non-manual workforces separately.

Reasons given for industrial action
In both surveys we asked respondents what they thought were the main reasons for the most recent dispute and we coded their answers using the same broad categories as the Department of Employment's official records of stoppages of work due to industrial disputes.[7] However, unlike the official records which use further subdivisions to cater for multiple or complex 'causes', our coding system allowed multiple coding among the nine broad categories. Our aim was to compare the reasons given for non-strike action with those given for striking, to see the ways in which strikes fit into the more general pattern of industrial action. Using the same questions and coding system in both surveys allows us to assess changes in these patterns and Table 10.4 shows these comparisons within and between our two study periods for each section of the workforce.

These results are worthy of attention in several respects. From the 1980 figures it is clear that *pay* was the predominant reason for strike and non-strike action among both sections of the workforce and, notwithstanding a slight decline, it would appear that **in general terms** this was still the case in 1984. The exception in 1984 is the pattern for manual strikes, with half as many respondents giving *pay* as the main reason than in 1980. Indeed, *pay* was more likely to be given as the reason for non-strike action than for strikes among blue-collar workers in 1984. As we might expect, *pay* was more likely to be given as the reason for either form of action among blue-collar workers in cases where workplace-level bargaining was predominant, whereas for white-collar staff *pay* was more frequently given as the main reason in cases where multi-employer bargaining was predominant. It is also notable from Table 10.4 that at least a quarter of cases in each 1984 column were coded to the *miscellaneous* category, and that for manual strikes the figure is almost a half, which is more than those giving *pay* as the main reason.

Although it might be tempting to suggest that these *miscellaneous* cases should have been more rigorously re-classified among the other eight specific categories, this would be to miss the significance of the finding itself. The *miscellaneous* category covers not only 'causes' in

Table 10.4 Reasons given by worker representatives for most recent industrial action

Column percentages

	Most recent strike of one day or more				Most recent non-strike action			
	Manual		Non-manual		Manual		Non-manual	
	1980	1984	1980	1984	1980	1984	1980	1984
Pay: wage rates & earnings	59[1]	32	61	51	41	38	56	53
Pay: extra wage & fringe benefits	12	7	1	*	4	8	5	4
Duration & pattern of working hours	20	3	2	—	20	9	6	3
Redundancy issues	3	6	12	5	5	6	8	8
Trade union matters	6	5	2	19	6	2	5	2
Working conditions and supervision	2	1	*	2	3	3	1	2
Manning & work allocation	6	10	9	9	21	10	22	15
Dismissal & other disciplinary measures	6	2	3	1	1	1	*	*
Miscellaneous	6	47	6	25	7	24	5	24
Miscellaneous only[2]	5	43	3	19	3	22	3	17
Not answered	7	*	12	3	7	9	4	6
Base: establishments where industrial action of type specified was reported by relevant worker representative								
Unweighted	185	152	70	143	212	237	207	233
Weighted	77	51	26	115	96	91	102	151

[1] See Note E.
[2] Cases where the reason given was coded to the miscellaneous category only.

the official Department of Employment coding scheme, it also had to accommodate in our data disputes that might be regarded as **political** by the Department of Employment and, therefore, not recorded in the official figures for stoppages of work due to **industrial** disputes. For example, it would appear that those sectors where *pay* was least frequently given as the main reason for manual strikes in 1984 were also those where *miscellaneous reasons* were most common, namely in the public and services sectors. In fact over 80 per cent of the *miscellaneous reasons* cases occurred in the **non-manufacturing** classes of the *Standard Industrial Classification* and nearly a third of these fell within the Postal Services and Telecommunications category. The pattern is very similar for manual non-strike action. It seems likely that these cases refer to the disputes related to privatisation[8] within that sector, which may go some way towards explaining the smaller proportion of manual strikes in 1984 for which *pay* was given as the main reason.

Action over the *duration and pattern of working hours* declined in importance between 1980 and 1984, particularly for manual workers, and in 1984 was more likely to take the form of non-strike action than striking for both sections of the workforce. It should be emphasised, however, that the 1980 figures are partly a reflection of the widespread engineering dispute which was partly about hours of work.

Behind *pay*, the second (single) most common reason given for white collar strikes in 1984 was *trade union matters* which probably refers, in many cases, to the action over the banning of trade unions at GCHQ at Cheltenham. Indeed, as much of the extensive sympathy action related to this issue lasted less than a single day, and would therefore not have been covered by our detailed questioning, it would seem likely that our results understate the significance of trade union-related reasons for (all) white-collar strikes in 1984. However, the preference for strikes rather than more 'cut-price' forms of action over this issue is particularly evident from Table 10.4, even allowing for the fact that the survey results exclude the shorter strikes associated with it.

Although both groups of workers were likely to use non-strike action in relation to *manning and work allocation* issues in 1980, in 1984 blue-collar workers were equally likely to use either form of action. Similarly, in 1984 *redundancy* issues among manuals were likely to be contested by either form, whereas previously there was a preference for non-strike sanctions. By contrast, white-collar employees seemed less likely to strike over this issue in 1984 than in 1980, and were more likely opt for non-strike action.

Although it was still uncommon for non-strike sanctions to be used over *dismissal and disciplinary issues*, in 1984 both groups of workers also seemed less likely to strike over this than in 1980 which may reflect the greater availability of formal procedures for dealing with disputes of this kind in 1984 than in 1980 (see Chapter 7). As far as issues related to working conditions and supervision were concerned, blue-collar workers seemed less likely to strike than previously although they still had a preference for non-strike action, while white-collar staff were much more likely to use both forms of action than previously.

Duration and continuity

As Table 10.5 shows, and as might be expected, non-strike action during both study periods was undertaken for considerably longer periods than strike action, regardless of the section of the workforce involved, with the vast majority of instances lasting longer than a working week. The proportion of establishments reporting very short strikes increased substantially over the period with practically all the (recent) white-collar strikes of one day or more lasting just the single day in 1984, and the extent of one-day manual strikes almost doubling over the period from 31 per cent to 59 per cent of establishments with a strike of one day or more. This is consistent with the view[9] that trade unionists may be resorting to a form of 'cut-price' strike action in the mid-1980s as being the most efficient sanction, rather than longer strikes which may be effective but costly to organise, and non-strike sanctions which are less costly but also less effective. One reason for this may be that in recent years stoppages which seemed likely to last some considerable time have increasingly been terminated at an early stage by employers initiating legal action.[10]

The bulk of the non-strike action in 1984 was conducted over consecutive days, the unusually high figure for manual strikes over intermittent days in 1980 reflecting the nature of the engineering dispute during that period. But it is still of interest that intermittent strikes, a novel type in 1979/80, were still being used in 1983/84.

Locality of action

We defined industrial action as 'local' if only employees from the sampled establishment were involved in the dispute, and although a minority of establishments reported the most recent **strike** as 'local' in both surveys, the overall pattern changed substantially between the two study periods, as we can see from Table 10.6. Overall, around one fifth of strikes among either section of the workforce were local in 1980, but almost half the cases of manual non-strike action involved only the sampled establishment as against a tenth of cases for white-collar staff. From Table 10.6 it is clear that, regardless of sector, manual strikes were much more likely to be local in 1984 than

Table 10.5 Reports by worker representatives of most recent industrial action in relation to duration and whether on consecutive or intermittent days

Column percentages

| | Most recent strike of one day or more | | | | Most recent non-strike action | | | |
| | Manual | | Non-manual | | Manual | | Non-manual | |
	1980	1984	1980	1984	1980	1984	1980	1984
Duration in working days								
1	31	59	67	91				
1–3	47[1]	77	77	95	24	21	9	12
4–5	10	4	1	3	8	6	6	3
6 or more	42	17	10	2	57	48	56	44
Other answers[2]	*	2	12	—	11	25	29	41
Action over consecutive intermittent days								
Consecutive days	46	80	(64)[3]	(92)	95	92	90	96
Intermittent days	54	20	(36)	(2)	4	5	7	2
Not answered	—	—	—	6	*	3	3	2
Base[4]: establishments where worker representatives reported the most recent action of type specified in column heads								
Unweighted	185	152	70	143	212	237	207	233
Weighted	77	51	26	115	96	91	102	151

[1] See Note C.
[2] Includes cases where either no information was available or the action was still in progress.
[3] See Note B.
[4] In the second half of the table the base changes to establishments with action lasting two days or more.

Table 10.6 Extent to which industrial action was local[1]

Percentages

	All sectors		Private sector		Public sector	
	1980	1984	1980	1984	1980	1984
Manual strike action	17	32	23	68	(2)[2]	11
Unweighted	*185*	*152*	*143*	*68*	*42*	*84*
Weighted	*77*	*51*	*56*	*19*	*22*	*32*
Non-manual strike action	21	1	(33)	§[3]	(12)	*
Unweighted	*70*	*143*	*37*	*16*	*33*	*127*
Weighted	*26*	*115*	*11*	*2*	*15*	*113*
Manual non-strike action	47	61	47	76	46	39
Unweighted	*212*	*237*	*162*	*150*	*50*	*87*
Weighted	*96*	*91*	*70*	*54*	*27*	*37*
Non-manual non-strike action	9	10	35	59	3	6
Unweighted	*207*	*233*	*73*	*63*	*134*	*170*
Weighted	*102*	*151*	*18*	*11*	*84*	*140*

All bases: establishments where worker representatives reported action of type specified.

[1] Local industrial action was action confined to the sampled establishment and the percentages in the table represent the proportion of establishments where the most recent industrial action specified was local.
[2] See Note B.
[3] See Note A.

in 1980. At the same time, however, the change in the pattern for white-collar strikes was much larger and in the opposite direction. Whereas a fifth of white-collar strikes were local in 1980, in 1984 practically none of them was, with the vast majority of them being in the public sector. Previous authors have noted the tendency for trade unionists within public services to engage in either 'selective' strike action at strategic workplaces, such as revenue collection, or short but **widespread** strike action, or both.[11] The power of the 'cut-price' strike within public services would seem to lie in its extensiveness, in terms of the number of workplaces affected. Our data suggest that such a strategy may have been used by a number of unions within the public services sector, on a number of occasions in 1983/84. As we might expect, blue-collar strikes were much more likely to be local in cases where workplace-level bargaining was predominant. However, for both sections of the workforce, the overall extent of local **non-strike** action increased over the period, particularly for blue-collar workers within the private sector. It is particularly notable from

Table 10.6 that although almost all white-collar strikes in 1984 were widespread stoppages, the tendency for white-collar workers to engage in local non-strike action in either the public or the private sector almost doubled between the two study periods. However, with the exception of white-collar strike action, local industrial action in 1983/84 tended to be concentrated within the private sector of the economy. To a lesser extent this was also true in 1980.

Incidence of first-time action
The results from both surveys show that in general terms only a minority of representatives of either blue-collar or white-collar workers reported that their section of the workforce had taken part in industrial action for the first time (Table 10.7). In 1984 slightly fewer establishments experienced first-time strike action among either section of the workforce than in 1980. The pattern for non-strike action, however, is rather different which in turn means that the overall pattern of first-time industrial action fluctuated quite sharply between our two survey periods. In 1980 manual workers were much more likely to have engaged in non-strike action for the first time than strike action, and the incidence of first-time non-strike action was at that time more common than among white-collar employees. Howev-

Table 10.7   Proportion of cases of industrial action where employees were taking action for the first time

Percentages

	1980	1984
Strike action		
Manual	34	30
Unweighted	*185*	*152*
Weighted	*77*	*51*
Non-manual	38	31
Unweighted	*70*	*143*
Weighted	*26*	*115*
Non-strike action		
Manual	50	18
Unweighted	*212*	*237*
Weighted	*96*	*91*
Non-manual	38	24
Unweighted	*207*	*233*
Weighted	*102*	*151*

All bases: establishments where worker representatives reported action of type specified

er, the figures indicate that the proportion of establishments with non-strike action where employees were taking action for the first time declined sharply, particularly for manual workers, and that the incidence in 1984 was slightly more common among white-collar employees (Table 10.7). Although first-time strike action was still particularly common in small establishments, for white-collar employees it was also likely in very large establishments.

The extent of 'official' and 'unofficial' industrial action in 1983/84
In the absence of other statistical sources, it was decided to include a question in the 1984 survey on the extent to which industrial action was made 'official' by the union or unions concerned. Twenty years ago the Donovan Commission considered the extent of official and unofficial stoppages on the basis of data collected by the then Ministry of Labour. As with the current Department of Employment stoppages data, the figures used by the Commission referred to the number of individual stoppages, each of which may have affected several establishments, whereas the survey results reported here refer to the number of **establishments** affected. The Commission's report suggested that their figures for official and unofficial stoppages were 'liable to a margin of error' for various reasons, including the fact that a strike might be made official some time after it was first recorded by the Ministry.[12] Indeed, it was for these very reasons that details of stoppages of work known to be official ceased to be published by the Department of Employment after 1981.[13] However, this particular difficulty did not arise in our survey because respondents were asked whether the action was '*made official by the union* **at any stage**'. We

Table 10.8   Extent to which manual strikes were made official in 1983/84 by broad sector

Column percentages

	All establishments	Private sector	Public sector	Manufacturing	Services
Manual					
Strike made official	61	33	78	26[1]	72
Strike remained unofficial	38	66	22	74	28
Status not reported	*	1	—	1	—
Base: establishments with recent manual strikes of one day or more as reported by manual worker representatives					
Unweighted base	*152*	*68*	*84*	*64*	*88*
Weighted base	*51*	*19*	*32*	*12*	*39*

[1] See Note C.

now turn to look at the results of this new question, which covered both strikes and non-strike action, in relation to other characteristics of reported industrial action in 1983/84. As with the general findings on industrial action reported earlier, the figures reported here tend to reflect the effects of the disputes within Division 9 of the *Standard Industrial Classification* during 1983/84, particularly in the Education and Public Administration sectors. Although coal mining was excluded from the 1984 sample (as it was in 1980), the results are still likely to reflect the indirect effects of the 1984/85 dispute within that industry, such as sympathy action among trade unionists within other sectors.

Official and unofficial strikes

Table 10.8 shows that in 61 per cent of cases, blue-collar strike action in 1983/84 was at some stage made official by the union concerned. Worker representatives in a further 38 per cent of cases said the strike action remained unofficial, leaving less than one per cent who had difficulty in reporting the status of the action. As we show later, however, a much higher proportion had difficulty in reporting the status of non-strike action. The extent to which manual strike action was made official was independent of either size of establishment or trade union membership density. But strike action was more likely to have been made official in the public and service sectors of the economy and in workplaces where the most important bargaining level was above the individual workplace. More specifically, in 1984 respondents in about two thirds of establishments affected by manual strikes in the private sector, and almost three quarters in manufacturing, said they remained **unofficial**. As we might expect, unofficial blue-collar strikes were much more likely to be local than official strikes, but they were also more likely to involve employees who had taken industrial action before.

Looking at the reasons given for blue-collar strikes in terms of whether or not they were made official (Table 10.9) it seems that strikes over *pay* were almost equally likely to take either official or unofficial forms, although those concerned with *extra wage and fringe benefits* were more likely to be unofficial. This may reflect the continuing significance of informal bargaining at local level designed to make marginal improvements to pay packages agreed at industry or national level. Strikes over *trade union matters* and the *duration and pattern of working hours* were almost wholly unofficial while those concerned with *manning and work allocation*, which in overall terms almost doubled over the period (see Table 10.4), were exclusively official. Bearing in mind our previous discussion of the nature of the disputes arising from *miscellaneous reasons*, over half of the cases of

Table 10.9 Main reasons for official and unofficial strikes among manual workers in 1984

Column percentages

	Official strikes	Unofficial strikes
Reason given for strike		
Pay: wage rates & earnings	30[1]	35
Pay: extra wage & fringe benefits	3	13
Duration & pattern of working hours	*	8
Redundancy issues	9	1
Trade union matters	1	12
Working conditions and supervision	*	3
Manning & work allocation	17	*
Dismissal & other disciplinary measures	1	4
Miscellaneous	54	36
Miscellaneous only[2]	53	27
Not answered	*	—
Base: establishments with strikes of one day or more among manual workers		
Unweighted	*79*	*71*
Weighted	*31*	*19*

[1] See Note E.
[2] Cases where the reason given was coded to the miscellaneous category only.

official blue-collar strikes in 1983/84 were due to *miscellaneous reasons*, a substantial proportion of which were accounted for by disputes within the Postal Services and Telecommunications sector. *Miscellaneous reasons* were given in just over a third of cases of unofficial blue-collar strike action in 1983/84.

We noted earlier that the bulk of white-collar strikes in 1984 occurred within the public services sector, and that all of them were 'widespread' rather than 'local'. The new question in the 1984 survey also enables us to say that practically all of these strikes were made official by the white-collar unions concerned, so that the characteristics of white-collar strikes reported earlier were in effect the characteristics of **official** strikes.

In overall terms, 20 per cent of establishments where white-collar representatives were interviewed were affected by official white-collar strikes in 1984, while the figure for blue-collar strikes, calculated in a similar way, was six per cent. Representatives in a further four per cent of workplaces reported unofficial blue-collar strike action while hardly any reported unofficial white-collar strikes.

Official and unofficial non-strike action

Of the most recent cases of **manual** non-strike action, worker representatives in a total of 38 per cent of establishments said that the action was at some stage made official by the union or unions concerned (Table 10.10). A further 54 per cent said the action remained unofficial. As with strikes, non-strike action among manual workers was more likely to have been made official in the public sector than the private sector and in service sector establishments than in manufacturing. Put differently, about two thirds of cases of recent non-strike action in both the private and manufacturing sectors remained unofficial.

Table 10.10   Extent to which non-strike action was made official in 1983/84 by broad sector

Column percentages

	All establishments	Private sector	Public sector	Manufacturing	Services
Manual					
Action made official	38	30	50[1]	30	44
Action remained unofficial	54	65	37	66	45
Status not reported	8	5	12	4	11
Base: establishments with recent manual non-strike action of one day or more as reported by manual worker representatives					
Unweighted	*237*	*150*	*87*	*134*	*103*
Weighted	*91*	*54*	*37*	*39*	*52*
Non-manual					
Action made official	90	44	94	40	93
Action remained unofficial	8	52	5	55	5
Status not reported	2	4	1	5	1
Base: establishments with recent non-manual non-strike action of one day or more as reported by non-manual worker representatives					
Unweighted	*233*	*63*	*170*	*60*	*173*
Weighted	*151*	*11*	*140*	*8*	*143*

[1] See Note C.

In only ten per cent of cases was the official non-strike action the first time that the relevant sections of the manual workforce had taken action, although the figure was much higher in manufacturing (17 per cent) than services (seven per cent). By contrast, first-time action was reported in just over a quarter of cases of unofficial action (and in just under a third of cases in both the private and manufacturing sectors).

In other words, and in contrast to the pattern for strikes, it was **unofficial** non-strike action that was most likely to involve manual workers who had not taken action before. In just under a third of cases the official non-strike action involved only employees from the affected establishment, again particularly within the private and manufacturing sectors. However, unofficial action was much more likely to be local, with employees from elsewhere being involved in only ten per cent of cases. This is similar to the pattern for strikes.

Looking at the particular types of official non-strike action taken by blue-collar workers in 1983/84, by far the most common was the overtime ban (76 per cent of affected establishments), followed by blackings (15 per cent) and working to rule (14 per cent), with 'others' (go-slows, lock-outs, work-ins/sit-ins etc.) numbering six per cent. (Percentages add up to over 100 because more than one type of action would be involved.) This overall pattern was the same for unofficial action, but with overtime bans being proportionately less, and the rest proportionately more important (overtime bans, 57 per cent; working to rule, 17 per cent; blackings, 16 per cent; and 'other', 12 per cent). However, non-strike action was more likely to take more than one form when it was made official, unofficial non-strike action typically taking a single form.

As an extension to the foregoing discussion it is interesting that in eight per cent of cases, far more than the figure for strikes, manual worker representatives had difficulty in reporting whether the action was official or unofficial. Those in the service sector, particularly in public services, had more difficulty than those in either private manufacturing or in the nationalised industries in reporting the status of the action. Apparently, even local representatives, who may well have organised or at least taken part in the action, sometimes found it difficult to be at all precise about something which might be assumed to be fairly unproblematic. There may have been a number of reasons for this, such as difficulties of recall, which in turn may be related to the relative 'visibility' of official strike and non-strike action. Whereas union ratification of **strike** action may translate directly into practical action, such as in the organisation (or monitoring) of picketing for example, non-strike sanctions are perhaps more likely to elicit principled support from the relevant union rather than practical action. It may also be that official non-strike sanctions are often the precursors of official strikes, if such 'cut-price' actions are not seen to produce the desired outcomes in the short term. There may, of course, have been difficulties with the question itself; its meaning may not have been clear to respondents. However, this possibility would seem to be unlikely, given that very few respondents had difficulty answering an identical question in relation to strike action.

Taking the most recent cases of non-strike industrial action among white-collar workers, representatives in nine out of ten establishments said that they were at some stage made 'official' by the union concerned. A further eight per cent said they remained unofficial and only two per cent had difficulty reporting the status of the action. In almost a quarter of cases of official non-strike action it was the first time that the relevant sections of the non-manual workforce had taken industrial action. In 95 per cent of cases employees from **other** establishments were also involved in the action. Of those establishments where the most recent non-strike action remained unofficial, it was first-time action in just over a third of cases and remained 'local' in almost three quarters.

The most common form of official non-strike action among white-collar workers was the work to rule (43 per cent of workplaces), followed by overtime bans (38 per cent) and blackings (eight per cent), with 'others' numbering 11 per cent. The pattern for unofficial action is rather different, however, with overtime bans being reported in 56 per cent of cases, blackings in 24 per cent and working to rule in 20 per cent ('others' numbered less than four per cent). Interestingly, and in contrast to the pattern for manual workers, non-strike action among white-collar staff was more likely to take more than one form if it remained unofficial. Official non-strike action typically took a single form.

Table 10.11 summarises the overall extent of official and unofficial industrial action in 1983/84. Six per cent of establishments where manual worker representatives were interviewed were affected by official non-strike action among blue-collar workers in 1983/84 compared with nine per cent where there was unofficial action. One tenth were affected by official action of **any** sort and about the same number were affected by **unofficial** action of any sort. Official action of any sort among white-collar staff was much more widespread, being reported in almost one third of establishments where white-collar representatives were interviewed. Official non-strike action was reported in almost a quarter of establishments and very few (two per cent) reported unofficial non-strike action.

Picketing and secondary industrial action

In addition to the sections on non-strike action, a novel feature of the first survey was the inclusion of a substantial section of questioning on the incidence and impact of picketing. Throughout the 1970s a number of disputes became notable through the use of large-scale picketing, such as at Grunwicks and those within the coal mining industry in 1972 and 1974, but, prior to the 1980 survey, systematic information on picketing was unavailable. During the first survey the

Table 10.11   Overall extent of official and unofficial industrial action in 1983/84

Percentages

	Manual	Non-manual
Any official action	10[1]	31
Any unofficial action	11	3
Official strike action	6	20
Unofficial strike action	4	*
Official non-strike action	6	24
Unofficial non-strike action	9	2

Base: establishments where worker representatives from recognised trade unions were interviewed

	Manual	Non-manual
Unweighted	*910*	*949*
Weighted	*554*	*560*

[1] See Note F.

1980 Employment Bill was being debated in Parliament and the subsequent Employment Act changed the existing law on picketing and restricted lawful picketing to a person's own place of work. The results from the 1980 survey included two major industrial stoppages where picketing was again particularly evident, namely, in the steel and engineering industries. But the results referred to the period (up to August 1980) before the law was changed (in October 1980). The inclusion of a similar section of questioning in the 1984 survey allows us to monitor some aspects of changes in picketing behaviour between the two study periods.[14] Although picketing was again a particularly topical subject in 1983/84, due, for example, to the start of the protracted dispute within coal mining, it should be emphasised again here that the coal mining sector was excluded from both the 1980 and 1984 samples. But the 1984 results reported here are still likely to reflect to some extent the indirect effects of that dispute.

As in 1980, both managers and worker representatives were asked whether the establishment had been picketed within the last twelve months and, if so, on how many occasions. Subsequent questioning focused on the most recent occasion of picketing, including whether it was in connection with a dispute at that establishment, the greatest number of pickets present at any one time, the number of separate entrances picketed and who organised the picketing. The questioning also covered the effects of picketing and the proportion of pickets who were employed at the establishment in question.

Despite the overall increase in the proportion of establishments affected by strikes, the overall extent of picketing declined by almost a half between 1980 and 1984, from 11 per cent to six per cent of establishments (as reported by any of the three main respondents). As in 1980, managers in almost three quarters of cases reported just a single instance of picketing, a similar proportion to that where a single instance of strike action was reported. It is clear from Table 10.12 that in 1984 it was still the case that the larger the establishment the more likely it was to be picketed, regardless of whether or not it had been affected by strike action. As we shall see, this relationship also holds for each of the types of picketing considered here; primary picketing, secondary picketing and external secondary picketing.

Table 10.12   The extent to which establishments were picketed in the previous year, as reported by any respondent[1]

Percentages

| | All establishments | Number employed at establishment | | | |
		25–99	100–499	500–999	1000+
1980					
Picketing in previous year	11	7	18	34	54
Base: all establishments					
Unweighted	*2040*	*747*	*777*	*249*	*267*
Weighted	*2000*	*1511*	*420*	*43*	*26*
1984					
Picketing in previous year	6	3	13	23	34
Base: all establishments					
Unweighted	*2019*	*715*	*724*	*295*	*285*
Weighted	*2000²*	*1533*	*405*	*40*	*23*

[1] The percentages represent those establishments where either the manager or the manual or the non-manual worker representative reported picketing.
[2] See Note H.

As we might expect, the decline in picketing occurred in precisely those sectors where the incidence of strike action declined, namely in the private sector (down from 11 per cent to three per cent of establishments), and in manufacturing (from 18 per cent to three per cent). However, picketing did **not** increase in those sectors which did experience an increase in strike action between the two study periods. Public sector establishments were picketed in 12 per cent of cases (11 per cent in 1980) and the figure for establishments in the service sector was seven per cent (eight per cent in 1980). That the picketing in these sectors did not increase is unsurprising, given the nature of the disputes in 1984 compared with those in 1980. As we have seen, of major significance here is their relative duration: strikes in 1984 were much shorter than those in 1980, the vast majority lasting a single day or less, and they were concentrated among white-collar workers. An example here would be the strike action within the civil service and elsewhere in protest at the government's banning of trade unions at GCHQ which, in many cases, lasted less than one day, but nevertheless affected a large number of establishments. A similar pattern of short but widespread strike action was taken by the teachers in support of their pay claim. In these circumstances trade unionists may feel that the costs of mounting a comprehensive picket far outweigh any benefits that may accrue and given that picketing tactics may serve a variety of purposes,[15] a relatively small but 'symbolic' picket may have been seen as the most cost-effective tactic in these cases. The picture in 1980 was clearly very different, with blue-collar strikes in both steel and engineering lasting many, often intermittent, days so that picketing in those circumstances, although also operating 'symbolically' to sustain strikers' morale, would probably have been seen more conventionally by the unions concerned as a means of exerting more direct pressure on the employer to settle the dispute.

In line with the foregoing anaysis, picketing of head offices of multi-establishment organisations, and of single, independent establishments declined substantially (from 15 per cent to three per cent and from seven per cent to one per cent respectively), while there was a much smaller decline among (non-head office) branches of multi-establishment organisations (from 12 per cent to eight per cent). This general pattern of change is similar for each of the types of picketing considered below and broadly reflects the very different patterns of industrial action in 1979/80 and 1983/84.

Incidence of primary picketing and its relationship to strike action
Primary picketing was defined in the survey as picketing in connection with a dispute at the picketed establishment. Between 1980 and 1984 the overall proportion of establishments affected by primary picketing fell by almost half, from five per cent to three per cent of establishments, reflecting the general decline in picketing overall. The **pattern** of decline is also very similar, with substantial falls in manufacturing (from nine per cent to two per cent) and the private sector (from five per cent to one per cent), while primary picketing of both public and service sector establishments remained the same, at five per cent and three per cent respectively.

Similarly, the extent to which establishments experiencing strikes were affected by primary picketing fell by almost half, from 29 per cent to 15 per cent of cases (Table 10.13). This reflects a large decline in manufacturing from (33 per cent to 15 per cent) and in the private sector generally (from 35 per cent to 20 per cent), and a slightly smaller decline in services (from 26 per cent to 15 per cent). In 1984, therefore, primary picketing of strikes (of any duration) was no more common among manufacturing plants than it was among service sector establishments. The same pattern of decline is evident for strikes of less than one day (down from 20 per cent to 11 per cent overall), though slightly less marked for strikes of one day or more (from 36 per cent to 21 per cent). In other words, the decline in primary picketing occurred across the board and not just because more strikes in 1984 were short.

Table 10.13   The extent to which strikes were accompanied by primary picketing[1]

Percentages

	All establishments	Number employed at establishment			
		25–99	100–499	500–999	1000+
1980					
Primary picketing in previous year	29	21	37	31	45
Base: establishments where any respondent reported strike action					
Unweighted	*536*	*73*	*194*	*104*	*165*
Weighted	*264[2]*	*134*	*96*	*18*	*15*
1984					
Primary picketing in previous year	15	10	22	25	30
Base: establishments where any respondent reported strike action					
Unweighted	*601*	*129*	*194*	*118*	*160*
Weighted	*380*	*248*	*104*	*14*	*14*

[1] The percentages represent those establishments where any of the three main respondents reported primary picketing as a proportion of those establishments where any respondent reported a strike.
[2] See Note H.

The more precise measurement of strike duration in our second survey allows us to say that in 1984 strikes of one day or more but less than a week were primary picketed in 20 per cent of cases, while the figure was almost half (48 per cent) for strikes of one week or more. Although we do not have comparable data for 1980, if we take both the comparable questions on strike duration from both surveys and the additional questions from the 1984 survey, it is clear that in overall terms strikes are still more likely to involve primary picketing the longer the strike goes on.

Although primary picketing in 1984 was much less common in all sizes of strike-affected establishment than it was in 1980, particularly in those employing less than 500 people, it also appeared that the chances of a strike involving primary picketing were more closely related to the size of the establishment affected than was the case in 1980. The results are given in Table 10.13 and it would seem likely that the different industrial distribution of disputes in the two study periods may be part of the explanation here. It should be emphasised, of course, that the figures do not include the coal mining industry.

Characteristics of primary picketing

According to managers, there was no significant change between 1980 and 1984 in the average maximum number of pickets present at any one time (15 in 1980, 16 in 1984). The typical (median) maximum remained the same at ten (see Table 10.16). As Table 10.14 shows there was virtually no change in the proportion of establishments with between one and six, and between 21 and 100 pickets and a slight increase for those with between seven and 20. Mass picketing (101 or more pickets) was as rare in 1984 as it was in 1980, with one per cent of picketed establishments being affected.

Of course, these figures cover those cases where perhaps several entrances were picketed. If we take only those cases with a single picketed entrance, between 1980 and 1984 the maximum number of pickets in the typical (median) case remained the same at six. The average maximum also showed no significant change (12 in 1980; 11 in 1984). As in 1980, in one per cent of cases the maximum number was over 50. On the basis of the results from both surveys, therefore, it is clear that the difference between the median for all establishments and the median for those with a single picketed entrance (for each respective year) shows that the large numbers of pickets overall are at least partly explained by the presence of multiple entrances. Moreover, although the code of practice on picketing[16] was introduced after our 1980 survey, its effects were foreshadowed several months earlier via the parliamentary and public debate over the passage of the 1980 Act. It might be, of course, that our 1980 survey results reflected some anticipation of the code's recommended maximum number of pickets. Alternatively, the code might simply have incorporated previously accepted 'normal practice'. Without earlier evidence it is difficult to choose between these two interpretations.

In 1984 managers in the great majority of cases (74 per cent of establishments with primary picketing) said **all** the pickets were employed at the picketed establishment and the number who said that less than half were employed there was very small (five per cent). The

Table 10.14   Characteristics of the most recent primary picketing according to managers

Column percentages

	1980	1984
Maximum number of pickets		
1–6	46[1]	45
7–20	36	40
21–100	16	14
101+	1	1
Not answered	—	★
Number of gates picketed		
1	77	71
2	13	15
3	10	14
Organisers of picketing		
Stewards of same employer, various establishments	71[2]	94
Stewards at establishment	69[3]	93
Stewards of same employer, other establishments	3	7
Stewards of another employer	★	2
Any paid union officials	21	6
Employees themselves	8	2
No information	2	—
Base: establishments where managers reported primary picketing in previous year		
Unweighted	*124*	*66*
Weighted	*54*	*26*

[1] See Note C.
[2] See Note D.
[3] See Note E.

picture in 1980 was similar. As we show later, however, the pattern for secondary picketing is very different.

As in 1980, establishment-based shop stewards were the most frequently mentioned organisers of primary picketing in 1984. Indeed, the results show that they were much more likely to organise picketing in 1984, with 93 per cent of managers reporting their stewards as organisers compared to 69 per cent in 1980. In addition, and as we might have expected given the more widespread nature of strikes in 1984 than in 1980, the involvement of stewards from other establishments of the same employer more than doubled, from three per cent to seven per cent of establishments. Overall, stewards of the same employer based at either the establishment or elsewhere organised primary picketing in 94 per cent of cases in 1984 compared to 71 per cent in 1980. By contrast, the involvement of full-time officials declined by over two thirds, from 21 per cent to six per cent of establishments, partly reflecting less strike activity in those sectors where full-time officials are common.

Effects of primary picketing

In both surveys we asked respondents whether, on the last occasion, picketing prevented any of the following from entering or leaving the premises:

employees of the establishment;
contractors' employees working at the establishment;
goods or services being received;
goods or services being sent out.

In addition, our second survey included a category for *visitors to the establishment*, but to make the general results comparable with the 1980 survey, and given that only six per cent of managers reported it anyway, this item has been excluded from the changes discussed below. It should be emphasised that when we discuss the 'effectiveness' of picketing in what follows, our definition of 'effective' picketing relates to the four broad categories of effect asked about in both surveys.

In terms of its overall impact on the movement of employees, goods or services in or out of establishments, primary picketing was as effective in 1984 as it was in 1980, with **some** restriction of movement being reported in 59 per cent of cases. The prevention of goods or services being received was again the most common effect, prevention of despatch again being second most common. As in 1980, one or other of these effects was mentioned by managers in 53 per cent of picketed establishments, but the increases for **each item** in 1984 indicates that more establishments experienced both effects than in 1980. Table 10.15 gives the results.

Restriction of the movement of people, excluding visitors to the establishment, was relatively less widespread and declined overall from 36 per cent to 30 per cent of establishments between the two study periods. However, primary picketing was still as likely to prevent contractors' employees entering an establishment (and not all establishments would have had them) as it was to prevent employees of the establishment itself. At least **some** employees of the establishment were prevented from reporting for work in over a fifth of cases in both 1980 and 1984.

These aggregate figures hide some important changes within particular sectors. Although less than a quarter of all cases of primary picketing were in manufacturing in 1984, compared to 43 per cent in

Table 10.15   Effects of most recent primary picketing according to managers

Percentages

People, goods or services affected	1980	1984
Establishment or contractors' employees	36	30
Establishment employees	23[1]	21
Contractors' employees	17	18
Goods or services received or sent	53	53
Goods or services received	42	50
Goods or services sent out	37	41
Any of the above effects	**59**	**59**
Visitors to the establishment	..[2]	6
Not answered	★	—

Base: establishments where managers reported primary picketing in previous year

Unweighted	*124*	*66*
Weighted	*54*	*26*

[1] See Notes E and F.
[2] See Note J.

1980, the picketing itself was much more effective than previously. Although the number of cases is too small to draw firm conclusions, in 1984 about nine tenths of manufacturing establishments affected by primary picketing reported that it had some effect, compared to about two thirds in 1980, which also reflects increases on all four of the comparable categories we asked about. By contrast, although over three quarters of all cases of primary picketing were among service sector establishments in 1984, up from 57 per cent in 1980, the overall effectiveness of the picketing did not change between the two study periods, with 52 per cent of establishments reporting some effect. Although the numbers of cases are relatively small, restriction of movement of goods or services appeared to remain as common, affecting around a half, while the proportion reporting restriction in the movement of employees declined from around one third to about a fifth.

Secondary picketing
Secondary picketing was defined as picketing which was **not** in connection with a dispute at the picketed establishment. In line with the pattern for primary picketing reported above, the overall extent of secondary picketing declined from seven per cent to four per cent of

establishments between the two study periods, the bulk of the decline being among manufacturing and private sector establishments. Thus in 1984, secondary picketing was still slightly more common than primary picketing.

As in 1980, establishments experiencing secondary picketing were widely spread throughout the economy, although the incidence was rather more even across sectors in 1984. However, of the nine broad Divisions of the *Standard Industrial Classification*, only Other Services showed some increase in the extent of secondary picketing, reflecting increases in Public Administration from nine per cent to 12 per cent, and Miscellaneous Services from six per cent to ten per cent. This clearly follows from the predominance of widespread disputes within these sectors.

Characteristics of secondary picketing

Table 10.16 shows that, according to managers, the maximum number of secondary pickets present at any one time in 1984 was about twelve on average, compared with ten in 1980, and that the typical (median) figure fell from eight to six. There was a slight drop in the proportion reporting between seven and 20 pickets (from 38 per cent to 30 per cent), and a rather larger increase in the proportion reporting between 21 and 100 pickets (from six per cent to 11 per cent of workplaces affected by secondary picketing). This increase at the upper end of the range of picketing numbers explains why the average increased slightly while the median fell. As with primary picketing, mass secondary picketing (101 or more pickets) **outside the coal mining industry** was as rare as it was in 1980, with less than one per cent of picketed establishments being affected. The extent to which secondary pickets were employed at the establishment differed sharply from the pattern for primary picketing. Managers in just a quarter of affected establishments in 1984 said that **all** the pickets were employed at the establishment, while around a half said that **none** of them was. However, it is also worth mentioning that ten per cent of managers could not answer the question.

Changes in the **organisation** of secondary picketing are similar to those for primary picketing outlined earlier, with the involvement of full-time officials declining by two thirds (from 43 per cent to 13 per cent), while the involvement of stewards from various establishments of the same employer increased by about three quarters, from 34 per cent to 60 per cent of cases. The figure for stewards of another employer was up from two per cent to nine per cent of cases (Table 10.16).

Table 10.16   Comparison of primary and secondary picketing characteristics, as reported by managers

	Primary picketing		Secondary picketing	
	1980	1984	1980	1984
Maximum of pickets				Numbers
Median	10	10	8	6
Average	15	16	10	12
Organisers of picketing				Percentages
Stewards of same employer, various establishments	71[1]	94	34	60
Stewards at establishment	69[2]	93	27	34
Stewards of same employer, other establishments	3	7	9	31
Stewards of another employer	*	2	2	9
Any paid union official	21	6	43	13
Other	8	5	3	15
No information	2	—	16	9
Effects of picketing				
Employees entering or leaving	36	30	25	25
Goods or services in or out	53	53	53	18
Any effect	**59[3]**	**59**	**63**	**32**
Base: establishments where manager reported picketing of the type specified in column heads				
Unweighted	*124*	*66*	*158*	*129*
Weighted	*54*	*26*	*93*	*48*

[1] See Note D.
[2] See Note E.
[3] See Note F.

Effects of secondary picketing

In contrast to primary picketing, secondary picketing was generally much less effective than it was in 1980. The proportion of establishments reporting **some** effect fell by about half between 1980 and 1984, from 63 per cent to 32 per cent of cases. However, the numbers of picketed establishments reporting each type of effect changed over the period. There was a decline of two thirds in the proportion of establishments reporting some restriction on the movement of goods or services, with restriction of movement of people (excluding visitors) remaining the same at a quarter of cases (Table 10.16). A broadly similar pattern of change was reported in both manufacturing and services sectors, although whereas about half of all cases of secondary picketing were in each sector in 1980, in 1984 92 per cent of cases were in the services sector, again reflecting the different industrial distribution of disputes between the two study periods.

It should be emphasised that our surveys only allow us to quantify those **instances** where secondary (and primary) picketing had **some** effect on the movement of goods, services or people. They do not allow us to quantify the magnitude of the effects within the establishments themselves. We cannot, for example, distinguish between those cases where only ten per cent of employees were prevented from reporting for work from those where all were prevented from doing so. There may also, of course, be other effects of picketing besides the five types that we asked about, such as its 'symbolic' effect when union members are solidly out[17] or, more broadly, its contribution to the resolution of the dispute. However, issues such as these would be difficult to pursue using the survey method and in the absence of other statistical sources the Workplace Industrial Relations Survey series provides the best) measures of the effectiveness of picketing in Britain currently available.

Table 10.17   The extent to which establishments were affected by picketing of the type specified in the previous year, as reported by any respondent

		Percentages
	1980	1984
Any picketing	11[1]	6
Primary picketing	5	3
Secondary picketing	7	4
External secondary picketing	4	2
Base: all establishments		
Unweighted	*2040*	*2019*
Weighted	*2000*	*2000*

[1] See Note F.

External secondary picketing

External secondary picketing was defined as those cases of picketing where none of the pickets were employees of the establishment, and the picketing was not in connection with a dispute at the picketed establishment. As in 1980, half of all cases of secondary picketing were of this 'external' type, and the likelihood of an establishment being affected increased if it was larger and if it had substantial trade union membership among its employees. By way of summary, Table 10.17 shows the general pattern of decline for each of the three types of picketing we have been considering. The table shows that the proportion of establishments experiencing this **pure** form of secondary picketing declined by half between 1980 and 1984, from four per cent to two per cent of establishments, according to managers' accounts.

Secondary blacking

Secondary blacking was defined in two related ways: first, the blacking of goods or services by trade union members at the respondent's establishment in connection with a dispute elsewhere; and secondly, in those cases where there had been industrial action in the previous year, the blacking of the organisation's customers' or suppliers' goods or services in connection with a dispute at the respondent's establishment. These two questions look at opposite sides of the same coin and in overall terms, the proportion of establishments affected by blacking of either type declined from four per cent to three per cent between 1980 and 1984, according to management respondents. However, blacking in relation to a dispute elsewhere fell from four per cent to three per cent of establishments while blacking in relation to a dispute at the establishment declined even more, from four per cent to one per cent of establishments. A much narrower range of industrial sectors was affected by secondary blacking in 1984 than in 1980, and the incidence no longer appeared to be related to size of establishment.

Notes and references

1. Daniel W W and Millward N (1983) *Workplace Industrial Relations in Britain: The DE/PSI/SSRC Survey*, Heinemann Educational Books, London, pp.214-7.

2. Department of Employment (1981) *Employment Gazette*, July, p.288; Department of Employment (1985) *Employment Gazette*, August, p.296.

3. In the 1984 survey we also asked about relations between management and recognised trade unions. Industrial action was more likely where relations between them were reported as relatively poor.

4. Daniel W W and Millward N (1983) *op. cit.* p.226.

5. Blanchflower D and Cubbin J (1986) 'Strike Propensities at the British Workplace', *Oxford Bulletin of Economics and Statistics*, February, p.33. There is a difference in the definition of the presence of procedures between the two analyses, however. Daniel and Millward confined theirs to *agreed* procedures for resolving disputes about pay and conditions or discipline and dismissals that were written down and signed by both management and union representatives, while Blanchflower and Cubbin used the presence of any procedure (which of course the great majority of establishments have). Even so, the latter analysis adds strength to the view that the presence of formal procedures may be a symptom of proneness to industrial action, rather than a device to inhibit industrial action by institutionalising conflict.

6. Due to minor changes in question structure it was not possible to replicate Daniel and Millward's earlier definition of the presence of procedures (above). In the 1984 analysis we defined the presence of procedures as *agreed* procedures for resolving disputes about pay and conditions or discipline and dismissals that were set out in a written document. In other words, the 1984 definition does not exclude cases where the procedures were not jointly signed by both parties.

7. Department of Employment (1973) *Employment Gazette*, February, p.117.

8. The unweighted distribution of *miscellaneous reasons* for either manual or non-manual strike-action shows that almost two fifths of cases were related either to disputes over privatisation, or to the abolition of the metropolitan councils. Between one quarter (manual) and one third of cases (non-manual) referred to sympathy action with groups such as the miners or the nurses, and around a third in both cases referred to responses that could be recoded to our other specific categories. However, it should be emphasised that this listing includes **all** *miscellaneous* cases, not just *miscellaneous* **only** cases, so in some cases part of the answer will already have been allocated to one of the specific codes. It is significant that there were so few cases of disputes against privatisation, or even sympathy action among our 1980 sample that it was not then necessary to modify the coding frame adapted from the official records of strikes. We intend to revise the coding of *miscellaneous reasons* cases at an early stage to differentiate between the main sub-categories mentioned by respondents.

9. Batstone E (1984) *Working Order: Workplace Industrial Relations over Two Decades*, Blackwell, Oxford, pp.292-3.

10. Institute of Personnel Management (1984) 'Who's been using the law in industrial disputes?', *Personnel Management*, June, pp.32-6; Evans S (1985) 'Research Note: The Use of Injunctions in Industrial Disputes', *British Journal of Industrial Relations*, March, pp.133-7; Labour Research Department (1985) 'Rise in Legal Actions Against Unions', *Labour Research*, October, pp.259-61.

11. Kahn P, Lewis N, Livock R and Wiles P (1983) *Picketing: Industrial Disputes, Tactics and the Law*, Routledge and Kegan Paul, London, pp.137-9.

12. Royal Commission on Trade Unions and Employers' Associations (1968), *Report*, Cmnd. 3623 HMSO, London, p.97.

13. Hansard (1985) House of Lords *written answer*, 26th March, col. 1018.

14. Other aspects of changes in picketing behaviour have been studied by Kahn P *et. al.* (1983) *op. cit.*, and Evans S (1983) 'Picketing Under the Employment Acts', in Fosh P and Littler C R (eds) *Industrial Relations and the Law in the 1980's: Issues and Future Trends*, Gower, Aldershot.

15. Kahn P *et al.* (1983) *op. cit.* p.57.

16. Department of Employment (1980) *Code of Practice: Picketing*.

17. Kahn P *et al.* (1983) *op. cit.* p.58.

11   Summary and Conclusions

'The present study . . . provides as objective a corpus of findings as we are likely to have. When it is updated, it will give policy-makers, academics and commentators a valuable insight into change in an area where the dogmatic and the half-informed too often have ruled . . .'. So ran the *Financial Times* editorial when the report of our first survey was published. We hope the contents of this book will be judged equally favourably and that those who have awaited systematic, large-scale survey evidence on British industrial relations practices **over time** will find it of value. We stress the time dimension because it highlights the importance and uniqueness of the data that we have been using. No sample survey of British industrial relations practices has had a previous survey of **identical design** to draw upon for the measurement of change.[1] And no survey of British industrial relations practices has been as large, as comprehensive in its industrial coverage or as detailed in its questioning of managers and trade union representatives as the two surveys that we have been analysing. The Workplace Industrial Relations Survey series is a unique source of information on the changing – and enduring – nature of British industrial relations at the place of work.

This book is not an exhaustive account of the results of the survey series. A good deal of secondary analysis, to which we have referred at appropriate places in previous chapters, has been carried out and published on the 1980 survey; we anticipate more further analysis will be done on the 1984 survey and on the two datasets in combination. What we have set out to do in this book is give a general account of the main findings on questions asked in both surveys and on most of the new questions asked in 1984. The major, but intended, omission in our account is on the new section of questioning in 1984 which focused upon the introduction of technical change. The analysis of this important topic area, greatly enhanced by the availability of the other material from the survey, is reported in Daniel's separate, companion volume.[2]

A novel feature of the series, at least in terms of its British predecessors, is the addition of a panel element to the sample. Although it was small-scale and experimental,[3] the panel has already proved useful in the analysis reported here. By providing information on the same establishments in both 1980 and 1984, it has enabled us to say more about the pattern of change – or lack of it – than would have been possible if only the main cross-sectional samples were available. In Chapter 3, for example, we have used the panel sample to examine the extent to which trade union recognition varied over time for the same establishments. The fact that there appeared to be very little gross change helped us to choose between different possible explanations of the pattern of net change. In Chapter 4 the panel data helped us to come to a judgment about the effect of a change in question wording. Other uses of the panel data, particularly for causal modelling, are as yet unexplored. Much remains to be done before the full potential of the panel sample has been realised.

But our main source of data for this report has been the large, cross-sectional samples, covering over 2000 workplaces in each of the two years 1980 and 1984. We have used these data in a number of different ways. First, we used them to update our description of institutional industrial relations from 1980 to 1984. This in itself is worthwhile on matters for which there are no alternative sources of factual information; it can also supplement other research findings by, for example, providing a benchmark or typical case against which more detailed, case-study findings can be set. Secondly, we have used the data to describe changes or trends at the aggregate level. We have done this primarily with the workplace as our unit of analysis; but the survey design also enables us to describe changes in the number or proportion of employees in workplaces having particular practices or institutions. Where the arrangement or practice of interest is confined to a group of employees **within** a workplace, as it very often is, we have generally used the responses to more detailed questions about the numbers covered by the arrangement to be more precise about the change in employee coverage. Thirdly, change at the overall level can be disaggregated to see whether it has occurred in particular sectors of the economy or types of workplace; or occasionally no change at the aggregate level may be the result of contrary trends in different sectors or among different types of workplace. Fourthly, but less often, our parallel analyses of the 1980 and 1984 datasets have revealed new relationships, the disappearance of previous relationships or significant changes in the patterns of variation.

Some of the aggregate changes that we have identified were projected as trends on the basis of our first survey. By analysing the 1980 results on industrial relations practices in terms of characteristics such as ownership, industrial sector, size, workforce composition and so on, we provided pointers to subsequent developments. In analysing the data from both surveys we can not only test those projections but we can begin to unravel the different sources of change. Some changes can, by and large, be ascribed to structural factors, sometimes apparent in other industrialised countries besides Britain: for example, the decline of union membership, union recognition and the closed shop in the private sector is clearly associated with the falling numbers of large workplaces employing predominantly male, manual, full-time employees. The nature and direction of causality, if the relationship is a causal one, remains a matter for debate. Other changes would appear to be the outcome of particular parties to the industrial relations system having made particular decisions of policy or being better or less able to influence events: the much reduced scope of bargaining by recognised trade unions would seem to fall into this category. Changes in government policy, most clearly where legislation is involved, are another obvious category: the revision of closed-shop agreements to incorporate new exemptions and the growth of share-ownership schemes are examples. But most of the changes that we have decribed do not have simple, single-factor explanations, if, indeed, any of them do. In summarising, we distinguish these different sources of change where possible, but our main purpose in this chapter is to set out what we have found to be the distinctive patterns of change and stability in the industrial relations practices of British workplaces.

The context of workplace industrial relations

Although the individual workplace formed the focus of interest and questioning in our surveys, we are, of course, aware that not all industrial relations activity takes place at this level. But the workplace has a primary status in industrial relations in the sense that it provides the locus of the employment relationship. Employment relations between managers and workers are subject to influences and pressures from many sources – higher-level management, trade union national bodies, government and so on, as well as economic and social developments which cannot be ascribed to particular actors, either individuals or organisations. What may be seen as problems or issues by one set of actors may not be seen as such by others. And the information needed as the basis for policy decisions at any level are unlikely to be obtainable from a single piece of research. The Workplace Industrial Relations Surveys were conceived as a multi-purpose resource and we would expect consideration of many of the issues on which the survey data have a bearing to draw factual information from other sources, as well as the political and other judgemental bases for decision-making.

In Chapter 1 we sketched out some of the important elements of the context of industrial relations during the period to which our two surveys relate. We referred to the changes in government policy, particularly those enshrined in legislative change. We referred to the changing economic conditions, particularly in relation to employment. We showed that many of the changes in the structure of employment were apparent at workplace level through the changing composition and characteristics of our sample. There were fewer very large workplaces, particularly in manufacturing. Manufacturing employed a smaller proportion of employees. The public sector, although not expanding in absolute terms, employed a larger proportion of employees and comprised a larger proportion of workplaces. More employees were employed in white-collar occupations, largely reflecting the fall in employment in traditional manual occupations. Ethnic minority workers were employed in substantial numbers in fewer workplaces. Part-time employees formed a larger proportion of those employed, as did women. And as we showed through our analysis in Chapter 8, part-time employment grew essentially in the service sector while declining as a proportion of the workforce in manufacturing. Correspondingly, it was in non-manual employment that the growth in part-time working grew.

In industry and commerce our first survey was conducted at a time of rapidly declining output, particularly in manufacturing. This picture had changed substantially by the time of our second survey in 1984. Responses to questions on these matters confirmed this changing picture in our sample of establishments, but also revealed considerable variation between establishments in their economic circumstances. Variation was also apparent in establishments' experience of changes in the size of their workforce – those in the competitive parts of the private sector were more likely to have had substantial changes in numbers of employees (in either direction) than workplaces in monopoly industries or the public sector. Workforce reductions were reported considerably less frequently in the private sector in 1984 than in 1980.

So it can be seen that we have had a good variety of background material against which to set our description of the changing pattern of British workplace industrial relations practices. In summarising our findings we have necessarily been selective. We hope that our selection in this chapter will help the reader who has already read the substantive chapters to recall their main findings and encourage others to follow up points of interest in the main body of the report. We begin our summary by looking at management organisation for industrial relations at the workplace.

Management organisation for industrial relations
The structural arrangements made by management for the organisa-

tion and conduct of industrial relations at workplace level appeared to have changed little between our two surveys. In the great majority of workplaces the senior person dealing with personnel and industrial relations matters was someone with general management responsibilities. Specialist personnel or industrial relations managers were present in 15 per cent of workplaces in 1984, the same proportion as in 1980. They remained more common in larger workplaces and less common in the private services sector than elsewhere. They were also more common in foreign-owned workplaces and those that used advanced technology. But personnel specialists increasingly had relevant experience and formal qualifications for their work. The proportion reporting that they had relevant formal qualifications rose from 49 per cent in 1980 to 58 per cent in 1984. More of them had degrees of some kind and more had relevant degrees. Specialists were also more likely to have support staff in 1984 than before.

The lack of change in the extent to which workplaces had personnel specialists was matched at the top level of organisations. In industry and commerce there was little change in the extent to which boards of directors had a member with specific responsibility for personnel or industrial relations matters.

Managers at workplace level with personnel responsibilities appeared to have become increasingly involved with certain types of activity. More of them reported involvement with determining or negotiating pay and conditions of employment as well as payment systems and job evaluation. It is likely, too, that more were involved in dealing with industrial relations procedures because the existence of formal procedures, including those dealing with discipline and dismissals, had increased. These were also the subjects – pay determination, disciplinary cases and procedures – upon which workplace-level personnel specialists most frequently consulted senior personnel managers at higher levels in their organisation. The formalisation of procedures was already observable as a trend before 1980, but it appears to have continued since, particularly in smaller workplaces, and must partly be a reflection of the legislative changes that have been made.

The impact of industrial relations and employment legislation was certainly the single most common contextual factor that personnel managers cited in 1984 as having recently enhanced the role of personnel management. This was particularly the case in the private services sector where formal procedures had been less common in 1980. Economic circumstances, in particular those of their own workplace, were also a reason given by personnel managers for saying that their influence over management decision-making had recently increased. Reports of increased influence were more common where there had been a large increase in the size of the workforce or where there had been substantial redundancies. No doubt some of the claims by our respondents that the influence of the personnel function over management decision-making at their establishment were exaggerated – we are relying on retrospective questions in 1984 here – but some of the preponderance of reported increases in influence could be accounted for by the declining influence of trade unions. Recognised trade unions, manual and non-manual, were reported as being involved in the joint regulation of non-pay issues to a much smaller extent in 1984 than in 1980. This reduction in the scope of collective bargaining was particularly noticeable in the private sector and in relation to joint regulation at workplace level. And it was in the larger workplaces, where recognised trade unions were most common, that personnel managers were more likely to say that their own influence had increased.

This picture of the organisation of personnel and industrial relations work relies upon the reports of our principal management respondent in the two surveys – the senior person at the establishment responsible for such matters, only infrequently a personnel specialist. In the 1984 survey we interviewed another manager besides our principal management respondent – a works manager in manufacturing plants that had a personnel specialist. In these, mainly large, manufacturing plants we found that works managers spent a considerable amount of time on personnel matters, about a quarter on average. They felt that departmental managers had most influence over decisions affecting people when it came to recruitment and appointment or to disciplinary cases. On the other hand, they reported that the personnel function at their establishment had greater influence than departmental managers in relation to collective disputes. Works managers also said that personnel management was more frequently involved in the introduction of *organisational change* than of *technical change*. Even when they played a role they were frequently brought in only at a relatively late stage. It seems that the view of personnel management as largely a trouble-shooting function has considerable support in this important sector of the economy.

Returning to the more general picture of management organisation, it was clear from our principal management respondents' accounts that there were important differences between workplaces that recognised trade unions for at least part of their workforce and those that did not. The difference was not in whether those workplaces had a personnel specialist at all, but in the nature and resources of the function. Specialists at workplaces with recognised unions were more likely to have formal qualifications for the work and they were more likely to have support staff. The presence of recognised trade unions does appear to elicit a greater investment in personnel expertise at workplace level.

Trade union representation

In our report on the first survey in our series we suggested that 1980 might prove to be a turning-point in British industrial relations. Where we were able to make comparisons with earlier survey results, or had retrospective data from 1980, there were strong indications of increasing trade union involvement in the conduct of labour relations at workplace level up to that time, or thereabouts. Few of these trends are apparent from our comparisons between our two surveys in 1980 and 1984 and many of them appear to have reversed. In other areas the picture is largely one of stability.

Our first measure of the involvement of trade unions in the affairs of workplaces was the mere presence of trade union members. There was little aggregate change in this, but that was not generally the case at the sectoral level. The public sector showed no change – virtually every establishment had union members. But in private manufacturing there was a striking decline in the proportion of workplaces with trade union members, particularly manual union members. Our panel data suggested that there was little gross change in whether workplaces had union members present and so the net decline in manufacturing seemed to be a structural change, reflecting the higher rate of closure of large manufacturing plants in industries with strong trade union traditions. By contrast, workplaces in the private services sector were marginally more likely to have union members present in 1984 than in 1980. There was thus a convergence of the two parts of the private sector, manufacturing and services.

A more conventional measure of trade union presence is *union membership density*; in our terms, the proportion of an establishment's workforce belonging to a trade union or staff association. Unfortunately we did not collect complete information on trade union membership among part-time employees in the 1980 survey and so direct measures of changing union density are not available. However, the 1984 results, which are complete, do enable us to present in Chapter 3 some breakdowns of trade union density by industry that are more detailed than those previously available from other statistical sources. The results confirmed in the most unequivocal manner the very strong connection between union density and the size of workplaces, as well as the particularly low density figure for smaller firms. They also showed that private sector workplaces that had contracted substantially between 1980 and 1984 were the ones with the highest union densities. We do not imply any causal connection here, but the correlation does suggest strongly that the greater loss of employment by large, highly unionised workplaces is a major factor behind the contraction of trade union membership since the end of the 1970s. Our analysis in Chapter 3 also supports the notion that the relative growth in part-time employment is another factor behind falling union membership.

Some of the changes in the extent of trade union membership at workplaces carried over into the changing pattern of trade union recognition, perhaps one of the most fundamental and enduring features of institutional industrial relations. Again stability characterised the public sector, trade union recognition for both manual and non-manual workers being virtually universal. In private manufacturing the proportion of establishments with one or more recognised unions dropped from 65 per cent in 1980 to 56 per cent in 1984. Within the engineering and vehicles sector the drop was even greater. Virtually all of this decline within manufacturing industry was in respect of manual workers and was attributable to the falling proportion of workplaces with union members present; managements in those workplaces with members present were no less likely to recognise the appropriate unions. In private services the trend was, if anything, in the opposite direction, there being marginal increases in recognition for both manual and non-manual workers.

Our panel data revealed that establishments, or at least larger ones,[4] were very unlikely to grant or withdraw recognition between 1980 and 1984. This confirmed our view that the decline in recognition in manufacturing industry was largely the result of the changing composition of that sector. The lack of gross change, particularly of establishments in which recognition was granted during the period, may also be relevant to consideration of the legal changes that were made in 1980 regarding trade union recognition. The Employment Act of 1980 repealed sections 11 to 16 of the Employment Protection Act 1975 which established a statutory procedure, involving ACAS in its initial stages, for dealing with trade union recognition issues. Our 1980 survey included questions on how recognition had been brought about in cases where formal recognition agreements had been signed in the previous five years, roughly the period during which the statutory procedures operated.[5] Only very small proportions of these cases had involved ACAS (one per cent of cases involving manual unions, three per cent involving non-manual) and none of these involved the statutory procedure, according to managers' reports.[6] These questions were omitted from our 1984 survey and two new questions were inserted asking, where there were no union members present, whether unions had attempted to recruit members and whether they had made a request for recognition within the previous five years. Managers reported that there had been requests for union recognition in four per cent of these cases for manual workers and three per cent for non-manual workers. In cases where there were already recognised unions for some workers but not all, 11 per cent of managers reported a request to extend recognition to some of the remaining groups of manual workers. The equivalent figure for non-manuals was 14 per cent. Thus trade unions appear to have made requests to represent workers in a significant minority of cases where they did not already do so. How many of these requests might have involved the statutory provisions if they had remained is not a question that can be answered from such evidence as we have. However, as the statutory procedure was involved in none of the cases reported in our 1980 survey of recognition being formally agreed between 1975 and 1980, the likelihood is that it would be few.

Besides the net decline in the proportion of private sector workplaces with recognised trade unions, noted earlier, there were also some changes in the *pattern* of recognition between the two surveys. Foreign-owned establishments were more likely to recognise trade unions in 1984 than in 1980, the proportion rising from 45 per cent to 54 per cent in respect of manual workers. This arose from a higher proportion having manual trade union members present. The similar increase in respect of white-collar employees was because those that had union members were more likely to recognise unions for them. Another change in pattern concerned the employment of ethnic minority workers. In 1984 workplaces with a relatively high proportion of ethnic minority workers were less likely to have recognised manual trade unions or to have union members present. No such difference was apparent in 1980.

Multi-unionism was one of the features of trade union representation that appeared to have changed very little between our two surveys. The pattern of variation across the different sectors of the economy was stable. There was also little change in the extent to which unions negotiated jointly or separately where there were several of them. A striking feature of the analysis of multiple bargaining units was that foreign-owned establishments were less likely to have them than their UK-owned counterparts in the private sector, even when workplaces of a similar size were compared.

Our comparisons between the two surveys showed a rather unexpected change in the numbers of trade union lay representatives in the economy as a whole. Given the substantial drop in union membership during the period, our finding that there had been a slight *increase* in the number of lay representatives required some explanation. The explanation was to be found in several related changes. To begin with, more representatives in 1984 were non-manual than in 1980 and a clear majority were employed in the public sector, both these shifts reflecting the changing composition of employment. Indeed, substantial increases in the numbers of lay representatives were reported in the public sector and in private services where non-manual employment predominates. These increases amounted to more than the reduction of the number of representatives in manufacturing. The manufacturing sector showed a particularly sharp drop in the number of manual shop stewards, despite the fact that more plants with recognised unions had stewards present. Workplaces with recognised non-manual unions were more likely to have lay representatives at the workplace than before, part of a general strengthening of white-collar union organisation at the workplace. This was also apparent in relation to full-time lay representatives: non-manual ones became more common, while manual full-time convenors or senior stewards became much less numerous. But on balance there were as many full-time lay representatives in 1984 as in 1980. Thus both the numbers of lay representatives and of full-time representatives at the workplace did not decline in the way that overall trade union membership declined. Shop stewards, and their non-manual counterparts, had fewer members on average to deal with than before.

The closed shop

Comparison of the results from our two surveys showed a marked decline in the number of employees working in closed shops, that is to say covered, in theory at least, by union membership agreements. (We did not attempt to assess the numbers working in 'approved' closed shops in 1984; that is, in closed shops which had been sanctioned by workforce ballots in accordance with recent legislation.) We estimated closed shop membership to be between 3.5 and 3.7 million in mid-1984. This represented a fall of about 1.2 million from mid-1980. The trend and the magnitude of our estimates were entirely consistent with those of other research based upon quite different methods of enumeration.[7]

The overall decline in closed shop membership did not affect different types of closed shop equally. It was manual, comprehensive, post-entry closed shops that became much less common; pre-entry and non-manual closed shops were present in the same, small proportions of establishments in 1984 as in 1980. But the membership of closed shops did not decline only by fewer establishments having a closed shop – it also happened because large establishments with closed shops in 1980 were much more likely to have shrunk, or closed, than workplaces that did not have a closed shop. Indeed, workplaces that had experienced large workforce contractions between 1980 and 1984 were three times more likely to have a closed shop than workplaces that had expanded by a similar amount. The most dramatic decline in both the number of closed shops and in the number of employees covered by them occurred in manufacturing industry, largely because of structural changes in that sector.

Although the closed shop existed in much the same types of establishment in 1984 as it did in 1980, there were some changes in these patterns. For example, within the nationalised industries there appears to have been a movement from comprehensive to partial closed shops. Single, independent establishments in the private sector, mostly small firms, were even less likely to have closed shops in 1984 than they were in 1980. Establishments with a concentration of ethnic minority workers had fewer closed shops in 1984 than other establishments, whereas in 1980 there had been no difference. Foreign-owned workplaces did not experience the decline in closed shop membership experienced elsewhere in the private sector.

There were some important changes in the characteristics of closed shops between our two survey dates. An increasing proportion were the subject of written agreements, particularly in the private sector. About a half of agreed closed shops contained exemptions in 1984, with changes in the type of exemption reflecting, albeit partially, the legislative changes since our 1980 survey. Only about two fifths of manual closed-shop agreements reported in 1984 had ever been revised. A similar proportion of agreements, whether revised or not, dated from 1981 onwards, corresponding roughly to the period after the introduction of the government's code of practice recommending the periodic review of closed shop agreements. New closed shops dating from 1983 or early 1984 were very rare, another part of the explanation for the overall decline in the practice.

On the basis of our 1980 survey we were able to show that the closed shop was not a necessary condition for the existence of check-off arrangements, although this had often been assumed to be the case. Our 1984 survey results show that check-off arrangements not only exist in 'open shops', they may also exist where there are no recognised trade unions. About a quarter of workplaces without recognised unions but with union members present had check-off arrangements according to management respondents. In workplaces with recognised unions the proportion with check-off rose during the four years between our two surveys to over four fifths. We estimate that the number of employees covered by such arrangements approached six million in 1984. The growth of non-cash wage and salary payments,[8] which may well be furthered by the repeal of the Truck Acts,[9] seems likely to have been a factor in this growth.

Trade union branch organisation

In Chapter 5 we used information from interviews with trade union representatives to describe the changing pattern of trade union branch organisation. For methodological reasons set out thoroughly in that chapter, our information is most easily interpretable in relation to branches that consist of members from a single workplace. Most of our comments in this summary refer to these *workplace-based branches*. They occurred in a quarter of the establishments in which we had a manual trade union respondent, a slight increase from the 1980 figure. However, they had become considerably more common in both private manufacturing and private services as well as in the nationalised industries; only in the public services sector had there been a shift to single or multiple-employer branches for manual unions. The pattern for non-manual unions was rather different. Workplace-based branches became more common in private services, less common in private manufacturing and in public services and were unchanged in the nationalised industries. The move towards workplace branches for both manual and non-manual unions in the private services sector is perhaps the most significant of these changes; but although it suggests a possible strengthening of workplace union organisation in private services we should remember that this sector generally had the least developed trade union representation of the four main sectors covered by our analysis.[10]

Workplace-based trade union branches changed in size dramatically between 1980 and 1984. Amongst manual unions their typical size dropped by a half, a much greater drop than the fall in aggregate membership of manual unions. By contrast, the typical size of non-manual workplace branches increased by half. Again this was greater than the aggregate change in membership because of changes in branch composition and the overall preponderance of geographically-based branches, especially in the public sector.

Trade union representatives were generally appointed by informal methods in 1984, as was also the case in 1980. A show of hands at a meeting of members was by far the single most common method. Non-manual representatives, who by 1984 outnumbered manual shop stewards, were more likely than manual stewards to be elected by some form of balloting procedure.

Contacts between trade union representatives

Meetings between manual shop stewards and other stewards of their union at their own workplace were less common in 1984 than in 1980, another indicator of the weakening of manual trade union organisation. There was no similar change for non-manual representatives. In multi-union workplaces joint union committees remainded a minority occurrence, declining noticeably in manufacturing industry for both manual and non-manual unions. There was an interesting change in pattern between the two years. Joint committees of manual stewards were very much more common in 1980 in establishments where pay bargaining took place at that level. But in 1984 the presence of joint stewards' committees was independent of the level of pay bargaining.

In Chapter 5 we use the term *single-employer combines* to refer to meetings or committees of representatives from more than one workplace of the same employer. Trade union representatives reported such combines with roughly equal frequency in the two surveys. Substantially fewer manual representatives did so in both private manufacturing and private services; the decline was particularly apparent among stewards of the largest manual unions. Non manual representatives in the public services sector reported much more frequent meetings than elsewhere, presumably a reflection of disputes in that sector at the time.[11]

Multi-employer combines were subject to similar patterns of change. Substantially fewer manual representatives in the private sector, both manufacturing and service industries, reported them in 1984 than in 1980. But they were reported more commonly in the nationalised industries and the public services sectors. Typically they met at least once every quarter.

The amount of contact between workplace representatives and their local full-time officials changed little between our two survey periods. But fewer stewards reported joint meetings with their local full-time official and local management. Contact with national union officers or the head office of their union was more common in 1984, although manual stewards in manufacturing were an exception to this trend.

Consultation, communication and employee involvement

Consultation and communication between management and employees, both entailing and not entailing trade union participation, were areas of change and innovation according to our findings. We began our analysis in Chapter 6 by looking at workplace-level consultative committees. There was no change in their extent in the economy as a whole: the proportion of workplaces where managers reported their existence was 34 per cent in both surveys.[12] Within manufacturing industry there was a drop from 36 to 30 per cent of establishments. By using the data from our panel sample and a retrospective question about the abandonment of committees, we were able to infer that the change was largely the result of the changing size structure of manufacturing, rather than a tendency for plants with committees to abandon them.

We extended our questioning in the 1984 survey to cover

consultative committees at levels above the sampled establishment where it belonged to a multi-establishment organisation. Such higher-level committees existed and had representatives from the establishment in about a quarter of cases. Combining these with those that had an establishment-level committee we calculated that 41 per cent of workplaces, employing 62 per cent of employees in the sample, had formal consultative machinery in 1984.

The composition of workplace-level consultative committees changed, partly reflecting the trend to non-manual employment: more committees covered only non-manual employees. Exclusive representation by trade union appointees declined, whereas a mixture of union and non-union representatives became more common. There were some notable changes in the major issues discussed by consultative committees. Pay and working conditions were less frequently reported by managers as the most important matter discussed, whereas employment issues were more frequently mentioned. For managers, production issues remained the most frequently mentioned category. However, trade union representatives were much more inclined to mention employment issues than managers in both 1980 and 1984. The most notable change between the two surveys was the increased prominence, reported by managers although not by trade union representatives, of industrial democracy, participation and consultation arrangements as issues that were discussed by existing committees. This reinforces our evidence on management initiatives to increase employee involvement, supporting the idea that there may have been further experimentation in this field.

Chapter 6 also contains findings from a new question on channels of communication which show that the presence of formal communication channels is strongly correlated with the quantity of information being given by management to employees. There were some significant changes of pattern in the amount of information given by management to employees. For example, in 1980 establishments in industry and commerce that were performing below average, according to managers' assessments, gave less than average amounts of information about their financial performance to employees; in 1984 below-average performers gave more information than the generality of establishments, along with those that were performing very much above average. In fact, average performers in 1984 gave the least amount of information to employees on all the six separate topics that we asked about. It seems that managements in industrial and commercial establishments that were performing poorly in financial terms were increasing the amount of information given to employees, including information on their financial performance. We noted also that foreign-owned workplaces were particularly forthcoming on the amount of information they gave to employees on the financial performance of their unit.

Another important feature of the 1984 results was that the biggest difference between managers' and trade union representatives' ratings of the amount of information given by management was on the issue of major changes in working methods or work organisation. Manual trade unionists were much less likely to say that they received a lot of information on this issue than managers were to say that they gave a lot of information. In his companion volume on technical change,[13] Daniel presents the results of more detailed questioning on recent technical changes affecting manual workers, showing clearly that management were less likely to consult manual workers about the introduction of new technology, especially where trade union organisation was weak or non-existent.

On the disclosure of information to trade union representatives for collective bargaining purposes we found little change between the two surveys. There may have been a slight reduction in requests for information under the provisions of the Employment Protection Act by manual trade union representatives, but there was little or no change in the case of non-manual representatives. It seems, therefore, that trade unionists did not reduce their requests for information under the legal provisions in response to the recessionary conditions faced by employers in the early 1980s.

Further light is shed on the issue of management-employee communication by responses to questions about initiatives taken by management to increase employee involvement. Increases in two-way communication were the type of initiative that increased most significantly between the two surveys, according to both managers and worker representatives. This change was evident in both parts of the private sector as well as in public services. Initiatives that entailed structural innovations, such as new consultative committees, showed no increase overall. The most common type of initiative taken by management to increase employee involvement thus changed significantly between the late 1970s and the early 1980s. There were also in 1984 some particular types of initiative that had not been mentioned in 1980, suggesting an increase in the variety of initiatives that managements were taking in this field. And although they were not frequently mentioned in this context, share-ownership schemes certainly became more widespread over the period 1980 to 1984. In fact the proportion of workplaces in industry and commerce whose parent company operated a share-ownership scheme rose from 13 per cent to 23 per cent. However, the rise in actual participation in such schemes was more modest, moving from five per cent of employees in the sector to seven per cent. More establishments were covered by schemes with 100 per cent eligibility, reflecting the fiscal encouragement of such schemes since the late 1970s.

Procedures

The trend towards more widespread and more formal procedures that we documented in our first report continued in the early 1980s. Procedures for dealing with discipline and dismissals were reported in 81 per cent of establishments in 1980 and 90 per cent in 1984. Analysis of the panel data left us in no doubt that many establishments without this type of procedure in 1980 had one in 1984. The increase occurred across all sectors and was apparent particularly in smaller establishments and small firms in the private sector where in 1980 such procedures had been least common. The continuing impact of the legislation and its accompanying code of practice is apparent. Legislation also appears to have had an impact in the area of health and safety. Procedures for dealing with health and safety issues were virtually as common as disciplinary procedures in 1984 (we have no information from the 1980 survey) and health and safety representation was present in an increasing proportion of workplaces.[14]

Disciplinary procedures also became more standardised in their application within establishments; in 1984 well over 80 per cent of establishments had a procedure that applied to all employees. More procedures were enshrined in written documents and the proportion of procedures that were agreed with trade unions where they had members present remained at about the same level. More procedures contained a provision for third-party intervention, although the specified body or person changed substantially. There was a drop in the proportion of disciplinary procedures that specified ACAS and a corresponding rise in various other specified third parties. In terms of the actual use of these third-party provisions, however, there was little change between the two surveys. It appears that the provision for third-party intervention in disciplinary procedures has been brought more into alignment with the pattern of use. Another indicator of the increasing use of procedures was that more trade union representatives in 1984 than in 1980 said that most disputes of this type were dealt with through the procedure.

Procedures for dealing with disputes over pay and conditions of employment also became more common and there was a slight increase in the extent to which they were written down and agreed with trade unions. Provision for third-party intervention was more frequently specified, but much of this increase was in provisions for intervention by higher-level management, trade union officials or both, rather than independent third parties. The actual use of

y provisions in pay disputes increased significantly in both
d private sectors. The use of ACAS was particularly marked,
ost other types of third party were used less frequently. Trade
representatives in the public services sector were much more
to express dissatisfaction with the operation of their negotiating
procedure, an unsurprising development in view of the widespread
industrial action in that sector at the time.

Pay determination

The pattern of pay determination in the British economy has been the
subject of considerable research in the past, although much of this
effort has been concentrated in manufacturing industry and upon the
pay of manual workers. Because of its comprehensive coverage, our
first survey was able to show the full variety of methods of pay
determination. Although this variety was still apparent in 1984 there
had been considerable change within the main sectors of the economy
over the period. In overall terms, the proportion of workplaces in
which the pay of at least some workers was determined by negotiation
with trade unions increased between 1980 and 1984, but this was
largely the result of the increased proportion of workplaces in the
public sector where trade union recognition is almost universal. In
private manufacturing the declining proportion of plants with
recognised manual unions implied that more manual employees in this
sector were having their pay determined unilaterally by management.
The levels at which collectively-determined pay were negotiated also
showed some shifts. Multi-stage bargaining became less common,
particularly for manual workers. The balance between plant bargaining and higher-level bargaining, often cited as the most significant
change in this area,[15] only shifted noticeably towards company-level
bargaining in the case of non-manual workers. In the private services
sector the pattern of pay determination changed little, except that
there was a shift towards company-level bargaining and away from
national or industry-wide bargaining for those groups of non-manual
workers whose pay was negotiated. An interesting feature of the
analysis in private services was that pay bargaining at the workplace
level, although uncommon, was associated with the use of advanced
technology. The increasing use of advanced technology in this sector,
particularly in the office, might suggest a movement in pay bargaining
practices towards the pattern in manufacturing.

Our analysis of changes in the pattern of pay determination relied
upon questions concerning the establishment as a whole or, where
unions were recognised, the largest bargaining units representing
manual and non-manual workers. New questions in our 1984 survey
about the employee coverage of recognised unions gave further insight

into the area of collective bargaining. The results showed that the great majority of managements that recognised trade unions did so in respect of all their manual workers. This was much less frequently the case for non-manual workers, no doubt reflecting the widespread exclusion of managerial and professional employees from collective bargaining arrangements in the private sector. For example, in private manufacturing 100 per cent coverage for manual workers was reported in three quarters of cases with recognised manual unions or roughly two fifths of all manufacturing plants; in the same sector the equivalent non-manual proportions were a third and a twelfth. Over the economy as a whole the coverage of collective bargaining naturally followed the pattern of trade union density, but the precise figures of coverage and density in our 1984 survey enabled us to show that coverage exceeded density by a substantial margin. We calculated that 71 per cent of employees were covered by collective bargaining, compared to 58 per cent who were members of trade unions or staff associations.

A further elaboration of our 1984 questioning on pay determination concerned the way in which national, multi-employer agreements influenced bargaining at the workplace level. This influence appeared to be very limited. More important was the influence of head office policy. In manufacturing industry, a majority of managers involved in workplace bargaining consulted higher-level management before the start of local pay negotiations and many of them did so during the course of negotiations. Local managers had more autonomy when negotiating the pay of white-collar staff (where their pay was subject to negotiation), presumably reflecting their lower salience in the overall cost structure. We also asked what factors influenced the amount of the most recent pay settlement. Unsurprisingly, the cost of living was the most frequently cited factor. More surprising was that the several measures of economic and financial circumstances that we had included in our interview schedules did not vary systematically with the factors influencing pay increases. Neither the establishment's recent financial performance, nor the trend in its output, nor the sensitivity of its product prices to the level of demand appeared to have any overall impact on the considerations that influenced pay settlements, even where managers were unconstrained by any trade union representation.

A final aspect of pay determination that we reported in Chapter 9 was the use of job evaluation to determine internal pay differentials.[16] In comparing the results of our first survey with previous work it appeared that the practice had grown during the previous decades. If there has been a growth in the use of job evaluation since 1980 it has been modest. The proportion of establishments with job evaluation remained constant at 21 per cent. However, those workplaces that did have schemes reported more schemes in 1984 than in 1980. There appeared to have been an extension of the practice to previously uncovered groups of employees so that the proportion of employees covered by job evaluation may well have increased.[17] The use of job evaluation remained much more common in workplaces owned by foreign firms, even when similar-sized workplaces were compared. Workplaces with recognised trade unions were also much more likely to have job evaluation. Given the latter association, the further expansion of job evaluation in the private sector would appear to be limited in view of the lack of growth of recognition in that sector.

Industrial action

In an important respect the data on industrial action differ from virtually all the rest of the material contained in our surveys. For the most part we have been describing and analysing changes in institutions or practices that have stability and continuity. On occasions we have illuminated the pattern of change by using the data from our panel sample for various purposes, but the level of gross change in arrangements such as trade union recognition, the closed shop, consultative committees and disciplinary procedures has been small. Most of the workplaces that had these features in 1980 also had them in 1984. By contrast, overt forms of collective conflict are spasmodic. We would have been surprised if many of the establishments that had experienced strikes or other industrial action in 1980 had also experienced them in 1984. We know from the official strike records that the industrial and regional distribution of strikes varies considerably from year to year. Our data also reflect this volatility. The differences between our 1980 and our 1984 results on this subject should therefore not be interpreted as possibly representing underlying trends, as many of the differences on the other topics can be. However, since on most of the features of industrial action that are measured in the survey series there is simply no alternative source of large-scale systematic evidence, the results from our two surveys provide an important source of information on this widely-discussed aspect of industrial relations.

Taking strikes and other forms of industrial action together, the year up to mid-1984 differed substantially from the year prior to our first survey. The picture of industrial action in 1983/84 was characterised by short strikes by non-manual workers in the public services sector, whereas the scene in 1979/80 was one of longer strikes by manual workers in the manufacturing sector. Overall, industrial action of any sort was reported in as many workplaces in 1984 as in 1980 (the actual proportions being 25 per cent and 22 per cent in 1984 and 1980 respectively), but this was largely the result of fewer, more widespread, short strikes in 1984. These results on the extent of industrial action of all types should not be confused with the picture of declining strike frequency portrayed by the officially recorded statistics of industrial stoppages for the same periods. In manufacturing, the dramatic drop between the two periods in the extent of longer strikes involving manual workers, combined with Batstone's observation of a similar change between 1978 and 1983, does support the suggestion that there is a trend away from the more costly type of sanction. Whether this mainly reflects the changing economic and labour market conditions of the early 1980s, or an increasing use of legal procedures by employers to curtail lengthy strike action, we cannot judge.

In other respects the patterns of industrial action in the two study periods were similar. The two most widely reported forms of non-strike action remained the banning or restriction of overtime working and working to rule. Pay and associated matters remained, by and large, the most frequently mentioned reason for both strike and non-strike action, but the 1984 results reflect disputes over privatisation and trade union matters in the public sector for which there was no parallel in 1980.

Many of these differences in the pattern of industrial action between the two periods were reflected in changes in the pattern of picketing. Indeed, as picketing is almost invariably connected with strike action rather than other forms of industrial action the pattern of picketing changed in relation to the pattern of strikes, but particularly in relation to the reduction in longer strikes. Thus the overall extent of picketing dropped by nearly a half between 1980 and 1984, from 11 per cent of establishments to six per cent. In manufacturing the drop was from 18 per cent of plants to three per cent. Both primary and secondary picketing were affected. But the nature of picketing, in so far as it was captured by our survey questions, did not change so markedly.

The typical maximum number of pickets was the same in both surveys; in cases where there was a single entrance the typical maximum reported was six, the recommended maximum in the code of practice. Primary picketing had some effect on the movement of goods or people in as many instances in 1984 as in 1980. But secondary picketing had such effects in a much smaller proportion of cases in 1984. These differences between the two periods should, however, be seen as differences, rather than trends, because of the volatility of industrial action from year to year.

Change and stability

Finally, a number of points that emerged from our analysis merit some reiteration. In the first place, we hope our analysis has demonstrated the value of a large-scale survey *series* as a resource for generating factual information about the changing, and enduring, institutions and practices of British industrial relations. If our two surveys had not been carried out to the same basic design, the measurement of change would have been compromised by a much greater number of methodological difficulties. If both surveys had not been large, only the most dramatic changes would have been detectable within the limits of sampling error. If they had not been virtually comprehensive in their coverage of industries and types of ownership we should have been painting a partial, and possibly misleading, picture. A shortfall on any of these features of the survey series would have severely handicapped the results that we have presented here – as well as those that will emerge from further analysis – as a resource for public discussion of industrial relations issues.

Many of the findings that we have summarised in this final chapter have been concerned with changes through time. Many of these changes have been marginal when set against the general picture of industrial relations structures and practices which the two sets of results portray. Others were too subtle to detect, but could well become visible as results from further surveys in the series are compared to results from the original one. Some of the changes that we have reported appear to have been largely a consequence of changes in the overall composition of workplaces in the British economy. Others appear to have been influenced by economic conditions or government policy. Yet others appear to have been brought about by actions or decisions by management, trade unions or employees. Only relatively rarely have we been able to adjudicate between possible explanations on the basis of particular combinations of evidence, both from within the survey datasets and from elsewhere. We hope additional and more focused analysis of the survey data, in parallel with other research material, will take discussion and debate further along the road from description to explanation and understanding. In the meantime – and until further systematic, large-scale survey evidence is collected and analysed – we anticipate that the changes and patterns of variation that we have identified will be a useful guide to the evolving character of British workplace industrial relations.

Notes and references

1. The two surveys carried out in the early 1970s by the Office of Population Censuses and Surveys could arguably be counted an exception. However, the unit of sampling

and analysis for those surveys was an *industrial relations situation* – defined as 'the establishment or that part of it which, for industrial relations purposes, was under the control of a single senior manager'. There was and is no known population of *industrial relations situations* so defined and the results could not and cannot be used to generalise from the sample to a defined population, the essential basis of survey research.

2. Daniel W W (1986 forthcoming) *Workplace Industrial Relations and Technical Change*.

3. The Steering Committee was helped in its discussions of whether to include a panel element in the study by a commissioned paper: Abell P and MacDonald K (1983) 'The contribution that panel analysis could make to industrial relations research', unpublished mimeo, Department of Sociology, University of Surrey.

4. It should be remembered, as we noted in Chapter 1 and again in Chapter 3, that because of the operation of a minimum size threshold of 25 employees at three separate points in time our panel sample is likely to under-represent workplaces near this threshold in terms of their size. Given that it is smaller workplaces where recognition requests are likely to arise (the great majority of larger workplaces already have recognised unions) the panel sample very probably understates the extent of gross change in the direction of increased recognition.

5. Daniel W W and Millward N (1983) *Workplace Industrial Relations in Britain: The DE/PSI/SSRC Survey*, Heinemann Educational Books, London, pp.30-33.

6. The majority of cases of requests for recognition were resolved voluntarily by ACAS during the lifetime of the statutory provisions. See Advisory Conciliation and Arbritration Service (1981) *Annual Report 1980*, ACAS, London.

7. Dunn S and Gennard J (1984) *The Closed Shop in British Industry*, Macmillan, London.

8. Incomes Data Services (1986) 'Moving to cashless pay', *IDS Study 361*, May.

9. Department of Employment (1986) 'The Wages Act 1986', *Press Notice*, 25 July.

10. See Chapter 3.

11. See Chapter 10.

12. We remind the reader here that proportions quoted in this report for the 1980 survey may differ from those given in our earlier report because of a revision to the weighting scheme. This is made clear in Chapter 1 and in the Technical Appendix. The effect of the revision is to increase the weighted proportion of small establishments and therefore reduce the overall proportions of characteristics correlated with establishment size. In the current example the effect is to reduce the proportion of establishments in 1980 with a consultative committee from 37 per cent to 34 per cent. Naturally, we have used comparable weighting schemes for the two surveys throughout our analysis in this book.

12. Where there were recognised trade unions, the patterns were very similar whether we used managers' accounts of the amount of information given or worker representatives' accounts of the amount they received.

13. Daniel W W (1986 forthcoming) *op. cit.*

14. See Chapter 6.

15. Brown W (1986) 'The changing role of trade unions in the management of labour', paper given to the Conference on the Role and Influence of Trade Unions in a Recession, Queen Mary College, London, January; Batstone E (1984) *Working Order*, Blackwell, Oxford, pp. 202-4.

16. The datasets also contain information on the extent of payment-by-results systems,

work study, profit-sharing, value-added bonuses and share-ownership schemes. Share-ownership schemes have been covered in Chapter 9 and there was extensive analysis of the first two items in our first report.

17. As we stated in Chapter 9, more precise estimates of the employee coverage of job evaluation are possible with the survey data, but have not yet been made.

Technical Appendix[1]

The emphasis in this appendix is on the design and execution of the 1984 survey, although comparisons are made with the 1980 survey where appropriate. A summary of the design and execution of the 1980 survey was included as Appendix B of the earlier report.[2]

The sampling frame and the sample
The sample design for the 1984 survey closely followed that developed for the 1980 survey. The sampling frame was the Department of Employment's 1981 *Census of Employment*; for the 1980 survey it was the Census conducted in 1977. As in 1980, all census units recorded as having 24 or fewer employees were excluded, as were units falling within Agriculture, Forestry and Fishing (Division 0) of the *Standard Industrial Classification (1980)*. Otherwise all sectors of civil employment in England, Scotland and Wales were included in the sampling universe – public and private sector, manufacturing and service industries. In 1984, as in 1980, differential sampling fractions were used for the selection of units of different sizes (in terms of numbers of full-time and part-time employees: 25 to 49, 50 to 99 and so on).

A census unit is in most cases a number of employees working at the same address who are paid from the same location by the same employer. The requirement of the survey design was for a sample of *establishments*, that is, of individual places of employment at a single address and covering all the employees at that address of the identified employer. In general there is a sufficient degree of one-for-one correspondence between census units and establishments for the census to serve as a viable sampling frame for the survey series. However, in some cases census units refer to more than one establishment, and in others to just part of an establishment. In later paragraphs we describe the procedures developed in 1980, and refined in 1984, for dealing with these difficulties.

At the time of the design of the 1984 sample, the 1981 *Census of Employment* files contained just over 135,000 units recorded as having 25 or more employees, which is about the same number as were recorded in the 1977 Census and used for the 1980 survey. From these files a stratified random sample totalling 3640 units was drawn; in

1980 the figure was 3994 units. The sample was smaller in 1984 for two reasons. First, our target number of establishments at which interviews were required was 1850, rather than 2000 as in 1980. Secondly, as only 300 or so units of the 'reserve pool' of 1000 units were used in 1980 and the 1980 experience gave a good guide to the extent of out-of-scope and non-responding addresses, we could reduce the size of the reserve in 1984. Consequently, the 1984 reserve pool as selected was just 513 units (target 520). In the event none of them was used.

Differential sampling fractions were used for selection within each of seven size bands, the size bands being determined by the number of full and part-time employees recorded as being present. Within each size band the census units were initially stratified by: the proportion of *male* employees, within the proportion of *full-time* employees, within the *Activities* of the *Standard Industrial Classification (1980)*. From the resultant list, samples were selected by marking off at intervals from a randomly selected starting-point, the list being treated as circular. The numbers of census units, sampling fractions and subsample sizes are given in Table A.1, with the figures for 1980 alongside for comparison.

Table A.1   Sampling fractions and numbers of census units drawn

Numbers

	No. of units in census		Sampling fraction		Sample selected	
	1980	1984	1980	1984	1980	1984
No. of employees recorded at census unit:			(1 in ...)			
25–49	66,959	70,000	79	92	849	760
50–99	33,881	33,288	42.5	51	799	650
100–199	18,340	17,625	26	28	700	620
200–499	10,649	9,880	15	16	699	600
500–999	3,098	2,796	6	6	499	500
1000–1999	1,332[1]	1,169	5.5	3.3	249	360
2000+	571[1]	484	3	3.3	199	150
Total	134,825	135,242	33.7	37	3,994	3,640

[1] Estimated subdivision.

As the table shows, the range of sampling fractions employed was greater than in 1980, reflecting a decision to generate fewer interviews in the lower size bands and more in the higher size bands. The extent to which this was achieved is detailed in later paragraphs. As the number of establishments at which interviews were achieved was comfortably in excess of the target there was no recourse to the reserve pool; however, a number of reserve pool units within SIC Class 79 were mistakenly included in the lists of establishments sent to employers in that sector at an early stage of the fieldwork. It was considered inappropriate to withdraw these cases once interviewing had begun, but minor modifications were made to the weighting procedures at the analysis stage to compensate for the over-selection of units within this SIC Class. Leaving aside the remaining 486 units in the reserve pool, the total number of addresses used was therefore 3154 (compared to 3307 in 1980). As in 1980, however, certain groups of these census units were withdrawn prior to fieldwork for reasons which we outline below.

In 1980 we developed procedures both for recontacting those bodies which had made a *Census of Employment* return for a grouping considerably larger than a single establishment and for resampling such 'aggregate returns' to generate usable survey units.[3] Typically this might be a single return for a complete local education authority rather than a return for each school or college within the authority. We used the same procedures in 1984 and 57 such aggregate returns were identified (there were 48 in 1980) of which 17 were found not to be either individual establishments or a number of establishments. (Typically they were all the peripatetic teachers in an education authority.) In a further 18 cases (28 in 1980) the authority refused or was unable to provide the information. Resampling the remaining 22 cases along the lines developed in 1980 generated a further 55 units to be added to the survey sample compared to 25 in 1980. In other words, the net effect in 1984 was to decrease the sample size by two (57 minus 55), compared to a decrease of 23 (48 minus 25) in 1980.

Although a census unit consists of employees at the same establishment who are paid from the same location, we found, as in 1980, that in some instances a single establishment was represented by more than one census unit, thus giving it a greater chance of selection than single census units of the same size. However, it was again the case that in the majority of these 'multiple census units' only a single unit from a group of units that comprised an establishment was included in the sample. We compensated for these inequalities of selection by individual weighting of the case. This is described further in the section on weighting of the data later in this appendix. In those cases where more than one census unit **in the sample** represented an establishment, it was necessary to delete all but one of any such groups and adjust the weighting for the remaining unit. This procedure resulted in 21 units being deleted from the sample, compared to 61 in 1980. In fact 11 of these were discovered during fieldwork and are referred to here as a matter of convenience.

In parallel with the main cross-sectional sample described so far, an experimental 'panel' subsample of addresses was drawn from the 1980 achieved sample and included in the fieldwork. The sampling procedures followed in the selection of this panel and the response rates achieved are summarised in a later section, but it is worth noting at this point that, of the 210 addresses selected, 14 were found to duplicate addresses in the main 1984 sample and were therefore withdrawn.

Before the start of fieldwork, a further 43 census units were also eliminated from the 1984 sample, of which 19 were outside the scope of the survey. Those deemed to be out of scope included all within Class 0 of the *Standard Industrial Classification* (Agriculture etc.),[4] merchant ships and other offshore workplaces, as well as all units in Northern Ireland. We also excluded 19 units because approaches had been made either to those addresses or to addresses in the same organisation during the course of piloting and development, and two units were eliminated because the addresses had been printed out incompletely or obscurely. (There were 36 of these in 1980.) Three units were withdrawn as duplicated addresses, compared to eight in 1980. Finally, all addresses in the coal-mining industry were withdrawn at the start of the fieldwork because of the continuing industrial dispute in that sector and the consequent unlikelihood of successful interviewing.

Questionnaire development and fieldwork

A pilot survey of 56 establishments was conducted during December 1983 and early January 1984. Establishments with fewer than 100 employees were excluded, but otherwise the sample was intended to cover a range of establishments of different sizes and from different SIC groups. The pilot survey covered not just the content and length of the questionnaires (management, works management and worker representatives), but also the contacting procedures and the reaction to two enclosures that it was proposed to send with the initial contact letter from the Department of Employment. The first of these enclosures outlined procedures for the protection of the respondents' anonymity, the second described the publication of *Workplace Industrial Relations in Britain*, the report on the 1980 survey. Letters were sent out from the Department of Employment in mid-November 1983 and eight interviewers were given a notional target of ten establishments. The addresses had been drawn from the 1977 *Census of Employment*, the sampling frame for the 1980 survey. Of the 56 establishments at which a main management interview was achieved, 22 yielded completed interviews with one or more worker representatives. Six interviews were also conducted with works managers. In addition to the modifications to the questionnaires, the pilot also gave general support to the two enclosures sent out with the initial contact letter and therefore both were used, with only minor modifications, in the main survey.

The interviewing for the main survey was carried out by 117 interviewers after initial contact had been made by letter from the Department of Employment. Five of the interviewers were SCPR employees, being members of the field staff. Apart from three relatively recently recruited interviewers, the remaining 109 were experienced interviewers from SCPR's regular interviewing panel. All had been trained by SCPR's field staff and 46 of the 117 had also worked as interviewers on the 1980 survey. Before fieldwork began, seven briefing conferences were conducted jointly by members of the research team from the Department of Employment, the Policy Studies Institute and SCPR. One hundred and five interviewers attended this series of conferences during early March 1984. The remaining twelve were briefed at four supplementary conferences by SCPR research and field staff during April and May.

At the time of the briefing conferences around 2000 addresses were available for passing to interviewers. Of the remaining 1150, some 350 had been withdrawn because the addressees had contacted the Department of Employment either to refuse, or to demonstrate ineligibility. The remaining 800 addresses were set aside and approached later during a second wave of contacts. These addresses had been screened out, on the basis of experience gained from the 1980 survey, as being one of several establishments belonging to a single organisation for which a single preliminary approach to the head office of the organisation was thought appropriate. Of these 'second-wave' addresses, 130 were from central government establishments, 260 from the nationalised industries, 100 from local authorities and the remainder from the private sector. Preliminary contacts with the relevant head offices were made by the researchers based at the Department of Employment or at the Policy Studies Institute; in some cases there was further contact by a small specialised interviewing unit set up within SCPR. Once head office approval had been secured – frequently it involved a courtesy visit and a separate head office interview for background material – the establishment addresses were handed over to the main interviewing panel.

Fieldwork began immediately after the main interviewer briefings and continued until October 1984. Although interviewing started some six weeks earlier than in 1980, the delays encountered in arranging second-wave interviews meant that the 1984 fieldwork was not complete until a few weeks later in the year. However, the bulk of the fieldwork was conducted over the same period in both the 1980 and 1984 surveys with a median date in May.

In both surveys fieldwork quality control was carried out by a postal check on a random subsample of establishments after the fieldwork period was over. Over 40 per cent of the forms returned were without comment (in 1980 it was about half) and the replies of those respondents' who did comment have been summarised in the more detailed technical report produced by SCPR and lodged at the ESRC Data Archive at Essex University. In addition to these postal checks the first batch of questionnaires received in field offices from each interviewer in the 1984 survey was subject to intensive checking by clerical staff. Any errors were documented and reported to both the interviewer and the relevant regional supervisor, whose task it was to follow up and check that misunderstandings were clarified and appropriate action taken by the interviewer.

Overall response

The outcome of the sampling, initial approach and fieldwork operations in 1984 may be judged from the summary statistics in Table A.2, with the equivalent 1980 figures alongside for comparison. As in 1980, ineligible or out-of-scope addresses fell into three main groups: those which were found to have closed down between the taking of the Census (1981) and interviewing (1984), of which there were 180, a somewhat higher proportion than in 1980; those of establishments which were found to have fewer than 25 employees, of which there were 178, about the same as 1980; and those which were found to be vacant or demolished premises or where the establishment had moved, leaving no trace of its new whereabouts, of which there were 42, slightly fewer than in 1980.

Table A.2   Summary of fieldwork response

Numbers

| | Addresses | |
	1980	1984
Initial sample	3307	3154
Resampled units[1]	25	55
Total sample	3332	3209
Less:		
Withdrawn at sampling stage	205	135
Ineligible/out-of-scope	376	449
Non-productive addresses	686	606
Interviews achieved	2040	2019

[1] Units resampled from aggregate census returns.

Non-productive addresses fell into three main groups: those for which a refusal was received at the Department of Employment in response to the original letter sent out, of which there were 220 cases (roughly two thirds of the expected number, based on 1980 returns); those for which a refusal was received by the SCPR interviewer or at SCPR offices, of which there were 316 or just over 13 per cent of all addresses passed to interviewers (compared to almost ten per cent in 1980); and those at which no effective contact was made (41 cases) or at which questionnaires were completed but could not be used (29 cases).

The overall response rate, judged by the completion of at least a satisfactory management interview, was 76.9 per cent. This is some two percentage points higher than that achieved in 1980. As a fieldwork operation, setting aside those addresses that were not issued to interviewers, the response rate achieved was 84 per cent. The overall response rate was analysed by region, industrial activity and establishment size. In regional terms there was much less variation in response than in 1980, ranging from 74 per cent in the West Midlands to 82 per cent in the North. The remaining regions lay within the range 75 per cent (Greater London) to 81 per cent (North West). As in 1980, however, the range of response rates for different industrial sectors was rather greater, from 66 per cent in 'Other manufacturing' to 91 per cent in 'Energy and water supply' (which, as noted earlier, **excludes** coal mining). In the main, however, the response rates fell within the range 72 per cent to 85 per cent. There was a greater variation in response rates for different sizes of establishment than in 1980, from 71 per cent in the smallest workplaces (25-49 employees) to 85 per cent in workplaces employing between 1000 and 1999 people. The results are given in Table A.3 and it is clear that the improvement to the overall response rate occurred among establishments employing 200 or more people.

Response among worker representatives and works managers
Within the 2019 establishments at which interviews were obtained with management respondents in 1984, manual negotiating groups were identified in 1327 cases (1334 in 1980) and non-manual in 1367 cases (1255 in 1980). In a small number of establishments (not included in the figures above) negotiating groups were not positively identified, although it was apparent from subsequent answers that management at the establishment did recognise one or more trade unions for negotiating purposes. Typically, the reason for such ambiguity was that negotiations took place at a higher level in the organisation. The numbers of such establishments were 78 in respect of manual recognition (31 in 1980) and 31 in respect of non-manual

Table A.3 Response rate in relation to size of establishment

Percentages

| | 25-49 | | 50-99 | | 100-199 | | 200-499 | | 500-999 | | 1000-1999 | | 2000+ | |
	1980	1984	1980	1984	1980	1984	1980	1984	1980	1984	1980	1984	1980	1984
Response rate	73	71	72	72	75	75	75	82	78	82	80	85	77	81

recognition (27 in 1980). In a further 174 cases there was no manual trade union representative at the sampled establishment and in 205 non-manual cases an equivalent situation existed. In the remaining cases – those where appropriate representatives existed at the sampled establishment – interviewers were required to seek an interview with the representative of the primary negotiating group for manual employees and, separately, with the representative of the primary negotiating group for non-manual employees.

In all, 910 interviews with primary manual representatives were achieved and 949 with primary non-manual representatives. At those establishments where worker representatives were present, the overall response rates were 79 per cent for manual representatives (84 per cent in 1980) and 82 per cent for non-manual representatives (85 per cent in 1980). Table A.4 shows the reasons for non-response among worker representatives in both 1980 and 1984. As in 1980, the major reason for failing to obtain an interview was the refusal to grant permission by management, although the proportion of these cases declined slightly in 1984. Taking as a base those establishments where interviews were not obtained but were required, management refusals to allow manual representatives to be interviewed fell from 53 per cent to 50 per cent, and the figure for non-manuals declined from 52 per cent to 47 per cent. However, it is significant that the number of refusals from worker representatives themselves increased substantially in 1984. If we take the two categories of *refusal by representative* and *never available* as our measure of worker representatives' unwillingness to be interviewed, this element of non-response among manual representatives increased from 13 per cent in 1980 to 38 per cent in 1984. The increase among non-manual representatives was even more marked, from 7 per cent in 1980 to 41 per cent in 1984. It seems likely that trade union opposition to government policy on industrial relations contributed to the increase in refusals among worker representatives, particularly as the Department of Employment was clearly identified as a major sponsor of the survey.

Interviewers were also required to conduct additional interviews with the works manager at those manufacturing plants where the main management respondent was a specialist in industrial, employee or staff relations or in personnel. Such specialists were present in 365 of the 561 manufacturing plants in the 1984 sample, but in 15 of these there was no works manager present at the establishment. Of the remaining 350 establishments, works managers were successfully interviewed in 259 cases, a response rate of 74 per cent. The most common reason for non-response was a refusal by the main management respondent. However, the dataset includes a total of 276 works manager interviews because an additional 17 interviews were

Table A.4   Reasons for non-response among worker representatives

Percentages

	Manual representatives		Non-manual representatives	
	1980	1984	1980	1984
Reason why interview with worker representative not achieved				
Refusal by management	53	50	52	47
Refusal by representative	9	20	5	23
Never available (no reason given)	4	18	2	18
Refusal by union	..	1	..	—
Broken appointment	5	2	5	2
Ill/away for duration of survey	13	6	10	8
Other reason	17	3	25	4
Base: establishments where interviews with worker representative not achieved				
Unweighted	*187*	*243*	*167*	*213*

carried out at manufacturing establishments where the main management respondent had **not** been coded as a personnel or industrial
relations specialist. Strictly, this is a matter of interviewer error, but
may also reflect the situation at the establishment. The research team
examined these questionnaires during the coding and editing stages
and decided to include them in the dataset, taking into account the
element of arbitrariness in the definition of the circumstances in
which these interviews were required.

Coding and editing of the data
Coding and editing of the questionnaires was carried out between
June and December 1984. As many of the open-ended questions used
in the 1980 survey were repeated in 1984, the previous coding frames
could be used with relatively little modification. In 1980 rigorous
structure checking of all questionnaires was undertaken prior to
general coding and editing and this was repeated in 1984. Questionnaires were checked where there were obscurities in the relationship
between the interviews achieved with worker representatives and the
data relating to union recognition as described in the management
questionnaire. Additionally, questionnaires in which there was a
mismatch between the sampled size and SIC Division of the
establishment and the information obtained at interview were
checked. Any questionnaires showing extreme values or unusual
combinations of data were referred to the research team who resolved
the queries or arranged for the questionnaires to be returned to

interviewers for further clarification. In 22 cases questionnaires were rejected as too incomplete or obscure to be usable.

As in 1980, particular attention was paid to the *Basic Workforce Data Sheets* (*BWDS*). The absence of these or obscurities or inconsistencies in their completion were the most common reasons for returning questionnaires to interviewers. In a number of cases the research team were able to modify the *BWDS* figures on the basis of information contained in the body of the questionnaires. Table A.5 summarises the extent to which the research team was able to remedy minor inconsistencies and deficiencies in the *BWDS*, but there were also 17 further cases where the *BWDS* was missing but for which it was possible to create a skeleton *BWDS* on evidence contained in the questionnaire. All these cases are identified on the dataset with appropriate codes.

Table A.5   Adjustments to the *Basic Workforce Data Sheet*, 1984

	No. of questionnaires
Adjustments to:	
Question 1 (manual employees)	125
Question 2 (non-manual employees)	252
Question 3 (manual employees: subcategories)	148
Question 4 (non-manual employees: subcategories)	278

Computer editing of the data was carried out in two stages. The first edit program consisted of a rigorous check of ranges and filters and questionnaire structure, while the second comprised a number of logic checks, checks on extreme values and on relatively complex relationships between different sections of the questionnaires. After the questionnaire data had been edited and cleaned, a considerable amount of further computer-file manipulation had to be carried out in order to calculate and add the weights described in the following section. The complete data file incorporating weighting was handed over to the research team on 16 April 1985. Further detailed work on the file was also carried out in order to provide an anonymised version for the ESRC Data Archive at Essex University. The anonymised tape was lodged at the Archive at the begining of August 1985.

Weighting of the data
All the results presented in the main text of this report, unless otherwise specified, were adjusted by weighting factors derived from two separate stages of calculation. The first stage compensated for the inequalities of selection that were introduced by the differential

sampling of census units according to their number of employees.[5] This first stage of weighting is imperative, otherwise the results from each size stratum simply cannot be added together to provide a meaningful aggregate. The second, and additional, stage of weighting was applied to adjust for the observed under-representation of small establishments in the distribution resulting from the first stage. Details of the two stages are discussed in turn.

In cases where the sampled census units corresponded precisely to an establishment (85 per cent of cases), the first stage of weighting involved applying a *stratum weight* corresponding to the inverse of the probability of selection of census units in that size stratum. In the remaining cases an individual weight was calculated, reflecting the fact that establishments comprising more than one census unit had an increased probability of selection. Such cases were identified using the same procedure as that developed in 1980. This entailed listing all census units in the same postcode as all those in the achieved sample and then combing the lists for any instances of units of the *same employer with the same postcode* as those in the achieved sample. This procedure revealed 300 such multiple census unit establishments among the achieved sample, whereas in 1980 the equivalent number was just 76. The increase reflects the fact that the use of postcodes has increased in the intervening years and that, therefore, the operation was considerably more comprehensive than previously.

We referred earlier to the erroneous inclusion of 27 units from the reserve pool in the lists of establishments sent to employers in Class 79 of the *Standard Industrial Classification* at an early stage of the fieldwork. In effect this meant that the units in that section of the sample listing had a higher probability of selection than other units in their size bands. All interviews achieved at establishments in that section, most of SIC Class 79, received a weight reduced by one seventh.

The second stage of weighting compensates for the fact that the achieved sample includes too few small establishments. This point is illustrated by Table A.6, which shows the structure of the 1984 (and 1980) achieved samples after applying the first weighting, compensating for unequal probabilities of selection. For comparison we also show the structure of the complete *Census of Employment* (1977 and 1981) in similar terms, both unadjusted and after adjustment for changes between the compilation of the census and the survey fieldwork. This adjustment was done by withdrawing from each size band the proportion of units that was found during the surveys either to have closed down or to have fallen below the threshold of 25 employees in the intervening period.

The differences between the weighted 1984 sample and the adjusted

Table A.6 Comparison by size band of weighted sample (first weighting only) and population

Percentages

| | Weighted sample | | Census of Employment units | | | |
| | | | Sample | | Adjusted[1] | |
	1980	1984	1980	1984	1980	1984
Number of employees in census unit at time of census:						
25–49	45.0	46.3	50.2	51.9	45.6	47.6
50–99	26.6	26.0	25.1	24.7	26.9	26.0
100–199	15.4	15.0	13.2	12.9	14.5	14.6
200–499	8.7	8.7	7.7	7.2	8.6	8.0
500–999	2.6	2.6	2.6	2.0	2.9	2.4
1000–1999	1.2	1.0	0.9	0.9	1.0	1.0
2000+	0.4	0.4	0.4	0.4	0.5	0.4
Base for percentages	2000	2000	137,925	136,599	137,925	136,599

[1] The data have been re-percentaged to take into account the proportion of census units in each size band that were found to have either closed down or to have become ineligible on grounds of having too few employees in the period between the completion of the census returns (1977 or 1981) and fieldwork (1980 or 1984).

1981 *Census of Employment* figures reflect small variations in response by size band. However, the differences are not substantial and if we define the '1984 WIRS population' as being those establishments which existed in 1981 and 1984, we can be confident that the sample is representative, within the limits of sampling error. However, the time-lag between the census (1981) and fieldwork (1984) means that the (adjusted) census definition of the population will understate the extent of 'new' and therefore *smaller* workplaces in 1984. The second stage of weighting involved applying further weights which attempted to compensate for this effect. Ideally, we would have matched the size distribution of the sample to the 1984 *Census of Employment* size distribution; unfortunately this was not available during the course of our analysis. Further details are given in a note available from the ESRC Data Archive. The additional factors derived from the second stage of weighting are incorporated into a single set of weights, representing both stages, which are referred to as the *second weighting scheme*. It is this that we have applied throughout.

Further refinements to the weighting scheme have been considered, particularly to compensate for the differential response rates between different sizes of establishment, different regions and different industry categories. None of these differences was especially large, and the fact that the population data were out of date suggested that any such adjustments might themselves contain biases. It was decided to await the 1984 Census information before considering any further adjustments.

The match between the sample using the second weighting scheme and the adjusted population is given in Table A.7. The grossing-up factor was 68.3.

Table A.7   Comparison of sample and estimated population after second weighting, 1984

	Adjusted population, 1984		Survey sample after second weighting	
	Employees	Employees per unit	Employees	Employees per unit
Size of unit				
25–49	2,366,154	33.4	2,517,790	35.5
50–99	2,282,875	67.7	2,329,866	69.1
100–199	2,405,238	135.5	2,439,865	137.3
200–499	2,916,315	295.2	2,925,166	295.8
500–999	1,824,145	674.6	1,789,688	662.9
1000+	3,149,512	2004.8	2,889,687	1853.0
Total	14,944,329	109.4	14,892,042	109.0

The panel sample

The panel dataset for the 1984 survey contains two types of case – *chance repeats* and *deliberate selections*. The chance repeats were cases where the same establishment had occurred by chance in each of the two main samples and by extensive checking of productive addresses the repetition had been discovered after the completion of fieldwork. The 96 such cases have been retained in the 1984 main sample unchanged but have also been included as part of the panel dataset. In the panel dataset they have been given weights that reflect the combination of their probabilities of selection on the two occasions. In all other respects they are part of the main cross-sectional sample and have been included in the discussion in the earlier sections of this appendix.

The deliberate selections were sampled in a separate operation and their response and weighting require separate description. They were selected from the 2040 establishments at which interviews had been successfully carried out in 1980 on the basis of a stratified random sample with a sampling interval of one in ten. Thirteen of the cases thus selected proved to be ones where there had been an indication at the end of the 1980 management interview of reluctance to participate in further interviewing. These were replaced by further random selections to provide a planned sample of 210 addresses. Fourteen cases were found to be duplicates with the main sample and were treated as panel cases and removed from the main sample. Interviews were achieved at 141 of the 210 establishments selected. Two were subsequently rejected as incomplete or doubtful panel cases. Of the remaining addresses 35 were found to be out of scope (mostly closed down or less than 25 employees) and the rest were refusals or cases of no contact. The 1980 characteristics of out-of-scope cases show, as would be expected, that they were grouped among the smaller establishments in the 1980 sample. The response rate was also somewhat lower for small establishments. The deliberate selections have been given weights that reflect their probability of selection in 1980 and the subsequent one in ten selection in 1984. The weights for both parts of the panel sample have subsequently been scaled to bring the weighted sample size to 200, approximately that of the unweighted achieved panel sample in total.

The overall response rate for the deliberate selection panel cases was 79 per cent. Worker representative interviews were obtained in 86 per cent of cases where manual worker interviews were required, and 84 per cent where non-manual interviews were required; the reasons for non-response were very much the same as in the main sample.

Sampling errors

Sampling errors for the main cross-sectional sample are somewhat larger than for a simple random sample of equivalent size, owing to the disproportionate sampling of larger establishments. Sampling errors were calculated for a number of variables in the 1980 survey and ranged from 0.4 per cent to 1.4 per cent. Given the very similar design and sample size of the two surveys, sampling errors for the 1984 survey are unlikely to be very different. Work is proceeding and will be reported via the ESRC Data Archive.

Notes and references

1. The material on the 1984 survey contained in this appendix is largely based upon technical reports written by Colin Airey of Social and Community Planning Research. For the 1980 survey the technical report was written by Colin Airey and Andrew Potts. Denise Lievesley of the Survey Methods Centre provided material on sampling and on the weighting of the data. The full documents are available from the ESRC Data Archive.

2. Daniel W W and Millward N (1983) *Workplace Industrial Relations in Britain: The DE/PSI/SSRC Survey*, Heinemann Educational Books, London, pp.321-33.

3. *Ibid*, p.323.

4. These should have been screened out of the original sample, but appear not to have been.

5. These weighting factors are also contained in the data records held at the ESRC Data Archive.

Index